Pewter
in Pennsylvania German Churches

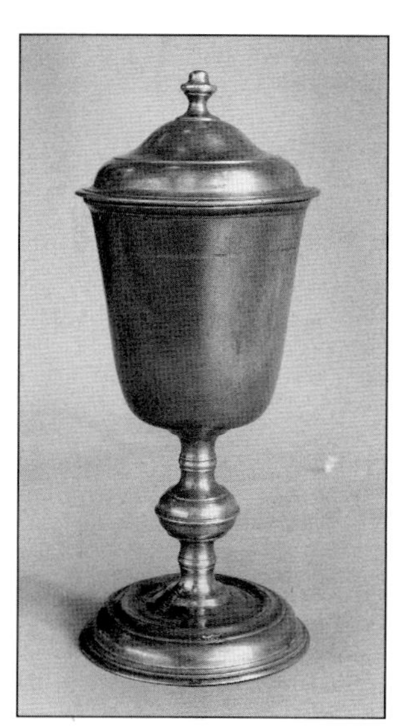

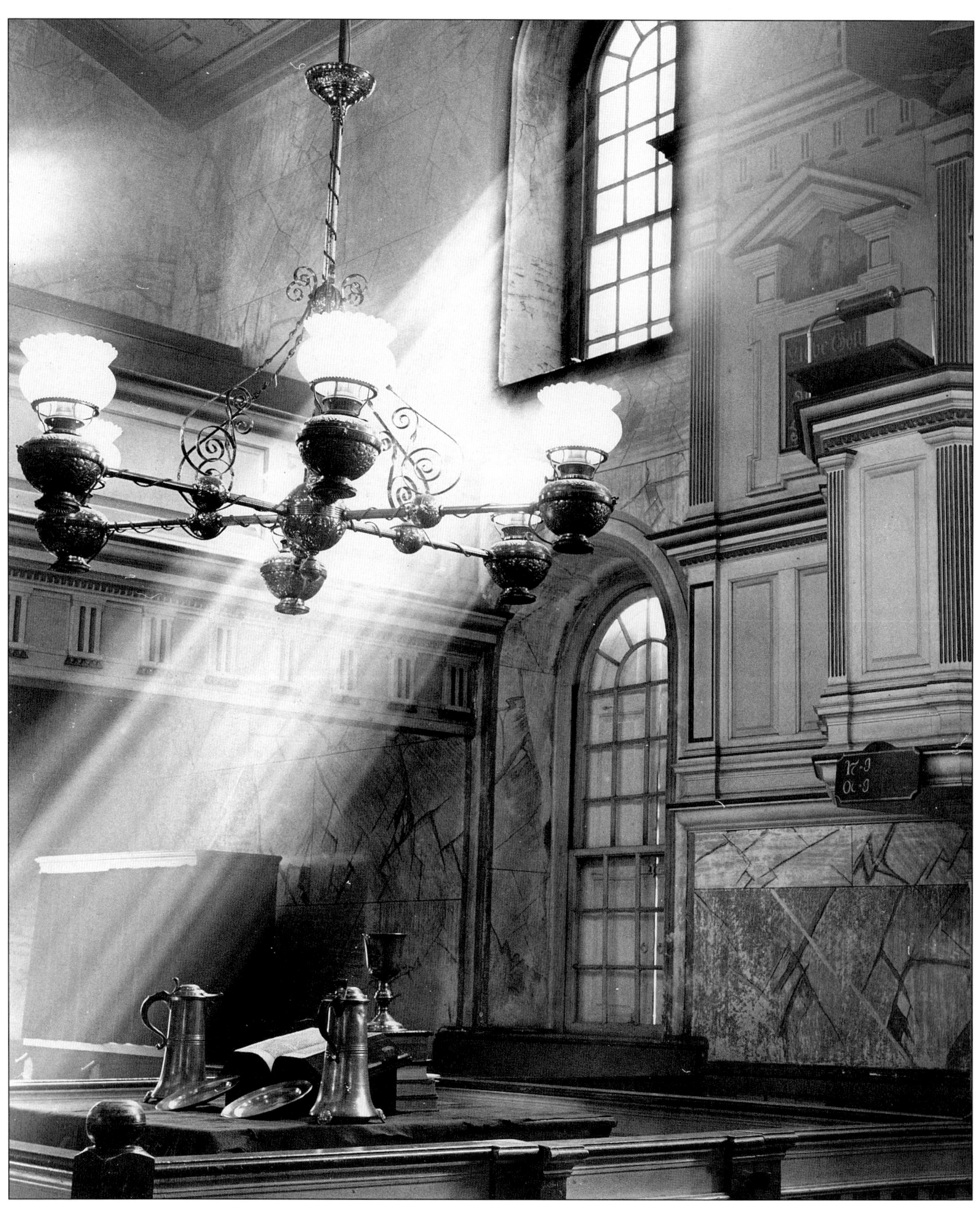

Interior of Bindnagle Lutheran Church, Lebanon County, Pa.
Photograph courtesy of Eric de Jonge.

Pewter
in Pennsylvania German Churches

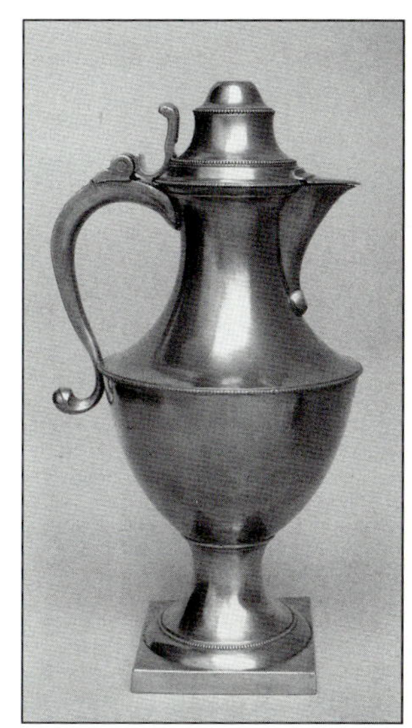

by Donald M. Herr

Best wishes to Dick Worth
Enjoy!
Donald M. Herr

The Pennsylvania German Society
Birdsboro, Pennsylvania
Volume XXIX

1995

Edited by Willard Wetzel

Designed by Beth Oberholtzer
Copyedited by Vandora Elfrink
Indexed by Lisa Thickett
Photography by
Donald Herr
Jonathan Charles
Museums as designated
Expanded flagon designed by Rick Bowman

Library of Congress Catalog Card Number 95-70952
ISBN: 0-911122-60-5

Printed and bound in the United States of America
by Science Press
Ephrata, Pennsylvania

Contents

Foreword

When we look at the illustrations in this book, what a world of imagery appears before our eyes! Winged cherubs and flying, trumpeting angels remind us of tombstone motifs in our colonial churchyards. Floral borders, birds, tulips and eagles, deer, hearts and crowns reveal kinship with Pennsylvania German fraktur decoration. Specific religious symbols range from the lamb and banner (symbol of the Moravian Church) to the instruments of the passion depicted on altar candlesticks made by Lancaster's Johann Christoph Heyne for Roman Catholic churches in the Colony. Secular symbols include coats-of-arms, and curious coinlike profiles of British sovereigns William and Mary as the Prince and Princess of Orange. Inscribed on the pewter vessels of the churches, as on fraktur, are records of the sources of pewter, as well as biblical commands and words of spiritual comfort.

This volume authoritatively presents the world of Pennsylvania German church pewter, with attention to forms, decoration, origins, production, and makers. Represented in the places of origin of our church pewter are not only Philadelphia and Lancaster, but also New York, New England, the British Isles, and the European continent. Yet among the stars in the galaxy of artist-craftsmen in the book—all of whom the author treats in concise bibliographical sketches—are the unmatched Pennsylvania German pewterers Johann Christoph Heyne (1715–1781) of Lancaster and William Will (1742–1798) of Philadelphia.

Filling a void in the study of Pennsylvania German material culture—the pewter vessels, patens and candelabra used ritualistically by our Colonial and Federal-period churches of Pennsylvania—Dr. Donald Herr offers us a surprising glimpse into a world of form and symbolism understood earlier by our Pennsylvania German ancestors but now largely forgotten. The product of Dr. Herr's years of study and research is indeed a treat for the eyes!

During the eighteenth century most Pennsylvania German congregations purchased or received pewter communion services through donation. The sacrament of Holy Communion was central to the ritual of all the Pennsylvania German churches including the Lutherans and Reformed as well as the Mennonites, Brethren, and Amish. The chalice, the common cup, from which the parishioners partook of the communion wine was a symbol of the spiritual community formed by church membership. This eighteenth century sense of spiritual community was reflected also in the seating plans of the pioneer church buildings, where parishioners were seated according to age and gender. Nuclear families did not sit together as is customary today. The eighteenth century seating arrangement pointed beyond the nuclear family and the individual to the overarching unity of God's family. In God's house all were children of God.

In the twentieth century the older sense of church as symbolized by seating arrangements often has been replaced with the nuclear family seating arrangement. At the same time, individual communion cups were developed because of concern for health factors. Furthermore, other metals—including gold and silver-plated ware—replaced pewter as the material from which ecclesiastical vessels were produced.

With these developments, the older pewter communion sets largely went into oblivion—into church closets, bank vaults, museum storage, and private collections. Many were irretrievably lost.

It is a pleasure for the Pennsylvania German Society to offer Dr. Herr's volume on the rich church pewter heritage—individual, family, and institutional—for study and viewing pleasure. We express our deep indebtedness to all the congregations whose pewter treasures are pictured in this volume and to their pastors and staffs, whose friendly cooperation, along with Dr. Herr's indefatigable research, have made this book possible.

DON YODER
University of Pennsylvania
November 15, 1994

Preface

THE USE OF PEWTER IN EIGHTEENTH CENtury Pennsylvania German churches has been a neglected aspect in the study of Pennsylvania German culture. No comprehensive study has been written, partly because historians of Pennsylvania German culture have lacked a knowledge of pewter and pewterers and partly because historians frequently focused on liturgy and neglected the origins and makers of the sacramental vessels.

The purpose of this book is to document early pewter that was used by or is still owned by Pennsylvania German churches founded in the eighteenth century. I personally enjoyed finding rare pewter forms that I had never seen before, many of which are photographed and documented in this volume for the first time. Another equally important outcome of this project was the identification of the makers, the period of their production, and their countries of origin. But perhaps the most significant outcome of this study, and the most pleasurable for me, was the opportunity to inform pastors, church historians, and members of the congregations about the rarity of these church treasures and the need for care and safekeeping.

Fifteen pewter communion and baptismal sets from Lancaster area Lutheran churches were assembled on October 13, 1972, at Holy Trinity Lutheran Church in Lancaster. The occasion was a meeting of the Pennsylvania regional group of the Pewter Collectors' Club of America. Sets were documented, measured, photographed, and insured. This information was conveyed to the participating congregations. At least two new forms were discovered that day, and the meeting benefitted both pewter scholars and the respective churches.

In 1975, the exhibit was repeated at Holy Trinity Lutheran Church with the addition of Reformed Church and Church of the Brethren pewter sacramental vessels. At this meeting, Frederick S. Weiser suggested that a survey of pewter in Pennsylvania German churches should be conducted.

In 1986, the subject was discussed as a volume for the Pennsylvania German Society and the project started the following year. The survey of early pewter in eighteenth century Pennsylvania German churches included churches of Germanic background that were in existence in 1800 or earlier. Lutheran, Reformed, Moravian, Church of the Brethren, Mennonite, and Roman Catholic denominations were included in the survey. The project included the areas settled by migration of Pennsylvania Germans in Maryland and the Shenandoah Valley of Virginia.

Charles H. Glatfelter's *Pastors and People: German Lutheran and Reformed Churches in the Pennsylvania Field, 1717–1793,* Volume I, was invaluable in sorting out the Lutheran and Reformed congregations from their early beginnings in Pennsylvania to the establishment of independent Lutheran and Reformed denominations in the United States after the Revolution. Churches with unsubstantiated claims of being founded in the eighteenth century were not included in the survey. Yearbooks of the Lutheran (now Evangelical Lutheran Church in America), Reformed (now

United Church of Christ), Mennonite, Moravian, Church of the Brethren, and Roman Catholic denominations were useful in locating congregations in existence prior to 1800. The name "Evangelical Lutheran Church in America" has been shortened to "Lutheran Church" in the text.

Each individual church was contacted and arrangements were made to document the congregation's pewter. These meetings took place at a church, or at a bank, home, or museum, and in one instance, even at an elementary school. Documentation included identifying the maker, noting working dates, and measuring and photographing the sets and individual pieces. Engraving, donors' names, initials, and other details were noted and photographed.

The documentation was entered into a computer database. The survey established that 178 congregations have pewter or know its whereabouts and that 391 no longer have it in their possession. Thirty-one percent of the 569 congregations surveyed still retain their sacramental vessels. A list of those congregations that have pewter and those that do not is found in the Appendixes.

Initially, the project was limited to pewter in Germanic background churches within the Commonwealth of Pennsylvania. Then the project was enlarged to include surrounding areas into which Pennsylvania Germans migrated; however, the bulk of the surviving pewter was within the Commonwealth.

In order to limit the project to early pewter, a church had to be founded by 1800 to be included in the survey. Silver-plated ware of the nineteenth century is not included in the survey.

Many rare pewter forms and marks not previously published are included here for the first time. Nine different flagon forms made by Philadelphia pewterer William Will are included. Six have not been previously illustrated. Lancaster pewterer Johann Christoph Heyne's known pieces, desirable to collectors, increased by twenty-nine as a result of the survey. The only known eighteenth-century coffeepot made by New York pewterer John Will, and likely the earliest marked American coffeepot, and accompanied by the only known oval platter by that maker, is the property of a Pennsylvania German church. Photographs coupled with dimensions and mark references should be of value to readers with a casual interest in pewter, as well as to pewter scholars. It is hoped that the readers of this book will have gained some knowledge of these wonderful and rare pewter forms, still surviving today, that were used in eighteenth-century Pennsylvania German churches.

DONALD M. HERR
Lancaster, Pennsylvania
July 1, 1995

Acknowledgments

THE AUTHOR DEEPLY APPRECIATES THE VALUable assistance of the following people for this project: Robert E. Asher, Kenneth Barkin, C. Richard Beam, Jan F. H. H. Beekhuizen, Richard L. Bowen, Jr., Lester P. Breininger, Jr., Raymond J. Brunner, David P. Cunningham, Eric de Jonge, Richard Druckenbrod, Curtis W. Dubble, Corinne Earnest, Kenneth Ferguson, Jan A. Gadd, Ellen J. Gehret, Martha A. Herr, Charles and Tandy Hersh, Clarke E. Hess, Wayne A. Hilt, Ronald F. Homer, Peter Hornsby, Robert G. Hostetter, Emyl Jenkins, Joan Johnson, Alan G. Keyser, Richard and Rosemarie Machmer, Heinz M. Markert, Derik A. Mundill, Larry M. Neff, William Oosterman, Albert J. Phiebig, Ruthann L. Richards, Ian D. Robinson, William L. Scollard, Karl Schöppl, Donald A. Shelley, Charles V. Swain, Frederick S. Weiser, and Mark B. Winchester.

The following institutions and their staffs kindly shared information and made their pewter available for study: Catholic Archives, Diocese of Harrisburg, Kathy Signor; Ephrata Cloister, Ephrata, Pa., Nadine Steinmetz, Curator, Clarence E. Spohn; Evangelical and Reformed Historical Society of the United Church of Christ, Lancaster, Pa., John Payne, President, Kay Schellhase, Archivist; Friends of Historic Peace Church, Shiremanstown, Pa., Miriam Miller, President; Henry Ford Museum and Greenfield Village, Dearborn, Mich.; Henry Francis du Pont Winterthur Museum, Winterthur, Del., Dwight P. Lanmon, Director, Donald L. Fennimore, Curator, Philip D. Zimmerman; Heritage Center of Lancaster County, Lancaster, Pa., Peter S. Seibert, Director, Wendell R. Zercher, Curator, Patricia J. Keller, Director/Curator, Susan S. Messimer; Historic Bethlehem, Inc., Bethlehem, Pa., Ralph G. Schwarz, Director, Charles A. LeCount, Curator; Historical Center, Juniata Mennonite District Historical Society, Richfield, Pa., Noah L. Zimmerman, Director; Historical Society of Carroll County, Westminster, Md., Jay A. Graybeal, Curator; Historical Society of Frederick County, Frederick, Md., Judith Proffitt, Curator; Historical Society of Pennsylvania, Philadelphia, Pa., Elizabeth Jarvis, Curator; Historical Society of York County, York, Pa., Janet Deranian, Curator; Lancaster Mennonite Historical Society, Lancaster, Pa., Carolyn C. Wenger, Director; Lebanon County Historical Society, Lebanon, Pa., Chris Mason, Curator; Lutheran Archives Center at Philadelphia, John E. Peterson, Curator; Mennonite Historians of Eastern Pennsylvania, Harleysville, Pa., Joel D. Alderfer, Librarian/Curator; Moravian Archives, Bethlehem, Pa., Vernon Nelson, Archivist; Moravian Congregational Archives, Lititz, Pa., Doris M. Johnson, Curator; Moravian College, Reeves Library, Bethlehem, Pa., Thomas Minor, Director, Bonnie Falla, Reference Librarian; Moravian Historical Society, Whitefield House, Nazareth, Pa., Susan M. Dreydoppel, Executive Director; Moravian Museums and Tours, Bethlehem, Pa., Charlene D. Mauers; Museum of Early Southern Decorative Arts, Winston-Salem, N.C., Frank L. Horton, Director Emeritus; Pennypacker Mills, Schwenksville, Pa., Elizabeth Gamon, Curator, Linda Christy, William Brobst; Schwenkfelder Museum and Library, Pennsburg, Pa., Dennis K. Moyer, Director; State Museum of Pennsylvania, Harrisburg, Jonathan Cox, Curator; Strasburg Heritage Society, Strasburg, Pa., Grace Stirba; Washington County Museum of Fine Arts, Hagerstown, Md., Jean Woods, Director; Brethren Heritage Room, Zug Memorial Library, Elizabethtown College, Elizabethtown, Pa., Hedda Durnbaugh, Archivist.

Pastors, church historians, and others who aided the project include:

Maryland

CARROLL COUNTY—Pipe Creek Church of the Brethren, Linwood, Terry K. Clark, Wanda Mills Clark, Stanley T. Diehl; St. Luke's Lutheran Church, New Windsor, Darrell L. Layman, Betty Munshaur.

FREDERICK COUNTY—Apple's United Church of Christ, Thurmont; Evangelical Lutheran Church, Frederick, Walter P. Fogarty, Phillis Knill, Kathryn Long; Glade United Church of Christ, Walkersville, Robert R. Rock.

WASHINGTON COUNTY—Zion Evangelical and Reformed United Church of Christ, Hagerstown, Jack D. L. Cook, R. H. Winters, David Schwartz.

Pennsylvania

ADAMS COUNTY—Bender's Lutheran Church, Biglerville, Elizabeth Devan; Emmanuel United Church of Christ, Abbottstown, Dean M. Bobb; Flohr Lutheran Church, McKnightstown, Douglas Y. Boden, Bonnie Baker.

BERKS COUNTY—Allegheny Union Church with Lutheran and United Church of Christ congregations, Mohnton, Elmer B. Reinhold, Jr., Rebecca A. Brenner, Charles J. Charles; Bally Mennonite Church, Bally, Roy K. Yoder, Drollene Gehman, Melvin and Sarah Gehman; Bern Union Church with Lutheran and United Church of Christ congregations, Leesport, Loretta W. Roberts, David Eicher; Christ Little Tulpehocken United Church of Christ, Bernville, Herman Lutz; Christ Lutheran Church, Spangsville, Robert R. Mitchell, Jr.; Epler's United Church of Christ, Leesport, Evelyn J. Aurand, John and Esther Blatt, Christine Pifer-Soote; Friedens Lutheran Church, Stony Run, Mark, D. Bernecker, Richard Schmidt; Jerusalem (Red) Union Church with Lutheran and United Church of Christ congregations, Kempton, Ernest Flothmeier, Larry Hemsley, Clarence Kunkel; St. John's United Church of Christ, Sinking Spring, W. R. Miller; St. John's (Hain's) United Church of Christ, Wernersville, Peter P. Goguts, Catherine M. Scheidy; St. Paul's Lutheran Church, Hamburg, Walter P. Fetterly; Salem United Church of Christ, Spangsville, Joan Jones, Eleanor Shaner; Schwartzwald United Church of Christ, Reading, Clyde E. Huber; The Most Blessed Sacrament Catholic Church, Bally, Charles Storm; Trinity Lutheran Church, Reading, Elton P. Richards, Jr.; Zion (Moselem) Lutheran Church, Kutztown, Donald B. Landis; Zion St. John's (Reed's) Lutheran Church, Womelsdorf, Gunther J. Stippich, Barbara Shade; Zion (Spies) United Church of Christ, Reading, Arlan M. Bond.

BUCKS COUNTY—Blooming Glen Mennonite Church, Blooming Glen, Truman H. Brunk, Jr., Robert L. Shreiner, William Gross, Jody Moyer, Arlan Lapp; Deep Run Mennonite Church, Perkasie, John M. Ehst; East Swamp Mennonite Church, Quakertown, Jonathan F. Yoder, James Gerhart; Line Lexington Mennonite Church, Line Lexington, Robert G. Walters, Lowell H. Delp; St. John's (Schuetz's) Lutheran Church, Spinnerstown, R. Bruce Todd; Springfield Mennonite Church, Pleasant Valley, Gregory Stenson, Irwin Miller; Swamp Mennonite Church, Quakertown, William A. Brunk.

CARBON COUNTY—St. John Lutheran Church, Palmerton, Jody L. Neifert.

CENTRE COUNTY—Salem Lutheran Church, Aaronsburg, Rosalie N. Smith, Ralph D. Musick; St. Peter's Lutheran Church, Rebersburg, Shirley Rishel.

CHESTER COUNTY—East Vincent United Church of Christ, Spring City, Paul H. Curvey, Pauline Keller.

CUMBERLAND COUNTY—Friedens (Peace) St. John's Lutheran Church and St. Paul's United Church of Christ, Grantham, Miriam Miller; Salem (Stone) United Church of Christ, Carlisle, George Bahner, Robert Alspaugh.

DAUPHIN COUNTY—Colonial Park United Church of Christ, Harrisburg, James W. Morris, Pat Rudy; Hannoverdale Church of the Brethren, Hummelstown, Earl E. Light; Hummelstown United Church of Christ, Hummelstown, Charles E. Doll, Jr.; St. Paul's (Sand Hill) Lutheran Church, Hershey, Steven R. Bowser; St. Thomas United Church of Christ, Harrisburg, Stephen A. Gifford; Salem United Church of Christ, Harrisburg, D. Albert Myers, Mary R. Bottiglier, Paul W. Knappenburger, Ann Conrad; Stauffer Mennonite Church, Hershey, Carl H. Snavely; Zion Lutheran Church, Hummelstown, Ronald G. Van Blargan, Robert T. Fox, Jr.; Zion (Klinger's) Lutheran Church, Erdman, Walter J. Hafer, Jr., Irwin Klinger.

LANCASTER COUNTY—Bergstrasse Lutheran Church, Ephrata, Jay B. Eickhoff; Bethany United Church of Christ, Ephrata, Rickey L. Mearkle; Bossler's Mennonite Church, Elizabethtown, Simon P. Kraybill; Brickerville United Lutheran Church, Brickerville, William W. De Hass, W. Stevens Shipman, Kenneth L. Weaver; Chestnut Hill Mennonite Church, Landisville, J. Leon Eshleman; Christ Church United Church of Christ, Elizabethtown, P. Larry Potteiger; Christ Lutheran Church, Elizabethtown, Henri A. Eberly; East Petersburg Mennonite Church, East Petersburg, John B. Shenk; Good Mennonite Church, Bainbridge, Clair Nissley, Harold L. and Dorothy Risser; Holy Trinity Lutheran Church, Lancaster, Larry L. Lehman, Averil Christman, Jean Thorn, Edward S. Brubaker; Jerusalem United Church of Christ, Manheim, Ruth Mary Summy; Landisville Mennonite Church, Landisville, J. Samuel Thomas; Lititz Moravian Church, Lititz, Alden A. Ward; Mellingers Mennonite Church, Lancaster, A. David Buckwalter, Earl B. Groff; Muddy Creek Lutheran Church, Denver, William A. Martin; New Danville Mennonite Church, New Danville, Lindsay Harnish; Peace United Church of Christ, Denver, John C. Oliphant; Risser's Mennonite Church, Mt. Joy, Amos Risser, Gerald M. Heistand; St. John's Lutheran Church, Maytown, Robert M. Lescallette; St. Michael's Lutheran Church, Strasburg, Herbert A. Lohr; St. Stephen's United Church of Christ, New Holland, W. Lee Lawhead; Salem (Heller's) United Church of Christ, Leola, Donald M. Leonard; Shaarai Shomayim, Jack P. Paskoff; Swamp United Church of Christ, Reinholds, M. Craig Snow, Donald F. Geschwindt; Trinity Lutheran Church, New Holland, David L. Hunsberger, James Cox; Zion Lutheran Church, Manheim, Eric B. Stenman, Joanne P. Stenman.

LEBANON COUNTY—Bindnagle Lutheran Church, Palmyra, Heidi Neiswender; Gingrich's Mennonite Church, Lebanon, Abram N. Hoover; Hill Lutheran Church, Cleona, Clyde I. Fry, John D. Merkel; Millcreek Lutheran Church, Newmanstown, Norman J. Wilson; St. Jacob's (Kimmerling's) United Church of Christ, Lebanon, Allen F. Helwig; St. Luke's Lutheran Church, Schaefferstown, Larry Bergh, William W. Miller; St. Paul's United Church of Christ, Millbach, Park J. Ranck; St. Paul's United Church of Christ, Schaefferstown, Joseph P. Gyorke; Salem Lutheran Church, Lebanon, B. Penrose Hoover, Harry T. Richwine, Jr.; Salem United Church of Christ, Campbelltown, R. L. Christensen; Salem (Walmer's) Union Church with Lutheran and United Church of Christ congregations, Annville, Linda Lindenberg, Fred Weierbach; Tabor United Church of Christ, Lebanon, David C. Mark; Trinity Lutheran Church, Colebrook, Robert E. Custer; Zion Lutheran Church, Jonestown, Richard M. Olson, Eugene L. Shiffer, Craig J. Dorward; Zoar (Mt. Zion) Lutheran Church, Lebanon, Eugene L. Shiffer.

LEHIGH COUNTY—Ben Salem United Church of Christ, Andreas, Paul W. Cope; Christ's Church (Lowhill) United Church of Christ, New Tripoli, Ruth Schaefer, Ralph Zettlemoyer; Egypt United Church of Christ, Whitehall, Bert A. Schory, Leonard E. Shupp, Charles Schultes, Alice Kuntz; Friedens Lutheran Church, Center Valley, John W. Tomlinson, Jr., Lee Izon; Heidelberg Union Church with Lutheran and United Church of Christ congregations, Slatington, David L. Hess; Jacob's United Church of Christ, Jacksonville, Scott L. Shay; Jerusalem Union Church of Western Salisbury with Lutheran and United Church of Christ congregations, Allentown, Carl R. Schmoyer, Gary Piatt; Jordan Lutheran Church, Orefield, Ralph F. Eberle, Jr.; Neff's Union Church with Lutheran and United Church of Christ congregations, Neffs, Thomas N. Thomas, Diane Selig; St. Paul's Lutheran Church, Allentown, F. Thomas Lichner; St. Paul's United Church of Christ, Trexlertown, Robert T. Stevens; Weisenberg Lutheran Church, New Tripoli, Raymond J. Hand; Zion Lutheran Church, Old Zionsville, Jeral W. Gade and Mary W. Gade; Zion United Church of Christ, Allentown, Raymond Butz.

MONROE COUNTY—Christ United Lutheran Church, Stroudsburg, Ralph A. Boyer IV, Jane Hunt Jones.

MONTGOMERY COUNTY—Boehms Reformed United Church of Christ, Blue Bell, Peter Taylor, D. S. Beall-Ellersieck, Harry Reiff; Emmanuel Lutheran Church, Pottstown, Martin L. Acker, Kathryn Hanley; Lower Skippack Mennonite Church, Skippack, Wilmer B. Denlinger, Roland Bean, Helen H. Patterson, George Pritchard; New Goshenhopen Reformed United Church of Christ, East Greenville, Antonio L. Villareal, C. L. Cain-Borgman, Richard Freed; New Hanover Lutheran Church, Gilbertsville, Richard Elliott, Edgar M. Cooper; Plains Mennonite Church, Hatfield, Gerald C. Studer; St. Luke's United Church of Christ, Trappe, L. Eugene Moyer; St. Paul's Lutheran Church, Ardmore, Edward Treichel, Elizabeth Lash; St. Paul's Lutheran Church, Red Hill, R. William Phillips; St. Peter's Lutheran Church, North Wales, Burlington B. Latshaw; Salford Mennonite Church, Harleysville, James C. Longacre, Willis A. Miller, John L. Ruth; Towamencin Mennonite Church, Kulpsville, Russell M. Detweiler, Harold M. Fly; Upper Skippack Mennonite Church, Skippack, Ray Freed; Wentz's United Church of Christ, Worcester, Jesse W. Deardorff, Ruth Yeakel, William John Ziegenfus.

NORTHAMPTON COUNTY—Central Moravian Church, Bethlehem, Willard Martin, Carol A. Reifinger; Emanuel Lutheran Church, Bath, Ray Walker, Dorothy Ruth; Emmaus Moravian Church, Emmaus, Richard Bruckart, Robert F. Engelbrecht; First United Church of Christ, Easton, John H. Thomas, George R. Eckstein; Hope Lutheran Church, Cherryville, Clark W. Kuntz II; Nazareth Moravian Church, Nazareth, David L. Wickmann; Salem United

Church of Christ, Bath, T. M. Burns, Victor G. Vogel, Jr., Jane Gilbert; Trinity Lutheran Church, Bethlehem, Harvey M. Weitzel, Stella Johnson; Zion's (Stone) United Church of Christ, Northampton, Willard W. Wetzel, Harold P. Smith.

NORTHUMBERLAND COUNTY—First United Church of Christ, Sunbury, Jonathan P. Albright; Himmel's Union Church with Lutheran and United Church of Christ congregations, Rebuck, P. W. Billow.

PERRY COUNTY—Trinity United Church of Christ, New Bloomfield, Joseph Darlington.

PHILADELPHIA COUNTY—St. Michael's Lutheran Church, Philadelphia, Janet S. Peterman.

SCHUYLKILL COUNTY—Christ United Church of Christ, New Ringgold, Dale M. Shellhamer; Friedens Lutheran Church, New Ringgold, William Koch; Friedens United Church of Christ, New Ringgold, Dale M. Schellhammer, St. John's Lutheran Church, Friedensburg, Paul E. Buzzard; Zion (Red) Union Church, with Lutheran and United Church of Christ congregations, Orwigsburg, Philip K. Smith, Robert Young.

SNYDER COUNTY—Cross Roads Mennonite Church, Richfield, Noah L. Zimmerman; St. Peter's Lutheran Church, Freeburg, David E. Bombay.

SOMERSET COUNTY—Holy Trinity Lutheran Church, Berlin, Melvin A. Kirk, Paul E. Pritts; Trinity United Church of Christ, Berlin, Carl W. Schwarm, Barbara Croner.

WASHINGTON COUNTY—Bethlehem Lutheran Church, Scenery Hill, Robert K. Brunk.

YORK COUNTY—Black Rock Church of the Brethren, Brodbecks, Gene L. Bucher, Donald Hubbell; Canadochly Lutheran Church, York, Melvin E. Dick; Christ Lutheran Church, York, Leonard R. Klein; Codorus Church of the Brethren, Loganville, Joseph A. Detrick, William I. Gould; Emmanuel United Church of Christ, Red Lion, Lester L. Ringer; Friedensaal Lutheran Church, Seven Valleys, J. Paul Kennedy; Old Historic Holtzschwamm Church, Thomasville, Harold and Nancy Hamme, Keith Myers; Paradise-Holtzschwamm United Church of Christ, Thomasville, Roger N. Cheney; Paradise Lutheran Church, Thomasville, Larry A. McConnell; St. Paul's (Wolf's) United Church of Christ, York, Richard McClain, John Wolf; St. Paul's (Zeigler's) Lutheran Church, Seven Valleys, James W. Weis; St. Peter's (Lischey's) United Church of Christ, Spring Grove, Maybelle Autland; Trinity (Roth's) United Church of Christ, Spring Grove, Philip K. Nace, Richard Graybill.

Virginia

FREDERICK COUNTY—Centenary United Church of Christ, Winchester, Gerald T. Stone; Trinity Lutheran Church, Stephens City, William Hogan.

ROCKINGHAM COUNTY—Rader's Lutheran Church, Timberville, John D. Yeich.

SHENANDOAH COUNTY—St. Paul's United Church of Christ, Woodstock, Jerrold L. Foltz; Zion Lutheran Church, Edinburg, John F. Tayler, Jr.

West Virginia

HAMPSHIRE COUNTY—Hebron Lutheran Church, Wardensville, Phillip C. Huber, Ruth Rudolph.

Finally, special thanks to the following individuals for their help and support over the years of the projects preparation:

Susan M. Cunningham designed a computer program for the project and facilitated the retrieval of the data.

C. Eugene Moore carefully edited the text and increased the clarity of the finished product.

Jean Woods read the manuscript and provided useful suggestions and support.

John Carl Thomas shared his enthusiasm for the pewter forms, not previously illustrated, found in the survey. He also read the text for subject accuracy.

Special appreciation is given to Don Yoder and editor Willard W. Wetzel for their suggestions and guidance with the project.

And most important of all, a special thank you to my wife, Patricia, and my family for their support and encouragement of this project through the years.

List of Abbreviations

A GREAT MANY SOURCES CONTRIBUTED TO the information in this book. Since 1934, the Pewter Collectors' Club of America has published a semiannual bulletin about newly discovered pewter forms, makers, and touchmarks. The club published *Pewter in American Life* in observance of its fiftieth anniversary. Ledlie I. Laughlin's monumental three-volume *Pewter in America, Its Makers and Their Marks* is considered the standard reference of American pewter. Charles F. Montgomery's *A History of American Pewter* and John Carl Thomas' *Connecticut Pewter and Pewterers* are the result of subsequent research.

The information in Howard H. Cotterell's *Old Pewter* (1929) on English, Scottish, and Irish pewter has been continually updated by articles in the British publication *Journal of the Pewter Society* and in the *Pewter Collectors' Club of America Bulletin*. Christopher A. Peal's *More Pewter Marks* and his addenda include more visible and new marks not found in Cotterell.

Erwin Hintze's seven-volume *Die Deutschen Zinngiesser und Ihre Marken* and Hanns-Ulrich's *Zinn* were useful for the identification of pewter from Germany. Karl Schöppl from Aachen provided current information about makers from his native land.

The third volume of Hugo Schneider's *Zinn: Die Zinngiesser der Schweiz und ihre Marken* was useful in identifying pewter from Switzerland.

Abbreviations used to identify pewterers and their marks in Pewter in Pennsylvania German Churches:

C = Cotterell, Howard H. *Old Pewter: Its Makers and Marks in England, Scotland and Ireland: An Account of the Old Pewterer & His Craft.* Rutland, Vt. and Tokyo, Japan: Charles E. Tuttle Co. 1963, 1st Edition pub. 1929 by B. T. Batsford Ltd., London.

D = Dubbe, B. *Tin en tinnegieters in Nederland.* Lochem BV: De Tijdstroom 1978, first printing Zeist, 1965.

H = Hintze, Erwin. *Die Deutschen Zinngiesser und Ihre Marken.* Bände 1–7. Aalen: Otto Zeller Verlagsbuchhandlung, 1964. Reprint of first edition, 1921–1931.

L = Laughlin, Ledlie I. *Pewter in America: Its Makers and Their Marks.* Boston: The Houghton Mifflin Co. 1940. I, II, Barre, Mass.: Barre Publishers, 1969. III. Barre, Mass.: Barre Publishing Co. 1971.

P = Peal, Christopher A. *More Pewter Marks.* Cringleford, Norwich, England: Peal, 1976.

S = Schneider, Hugo, and Kneuss, Paul. *Zinn: Die Zinngiesser der Schweiz und ihre Marken.* Bände III. Olten: Walter-Verlag AG, 1983.

ST = Scott, Jack L. *Pewter Wares from Sheffield.* Baltimore: Antiquary Press, 1980.

T = Thomas, John C. *Connecticut Pewter and Pewterers.* Hartford: The Connecticut Historical Society, 1976.

Abbreviations used to measure objects in the study:

H = height
TD = top diameter
BD = bottom diameter
L = length
W = width
D = diameter

Dimensions are recorded in inches.

Dates following the pewterer's name and location are approximate working dates. The information in this book represents an attempt to include the most current knowledge of pewterers and their production dates.

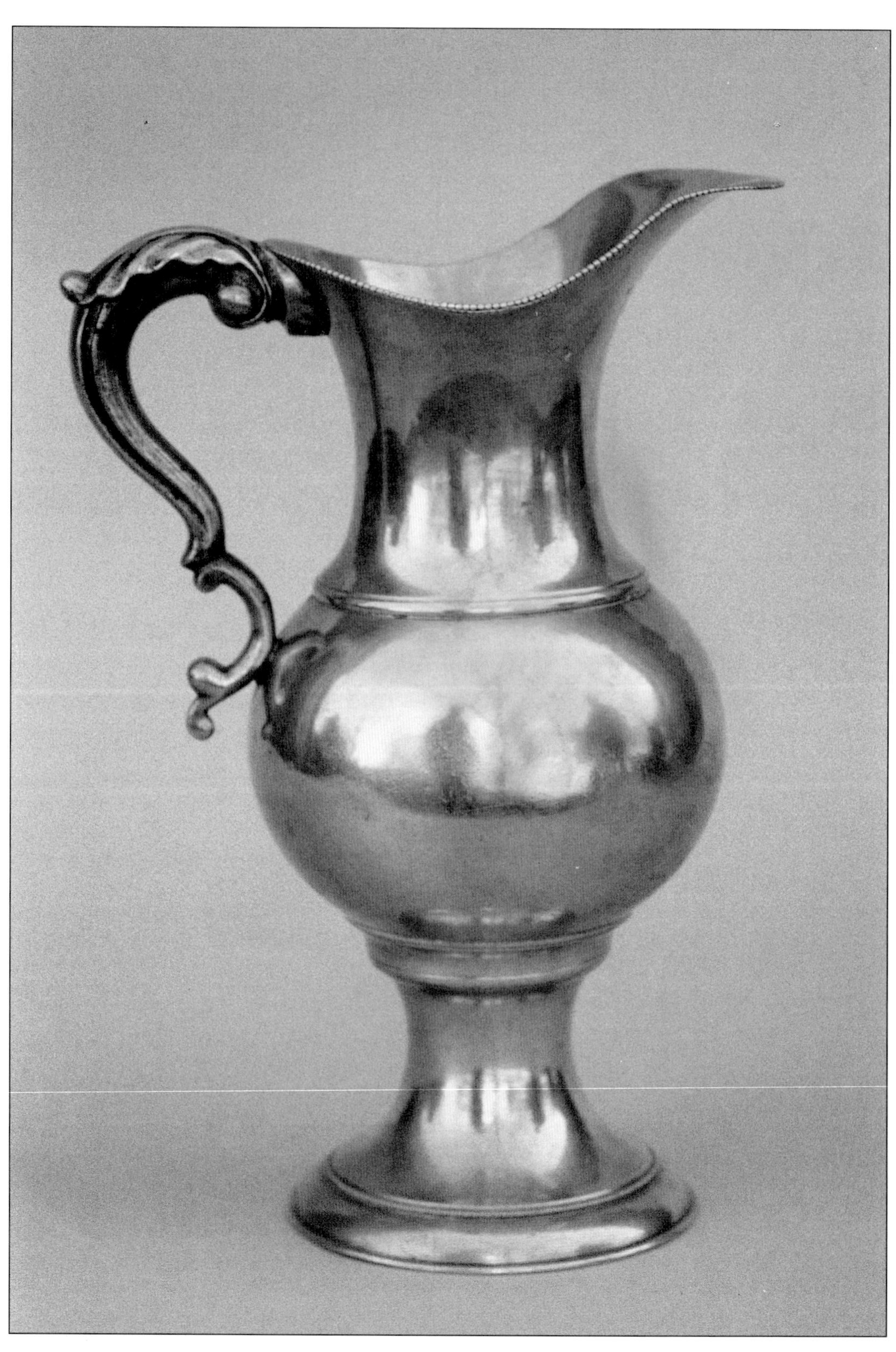

Ewer or pitcher attributed to William Will, Philadelphia, 1764–1798. H 10 3/4", TD 3 3/8", BD 4 1/4". St. Michael's Lutheran Church, Strasburg, Lancaster County, Pa.

CHAPTER 1

Pewter

COMPOSITION

Pewter is an alloy whose principal element is tin. Copper, lead, bismuth, and antimony, added in varying amounts, give the admixture its variable weight and hardness. As a rule, the larger the proportion of tin, the better quality the pewter.

Analysis of pewter made by certain eighteenth-century American makers revealed an extremely high tin content, often as high as 95 to 99 percent.[1] In general, increasing the lead content made the alloy softer, more malleable, and easier to cast and work. Examples of the softer alloy are spoons, plates, and measures. These forms were frequently made by country makers. Hardening agents such as copper, bismuth, and later antimony added rigidity and strength to the finished product. The addition of copper, frequently three percent, gave a fine texture, excellent surface quality and strength to the end product. Pewter of the best quality was used for flagons, tankards, plates, and dishes, as well as for other forms used in both the home and the church.

CONSTRUCTION

Most pewter objects were made by casting the melted alloy into molds, which were made of stone, clay and sand but most frequently of bronze (Figure 1), brass, and bell metal. The alloy was heated to 400–500° F and then poured into molds. The molds were coated with lubricants such as ocher, egg white, carbon, or pumice to aid the flow of the molten metal. The molds were then heated to the correct temperature to ensure an even coating of the metal into all parts of the casting. After cooling, the molds were opened and the casting removed. Surplus metal was removed and the casting was cleaned, scraped, and smoothed or burnished, using a lathe.

Bronze, brass, and bell-metal molds were costly and difficult to make but gave excellent results and could be used repeatedly.

Because the shape of each pewter vessel was predetermined by the shape of the mold, the styles of each pewterer's products were limited to the styles of the molds the pewterer owned, had access to, or selected. It must be clearly recognized, however, that the pewterer had little of the flexibility enjoyed by the silversmith, who hammered thin sheets

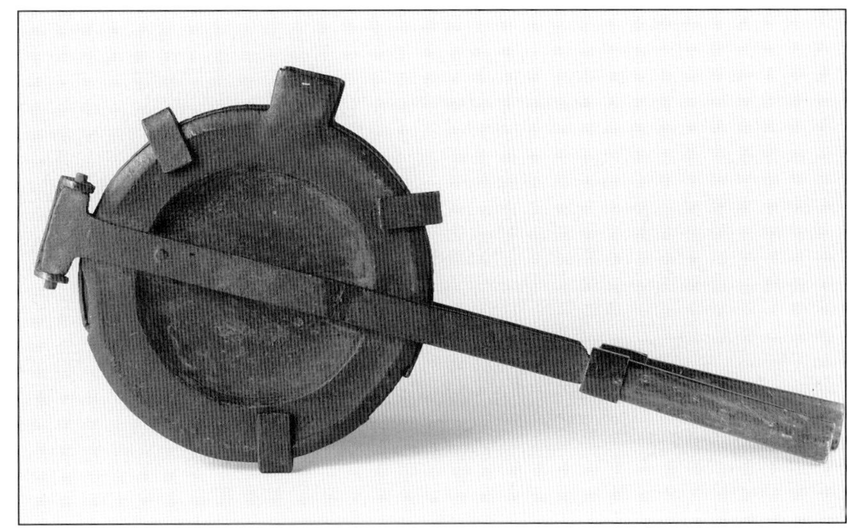

Fig. 1. *Bronze mold for casting pewter plates. Probably American, 1790–1820. Length 21″, Width 10 1/8″. This mold produced a plate 8″ in diameter. Courtesy, Winterthur Museum.*

1. Charles F. Montgomery, A History of American Pewter (New York: Praeger Publishers, 1973), 235.

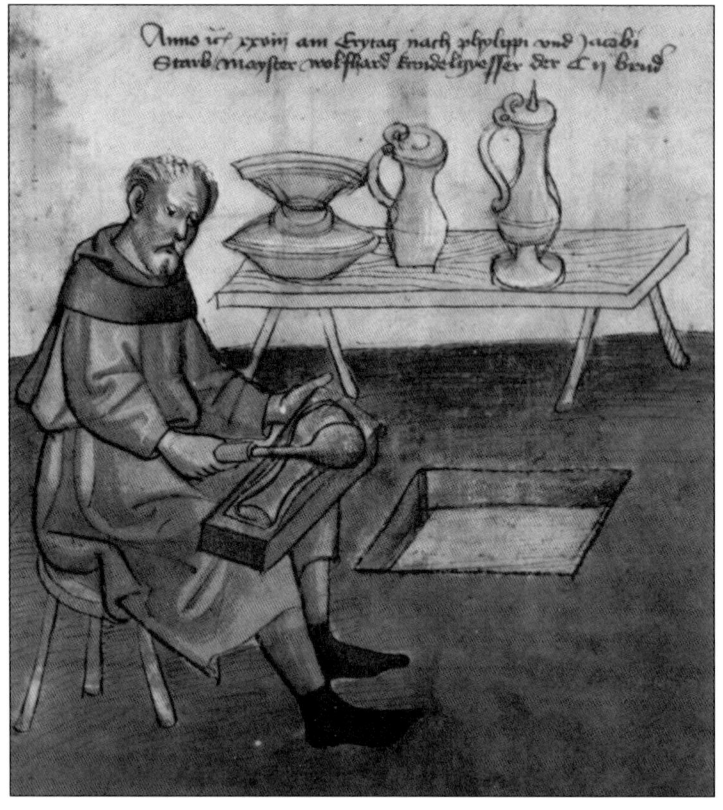

Fig. 2. *Casting the body of a flagon, 1428. Margarete Wagner,* ***Nürnberger Handwerker: Bilder und Aufzeichnungen aus den Zwölfbrüderhäusern 1388–1807*** *(Wiesbaden, Germany, 1977). Courtesy, The Library of Congress.*

of the more malleable silver into the designs that he offered to his customers.

Plates, dishes, and basins, collectively known as flatware, were made in one mold. Vessels such as flagons, tankards, mugs, chalices and beakers were called holloware. Holloware pieces required multiple molds and the finished parts were soldered together to make the resultant form. See figures 2, 3, and 4.

Fourteen molds were necessary to produce the various parts needed to assemble the flagon illustrated in Figure 5.

The booge (curved part of a plate, dish, or basin) was hammered, perhaps to strengthen it, on most British flatware. Hammering flatware was not a common practice in America or on the Continent.

The methods used in manufacturing pewter changed little over several centuries until the industrial revolution of the early nineteenth century. At that time, drop presses, powered by water and steam, were developed to stamp sheets of metal into forms. Powerful lathes then spun thin sheets onto a pattern, taking the design of that pattern.

Britannia metal is a term for an alloy that is harder, thinner, and lighter in weight than pewter of an earlier time. It can be made into sheets for mass production.

HISTORICAL BACKGROUND

Pewter has been in use for several thousand years. The Egyptians and Chinese were proficient in the art of making pewter. Written sources from classical antiquity reveal that the Romans used pewter plates. Several hundred pieces of Roman pewter have been excavated in Britain, suggesting a pewter industry of reasonable size in the third and fourth centuries.[2]

Tin mines, particularly those in the area of Cornwall, England and the Erzgebirge (Ore Mountains) areas of Saxony, such as Ehrenfriedersdorf, Wunsiedel, and Altenberg, provided the mineral ore cassiterite for the production of tin used

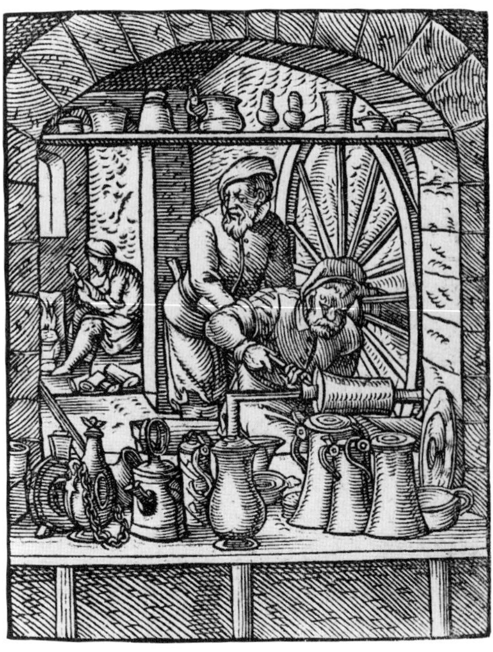

Fig. 3. *A pewterer is working at a lathe, smoothing the body of a flagon. Note the finished flagons in the foreground. Woodcut by Jost Amman,* ***Ständebuch*** *(Frankfurt, Germany, 1568). Courtesy, Trustees of the British Museum.*

2. Peter R. G. Hornsby, Rosemary Weinstein, and Ronald F. Homer, *Pewter: A Celebration of the Craft 1200–1700* (London: The Museum of London, 1989), 30.

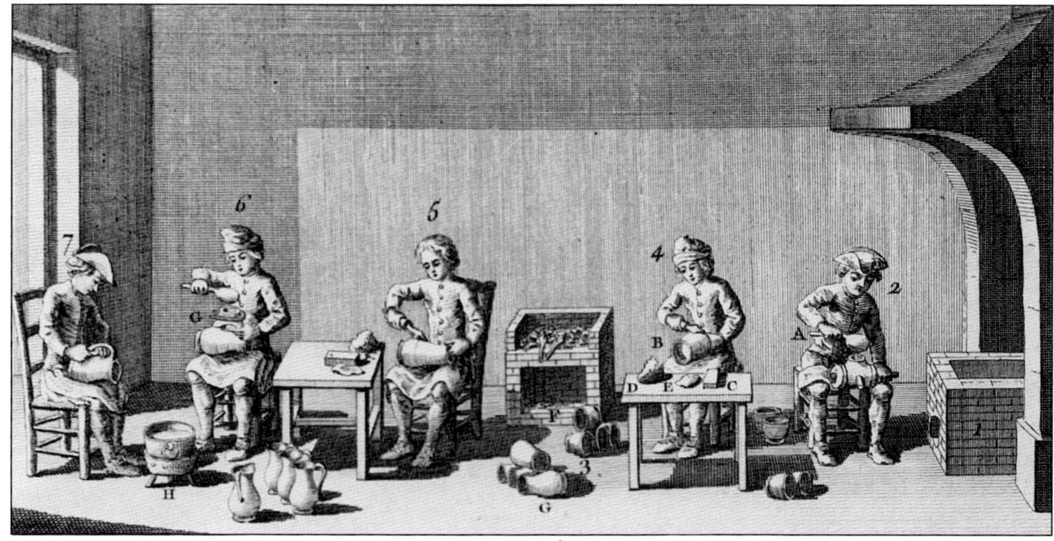

Fig. 4. *Interior of an eighteenth century pewterer's shop. Left to right: burnishing or smoothing the surface by hand, casting a handle onto a vessel, two workers soldering, and another pouring metal into a mold. Pierre Auguste Salmon,* ***L'Art du Potier d'Etain*** *(Paris, 1788). Courtesy, The Winterthur Library, Printed Book and Periodical Collection.*

by pewterers in the twelfth to the eighteenth centuries.[3]

The quality of the alloy and workmanship given to the finished product were controlled by strong trade organizations or pewterers guilds, in the British Isles and Continental Europe. In England, the London Company was a notably strong guild. An aspiring pewterer was required to serve an apprenticeship of seven years. He lived with his master, and was subject to the discipline of his master. After completing his apprenticeship, and before he was allowed to set out on his own, he had leave to strike his mark on the guild's touchplate and became a Freeman or Yeoman. Then, he may have worked for another pewterer as a Journeyman or opened his own shop. A select group, the Livery, was elected from the Freemen or Yeomanry. The London Company had various offices that included Renter Warden, Upper Warden, and Master.

There were no pewterers guilds in America. Colonial pewterers were not subject to the powerful trade organizations that existed in Europe.

An endless variety of objects for domestic and ecclesiastical use has been made by pewterers for more than six centuries. The majority of table utensils were made of pewter in the sixteenth and seventeenth centuries, the metal having

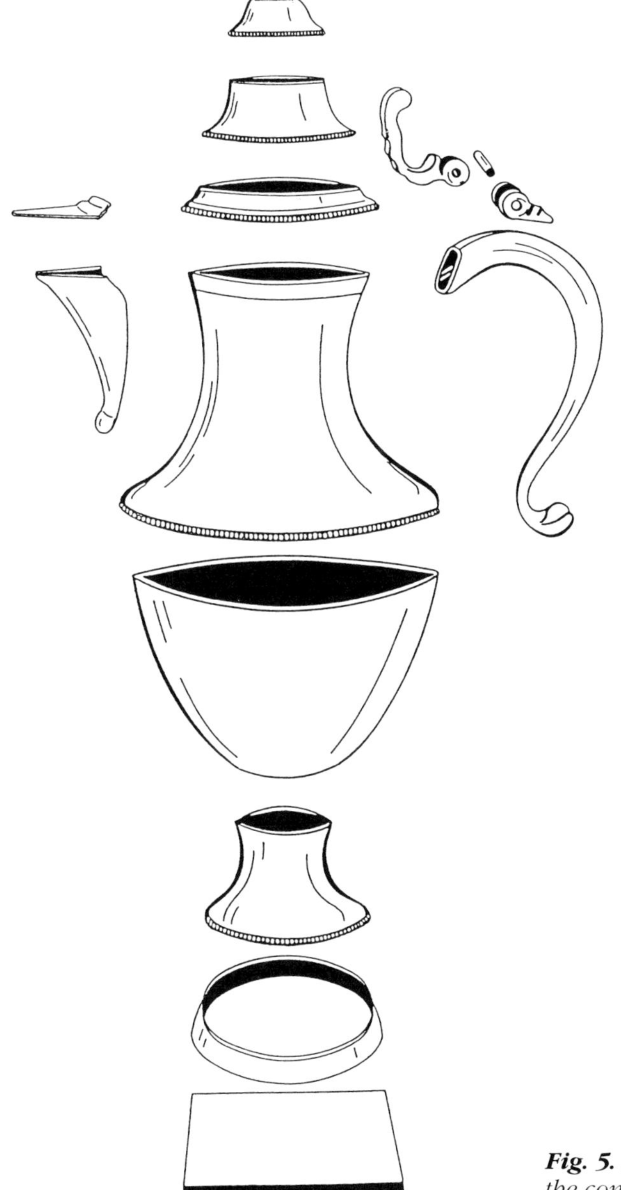

Fig. 5. *Diagram showing the construction of a flagon.*

3. H. Wilsdorf, W. Quellmalz, and G. Schlegel, *Das erzgebirgische Aijnn in Natur, Geschichte und Technik* (Altenberg, Germany: Altenberg Museum, 1983), 29, 31, and 34.

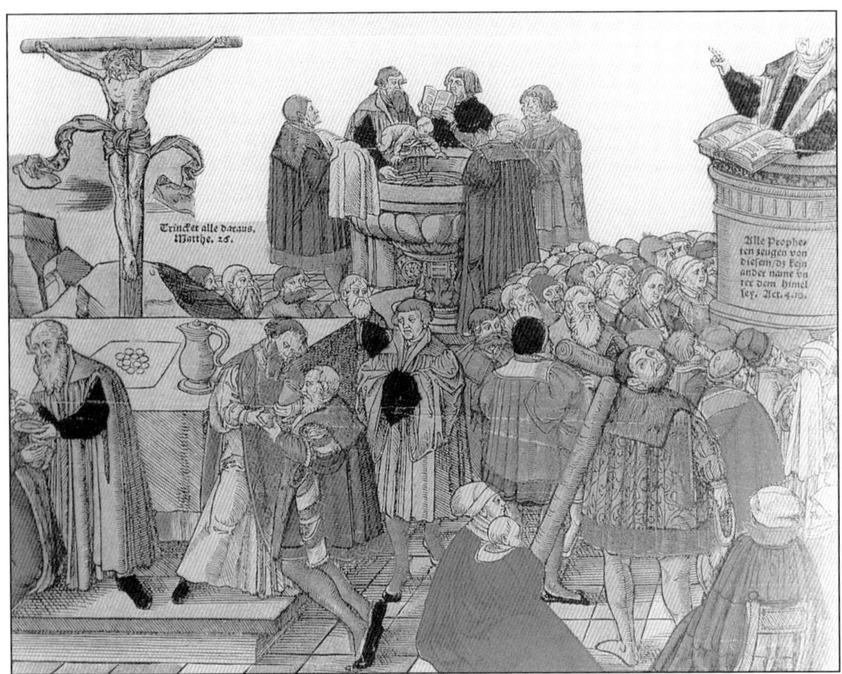

Fig. 6. *Detail of a woodcut by Lucas Cranach the Younger printed in Wittenberg, Germany, about 1535. Courtesy, William Oosterman.*

replaced wood and other organic materials. In England, pewter had become outmoded by fashionable pottery and porcelain by the end of the eighteenth century. The use of mugs in taverns, however, continued into the third quarter of the nineteenth century.[4]

In America, pewter was used widely in the last half of the eighteenth century and well into the first half of the nineteenth. Pewter competed with English imports such as delftware, salt-glazed ware, creamware, and Oriental export porcelain. Soft paste, such as Gaudy Dutch and later Gaudy Ironstone, were nineteenth-century export items popular with the Pennsylvania Germans.

In mid-nineteenth century America, pewter was made into nearly every conceivable form. The lighter, thinner metal was made into sanders, shaving boxes, shakers, cups and saucers, silhouette frames, nursing bottles, fluted bowls, and spittoons. The alloy itself became silver-plated, as were other base metals, satisfying the tastes of Americans in the third quarter of the nineteenth century.

USE OF PEWTER IN THE CHURCH

In England, pewter was used in churches as early as 1076.

> By a resolution passed by the council of Winchester in 1076, pewter (or tin) was allowed to be used for ecclesiastical vessels, but at a Council, held at Westminster a century later, the use of base metal was prohibited. In 1603, in the first year of the reign of James I, the Canons promulgated that the sacramental wine should "be brought to the table in a clean and sweet standing pot or stoup of pewter, if not of purer metal": this led to the considerable numbers of pewter flagons which we know to have been in church use from that time onward.[5]

Domestic use of the flagon form waned in England in the seventeenth century, while its use in the church increased. Pewter flagons were adopted by most parishes in the first half of the seventeenth century.[6] In the eighteenth century, flagons appear to have been used almost exclusively in the church.

In the Netherlands, church pewter rarely survived from the period before the Reformation in the early 1500s, since it was either destroyed during periods of iconoclasm or required to be handed over to the secular authorities.

Flagons found in paintings by Dutch artists of the fifteenth to seventeenth centuries present the use of the vessels in a domestic setting.[7] In that time period, flagons were probably used more frequently at home than in the church.

> For Protestant churches pewterers made communion flagons and

4. Peter R. G. Hornsby, *Pewter of the Western World (1600–1850)* (Exton, Pa.: Schiffer Publishing, Ltd., 1983), 27

5. The Worshipful Company of Pewterers, *A Short History of the Worshipful Company of London and a Catalogue of Pewterware in Its Possession* (London: Percy Lund, Humphries & Co., Ltd. 1968), 31.

6. Hornsby, *Pewter of the Western World (1600–1850)*, 77.

7. Hornsby, Weinstein, and Homer, Pewter: A Celebration of the Craft 1200–1700, 40.

beakers, dishes, offertory boxes, christening ewers and basins.[8]

The administration of the sacraments of baptism and communion in the Lutheran Church in sixteenth-century Germany is illustrated in Figures 6 and 7. Note the use of the common cup, a practice that continued in Pennsylvania German churches into the twentieth century. Sanitary concerns gradually decreed the use of individual cups. The communicant in the left foreground of the German print is receiving a wafer. In the background, an infant is being baptized by immersion. Note that an attendant is holding a towel.

Adult baptism, as conducted in the Mennonite Church of the Lamb in the eighteenth century, is depicted in a drawing from the Netherlands in Figure 8.

The sacrament of communion is being administered in Figure 9.

Lewis Miller, perhaps more than any other artist, chronicled the daily events in the lives of Pennsylvania Germans and others around him in York, Pennsylvania, and the surrounding area. He attempted to record the everyday life, customs, and dress of those with whom he came in contact, and the events in the city in which he resided. His birth is recorded in the records of Christ Lutheran Church of York as May 3, 1796. He spent most of his life in York, where he carefully recorded

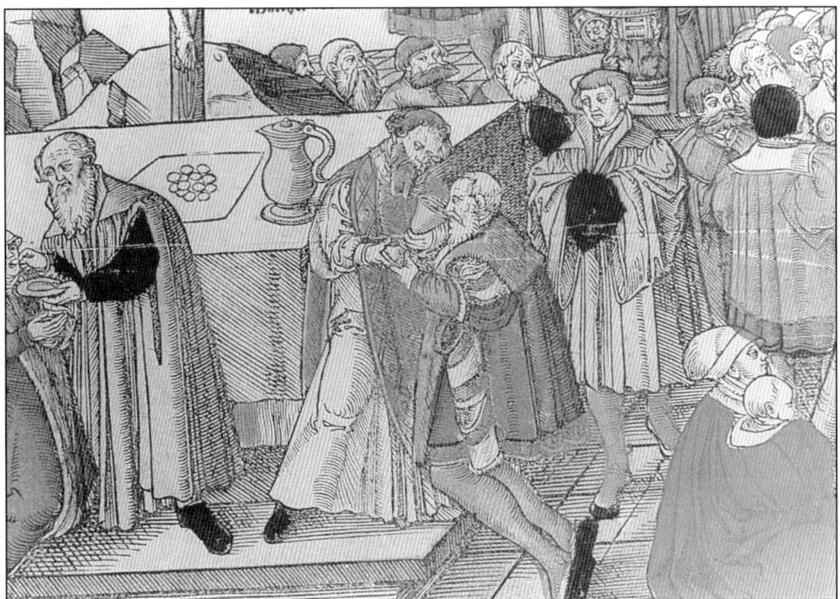

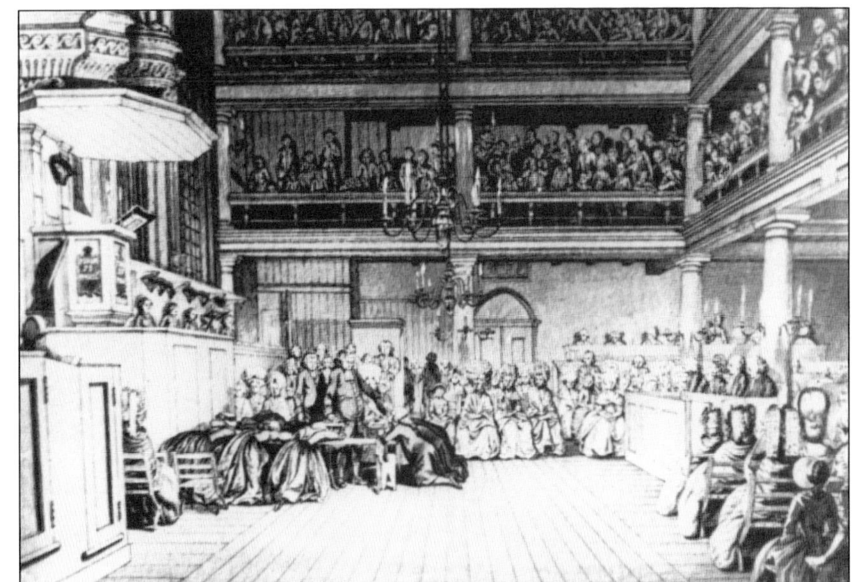

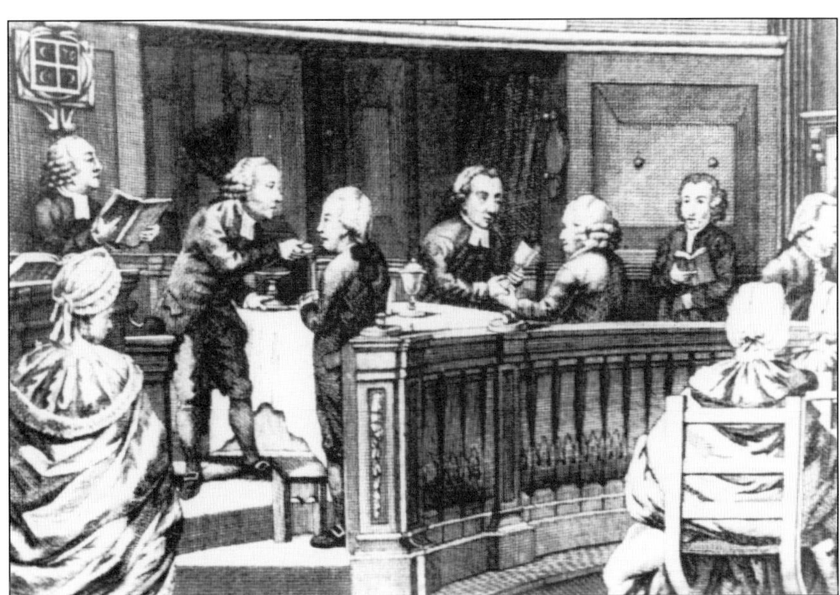

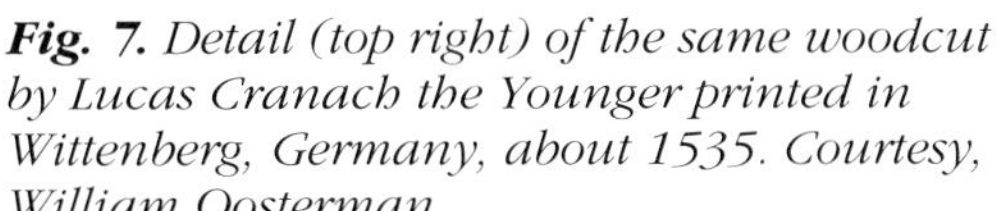

Fig. 7. *Detail (top right) of the same woodcut by Lucas Cranach the Younger printed in Wittenberg, Germany, about 1535. Courtesy, William Oosterman.*

Fig. 8. *Service of baptism (center right) in the Mennonite Church of the Lamb. Pen and wash drawing by P. Wagemaar, 1781. Courtesy, William Oosterman.*

Fig. 9. *Receiving the sacrament of communion (bottom right). Engraving by J. L. van Beek after a drawing by J. Meurs, 1785. Netherlands. Courtesy, William Oosterman.*

8. B. Dubbe, *Tin en tinnegieters in Nederland* (Lochen BV: De Tijdstroom, 1978, first edition Zeist, 1965), 468.

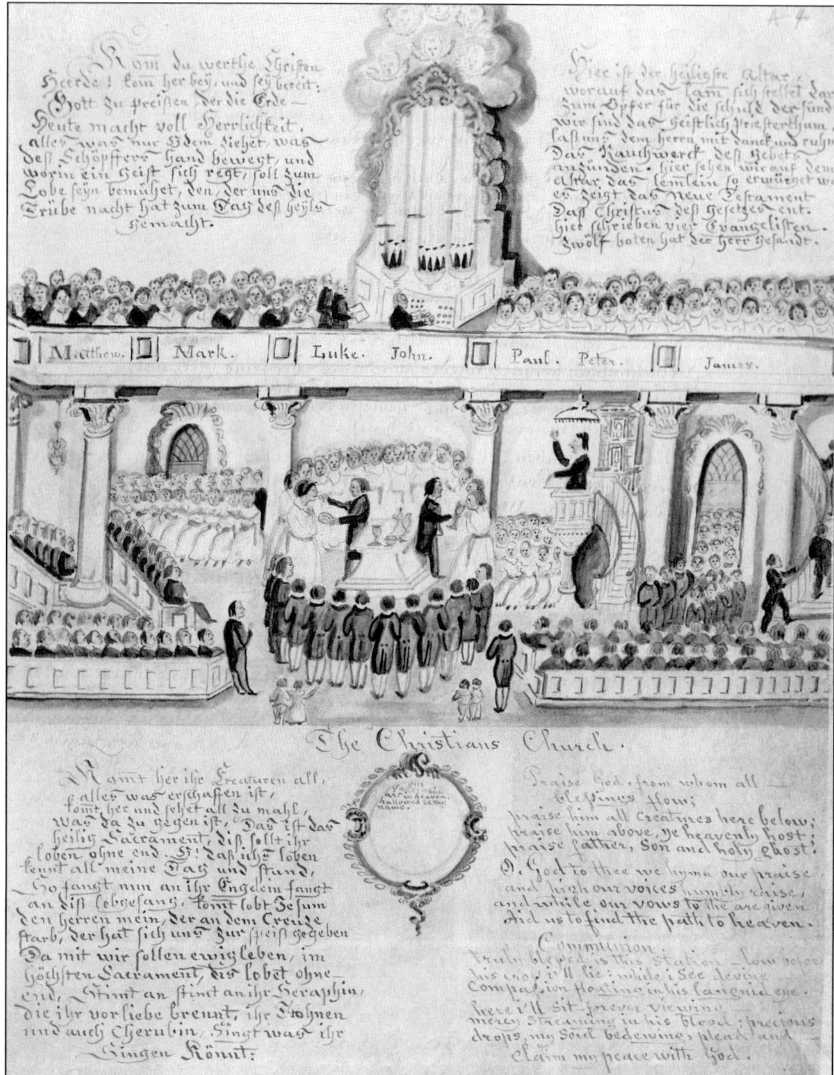

Fig. 10. *The service of communion depicted in a watercolor (left) by Lewis Miller, York, Pa. Miller made many watercolors between 1812 and 1880. In this drawing, "The Christians Church," Miller portrayed the separation of the sexes within the church and the minister conducting the service from his wine-glass pulpit. Assistants administer the sacraments to female communicants. Courtesy, The Historical Society of York County, Pa.*

Fig. 11. *Communion vessels and altar (below) used in the old Lutheran Church (Christ Lutheran) in York, Pa. Watercolor by Lewis Miller. Miller's "Record of the old Lutheran Church . . ." includes "The Altar in the old church as it Stood from 1753 to 1811." The altar has been prepared for the service of communion. A cloth, usually of homespun linen or cotton, covered the altar. The base of the altar was often solid, or closed, in Lutheran churches. Reformed congregations preferred an open communion table. The table top frequently was supported by turned legs. Courtesy, The Historical Society of York County, Pa.*

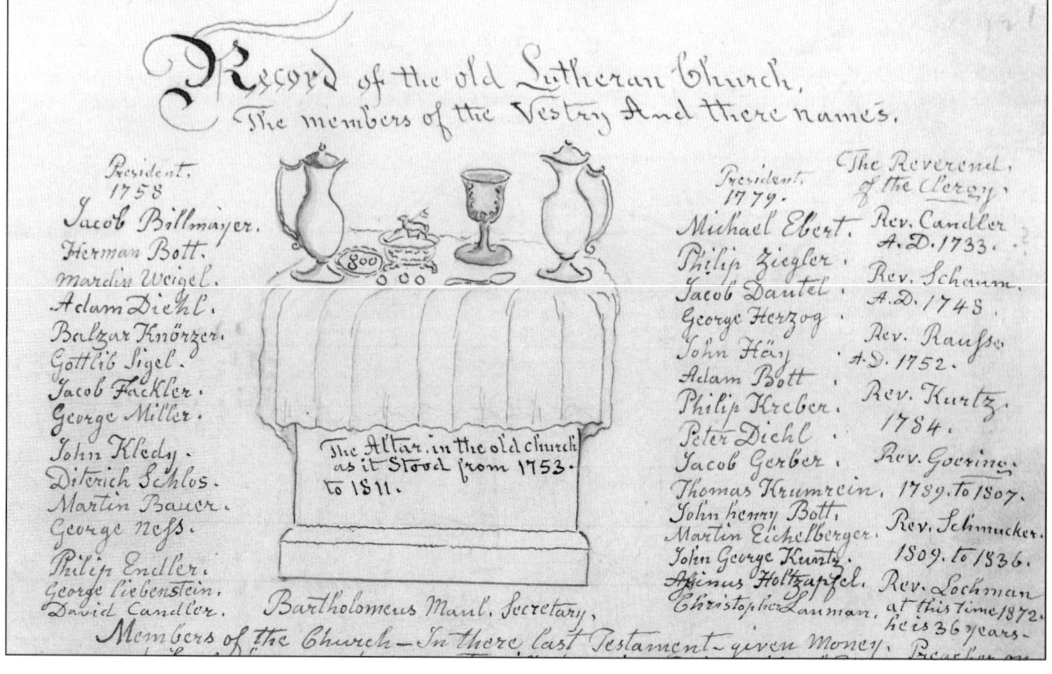
Record of the old Lutheran Church,
The members of the Vestry And there names.

President. 1758
Jacob Billmayer.
Herman Bott.
mardin Weigel.
Adam Diehl.
Balzar Knörzer.
Gottlib Sigel.
Jacob Fackler.
George Miller.
John Kledy.
Diterich Schlos.
Martin Bauer.
George Ness.
Philip Endler.
George liebenstein.
David Candler.

800

The Altar, in the old church as it Stood from 1753. to 1811.

President. 1779.
Michael Ebert.
Philip Ziegler.
Jacob Dantel.
George Herzog.
John Hay
Adam Bott.
Philip Kreber.
Peter Diehl.
Jacob Gerber.
Thomas Krumrein.
John henry Bott.
Martin Eichelberger.
John George Kuntz.
Albinus Holtzapfel.
Christopher Lanman.

The Reverend. of the Clergy.
Rev. Candler A.D. 1733.
Rev. Schaum. A.D. 1743.
Rev. Raufse. A.D. 1752.
Rev. Kurtz. 1784.
Rev. Goering. 1789. To 1807.
Rev. Schmucker. 1809. to 1836.
Rev. Lochman at this time 1872. he is 36 years.

Bartholomeus Maul. Secretary,
Members of the Church—In there last Testament-given Money.

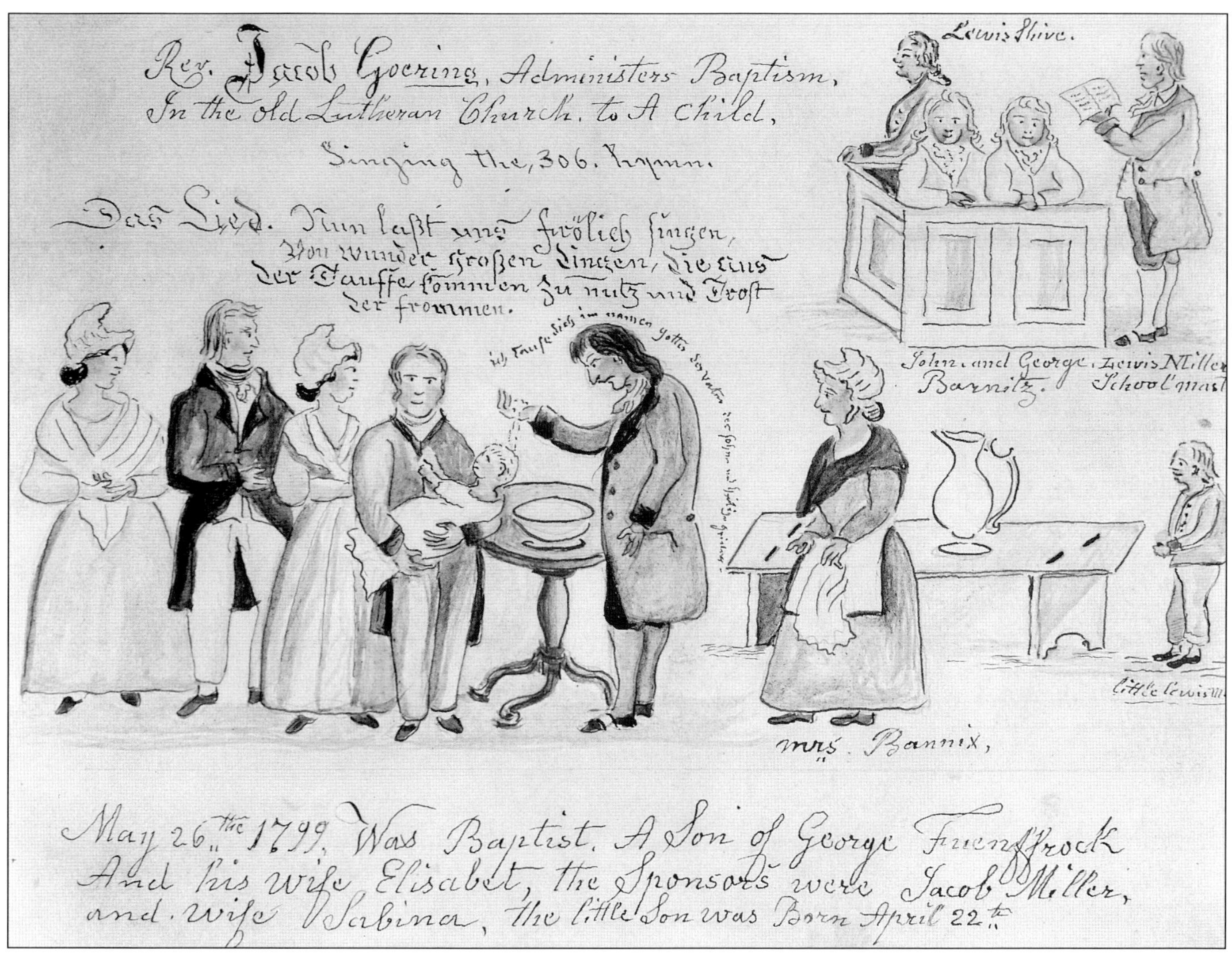

Fig. 12. *Baptism and vessels in the old Lutheran Church (Christ Lutheran) in York, Pa. Watercolor by Lewis Miller. Courtesy, The Historical Society of York County, Pa.*

his experiences with drawings and detailed texts. He traveled to Europe and later New York and eventually lived with his niece in Christiansburg, Virginia. He died there on September 15, 1882.[9]

Several watercolors by Lewis Miller give us some insight into the services of baptism and communion and the use of vessels in the nineteenth century by Pennsylvania Germans in York, Pennsylvania. Miller drew a church interior that included the service of Holy Communion in Figure 10. He depicts female communicants partaking of the bread and wine. In Figure 11, the altar of the old Lutheran Church in York is replete with a pair of flagons, a chalice, a host box, paten, and spoon. The old Lutheran Church in York is now Christ Church. The surviving holloware vessels in that church are silver and not pewter, but they do illustrate the use of sacramental vessels of a Pennsylvania German Lutheran Church in a contemporary setting. Figure 12 depicts a

9. Donald A. Shelley, "Introduction," *Lewis Miller: Sketches and Chronicles: The Reflections of a Nineteenth-Century Pennsylvania German Folk Artist* (York, Pa.: Historical Society of York County, 1966), xiii–xxii.

child being baptized in the old Lutheran Church in the same city.

Durs Rudy, Jr. (1798–1850) of Lehigh County, Pennsylvania, painted the service of baptism in Figure 13 about 1830. A flagon (used to hold the baptismal water) and a basin (made in a pottery style) are present in preparation for the baptism of an infant. In another depiction of infant baptism, Rudy portrayed a mug and a basin as baptismal vessels.[10]

FORMS USED IN THE CHURCH

A flagon is a tall receptacle from which wine or other liquids were poured into smaller vessels for drinking convenience. Flagons were used in churches and homes, with little or no difference between the form of the vessels. It is quite probable that some flagons bearing inscriptions of church ownership were previously used in the home. More likely they were presentation pieces. Quite a few flagons bear donors' initials and inscriptions that include "the gift of . . ."

Tankards are a lidded domestic form that frequently found church usage as receptacles for wine and hence took on the function of flagons.

Mugs are lidless vessels that were used in various ways in the home and tavern. Larger quart mugs were often used to hold wine or water in an ecclesiastical setting. Smaller sizes—pint, half pint and quarter pint—were used as the common cup, and on occasion in the service of baptism.

Beakers, with and without handles, were widely used in the home and in the church as the common cup.

A chalice is a drinking cup or goblet used to dispense the wine in the sacrament of the Lord's Supper. Chalices have stems. They were also used in the home.

Ewers or pitchers are ecclesiastical vessels used to hold the water for the sacrament of baptism. The liquid is then poured into a basin for ease of use.

Basins are used to hold the water for the sacrament of baptism prior to its usage on the recipient.

As in many churches, candlesticks are used on or near the altar in the Roman Catholic church.

A ciborium, pyx, or host box was used to hold the eucharistic wafers.

A paten is a plate used in the eucharistic service for the bread or host. Patens are frequently small in size and occasionally footed.

Spoons were used to partake of the Last Supper portion of the love feast in the Church of the Brethren, Mennonite, and Moravian churches.

10. Donald A. Shelley, *The Fraktur-Writings or Illuminated Manuscripts of the Pennsylvania Germans* (Allentown, Pa.: The Pennsylvania German Folklore Society, 1961), fig. 233; Jean Lipman and Alice Winchester, *The Flowering of American Folk Art 1776–1876* (New York: The Viking Press, Inc., 1974), fig. 143.

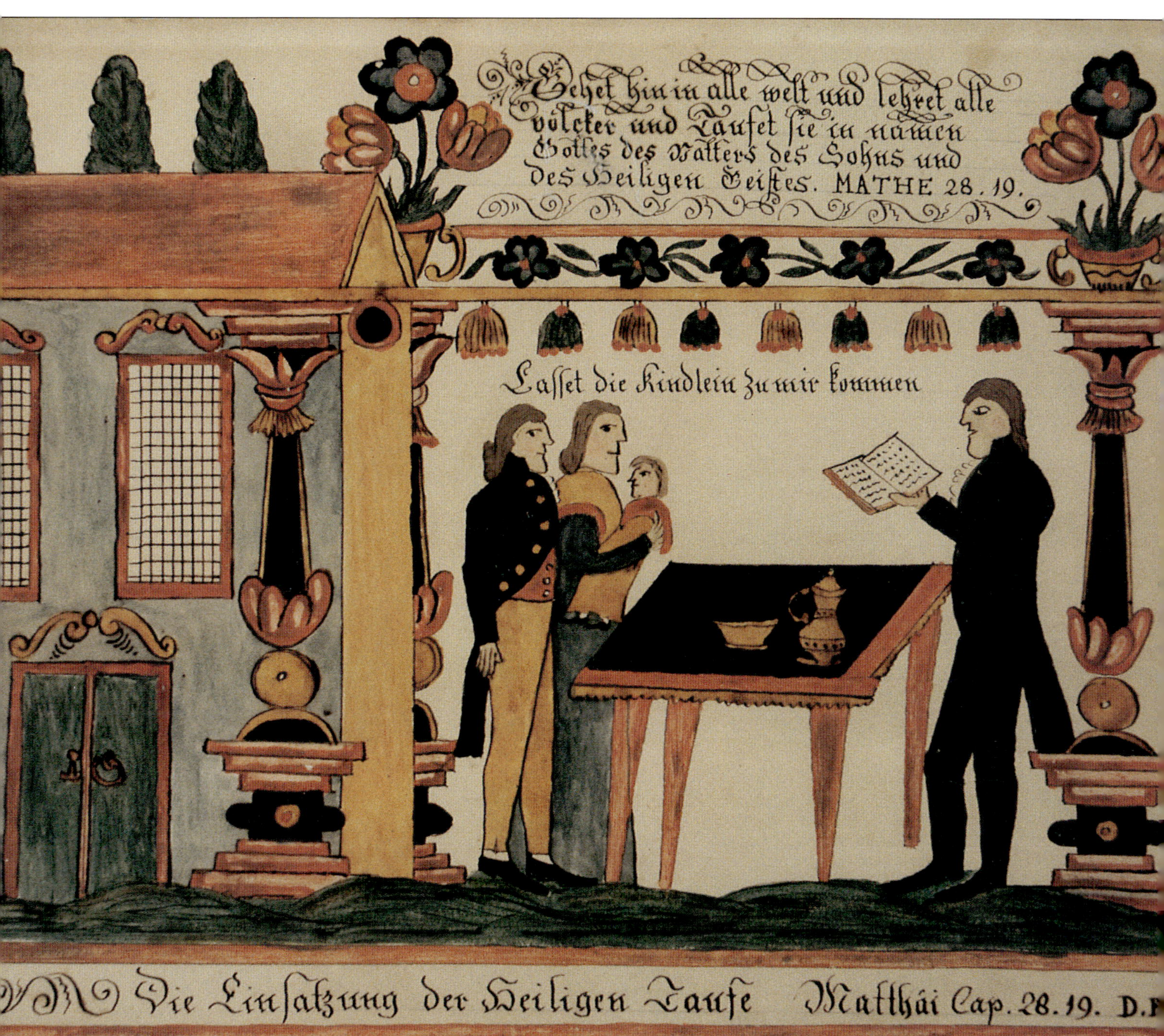

Fig. 13. *Infant baptism as depicted by Swiss emigrant Fraktur artist Durs Rudy, Jr., about 1830. Hand drawn, lettered, and colored on paper. Private collection.*

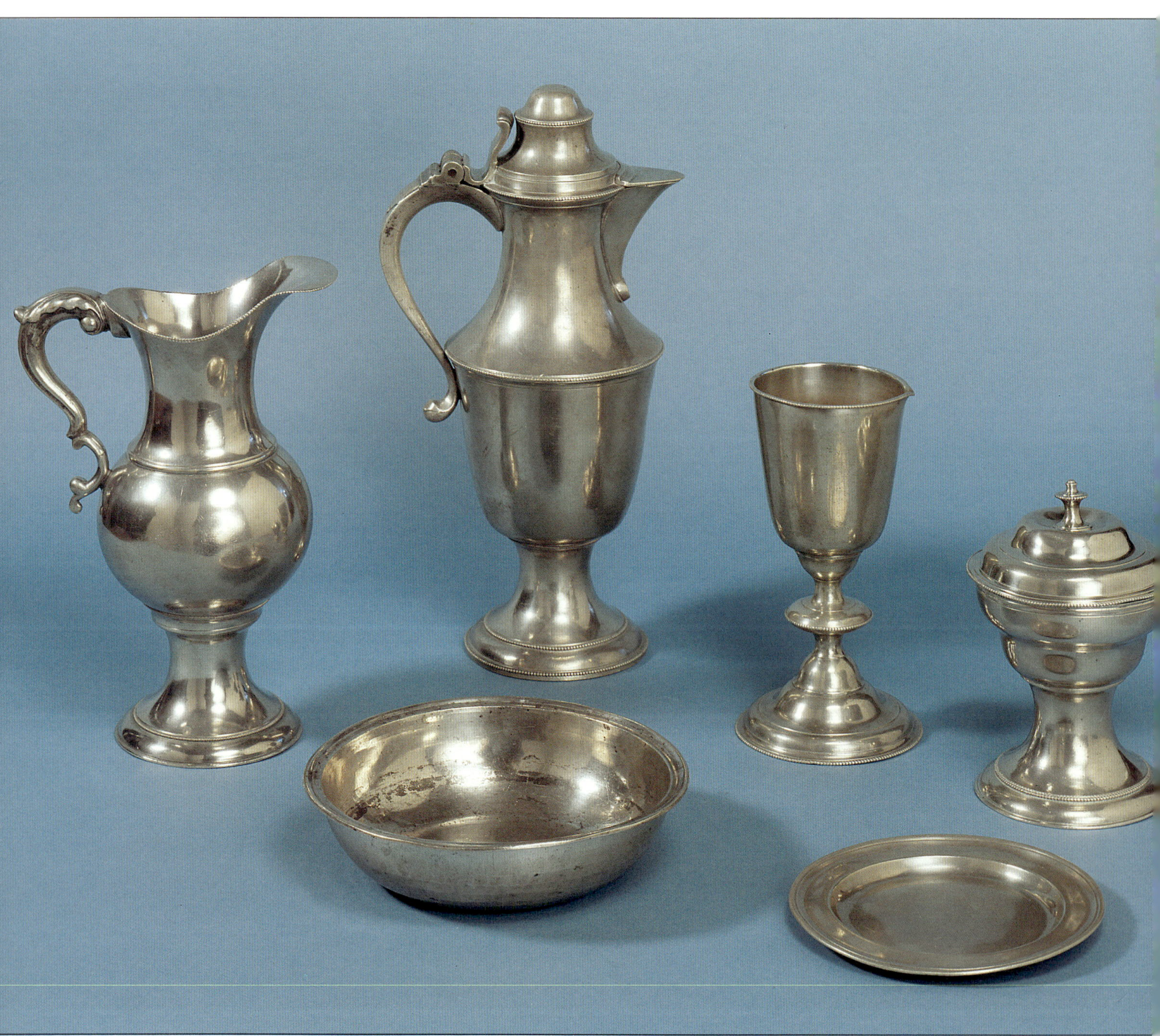

Fig. 14. *The ewer or pitcher is attributed to William Will, Philadelphia, 1764–1798. It has a double C-scrolled handle with acanthus leaf decoration. H 10 3/4″, TD 3 3/8″, BD 4 1/4″. The flagon is unmarked but also attributed to William Will. H 13 5/8″, TD 3 3/8″, BD 4 1/4″. The chalice is a form attributed to William Will. H 8″, TD 3 1/2″, BD 4 1/4″. The ciborium, with a sugar bowl body, has the same base as the ewer and flagon. Attributed to William Will, it is 7 1/8″ high with top and bottom diameters of 4 1/4″ and 4 1/8″. Johann Christoph Heyne, Lancaster 1752–1781, is the maker of the 6 3/8″ paten (L 532,533). The 8″ basin is marked Townsend and Compton (C 4800), a London firm working 1785–1810. St. Michael's Lutheran Church, Strasburg, Lancaster County, Pa.*

CHAPTER 2

The Pennsylvania Germans

Origins

REGIONAL DIVERSITY

From the first settlement of Germantown in 1683, a sizeable migration of German-speaking people into southeastern Pennsylvania continued into the eighteenth and nineteenth centuries. Nearly all these immigrants who came to Pennsylvania prior to the Revolution had left the southwestern provinces of the Holy Roman Empire (at that time there was not a national state called Germany) and Switzerland.[1] Many who immigrated to the New World were from the Palatinate, Württemberg, Hesse, Baden, Franconia, Zweibrücken, and Alsace-Lorraine. Other German-speaking lands of Europe contributed to the ethnic group known today as the Pennsylvania Germans, or Pennsylvania Dutch.

RELIGIOUS DIVERSITY

Pennsylvania's tolerance of religious diversity and promising land opportunities attracted many who sought relief from the religious and dynastic wars that followed the Reformation. Crop failures, craft restrictions, taxation, overpopulation, the desire to move on, and the advertising efforts of William Penn and his agents attracted many to Pennsylvania. Philadelphia became the preferred port of entry and southeastern Pennsylvania received and retained a heavy concentration of German-speaking immigrants. By 1790, more than one-third of the inhabitants of Pennsylvania were of Germanic background. Migrations continued into Maryland, the Shenandoah Valley of Virginia, the Piedmont regions of the Carolinas, and into Ohio and Ontario.

The religious diversity of Germans pouring into Pennsylvania in the eighteenth century presented a wide spectrum of Christian beliefs. At one extreme were the Roman Catholics. At the other extreme were the groups such as the Mennonites, Amish, Church of the Brethren, and other smaller groups. Between the two were the Lutheran, Reformed, and Moravian denominations.[2]

The majority of German settlers who came to Pennsylvania in the eighteenth century were, or considered themselves to be, associated with the Lutheran or Reformed denominations. Possibly 90 percent were affiliated with one or the other of these. In the following discussion, the Pennsylvania German religious

1. *Charles H. Glatfelter, Pastors and People: German Lutheran and Reformed Churches in the Pennsylvania Field, 1717–1793,* II, The History (Breinigsville, Pa.: The Pennsylvania German Society, 1981), 4.

2. Ibid., 9.

groups are listed in decreasing order based on the number of pewter pieces found in churches of that denomination. Examples of pewter forms used by these various denominations are illustrated.[3]

Religious Groups and Their Use of Pewter Vessels

THE LUTHERAN CHURCH

The efforts of Martin Luther (1483–1546) and others to reform the Roman Catholic Church in meeting the spiritual needs of its members led to the formation of the Lutheran Church in Germany. Banned from the Roman Catholic Church because of his departure from its doctrine and imprisoned because of his teachings, Luther was a major leader of the Protestant Reformation. Luther's Catechism, published in 1529, instructed followers in the fundamentals of Christian doctrine. His teachings, incorporated in the Augsburg Confession of 1530, provide the basis for the Lutheran belief that people can be saved by faith rather than good deeds. Luther believed that one is freed from sin through God's gift of grace through Jesus Christ on the cross, God's forgiving love, and the belief that the Bible has authority over all teaching in the church.

Lutherans have two sacraments: Baptism and the Lord's Supper. The Lord's Supper is also called the Eucharist or Sacrament of the Altar.

The Lutheran Church of eighteenth-century Pennsylvania is now part of the Evangelical Lutheran Church in America.

Lutheran pastor Henry Melchior Muhlenberg (1711–1787) lamented the shortage of chalices in the early years of our country, for he wrote in his diary on January 16, 1743:

> It is so very difficult for us to obtain a chalice here; there is none who is able or willing to make one, so as yet we do not have one. I might well wish for a pair of them, even if they were only copper or tin.[4]

Life was sometimes difficult for those traveling ministers and working conditions were less than comfortable, as Muhlenberg noted on April 18, 1762, when he was in Germantown:

> At nine o'clock rode to church. They had made seats by placing planks or flooring boards on the ground, but because neither roof, nor windows, nor doors had yet been made and quite a strong wind was blowing, it was very uncomfortable, even rather dangerous, to hold divine service and Communion in the building; but we could not do otherwise on account of the multitude of people . . . . After the sermon [I] addressed the confirmands briefly again, consecrated and administered the Holy Communion first to the young beginners and then to the rest, all together 119 in number. I was very much embarrassed because the wind was constantly threatening to carry off the consecrated wafers, which would have caused offense and given occasion for scandal. After this I baptized another child in the church and was finished toward three o'clock in the afternoon, but very tired and plagued with a headache.[5]

The scarcity of ministers available to meet the needs of German speaking congregations was mentioned in Jonas Heinrich Gudehus' observations in the early nineteenth century. Gudehus, a schoolmaster in the Zion Moselem Lutheran Church in Berks County, noted the matter in his writing as follows:

> The services of the Lutherans and the Reformed (about the others I concerned myself little) are very simple. Because the preachers have to preach every Sunday in at least two of their congregations and the churches of the same are often very far from one another, they have to hurry to get finished with these tasks, for after the same they often still have a long way to their home.[6]

3. Ibid., 9.

4. Henry Melchior Muhlenberg, *The Journals of Henry Melchior Muhlenberg*, I, trans. Theodore G. Tappert and John W. Doberstein (Philadelphia: Muhlenberg Press, 1942), 85.

5. Ibid., 507.

6. Jonas Heinrich Gudehus, "Journey to America," trans. Larry M. Neff, in *Ebbes fer Alle-Ebber—Ebbes fer Dich: Something for Everyone—Something for You* (Breinigsville, Pa.: The Pennsylvania German Society, 1980), 254.

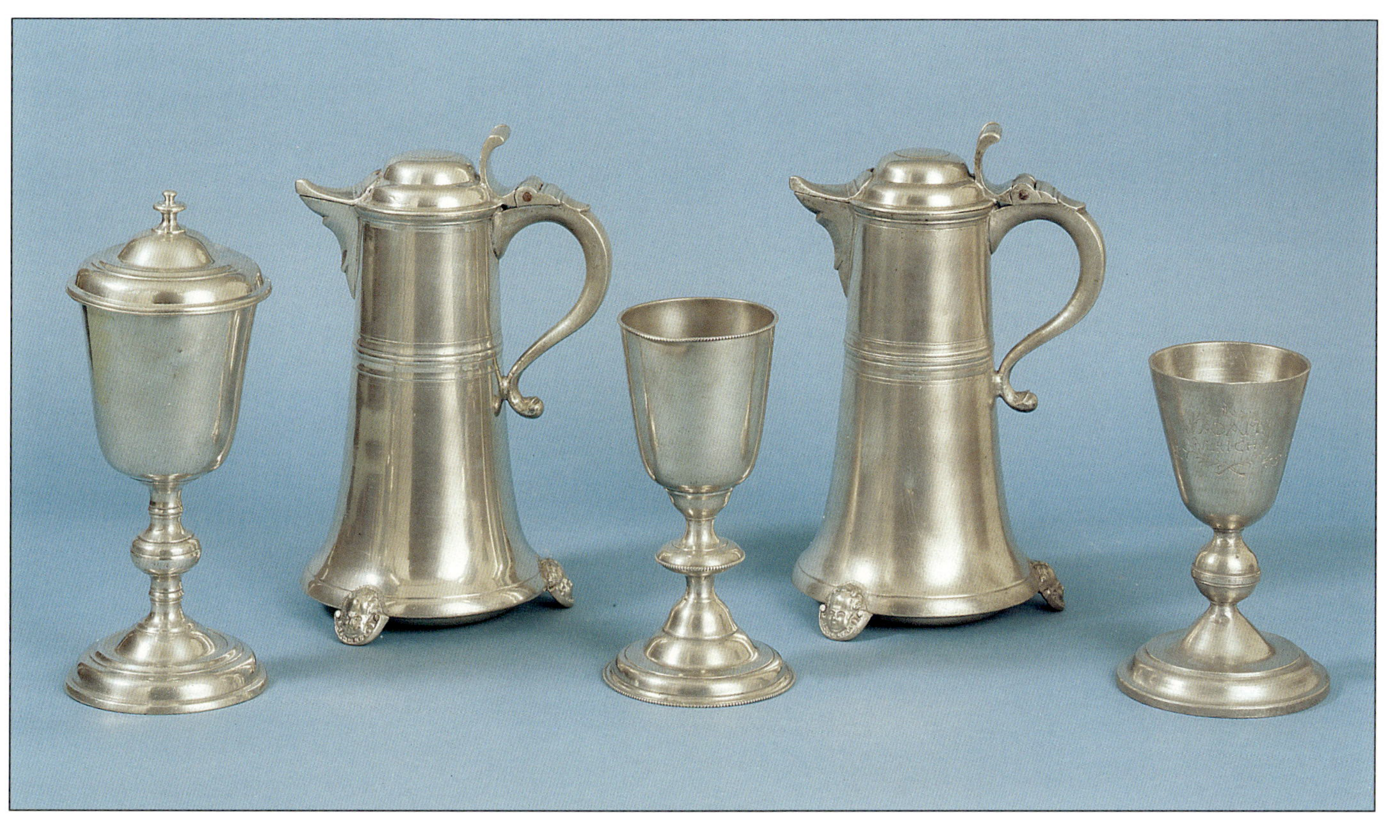

Fig. 15. *The chalice is attributed to Johann Christoph Heyne, Lancaster, Pa., 1752–1781. H 11", TD 4 1/8", BD 4 1/2". Both flagons are by Heyne and have the same marks and dimensions (L 530, 532). H 11 1/4", TD 3 1/2", BD 5 7/8". The chalice in the center is attributed to William Will, Philadelphia, 1764–1798. It is 8 1/8" high and has top and bottom diameters of 3" and 4 1/4", respectively. The chalice is engraved "Adam Ulrich 1745." It is unmarked and probably was made in Germany. H 7 1/4", TD 3 1/2", BD 4 5/8". A similar chalice, dated 1744, is owned by Zion Lutheran Church, also located in Lebanon County. Hill Lutheran Church, Cleona, Lebanon County, Pa.*

Gudehus also mentioned the infrequency of communion and the deposition of the unused wine:

> Communion is held once a year and the congregation takes care of the hosts and the wine. After the service the preacher, the elders and the schoolmaster drink the left over wine in the church.[7]

The exceptionally fine pewter communion and baptismal service in Figure 14 is an example of a set used in a Lutheran church. It is unusual in that the service contains a ewer, flagon, chalice, and ciborium made by the same maker.

The Hill or Berg Church, in Lebanon County, dedicated on August 12, 1744, originally was shared by both Lutheran and Reformed congregations. The Reformed group withdrew and built its own church in 1903–1904.[8] The Hill Lutheran church continued services at the original site and, as frequently happened, retained the old pewter communion and baptismal pieces. Sixteen pewter pieces, the largest number of any church in the survey, are owned by the Hill Lutheran church. The set includes five pieces by Lancaster pewterer Johann Christoph Heyne: two flagons, a chalice, a ciborium, and a paten. Figures 15 and 16.

7. Ibid.

8. Glatfelter, *Pastors and People,* I, *Pastors and Congregations,* (1980), 336.

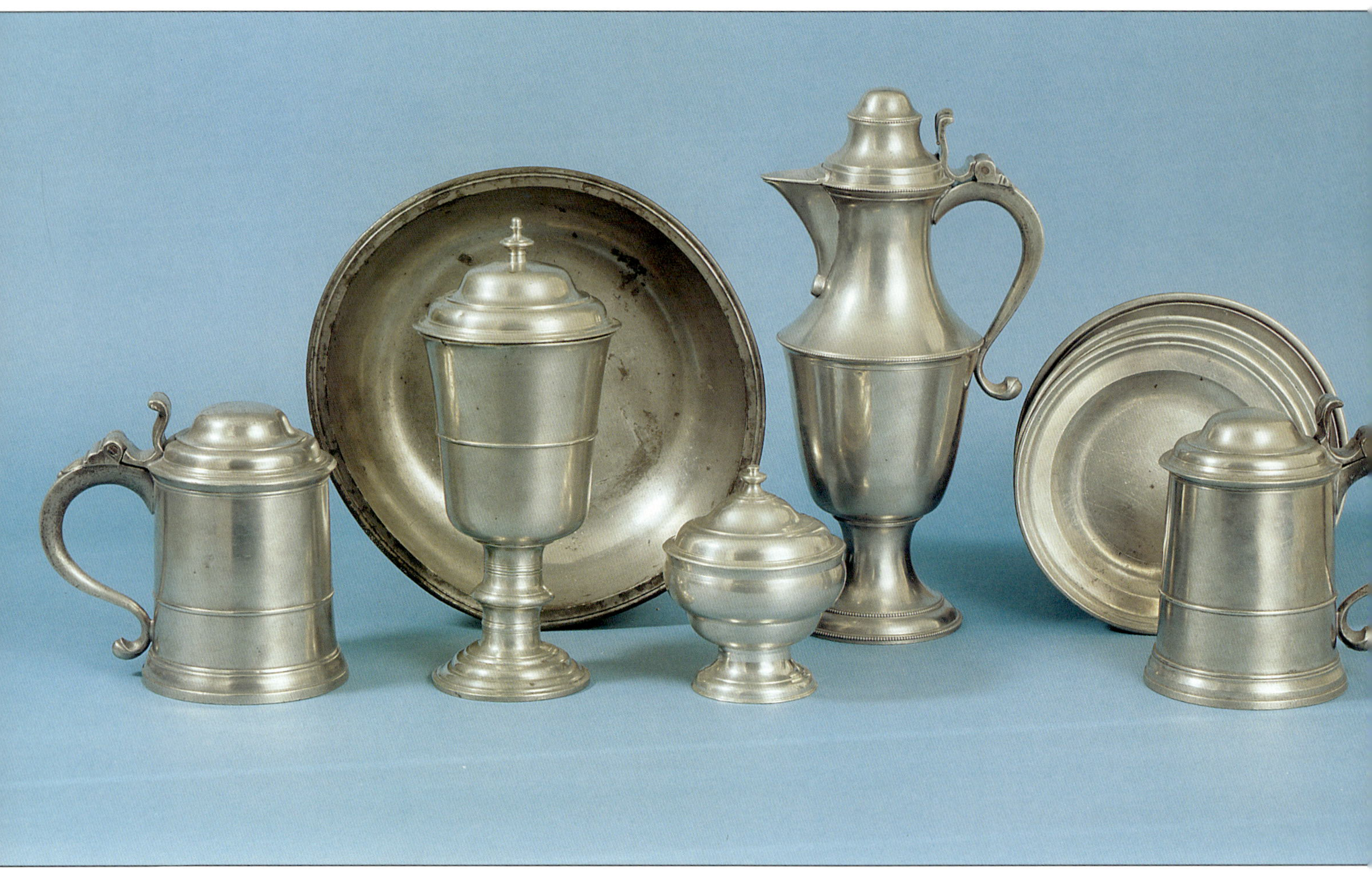

Fig. 16. *The quart tankard on the left was made by William Eddon of London (C 1503). Eddon worked from 1689 to 1745. H 7 1/4", TD 4 3/8", BD 5". Samuel Ellis is the mark on the 12" basin (C 1547). Ellis worked in London 1721–1773. The large lidded chalice is reminiscent of those made in Scotland or England 1750–1800. H 11", TD 4 3/8", BD 4 1/2" The rare sugar bowl or ciborium was made by Johann Christoph Heyne, Lancaster, Pa. 1752–1781, (L 533). H 5 1/2", TD 4 1/4", BD 3 1/4". The handsome flagon is one of three of this form found in the survey. It is attributed to William Will, Philadelphia, 1764–1798. H 13 3/4", TD 3 3/8", BD 4 3/8". The 8 1/2" plate is marked "A Carter" and was probably made in the West Country area of England approximately 1750 (P 825). Two plates bear the marks of Townsend and Compton of London, 1785–1810 (C 4800). They are 8" and 7 5/8" in diameter. The 7 3/4" plate is marked Love (L 868,869). It was probably made in Philadelphia 1750–1825. The quart tankard was made by William Charesley, London, 1729–1770, (C 888). H 7 1/8", TD 4 1/8", BD 5". Hill Lutheran Church, Cleona, Lebanon County, Pa.*

Few Pennsylvania German churches built in the eighteenth and early nineteenth-century have survived alteration. As congregations grew and membership increased, the need for more space frequently caused many sanctuaries to be divided into two floors. Bindnagle Lutheran Church, in Lebanon County, Pennsylvania, is an example of a Lutheran Church that has had few changes since its construction in 1803. Figure 17 gives us a glimpse of a church interior in that period of time with its intricate architectural details.

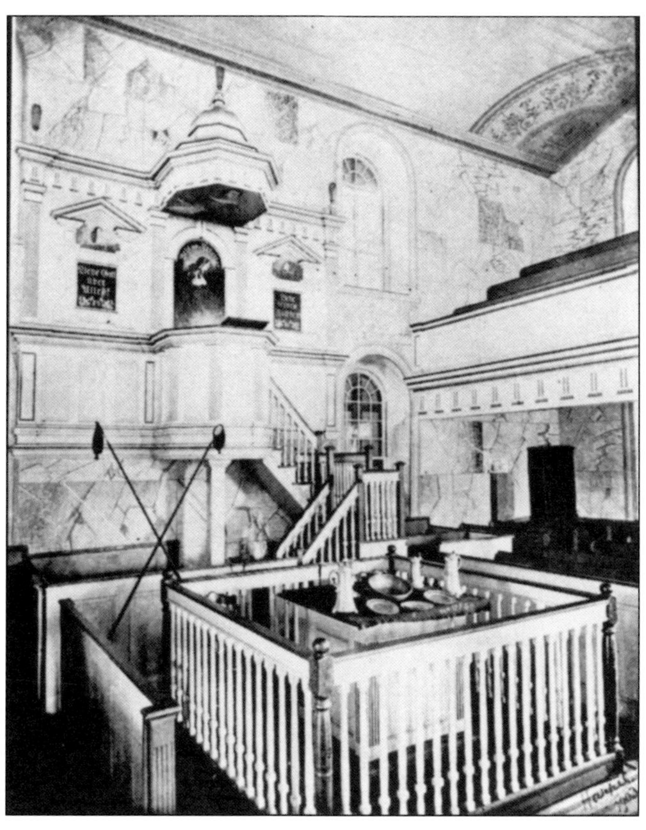

Fig. 17. *Interior of Bindnagle Lutheran Church. Note the pewter communion service on the enclosed altar. A "wine glass" pulpit, with its canopied sounding board above, is in the background. A painting of Christ is flanked by "Liebe Gott uber Alles" [Love God Over All] and* **"Liebe deine Nachsten"** *[Love your Neighbor]. The collection bags on long poles, or* **Glingelsecklein,** *had bells attached, perhaps to arouse drowsy parishioners at collection time. Bindnagle Lutheran Church, Palmyra, Lebanon Co., Pa.*

THE REFORMED CHURCH

In Zurich, in 1519, Huldrych Zwingli (1484–1531) initiated the Reformed Church. His views spread throughout Switzerland and southern Germany, where the Palatinate became its most important center. Differences in doctrine prevented a union of the Lutheran and Zwinglian churches. John Calvin (1509–1564) continued the Swiss Reformation and Protestant movement as it spread into France, the Netherlands, England, Scotland, and Ireland. In France, members of the Reformed Church and followers of Calvin were given the name Huguenots. The Reformed movement did not emphasize elaborate ceremonies in the church, and a few simple rites were considered godly. Creeds and confessions were relatively less important to members of the Reformed Church than to the Lutherans.

The Pennsylvania German churches of Reformed heritage adopted the name German Reformed Church, to differentiate themselves from the Dutch Reformed denomination in New York, New Jersey, and elsewhere. The word "German" was dropped from the title in 1869, leaving Reformed Church in the United States. It was this denomination that became part of the Evangelical and Reformed Church in 1934 and of the United Church of Christ in 1957.

The lack of qualified ministers in the New World was deplored by Reformed minister Michael Schlatter (1716–1790) in 1750 when he noted that thirty two congregations were without regular ministers; Lancaster, Cocalico, Donegal, Heidelberg, Egypt, Jordan, and Allemangel were among these. They were "only attended to when one of the few ministers in the country, by neglecting his own congregations, visits them once or twice a year by a tedious journey."[9]

Jacob Wentz and John Lefever each deeded about an acre of land to trustees in Worcester Township, in what is now Montgomery County, Pennsylvania, on January 2, 1762. The following year, the Reformed congregation built and dedicated a church that eventually became known as Wentz's Reformed Church.

9. Henry Harbaugh, *The Life of Rev. Michael Schlatter; with a Full Account of his Travels and Labors among the Germans in Pennsylvania, New Jersey, Maryland and Virginia Including His Services as Chaplain in the French and Indian War, and in the War of the Revolution. 1716–1790* (Philadelphia: Lindsay and Blakiston, 1857), 203–205.

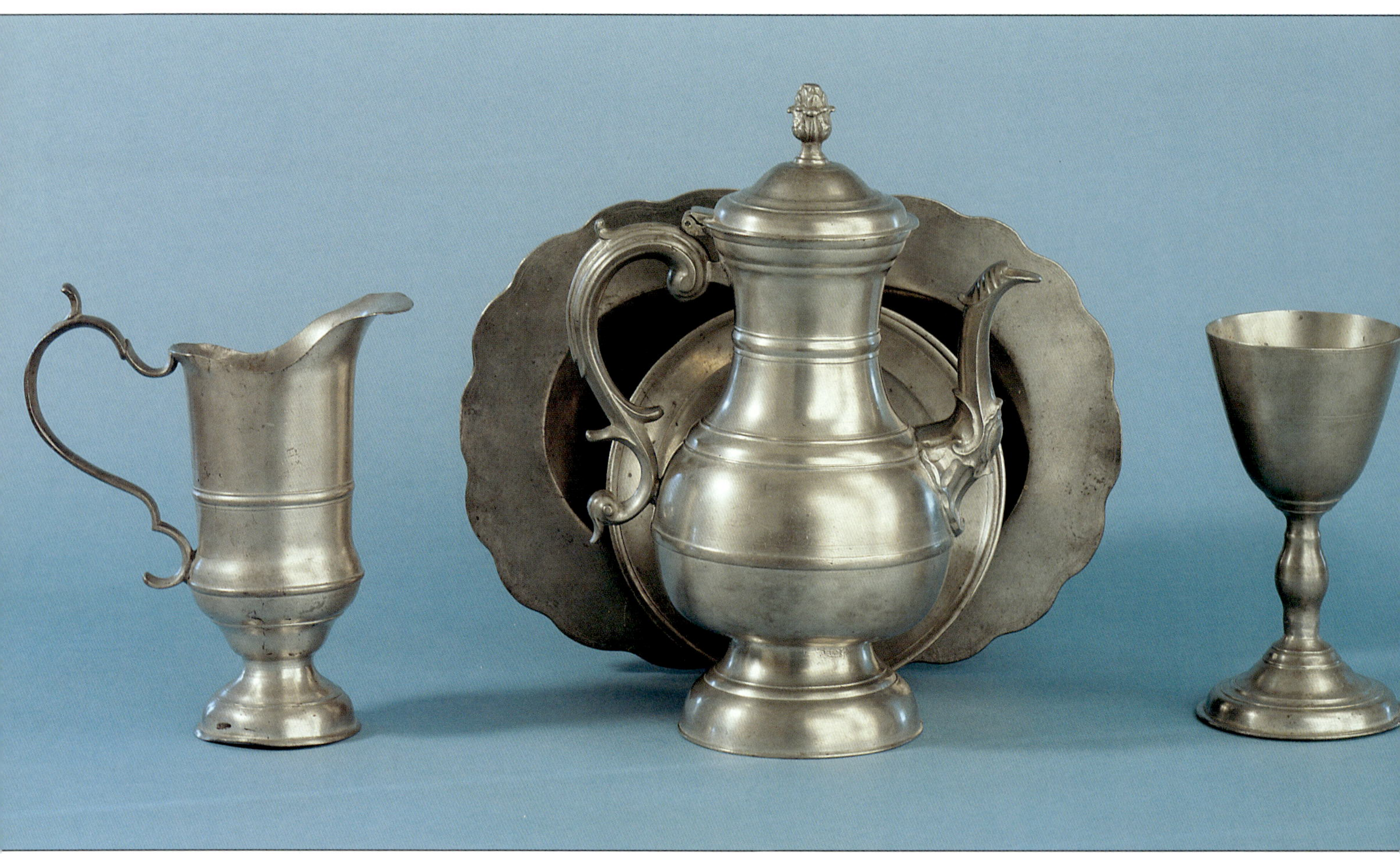

Fig. 18. *The rare and beautiful coffeepot (used here as a flagon), oval baptismal basin, ewer, and chalice are examples of the fine craftsmanship of John Will of New York. The thistle-shaped ewer is attributed to Will, who worked 1752–1774. A beaker was used to form the top portion of its body. H 9 1/8", TD 3 3/8", BD 3 3/8". The oval dish with scalloped edge is marked by John Will (L 481, 482). It is 14 1/4" in length, 10 1/4" wide and 1 3/8" high. The remarkable coffeepot used as a flagon is also marked by John Will (L 479). It is the earliest known marked American coffeepot. H 13 3/8" TD 4 1/8", BD 5". See the chapter on forms for a more detailed description of the pieces. Two plates bear the marks of John Townsend, London, 1748–1801 (C 4795). D 8 3/8". The chalice is unmarked but similar in form to others attributed to John Will. Wentz's Reformed Church (now United Church of Christ), Worcester, Montgomery Co., Pa.*

The pewter communion and baptismal service in Figure 18 may have been acquired in the early years of the congregation. As is usually the case, no consistory records have been found that confirm when and how it was acquired. Four of the pewter pieces were made by New York pewterer, John Will, who died in 1774.

On occasion, sacramental vessels were transferred from a defunct or inactive church to another church. Such is the case with the Zion's (Stone) Reformed church in Northampton County, Pa. On November 6, 1772, officers of the Indian Creek church agreed that:

> [Since the new Stone] church is now finished and we have abandoned the church at Jost Dreisbach's we deem it reasonable that we shall have no further use for the church vessels here, but desire to transfer them to the new Stone

> church. And that we hereby transfer and hand over the same to the Stone church . . . the baptismal dish, the chalice, the table cloth and the collection bags *(Glingelsecklein)* to be devoted there to the same use.[10]

The church received its name from its stone construction. A second stone building replaced the original in 1836. Both Lutheran and Reformed congregations worshiped there from 1772 until the Union arrangement was terminated in 1967.[11]

The Zion's (Stone) United Church of Christ pewter set is illustrated in Figure 19.

10. See Theo. F. Herman and John S. Stahr, eds., *The Reformed Church Review* (Philadelphia: Reformed Church Publication Board, 1914), 218. Also see Glatfelter, *Pastors and People I, Pastors and Congregations,* 388.

11. Information from Harold P. Smith, historian at Zion's Stone United Church of Christ, Northampton County, Pennsylvania. September 3, 1991. Also Milton H. Cole, History of Zion's (Stone) Church near Kreidersville, Pa. in Commemoration of the One Hundreth Anniversary of the building of the present church edifice, 1836–1936 (Allentown, Pa.: Schlechters, 1936).

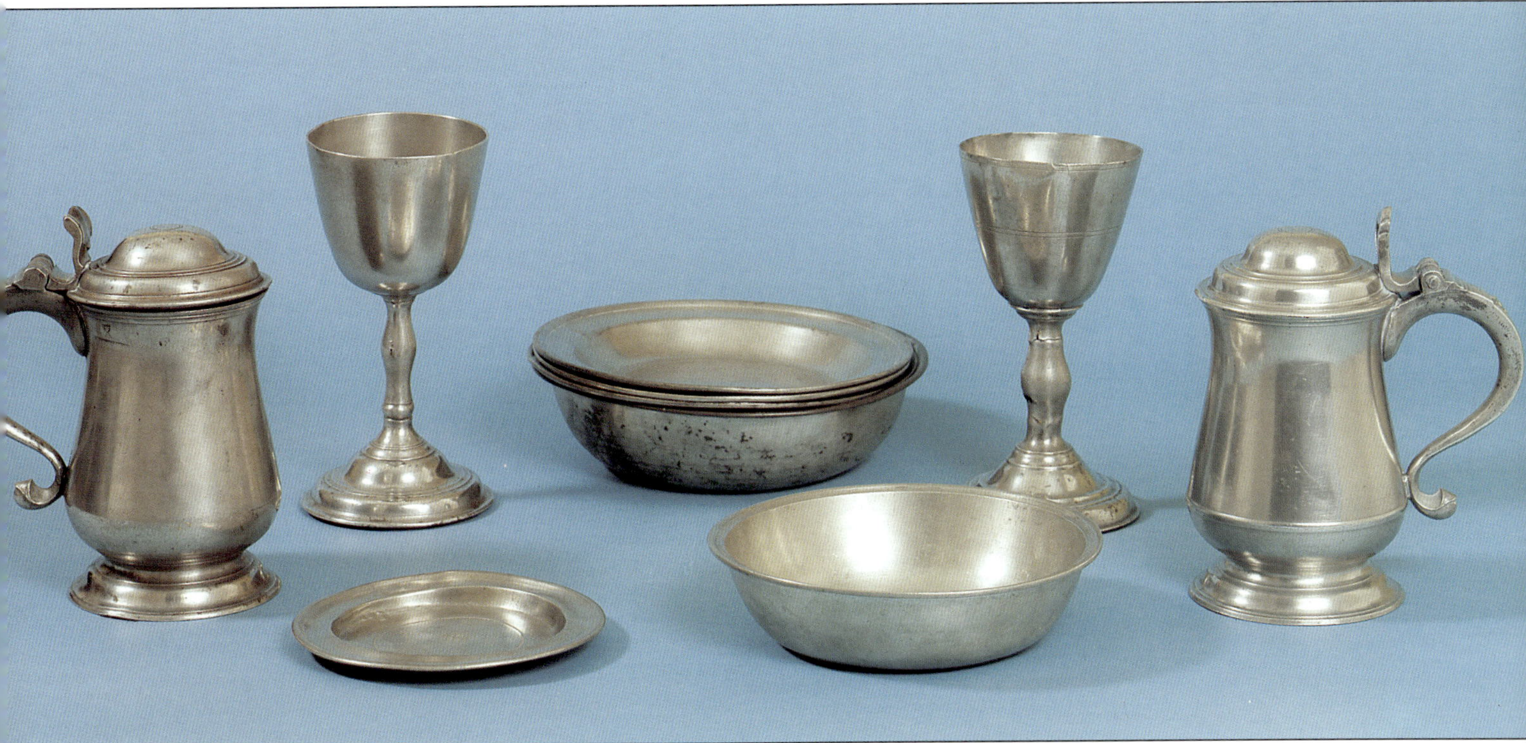

Fig. 19. *The quart tulip-shaped tankard on the left is attributed to William Will, Philadelphia, 1764–1798. H 8 1/8", TD 4 1/8", BD 4 3/8". The 6 1/4" plate or paten is marked by William Will, Philadelphia, 1764–1798 (L 534). The chalice is unmarked; but it is a form frequently found with other Will pieces and can be attributed to him with confidence. H 8 1/2", TD 3 7/8", BD 4 3/8". Henry Joseph of London (C 2686) made the 9" basin in the background. His working dates are 1736–1785. Three 8 5/8" deep plates are marked by Love and were probably made in the Philadelphia area about 1750–1825. John Will made the 7 7/8" basin in the foreground and marked it with his IW in a circle mark (L 481). He worked in New York City, 1752–1774. The chalice with the distinct flare to its cup is a form that has been attributed to John Will. H 8", TD 4", BD 4 1/8". William Will marked the tulip-shaped tankard with the band on its lower body with his large Philadelphia, William Will lamb and dove mark (L 535). H 8 1/8", TD 4 1/8", BD 4 3/8". Zion's (Stone) United Church of Christ, Northampton, Northampton County, Pa.*

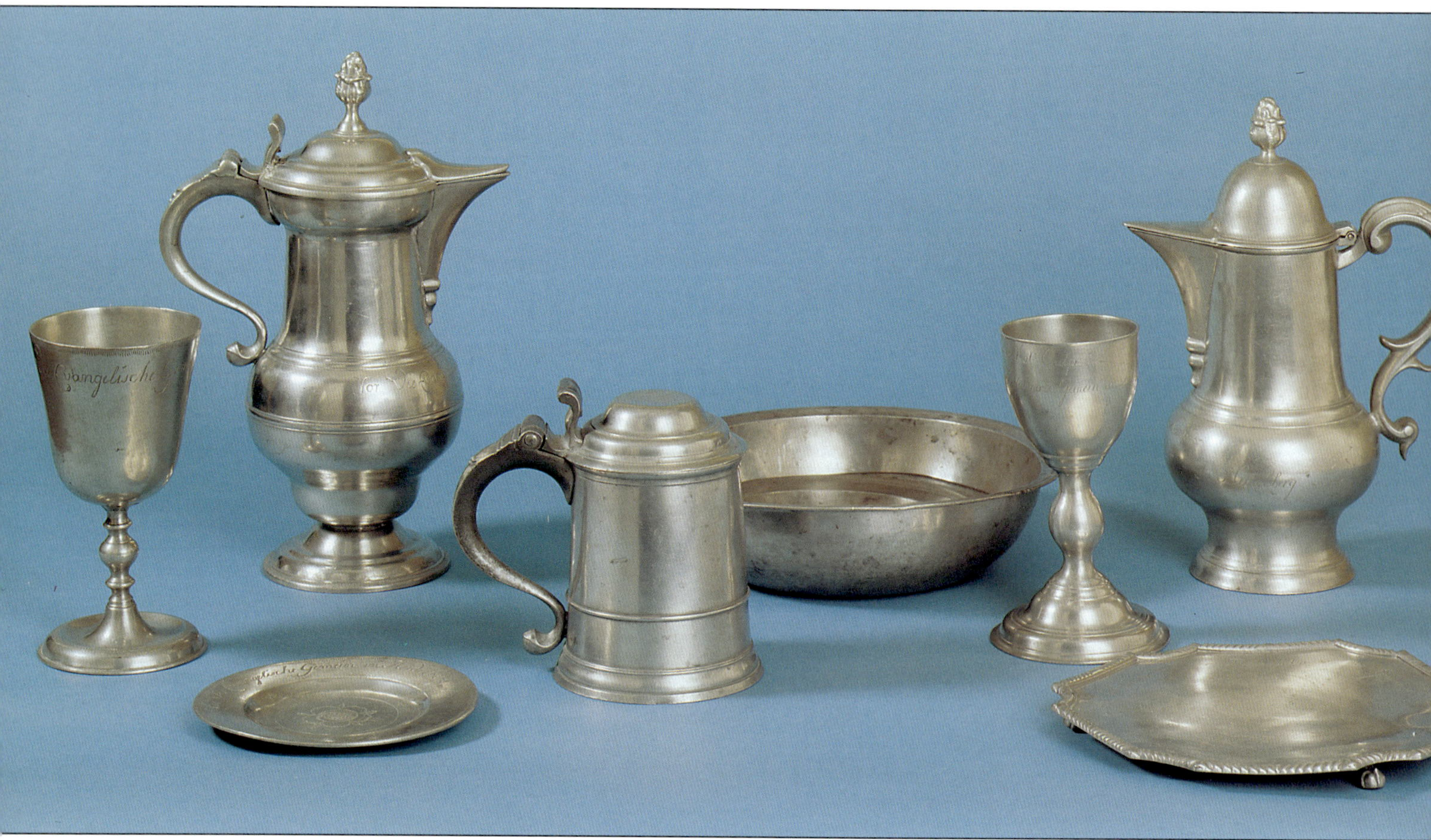

***Fig. 20.** The unmarked chalice may be of Pennsylvania or Continental origin and was probably made in the second half of the eighteenth century. H 7 5/8", TD 4", BD 3 7/8". The unmarked 6 1/4" paten was probably made in Philadelphia during the same time period. The flagon, attributed to William Will, Philadelphia, 1764–1798, has a body, spout and finial similar to marked examples by Will. The flagon, chalice, and paten are all engraved **"Vor Die Evangelische Gemein in Heidelberg 1767"** [For the Evangelical Congregation in Heidelberg]. The quart tankard is marked by John Bassett, a New York pewterer who worked 1720–1761 (L 458). H 6 3/4", TD 4", BD 4 7/8". The 10 3/4" basin was made by Samuel Jefferys, of London who worked about 1734–1739 (C 2607). Mathias Culp must have donated the chalice, flagon, and footed paten to the Reformed congregation, as they are similarly engraved with the donor's name and spelling variations of **"Vor die Reformirte Gemein in Heitelberg 1765"** [For the Reformed Congregation in Heidelberg 1765]. The chalice may have been made in Philadelphia by William Will. It is reminiscent of a form made by his father, John Will, and employs the use of a tankard lid for its base, a practice used by the Wills and other American eighteenth century pewterers. H 7 3/8", TD 3 3/4", BD 4 1/2". The footed paten is 9" in diameter and 5/8" high and rests on three ball and claw feet. William Will is the only American pewterer known to have used that foot design. He used the same style of feet on several marked pear-shaped teapots. The flagon is marked by William Will (L 538, 541). It is his only flagon that has a teapot hinge for its lid attachment. The foliate finial, domed lid and spout design have been found on other flagons by this maker. His brother Philip and father John used the same handle design and must have shared molds. William Will worked in Philadelphia, 1764–1798. The 1765 date on the flagon suggests that this form was made early in his career. H 12", TD 3 3/8", BD 4". Heidelberg Union Church, with Lutheran and United Church of Christ congregations, Slatington, Lehigh County, Pa.*

UNION CHURCHES

Numerous Lutheran and Reformed congregations shared a building and a cemetery for economical purposes. Each congregation had its own pastor and its own confession of faith or doctrinal basis. The two groups regarded themselves as closely related. Families in each group were often partly Lutheran, partly Reformed, but all members at one church. The "Union" churches sometimes shared the same pewter vessels. Occasionally, the vessels were engraved to identify congregational ownership, as is the case with the Heidelberg Union church pieces illustrated in Figure 20. A flagon, chalice, and paten are engraved "For the Lutheran congregation in Heidelberg 1767" and another flagon, chalice, and paten are engraved "Mathias Culp, For the Reformed congregation in Heidelberg 1765." The basin and tankard are not engraved and may have been shared by the congregations.

Another example from a Union church in which Lutheran and Reformed congregations shared the same building, and in this case the same pewter communion and baptismal vessels, is the set of a union church in Lehigh County, Pennsylvania. Fig. 21.

Fig. 21. *The unmarked chalice is of Pennsylvania origin, probably Philadelphia, 1800–1810. H $7\frac{5}{8}$″ TD $3\frac{1}{4}$″, BD $3\frac{1}{4}$″. The flagon is by William Will, Philadelphia 1764–1798. It is marked on the inside bottom (L 539). H $12\frac{3}{4}$″, TD $3\frac{7}{8}$″, BD $4\frac{1}{2}$″. The body form, foliate finial and Germanic pointed spout have been found on several other examples by this maker.* ***Flecheln,*** *or zigzag engraving, is found around the spout on both the body and the lid. The initials AB and GB and the date 1769 are found on its body. AB and GB may be the initials of parishioners Adam and George Blank. The $11\frac{3}{4}$″ unmarked basin is American or British in origin. The tulip-shaped quart tankard is marked by Cornelius Bradford (L 496). Bradford worked in New York City 1751–1753 and 1770–1785 and in Philadelphia 1753–1770. H $7\frac{7}{8}$″, TD 4″, BD $4\frac{3}{8}$″. Two small $4\frac{1}{8}$″ patens are unmarked as is a 6″ paten. A $7\frac{5}{8}$″ plate was made by Thomas Townsend and Henry Compton (C 1063) London, 1810–1855. Two $8\frac{3}{8}$″ plates were made by Townsend and Compton (C 4800), London, 1785–1810, and Thomas and Townsend Compton (C 1064), London, 1810–1815. Richard King (C 2750), London, 1745–1798 is the maker of an $8\frac{7}{8}$″ plate. His mark is found with that of Samuel Ellis (C 1547) London, 1721–1773, on another plate of the same size. A union church in Lehigh County, Pa.*

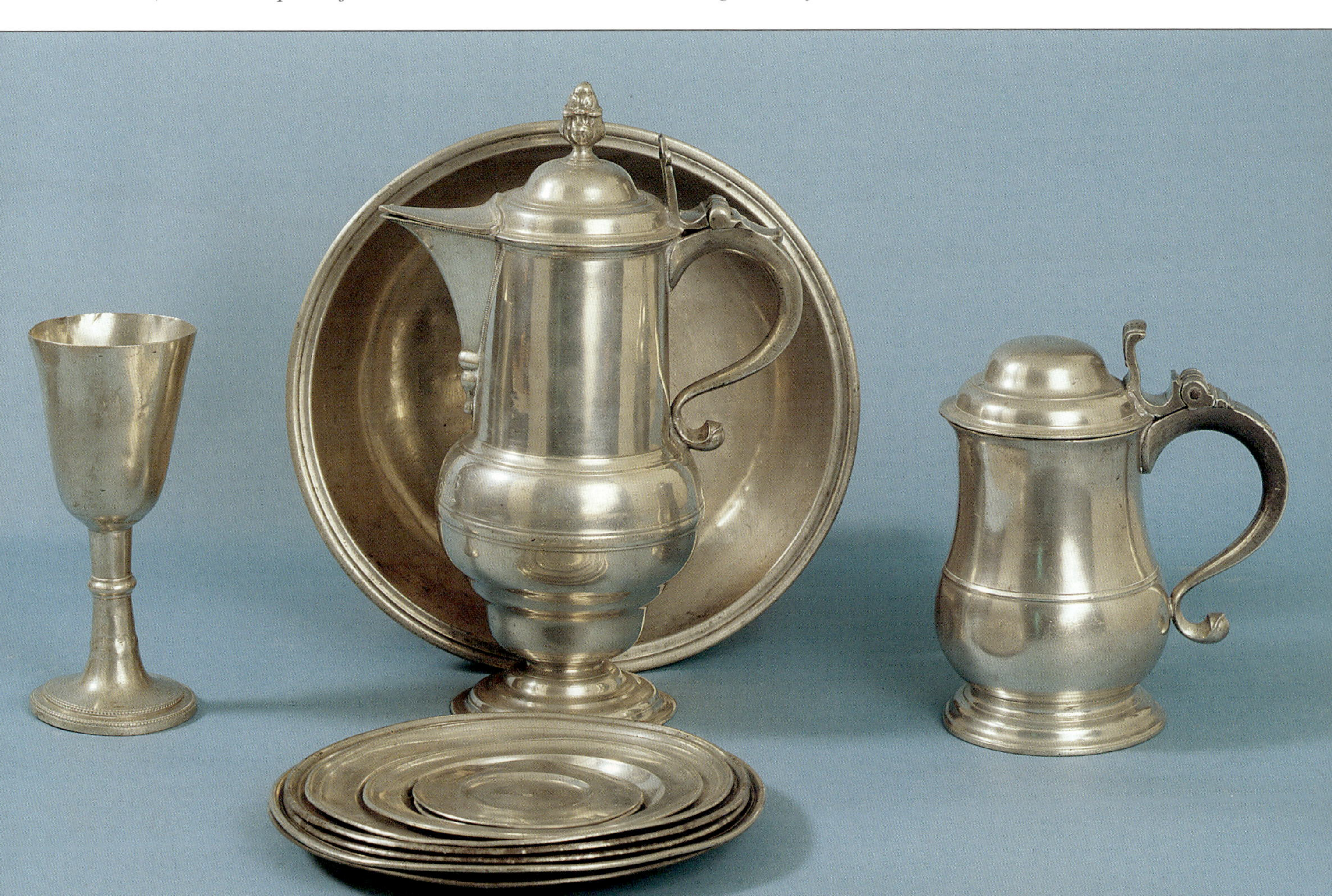

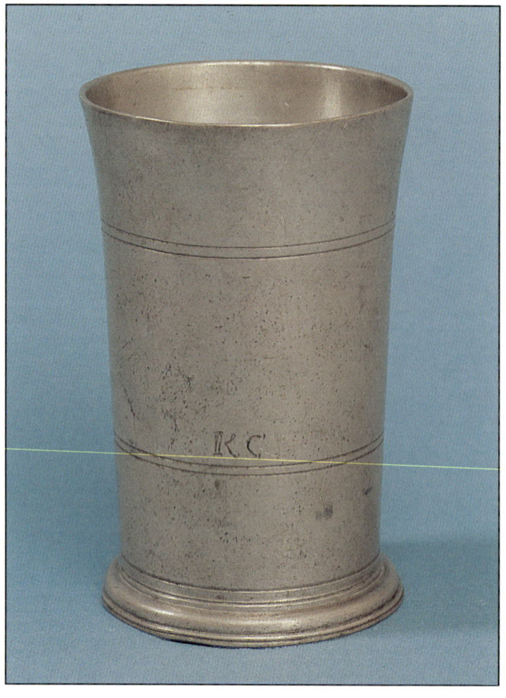

Fig. 22. *Beaker or cup by Robert Iles, London, 1695–1735 (C 2522). H 5 3/8″, TD 3 1/4″, BD 3 1/8″. The initials RC on the body of the beaker may be for River Corner Mennonite Church, a church served by a bishop in the same district that included Byerland and New Danville Churches. New Danville Mennonite Church, New Danville, Lancaster County, Pa.*

THE MENNONITE CHURCH

The Anabaptists had their beginnings in Zurich, Switzerland, in 1525 as dissenters from Zwingli's Reformed movement. In Holland, Menno Simons (1496–1561) renounced Catholicism in 1536 and adhered to the strict commands of the New Testament. The movement in Holland, Switzerland, and Germany eventually spread throughout northern and eastern Europe. Its followers became known as Mennonites.

The Mennonites were the main evangelical branch of the Anabaptist movement. Anabaptists held that infant baptism was invalid and believed in baptizing adult believers only. They were called Anabaptists (rebaptizers) because they rebaptized all who joined them. Anabaptists opposed war, military service, participation in government, and the swearing of oaths. Persecution drove them to more friendly states such as the Palatinate of the Rhine, where they were permitted to worship freely, but they were not allowed to erect meetinghouses until the nineteenth century.[12] Continued governmental restrictions encouraged their migration to North America.

Mennonites from Krefeld on the Lower Rhine arrived in Germantown (now part of Philadelphia) in 1683. A congregation eventually developed, and Germantown became the first permanent Mennonite congregation in America. In the eighteenth century, Pennsylvania received the bulk of the Mennonites who immigrated to the New World. During the next century, two migrations from Pennsylvania settled in Canada and the Midwest.

The Lord's Supper was served twice a year in nearly all Mennonite congregations. The Franconia Conference presently has communion once a year, usually in the spring.[13] In most Mennonite congregations, communion included footwashing in connection with the Supper and was preceded by the communion service.[14] Earthenware cups and pitchers were frequently used as communion vessels. Pewter cups (usually beakers or handled mugs) were also used in the communion service of eighteenth-century Mennonite churches in Pennsylvania. The bishop officiated at the service within a

Fig. 23. *Hans Herr House, Lancaster Co., Pa.*

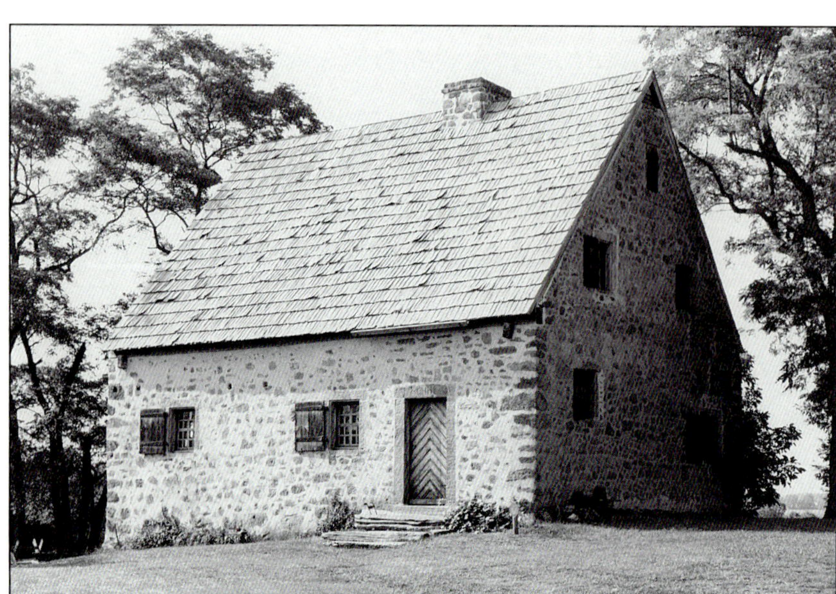

12. Don Yoder, "Sects and Religious Movements of German Origin," *Encyclopedia of the American Religious Experience: Studies of Traditions and Movements,* edt. Charles H. Lippy and Peter W. Williams (New York: Charles Scribner's Sons, 1988), I, 616.

13. John C. Wenger, *History of the Mennonites of the Franconia Conference* (Telford, Pa.: Franconia Mennonite Historical Society, 1937), 31.

14. *The Mennonite Encyclopedia,* II (1956) s.v. "Footwashing."

district and the deacon provided the cup.[15] Mugs were also used for baptism. The water was sprinkled and sometimes poured onto the head of the candidate. The early British beaker in figure 22 may have been used in the nearby Hans Herr house. The Herr house was built by Christian Herr in 1719 and served as an early meeting place for local Mennonites.[16] Figure 23.

Pewter basins were used for baptism by a few Mennonite congregations. In the ritual of baptism, some ministers dipped the water from a basin with their hands onto the candidate, others poured water from a pitcher onto the head of the recipient. Earthenware pitchers were frequently used for pouring. No pewter pitchers were found in Mennonite churches in this survey. Pewter basins were favored more by the Franconia Mennonite Conference, whose congregations are located in Bucks and Montgomery counties, than by the Lancaster Conference. The pewter basin and beaker in Figure 24 were made by the Palethorps of Philadelphia.

Communion cups were used as common cups sometimes into the twentieth century. A beaker attributed to Simon Edgell, who worked in Philadelphia, 1713–1742, is owned by the Deep Run Mennonite Church East of Bucks County, Pennsylvania. Two labels that accompany the beaker note: "Pewter Communion Cup from the Deep Run East Mennonite Congregation in Bucks County. The cup was given to the congregation in 1746 by William Allen, who sold land to the church in that year." Deep Run is the second oldest Mennonite Community in Bucks County. The cup was used until 1920.

THE CHURCH OF THE BRETHREN

Another group with Pietist as well as Anabaptist roots was the Church of the Brethren. Like the Mennonites and

15. Personal communication, Bishop David S. Thomas, December 29, 1990.

16. Steve Friesen, *A Modest Mennonite Home* (Intercourse, Pa.: Good Books, 1990), 89.

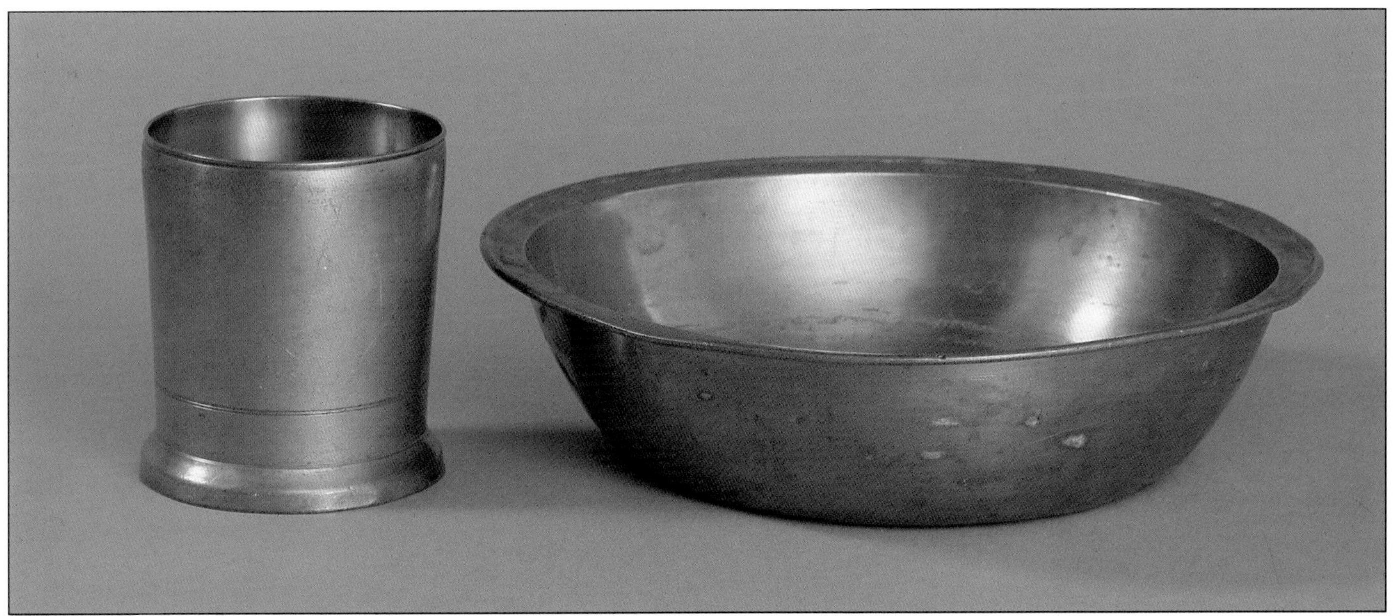

Fig. 24. *Beaker or cup made by Robert Palethorp, Jr., Philadelphia, 1817–1821 (L 560). This large beaker with no flare to the rim is made in the tradition of those made in the eighteenth century. Nearly all other beakers made by the Palethorps are smaller, have a curve or flare to their rims and follow the style of most beakers made in the nineteenth century. H 4", TD 3 1/2", BD 3 1/2". Two-quart basin used for baptism and made by the Palethorps of Philadelphia. Robert, Jr., his brother John H. and father Robert, Sr., worked in various combinations from 1817–1845 (L 561). H 2 1/2", TD 10 1/4". Blooming Glen Mennonite Church, Blooming Glen, Bucks County, Pa.*

Amish, they practice adult baptism. A Reformed Pietist named Alexander Mack, Sr. (1679–1735), was the founder in 1708 in Wittgenstein, Germany. The group migrated to Pennsylvania in 1719 and 1729 and settled in Germantown.[17] The first Brethren congregation in America was organized in Germantown on Christmas Day in 1723 when six people were baptized and the first love feast held.[18] (The love feast included the celebration of the Lord's Supper with a meal, footwashing, and the communion service.) From there the Brethren spread into rural areas of southeastern Pennsylvania, often settling among the Mennonites and Amish, some of whom were converted to the new movement.

The Brethren practiced baptism by threefold or trine immersion. Because of this practice they were sometimes called Tunkers, Dunkers, Dunkards or Dippers, from the German word *tunken* which means "to dip." Baptisms traditionally took place out of doors in a stream or lake. They asserted that "outdoor mid-winter baptisms in ice-covered water demonstrated the sincerity of the person baptized."[19] It was not until the last quarter of the nineteenth century that baptism in baptistries or "pools" became an accepted practice. One reason for this was "the Philadelphia Brethren congregation began baptizing new members in a pool (October, 1874) because the Delaware river had become very muddy except at high tide."[20] With the exception of the conservative offshoots, such as the German Baptist Brethren and Dunkard Brethren, modern Brethren use baptistries. The practice of baptism by immersion eliminated the need for baptismal vessels.

Communion in a broad sense includes the observance of the Last Supper or "love feast" that includes a service of footwashing to symbolize servanthood, a meal to symbolize brotherhood, and the Eucharist to celebrate salvation. The love feast includes the washing of feet, a meal (often with pewter spoons), and unleavened bread and wine. Unleavened bread was served on plates other than pewter, for pewter plates were not found in Brethren churches in the survey. Pewter cups were used for communion in Brethren churches. One cup was used for the men and another for the women. Indeed, pairs of pewter beakers or cups are found in Brethren churches today. Figure 25. Some congregations have blown-glass decanters that were used in the eighteenth century to store the wine prior to serving the communicants.

Pewter spoons were used in the love feast and a few have survived in Brethren churches. Figure 26.

The Ephrata Community was founded in 1732 by Johann Conrad Beissel, who

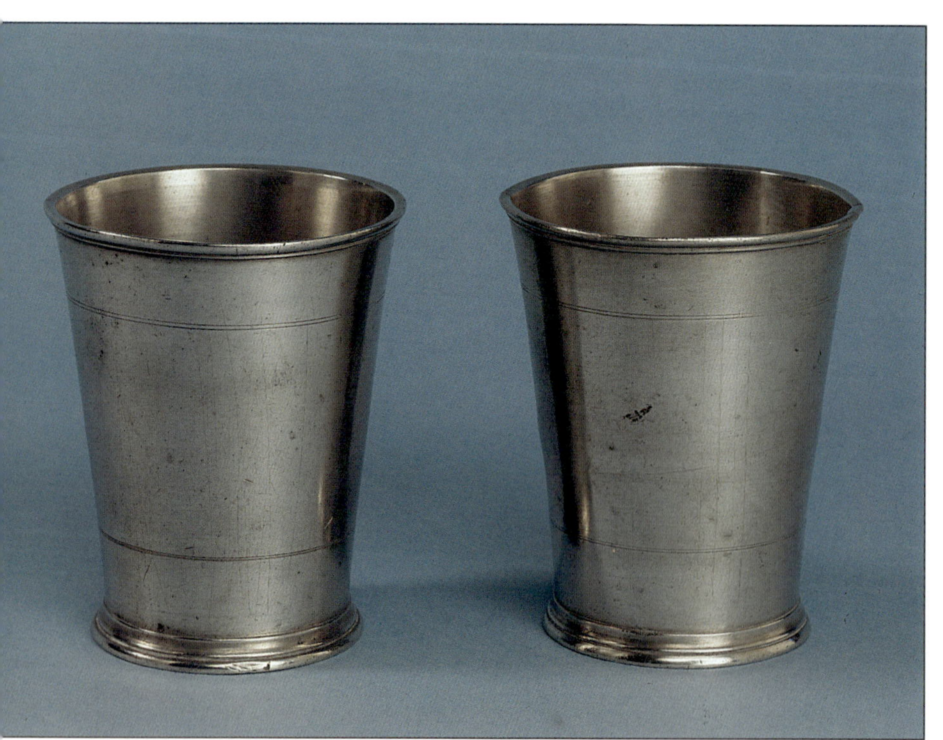

Fig. 25. *Pair of beakers or cups marked by Johann Christoph Heyne (L 530). Heyne worked in Lancaster, Pa., 1752–1781. Both beakers have the same dimensions. H 4 1/8", TD 3 3/8", BD 2 5/8". Codorus Church of the Brethren, Loganville, York County, Pa.*

17. Yoder, 620.

18. *The Brethren Encyclopedia* (1983), s.v. "Pennsylvania."

19. *The Brethren Encyclopedia* (1983), s.v. "Baptistries."

20. Ibid.

was not in agreement with the Brethren mainstream and had separated from what became the Conestoga Brethren congregation.[21] His followers worshiped on the seventh day and were known as Seventh-Day Baptists. The double cloister, with both monks and nuns, was similar to the double monasteries of the Middle Ages.[22]

The Snow Hill Cloister near Quincy, Franklin County, Pennsylvania, continued the beliefs of the Ephrata Community. Baptism was by trine immersion; and wooden communion vessels, not pewter, were used in that settlement.[23]

THE MORAVIAN CHURCH

The *Unitas Fratrum,* or Moravian Church, as it is known today, had its beginnings in the Slavic lands of Bohemia and Moravia. Persecuted followers of John Hus (1369–1415), a Bohemian reformer and martyr, found protection on the estate and castle, "Lititz," of Bohemian king George Podiebrad.[24] On March 1, 1457, the followers founded an organization later known as the *Unitas Fratrum.* A Protestant leader, Count Nicolaus Ludwig von Zinzendorf (1700–1760), provided refuge from war and persecution on his estate in Saxony. The town of Herrnhut, founded in 1722, became the world center of the enlarging missionary church.[25]

The first Moravian missionary in America arrived in Philadelphia on September 22, 1734.[26] After their first attempt at settlement in Savannah, Georgia, failed, they moved to Pennsylvania. Zinzendorf visited the newly organized congregation in Bethlehem on Christmas Eve of 1741. Moravian communities that flourished elsewhere in Pennsylvania, such as Emmaus, Nazareth, and Lititz, continue to this day.

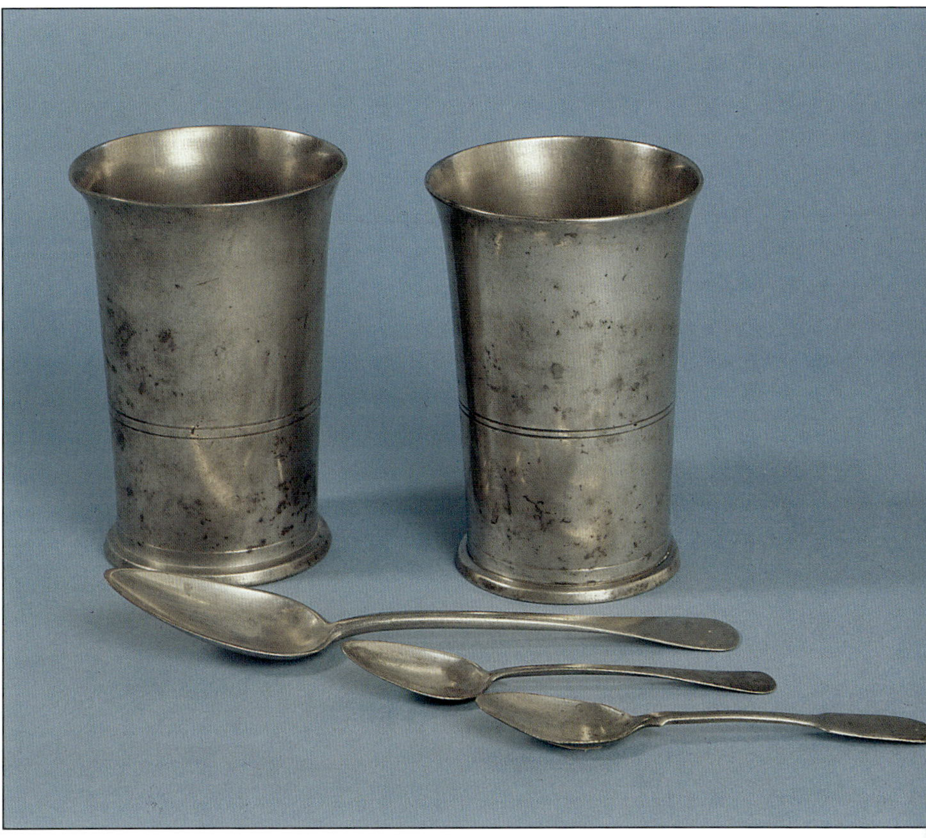

Fig. 26. *Pair of beakers attributed to the Boardmans of Hartford, Conn. Thomas Danforth Boardman and his brothers Sherman and Timothy and various partners produced pewter in Hartford, 1804–1873. Left H 5 1/8″, TD 3 1/2″, BD 2 7/8″. Right H 5 1/8″, TD 3 1/2″, BD 3″. Tablespoon by the Boardmans L 7 3/4″. Teaspoon by the Boardmans L 5 1/4″. Both marked "Best Britannia Metal." Teaspoon by John Yates, Birmingham, England, 1805–1852 (C 5340A). L 5 3/8″. Black Rock Church of the Brethren, Brodbecks, York County, Pa.*

The Moravians differed from the other Pennsylvania German groups in their insistence on planned towns centering around *Gemeinhaus* and school rather than dispersed farm settlements. (A *Gemeinhaus* was the congregational center, a large multipurpose building designed to house worship services and ministerial living quarters in the days before separate Moravian church buildings were erected.)[27]

In Bethlehem, services were first conducted in the *Gemeinhaus* in 1741. Ser-

21. *The Brethren Encyclopedia* (1983), s.v. "Ephrata Community."

22. Yoder, 624.

23. Information from Christ M. King, Trustee of Snow Hill Cloister, August 16, 1992.

24. Charles D. Kreider, *Moravian Faith and Worship* (Bethlehem, Pa.: Bethlehem Printing Co., 1920), 16.

25. Yoder, 622.

26. Mabel Haller, *Early Moravian Education in Pennsylvania: A Dissertation in Education Presented to the Faculty of the Graduate School of the University of Pennsylvania in Partial Fulfillment of the Requirements for the Degree of Doctor of Philosophy* (Nazareth, Pa.: The Moravian Historical Society, 1953), 5.

27. Yoder, 623.

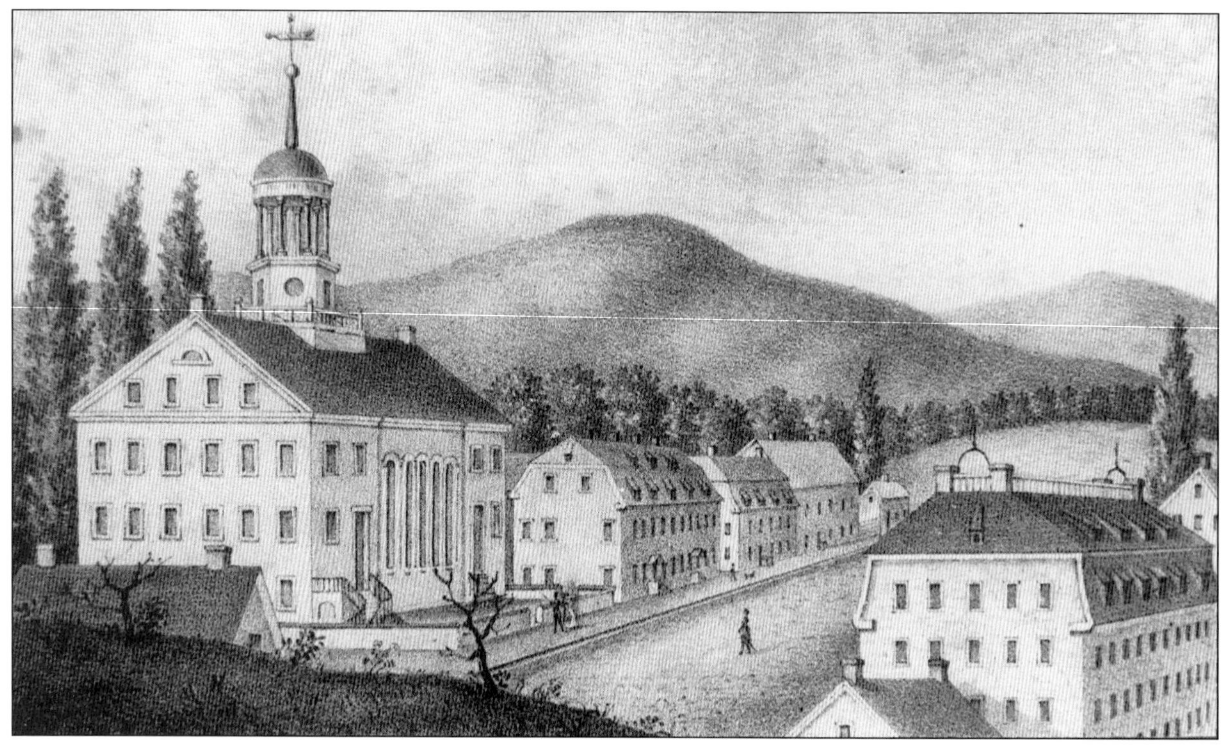

Fig. 27. *"Church & Young Ladies Seminary, at Bethlehem, Penna.," drawn by Samuel Reinke (1791–1875) and illustrated in* ***Twelve Views of Churches, Schools and Other Buildings, Erected by the United Brethren in America; with Brief Descriptions Annexed,*** *(1836). The large church (Central Moravian) was built next to the Gemeinhaus.*

vices were held in the 1751 chapel that adjoins the *Gemeinhaus* until the completion of the large church (Central Moravian) in 1806. Moravian minister and artist Samuel Reinke, included a view of the church and girls' school at Bethlehem in one of his drawings of churches, schools, and other buildings of Moravian communities.[28] Figure 27.

Education was stressed from the movement's beginning, and boarding schools for boys and girls were established in all Moravian communities. During the first decade of their settlement in Pennsylvania, 1740–1750, sixteen schools were established to educate both Moravian and non-Moravian pupils.

The love feast, a simple meal shared by all, was also a part of the Moravian celebration. "Moravian cakes and coffee were distributed, while the children sang some of the traditional hymns of the Church or some musical instrument played a chorale."[29] The love feast was often a festive event for students and was used to mark a special occasion in a pupil's life, such as a birthday, recovery from illness, arrival at or departure from school, as well as welcoming distinguished visitors, or commemorating religious or patriotic holidays.[30]

Ministers, teachers, and craftsmen, such as pewterer Johann Christoph Heyne, fulfilled both the spiritual and physical needs of the communities. Heyne was a Moravian minister as well as a pewterer. He journeyed to the Moravian settlement in Bethlehem shortly after his arrival in Philadelphia in 1742. He was in Lancaster by 1752 and worked there as a pewterer until his death January 11, 1781.

The chalice attributed to Heyne in Figure 28 has a short cup and large knop (enlargement found on the stem of chalices) as do others dated in the early 1750s. It was probably made early in his career as a pewterer.

28. *Twelve views of churches, schools and other buildings, erected by the United Brethren in America; with brief descriptions annexed* (New York: Lithography of Endicott, 1836).

29. Henry Emilius Stocker, *Moravian Customs and Other Matters of Interest* (Bethlehem, Pa.: Times Publishing Co., 1918), 72.

30. Haller, *Early Moravian Education in Pennsylvania,* 218–219.

The quart tankard in Figures 29 and 30 has a flat lid with a crenated (scalloped) lip. The painted surface is an unusual treatment of pewter for a piece that has been associated with ecclesiastical use. The marbleized treatment of its surface has floral swags and pendants and includes the initials F B on the lid, possibly for Franz Boehler. A label accompanying the tankard notes that the piece belonged to Franz Boehler, brother of Peter Boehler. Edmund de Schweinitz's *The Clergy of the American Province of the Unitas Fratrum* tells us more about Franz Boehler, who was born September 1, 1722, at Frankfurt on the Main.[31] An emigrant to America in 1752, Boehler was superintendent of the church school at Macungie (Emmaus) in 1755. He ministered to other Moravian communities in Pennsylvania, New Jersey, and New York. In 1771, he returned to serving again in Emmaus.[32] Boehler died June 4, 1806, while visiting the Moravian community in Lititz, and he is buried in the Moravian cemetery there.

31. Edmund de Schweinitz, *The Clergy of the American Province of the Unitas Fratrum*. Manuscript located at the Moravian Archives, Bethlehem, Pa.

32. Information from card file at the Moravian Historical Society, Whitefield House, Nazareth, Pa. Also see Donald L. Fennimore, "A Marbleized Pewter Tankard," *Pewter Collectors' Club of America Bulletin* No. 88 (March 1984), 302.

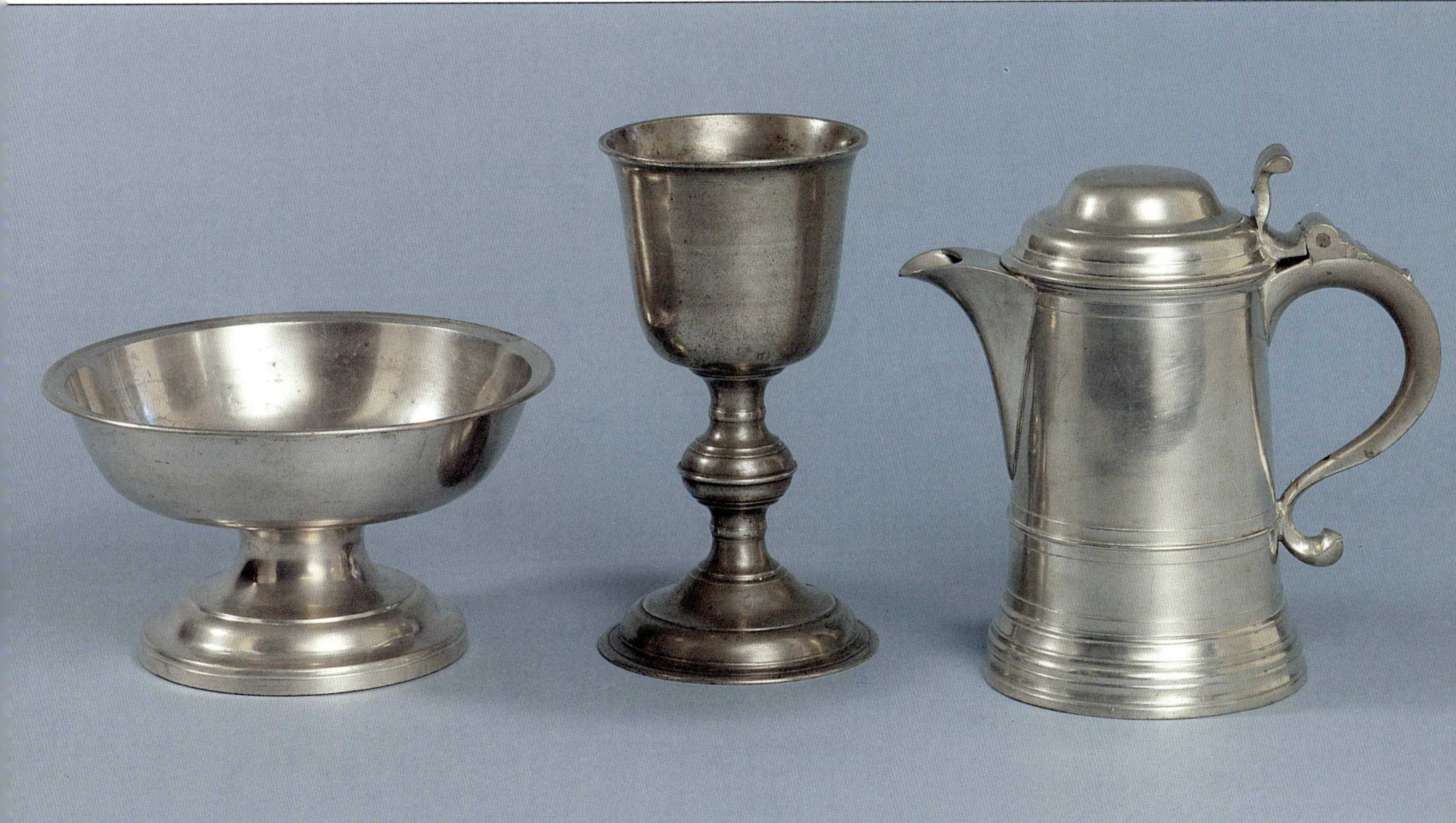

Fig. 28. *Footed baptismal basin marked Boardman Warranted made by Boardman & Company, Hartford, Connecticut, 1825–1827 (L 434). H 4 1/2", TD 8", BD 5 1/8". Chalice attributed to Johann Christoph Heyne, Lancaster, Pa., 1752–1781. H 8 1/8", TD 4 1/8", BD 4 3/8". Quart flagon by the Boardmans, Hartford, Conn., 1825–1827 (L 431), H 8 1/4", TD 4 1/8", BD 5". Central Moravian Church, Bethlehem, Northampton County, Pa.*

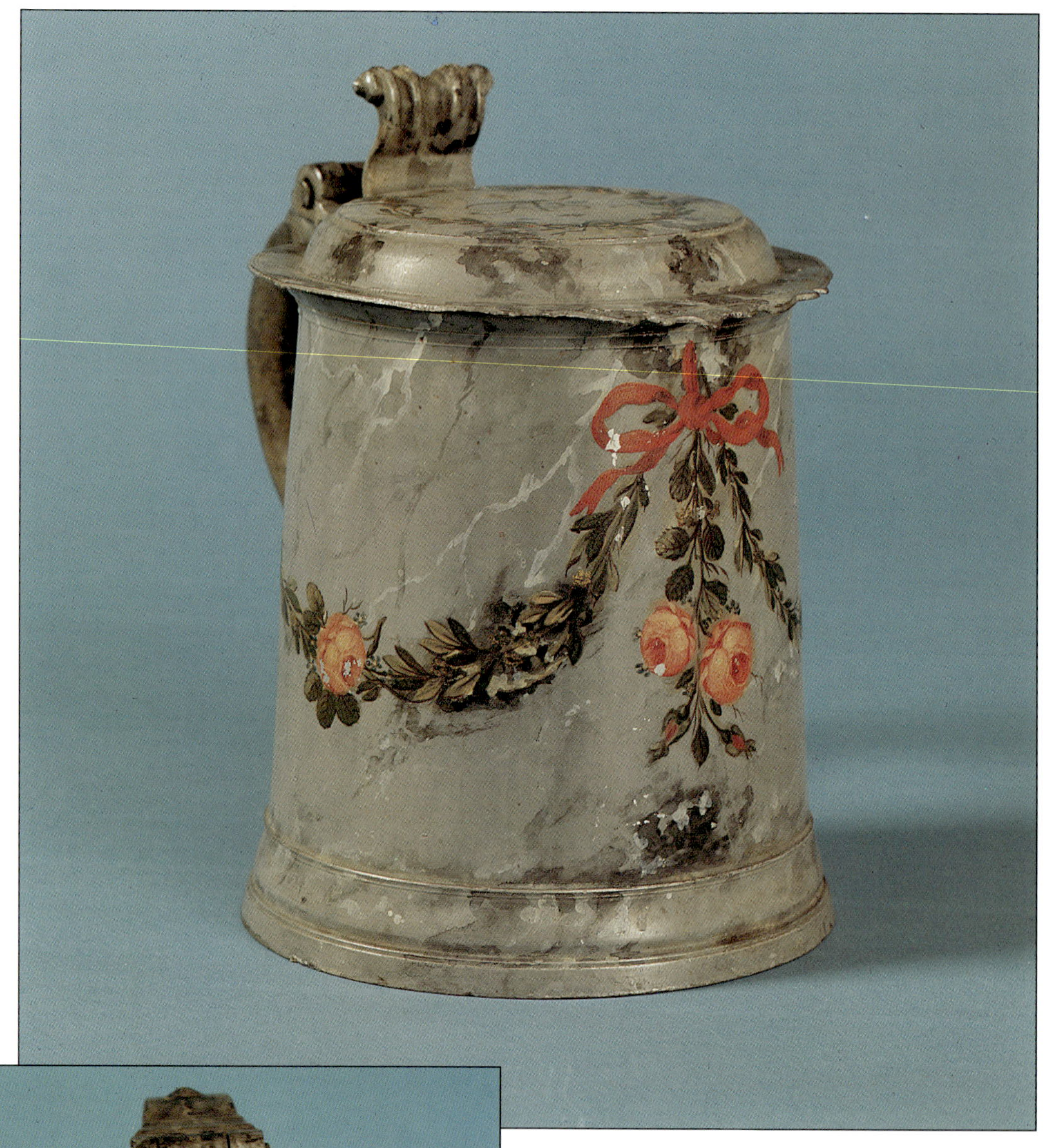

Fig. 29. *Quart tankard (right) made by William Kirby, New York, N.Y., 1760–1793 (L 499). H 7″, TD 4 3/8″, BD 5″. Emmaus Moravian Church, Emmaus, Lehigh County, Pa.*

Fig. 30. *The initials F B (below) painted on the lid of a quart tankard made by William Kirby.*

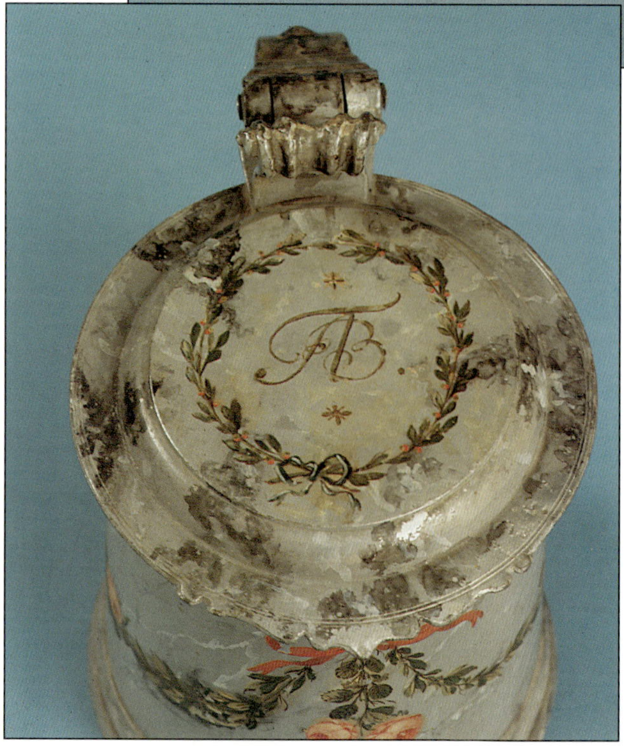

THE ROMAN CATHOLIC CHURCH

Western Europe was almost solidly Roman Catholic for the first 1,500 years of Christianity, up to the Protestant Reformation. Roman Catholics founded Maryland in 1634 and were later restricted by law in Maryland and in most other colonies. Those restrictions were not removed until after the Revolutionary War. The Catholic Church grew slowly in the colonies because of these restrictions and because most colonial immigrants were Protestants, since Catholics were by parliamentary action excluded from entering the British colonies.

By Catholic decree, sacred vessels were to be made of precious metals such as gold or silver.[33] Hence the absence of pewter vessels in colonial Pennsylvania German Catholic churches.

Candles have been documented as being used in the church as early as the fifth century. They are mentioned in the Book of Revelation (1:12). It was formerly prescribed that there should be six candlesticks on the altar—three on each side. They could be made of brass or bronze, silver-plated metals, pewter, or plain wood. Two pairs of candlesticks were found in the survey and all four have a history of usage in The Most Blessed Sacrament Catholic Church.[34] Figures 31 and 32.

OTHER GROUPS

Other groups of Pennsylvania Germans that were present in much smaller numbers in the Commonwealth before 1800 include the Amish and the Schwenkfelders.

The Amish

Jacob Ammann (1644–ca. 1735) was an Anabaptist leader from Switzerland who differed from the mainstream Mennonite movement. His followers became known as the Amish. The separation took place about 1693. Amish families began traveling to America in the 1730s.[35] They frequently settled among Mennonites and other plain-dressing people.

In the Amish community, communion is held in the spring and fall. There are no special designated vessels for communion, and pewter would not have been used. A cup for communion is taken from the kitchen, as is the pitcher for baptism.[36] The minister is chosen by lot and has no formal training. This is also the case with the bishop.

The Schwenkfelder Church

The Schwenkfelders are the followers of a sixteenth century Silesian Protestant

33. Peter M. J. Stravinskas, ed., *Our Sunday Visitor's Catholic Encyclopedia* (Huntington, Indiana: Our Sunday Visitor, Inc., 1991), 853.

34. Charles F. Montgomery, *A History of American Pewter: A Winterthur Book* (New York: Praeger, 1973), 210.

35. Yoder, 618.

36. Information from John A. Hostetler, February 2, 1990. Also see John A. Hostetler, *Amish Roots: A Treasury of History, Wisdom, and Lore* (Baltimore and London: Johns Hopkins University Press, 1989), 89, 182.

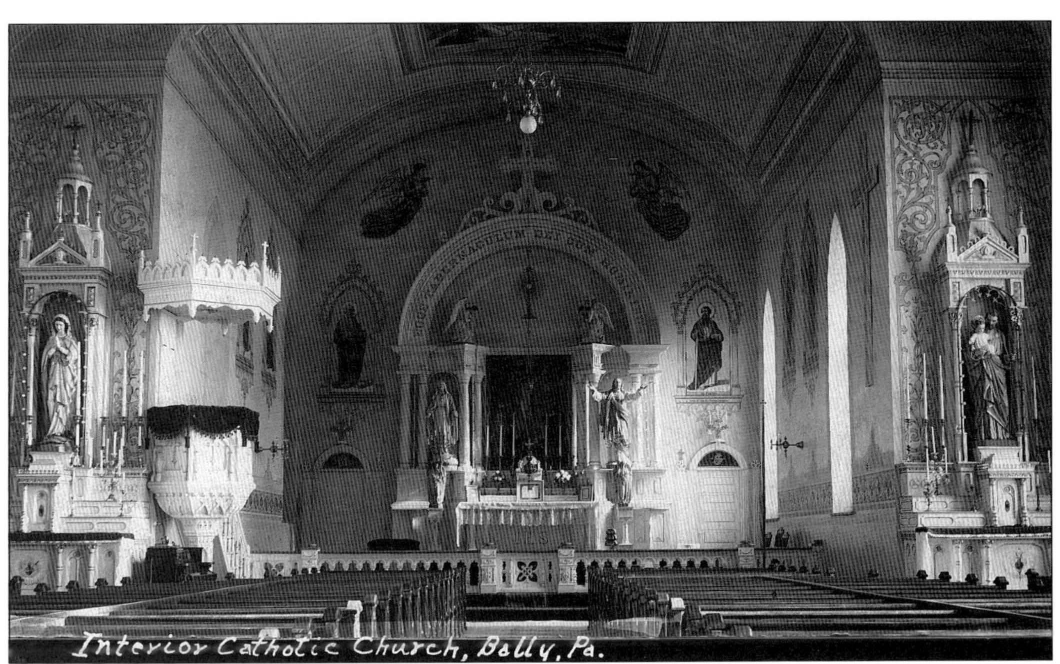

Fig. 31. *Interior of The Most Blessed Sacrament Catholic Church, Bally, Berks County, Pa., from a postcard postmarked 1911.*

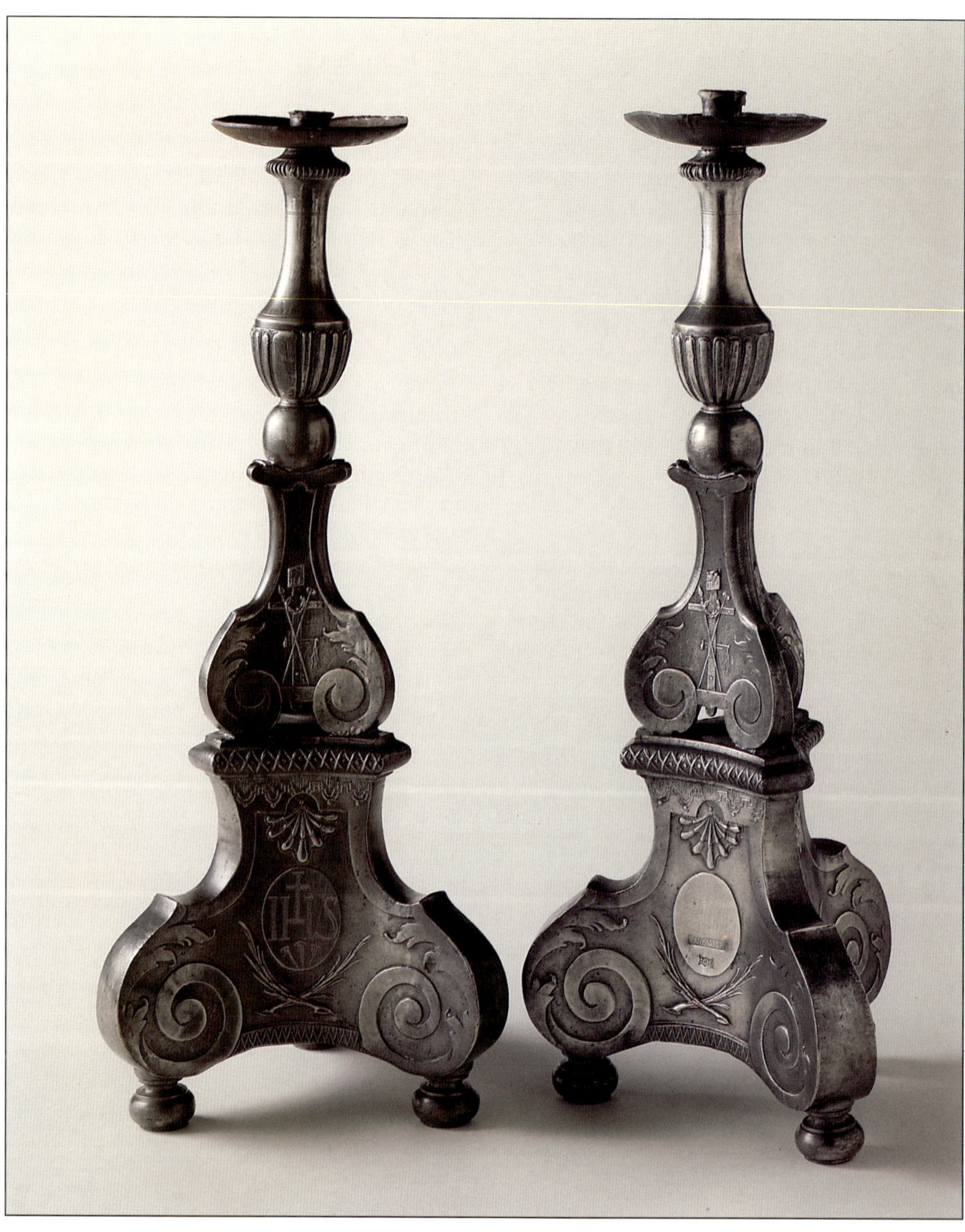

Fig. 32. *Pair of candlesticks by Johann Christoph Heyne, Lancaster, Pa. 1752–1781 (L 530,533). Left H 21¼", BD 8¾". Right H 22⅞", BD 8¾". Courtesy, Winterthur Museum.*

reformer named Kaspar Schwenkfeld von Ossig (1489–1561). Banished by the Roman Catholic government from Silesia, they received asylum on Count von Zinzendorf's estate in Bertelsdorf, just a few miles from the Moravian community of Herrnhut. Many migrated to Pennsylvania between 1734 and 1737.[37] They settled in the countryside about fifty miles north of Philadelphia, near the Moravians and Mennonites.[38]

From their beginning, the Schwenk-

37. Yoder, 222.

38. Horst Weigelt, "The Emigration of the Schwenkfelders from Silesia to America," in *Schwenkfelders in America: Papers Presented at the Colloquium on Schwenckfeld and the Schwenkfelders, Pennsburg, Pa. September 17–22, 1984,* ed. Peter C. Erb (Pennsburg, Pa.: Schwenkfelder Library, 1987), 13.

felders dispensed with the sacraments and for that reason had no use for sacramental vessels.[39] Baptism and communion were not practiced by the Schwenkfelders in Pennsylvania in the eighteenth century, hence the absence of pewter vessels from that period.[40] It was not until the nineteenth century that they resumed public usage of the sacraments.

Other religious groups from German speaking countries migrated to the New World in small numbers in the eighteenth century. Among them were Jews from Western Europe looking for the prospect of a better life. Many were merchants and traders in colonial times.

> there was no formal Congregation in colonial Lancaster. The census of 1790 lists only three Jewish households in Lancaster.[41]

Silver and bronze were used in the synagogue, not pewter.[42] Pewter seder dishes were used in the ceremonial dinner in the home and were not commonly used in the synagogue.

---

39. Yoder, 622.

40. Personal communication, Dennis K. Moyer, Director, Schwenkfelder Library, Pennsburg, Pa., March 13, 1994.

41. David Brener, *The Jews of Lancaster, Pennsylvania: A story with two beginnings* (Lancaster, Pa.: Congregation Shaarai Shomayim, Lancaster, Pa. in association with The Lancaster County Historical Society, 1979), 7.

42. Information from Rabbi Jack P. Paskoff, December 16, 1994.

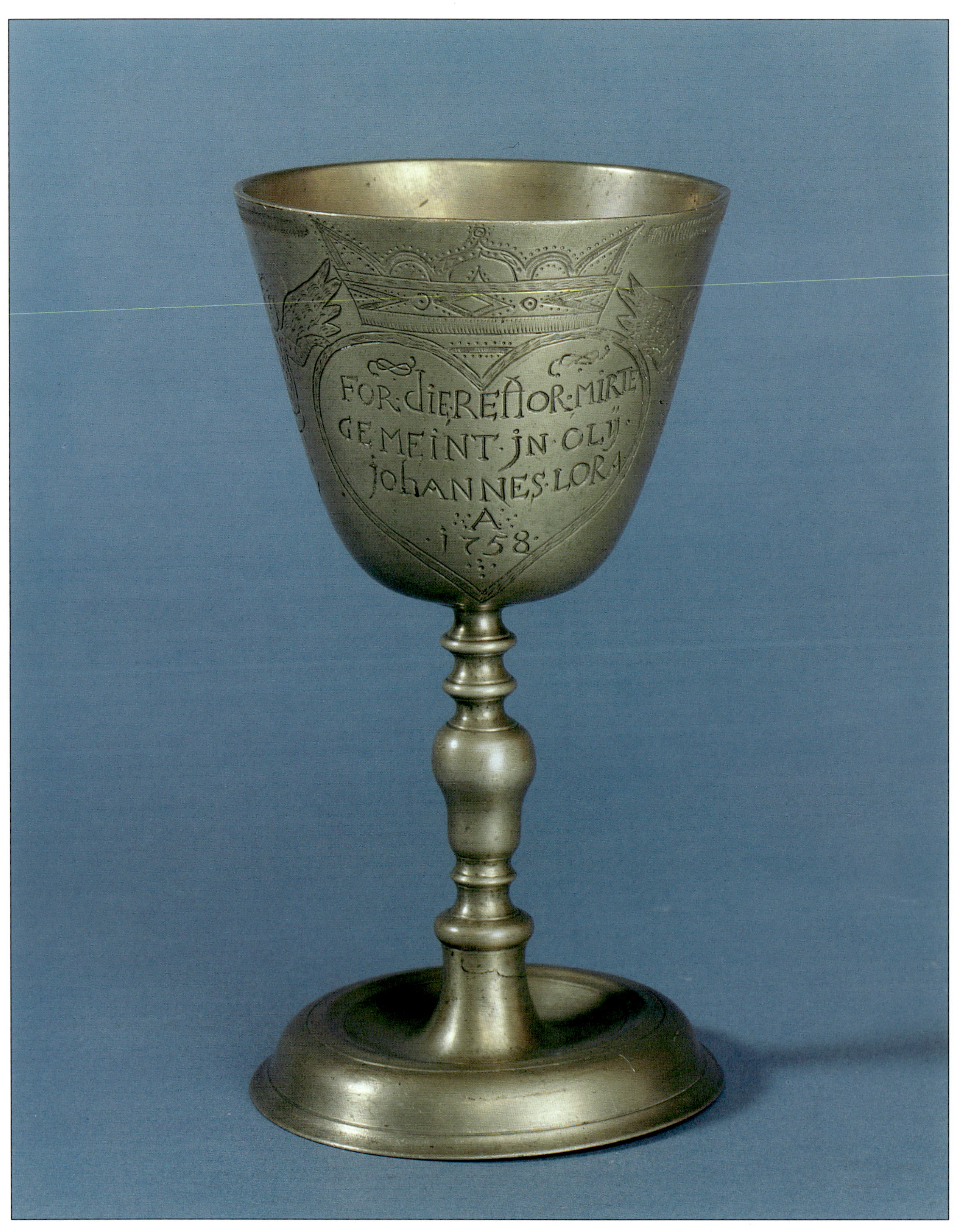

Fig. 33. *Chalice. American or Continental, 1758. H 7 3/8", TD 4", BD 3 7/8". Salem United Church of Christ, Spangsville, Berks County, Pa.*

CHAPTER 3

Vor Die Gemeinen

(For the Congregations)

DONORS AND CONTEXT

Parishioners frequently donated pewter vessels to the congregations for use in the sacraments of Holy Communion and Baptism, as attested by the many pieces bearing initials and dates inscribed on vessels owned by Pennsylvania German churches. Seventeen percent of the pewter in the survey bore dates and/or initials of donors, and some were clearly inscribed *Vor Die Gemeinen** [for the congregations] or *Das Geschenke zu* [the gift to] and included the names of the benefactors. This finding is in agreement with the theory that acquisitions were many times haphazard donations.[1] It contrasts with the conclusion of a study of silver in Anglican churches in New England that suggests that congregations decided on communion vessels long before the vessels were acquired.[2] That is not the case with the Pennsylvania Germans and their preference for pewter.

Birth and baptismal records were normally recorded in detail in church record books. Scribes, usually ministers, customarily included in their entries the date, the name of the person baptized, the names of the parents, and the names of the baptismal sponsors or godparents. Marriages were also recorded, though not always as often as the baptisms. Those united were not always members of the congregation or of the same faith. Consistory records are another story. They are often sparse and when they do exist, they often deal with building supplies, minister and schoolmaster concerns, and financial transactions that rarely mention communion and baptismal vessels.

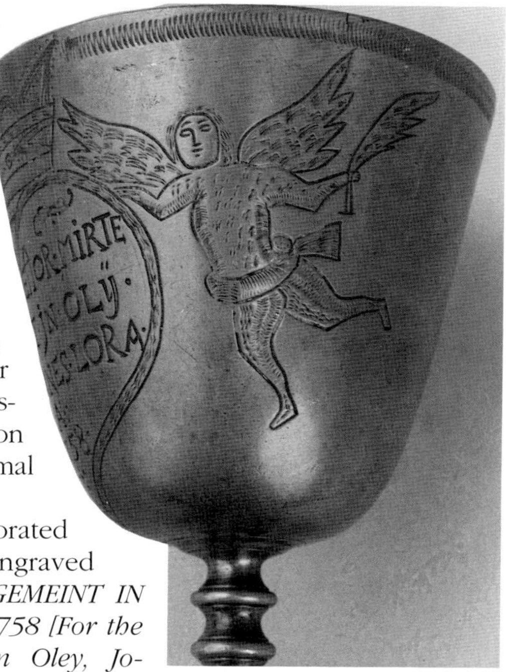

Fig. 34. Detail of one of a pair of angels engraved on chalice. Salem United Church of Christ, Berks County, Pa.

The profusely decorated chalice in Figure 33 is engraved *FOR DIE REFFORMIRTE GEMEINT IN OLY JOHANNES LORA A 1758 [For the Reformed congregation in Oley, Johannes Lora, in the year 1758].* The Reformed congregation in Oley dates from May 4, 1736, when John Philip Boehm administered the Lord's Supper to thirty-nine communicants. Johannes Lora donated the chalice in 1758. John Lorah purchased 247.5 acres of land in Amity township on June 1, 1740.[3] Amity township is a few miles from the church to

**Gemeinen* (congregations) is the Literary German equivalent of the Pennsylvania German *Gemee,* sometimes spelled *Gmee.* In worship, the Pennsylvania Germans often used Literary ("High") German.

1. Donald L. Fennimore, "Religion in America: Metal Objects in Service of the Ritual," *American Art Journal,* 10, no. 2 (November 1978), 29–30.

2. Barbara McLean Ward, "In a Feasting Posture: Communion Vessels and Community Values in Seventeenth- and Eighteenth-Century New England," *Winterthur Portfolio,* 23, no. 1 (Spring 1988): 3.

3. Morton L. Montgomery, History of Berks County in Pennsylvania (Philadelphia: Everts, Peck & Richards, 1886), 957.

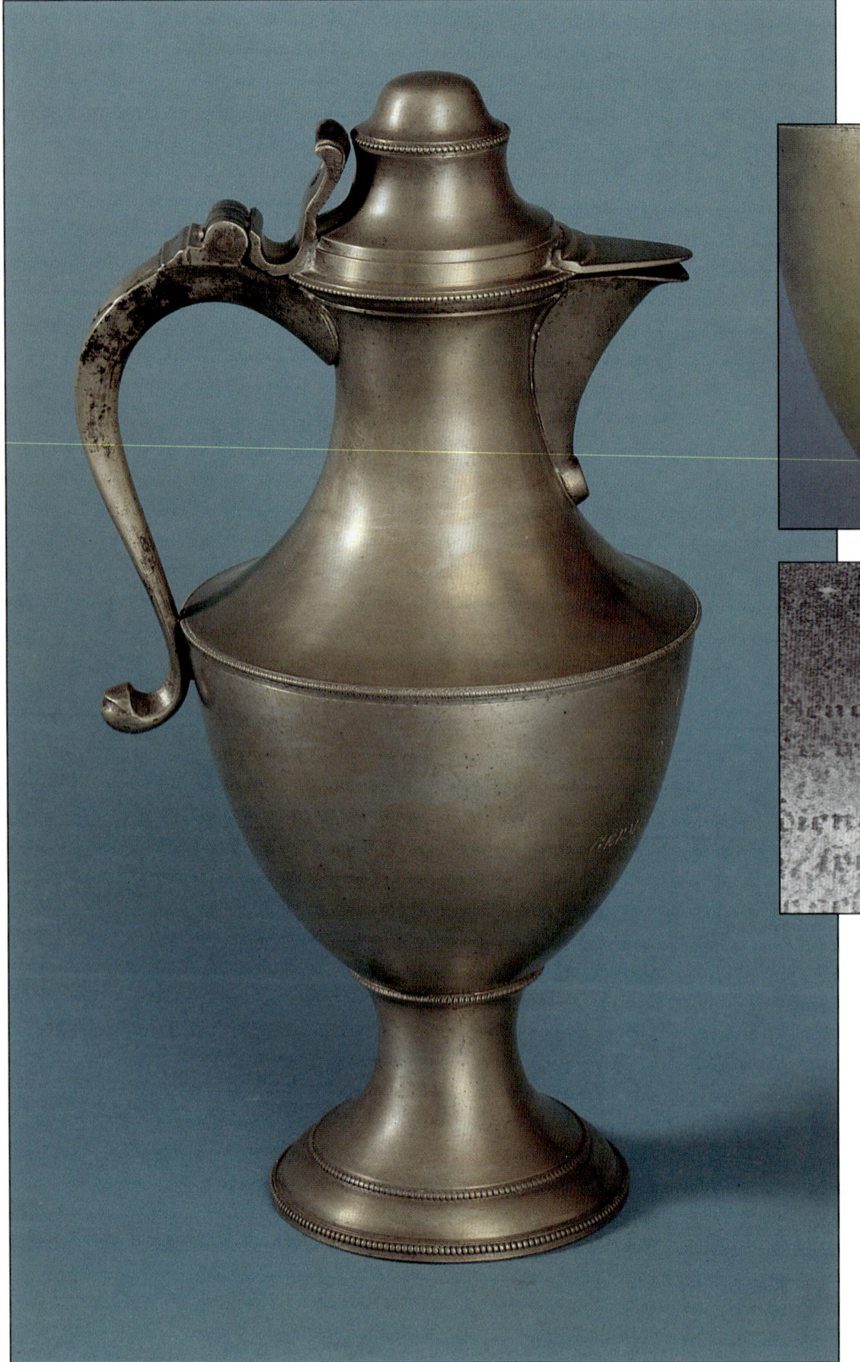

Fig. 35. *Flagon (above) attributed to William Will, Philadelphia, 1764–1798. H 13 1/2″, TD 3/8″, BD 4 3/8″. Salem United Church of Christ, Spangsville, Berks County, Pa.*

Fig. 36. *Detail (above top) of engraving on flagon. Salem United Church of Christ, Spangsville, Berks County, Pa.*

Fig. 37. *Detail (above) of tombstone of Daniel Udree, Salem Church Burial Ground.*

which the chalice belongs. A finely engraved heart, crown, and pair of angels decorate the body of this handsome chalice.

The church did purchase a baptismal basin. An entry in the church records of the Oley (Salem) Reformed Church for 1779 notes that Johannes Griesemer was paid 2 pounds, 12 shillings and 6 pence *vor tauf schissly (Schüssel)* [for a baptismal basin].[4] It is no longer in the posession of the church, and it is not known whether it was made of pewter.

The congregation also owns a large-bodied flagon (Figure 35) of Federal style attributed to William Will. It is engraved *THE GIFT OF / DANIEL UTRY Esq.r / TO THE / GERMAN REFORMED CHURCH / AT OLEY.*

Daniel Udree was the wealthy iron-master, owner of the Oley Furnace. He was a colonel in the Revolutionary War and led a battalion of Berks County militia in the Battle of Brandywine. He rose to the rank of major general in the War of

4. Church record of the Oley (Salem) Reformed Church, Oley, Berks Co., 1763–1860. Transcribed February 1933 by William J. Hinke. In the Evangelical and Reformed Archives of the United Church of Christ, Schaff Library, Lancaster Theological Seminary, Lancaster, Pa.

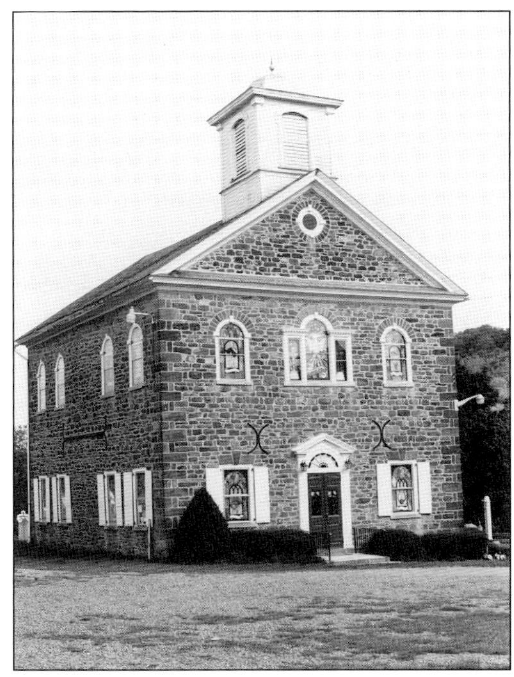

Fig. 38. *Jerusalem (Red) Union Lutheran and United Church of Christ congregations, Kempton, Berks County, Pa., built in 1812–1814. The color of the roof and doors provided the name by which it was known in the nineteenth century: the Red Church. The building has had few alterations and provides a setting in which the pewter vessels in the following figure were used.*

1812. He served several terms in the Pennsylvania General Assembly and two terms in Congress. His holdings included a farm, flour mill, and two furnaces that made him the largest taxpayer in the county in the final years of his life. His large tombstone, (Figure 37) in the cemetery by the church, notes that he was born in Philadelphia on August 5, 1751, and died on July 15, 1828.[5] The flagon that bears his name was made in Philadelphia about 1790.

An example of pewter given by a member of the congregation is illustrated by the inscription on a chalice in a set owned by the Jerusalem (Red) Union Lutheran and United Church of Christ congregations in Kempton, Berks County, Pa. (Figures 38 and 39) The building, pewter baptismal and communion set,

5. See P. C. Croll, *Annals of the Oley Valley in Berks County, Pa.* (Reading: Reading Eagle Press, 1926), for information about Udree. Eleanor Shaner, secretary of Salem United Church of Christ, brought the above information to the attention of the author.

Fig. 39. *Oval dish by William Will, Philadelphia, 1764–1798 (L 538, 539). H 1 5/8″, L 15 1/2″, W 10 1/2″, Brim 2″. Chalice probably Philadelphia, possibly William Will. H 9″, TD 4″, BD 4 1/2″. Flagon, Germany, Franconia district of northern Bavaria, 1743, H 11 3/4″, TD 3″, BD 5 1/2″. Engraved "CF CB 1743." Quart pitcher attributed to William Will, H 7″, TD 3 3/8″, BD 5 1/4″. The wrigglework decoration that adorns the top, base and handle attachments is very similar to that on the marked Will dish. Jerusalem (Red) Union Church with Lutheran and United Church of Christ congregations, Kempton, Berks County, Pa.*

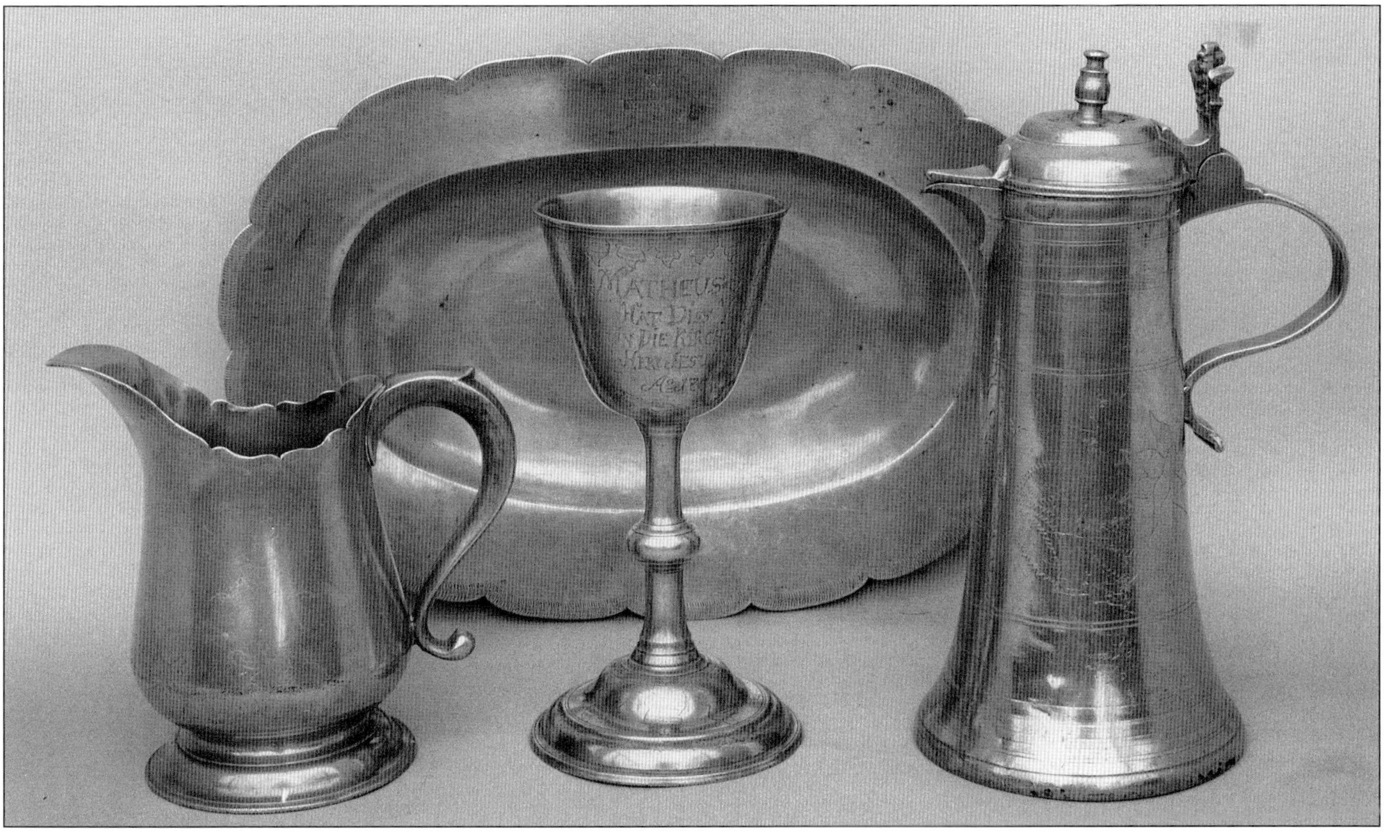

Fig. 40. *Cup of chalice donated by Matthias Probst in 1766. Jerusalem (Red) Union Church with Lutheran and United Church of Christ congregations, Kempton, Berks County, Pa.*

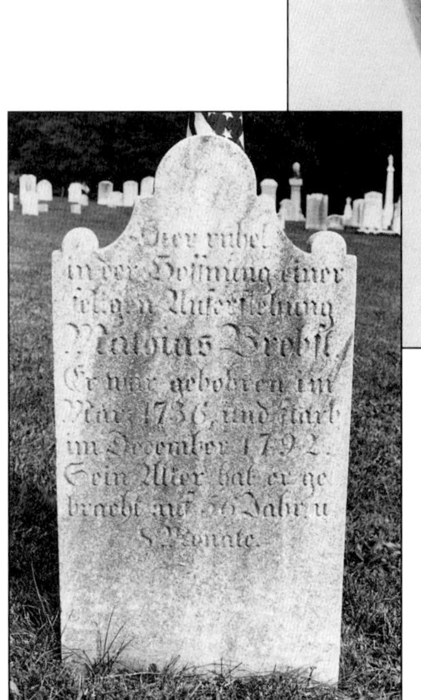

Fig. 41. *Gravestone of Matthias Brobst, born March 1736, and died 1792 at the age of 56 years and 8 months. Jerusalem (Red) Union Church, Kempton, Berks County, Pa.*

chalice, and information about the donor are included to put the situation into context.

The chalice is engraved *NEHMET HIN UND DRINCKET ALLE DRAUS DAS IST MEIN BLUT Math 26 MATHEUS PROBST HAT DISS VERERTH IN DIE KIRCHE DEIN HERN JESU MEIN A 1766.* [Take and drink ye all of it, this is my blood, Matthew 26. Matthias Probst has donated this chalice to the church of your Lord in the year 1766.]

Matthias Probst donated this chalice to the church two years before his minister Daniel Schumacher illustrated the title page of the church book for the Allemaengel Union (Lutheran and Reformed) congregations. Schumacher had apparently neither university training nor ordination but functioned widely as a Lutheran pastor.[6] One of the earliest entries in this church register notes the birth and baptism of Catharina Barbara Probst, born December 16, 1767, and baptized January 24, 1768. The parents were Matthes *(sic)* Probst and his wife, Maria Magdalena (Stammbach) Probst. In 1779, on the tenth Sunday after Trinity, Matthias Probst was elected an elder in the church.[7] A Matthias Probst served in the Revolutionary War in 1777. His tombstone is found in Section II, Row 5 of the church cemetery (Figure 41).

Pastor Schumacher withdrew from the Allemaengel congregation and he and his followers built the New Allemaengel or Friedens (White) Union Church nearby. The minister decorated the title page of the record book of the new congregation on May 20, 1771. He noted the following donations:

> Christian Hechler and his wife presented a cup and paten to be used in the Holy Communion, for the united congregation in the church in the year 1771.
>
> Jacob Bielman and his wife Eva a baptismal bowl and a baptismal can on the 20th Sunday after Trinity, 1771.
>
> Susanna Catharine Nargang presented a white figured altar cloth on the 23rd Sunday after Trinity, 1771, for the use of the united Lutheran and Reformed congregation at the communion.
>
> John Nicholas Mannebach presented to the church three pounds, and a black altar cloth, as a memorial to the Reformed and Lutheran congregation of himself, on the 16th Sunday after Trinity, 1773.

6. Frederick S. Weiser, "Fraktur," in *Arts of the Pennsylvania Germans,* ed. Scott T. Swank (New York: W.W. Norton & Co., 1983), 261.

7. Church Book of the Lutheran Church of Allemaengel, Albany Township, Berks County, 1768–1862. Transcribed by William J. Hinke, 1938. Evangelical and Reformed Church Archives of the United Church of Christ, Schaff Library, Lancaster Theological Seminary, Lancaster, Pa.

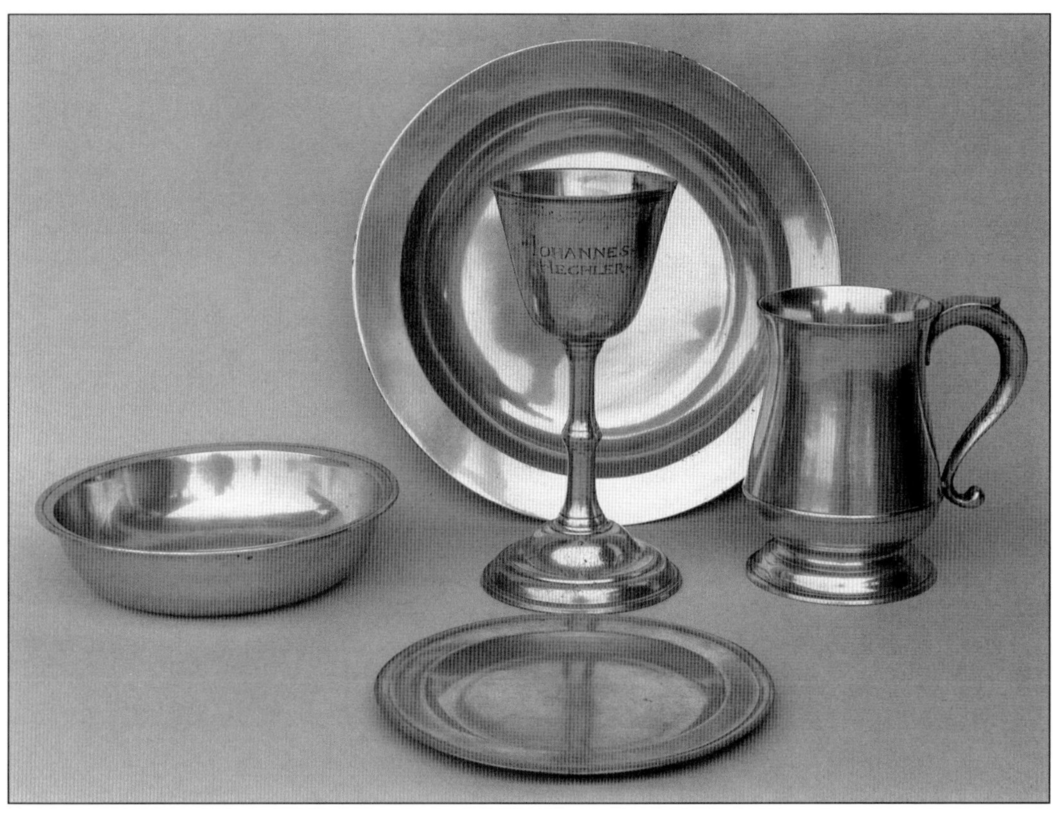

Fig. 42. *Basin marked* ***Love****, Philadelphia, 1750–1825 (L 868, 869). D 8″. Deep dish by Townsend and Giffin, London, 1777–1801 (C 4801). D 11 7/8″. Plate by Townsend and Giffin (C 4801). 7 7/8″. Chalice probably Philadelphia, possibly William Will, 1764–1798. H 9 1/8″, TD 4 1/4″, BD 4 1/2″. Quart tulip mug by William Will, Philadelphia, 1764–1798 (L 535). H 6 3/8″, TD 4 1/8″, BD 4 3/8″. Friedens Lutheran Church, Stony Run, Berks County, Pa.*

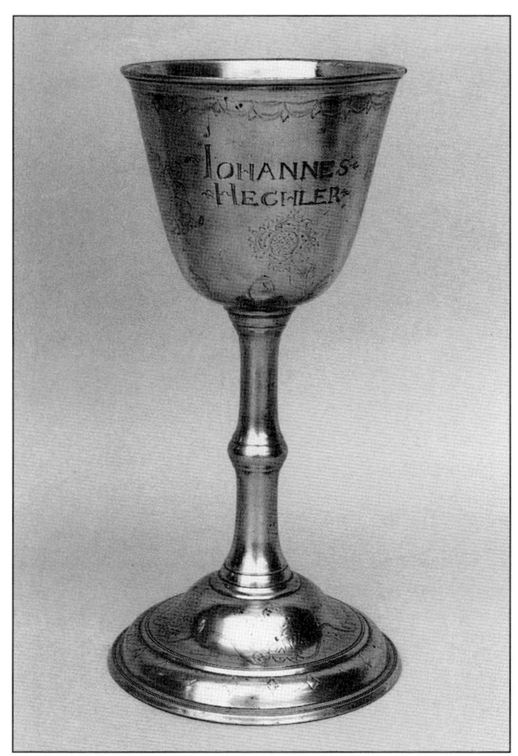

Fig. 43. *Chalice donated to the Lutheran and Reformed congregations by Johannes Hechler. The swag and diamond decoration around the lip of this chalice has been found on sugar bowls attributed to William Will. Friedens Lutheran Church, Stony Run, Berks County, Pa.*

> The three pounds are to be used for the erection of the cemetery.
>
> Our sister M.E.S. presented to this united congregation a collection plate, on the 22nd Sunday after Trinity, 1773.[8]

And indeed, the church owns a cup (chalice), a paten, a baptismal bowl, a can (mug), and a collection plate. Figure 42.

The chalice is engraved *JOHANNES HECHLER VOR DIE LUTHERISCHEN UND REFORMIERTEN E GEMINEN* [Johannes Hechler for the Lutheran and Reformed congregations]. Figure 43.

Aaron Levy, a Philadelphia Jewish merchant and land developer in upstate Pennsylvania, founded the village of Aaronsburg in the geographical center of Pennsylvania in 1786. In a generous ecumenical gesture, he provided land for a church building for his Protestant settlers.

8. Church record of the Friedens Union Church, Albany Township, Berks County, 1771–1876. Copied and translated by William J. Hinke, July 1933. Reformed Church Records at the Evangelical and Reformed Historical Society of the United Church of Christ, Schaff Library, Lancaster Theological Seminary, Lancaster, Pa. Also in H. S. Kidd, *Lutherans in Berks County: Two Centuries of Continuous Organized Church Life 1723–1923,* published by the Reading Conference of The Evangelical Lutheran Ministerium of Pennsylvania and Adjacent States (Kutztown and Reading, Pa.: William S. Rhode, 1923), 118.

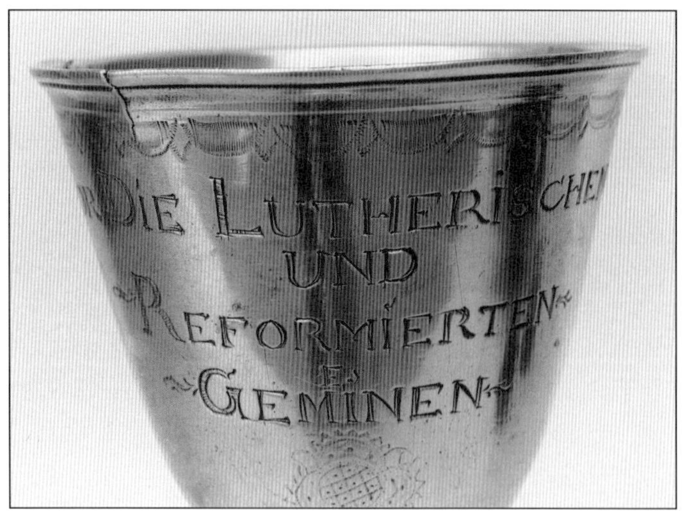

Fig. 44. *Detail of chalice. Friedens Lutheran Church, Stony Run, Berks County, Pa.*

At the same time he commissioned pewterer William Will to make a communion and baptismal set for a union church of Lutheran and Reformed congregations. His gift of a flagon, pitcher, chalice, and baptismal bowl by William Will is inscribed *DAS GESCHENKE ZU DENEN DEUTSHCEN GEMEINDEN IN ARENSBURG VON ARON LEVY,* [the gift to these German congregations in Aaronsburg from Aaron Levy]. Plans for the union church failed and the Lutherans erected Salem Church. The pewter set was probably made between 1789 (when land was granted to the Lutheran congregation) and 1794 (when the union plan was abandoned).

The set in Figure 45 is one of the finest of surviving American services.[9] It is an example of an entire set made by one pewterer and given by one donor. In this case the donor was not a member of the congregation but the town founder. This set once disappeared from sight:

9. In his *Pewter in America* (1971), Laughlin makes the judgment: "In some respects this is the finest of surviving American services." Plate 96. In the two decades since then, however, many equally fine services have been discovered in Pennsylvania German churches.

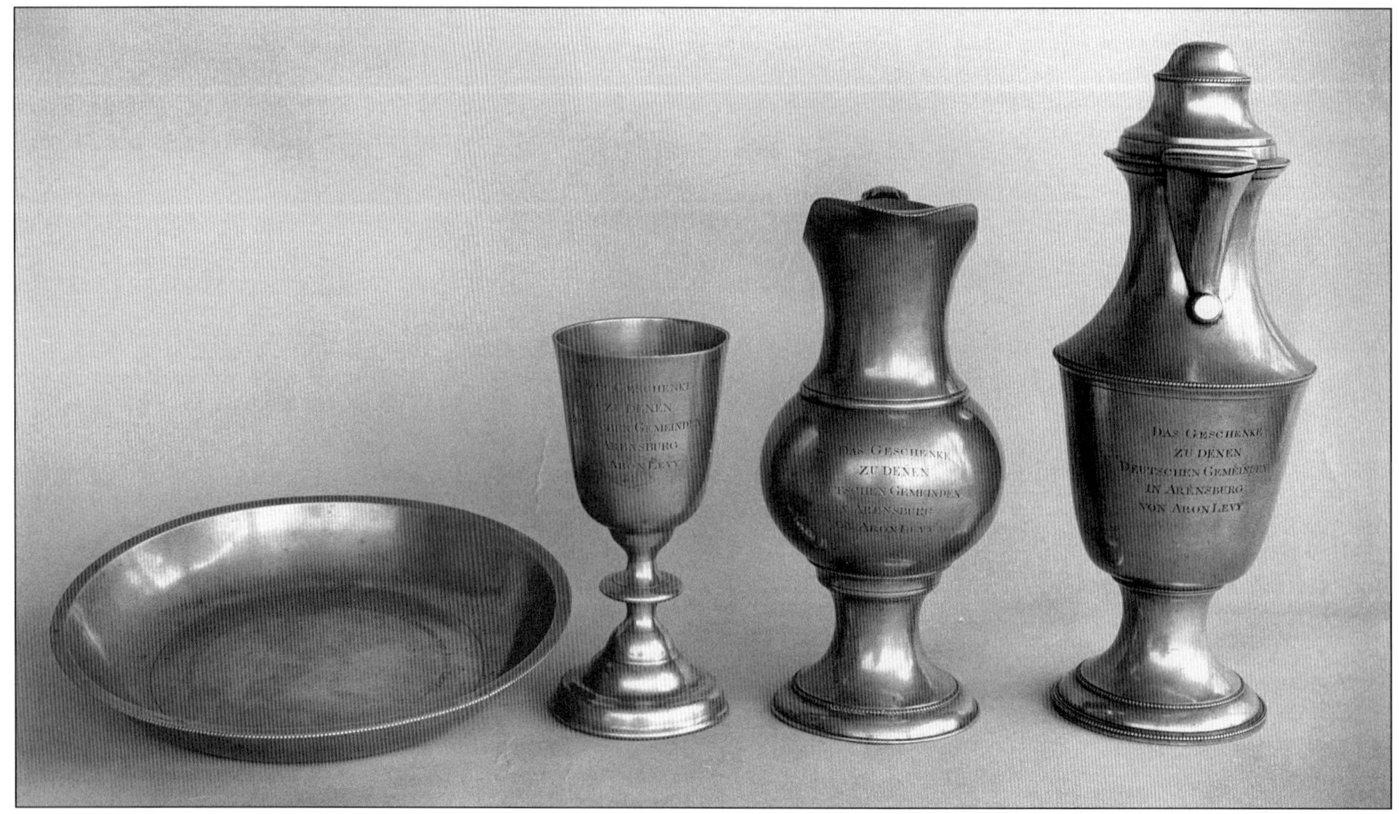

Fig. 45. *The baptismal basin is marked by William Will, Philadelphia, 1764–1798 (L 537,540). Chalice attributed to William Will, H 7 3/4", TD 3 1/2", BD 3 5/8". Ewer or pitcher attributed to William Will. H 10 7/8", TD 3 3/8", BD 4 1/4". Flagon attributed to William Will. H 13 7/8", TD 3 3/8", BD 4 3/8". Salem Lutheran Church, Aaronsburg, Centre County, Pa.*

In 1852 the original Salem Lutheran Church was torn down and replaced by the present building. Between 1869 and 1873 the latter was remodeled and, perhaps accidentally, the communion service was enclosed within a platform on which the pulpit stood. There it remained until 1917, when the church was again remodeled and workmen, tearing out the platform, found the forgotten pewter.[10]

Michael Weber and his wife, Anna Barbara, donated two flagons to the Lutheran Church in Heidelberg (Township), Lancaster (County), in 1764. They are similarly inscribed: *Michael Weber und seine Ehefrau Anna Barbara haben die Communion Kanthen in die Evange-*

10. Paul M. Auman, "New Finds in Old Pewter by William Will: The Aaronsburg Communion Service," *The Magazine Antiques* (April 1950); and John C. Thomas, ed., *American and British Pewter: An Historical Survey* (Clinton, N.J.: The Main Street Press, 1976), 102–3.

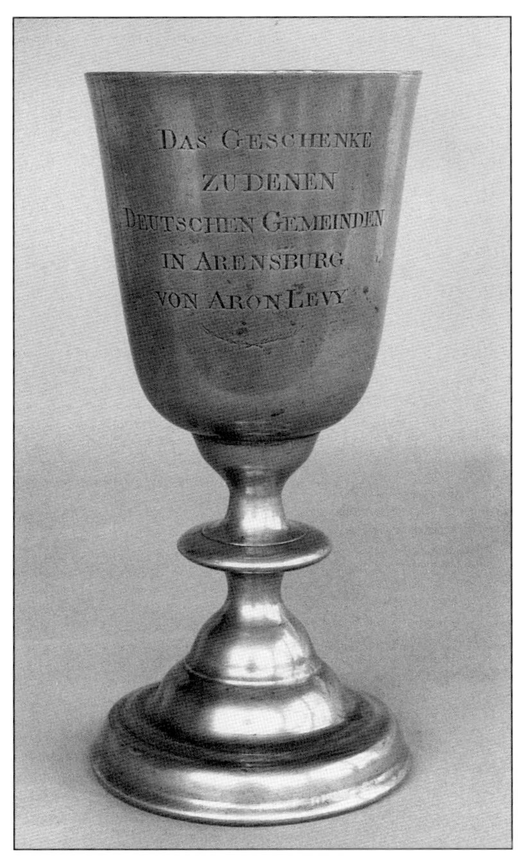

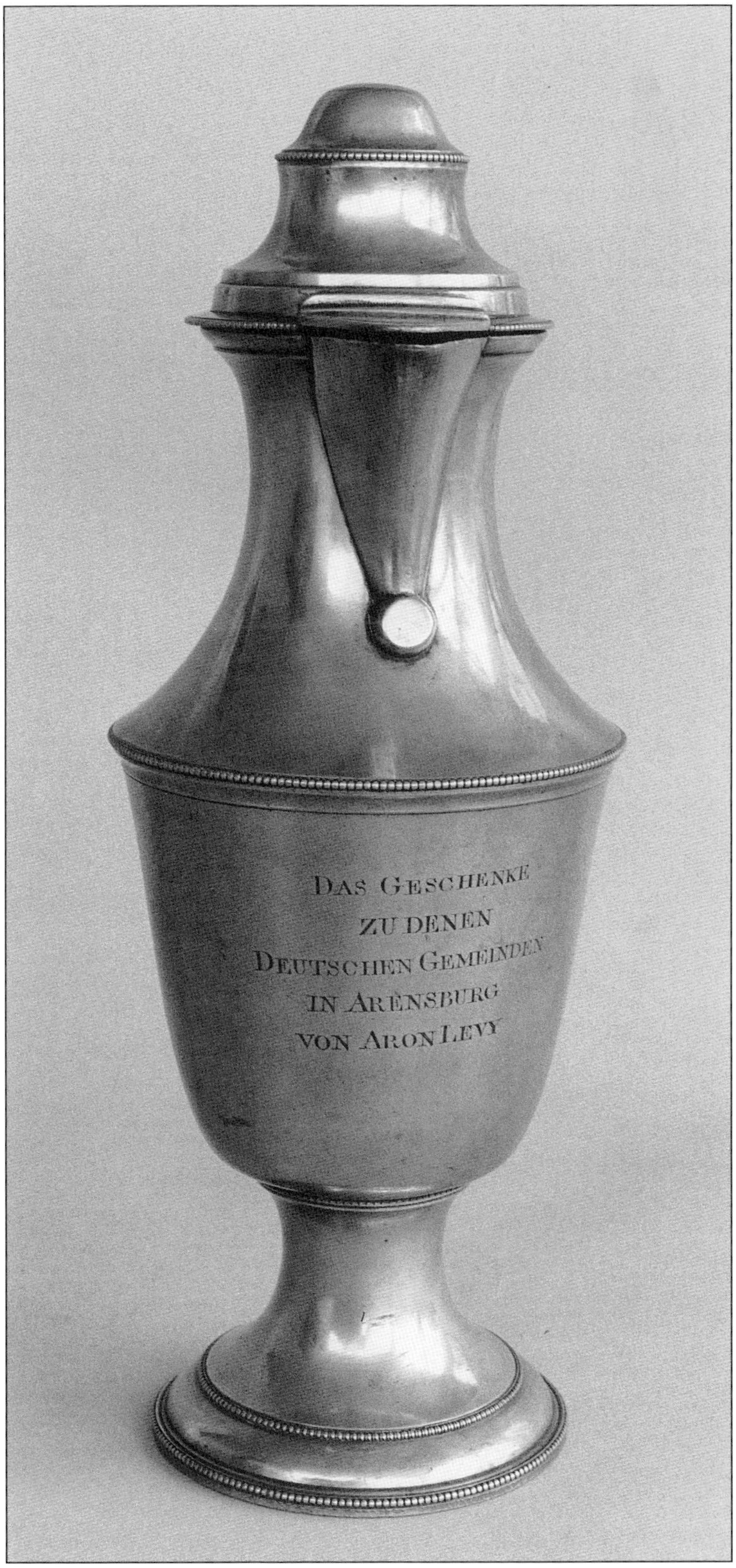

Fig. 46. *Flagon (above) attributed to William Will, Philadelphia, 1764–1798. Salem Lutheran Church, Aaronsburg, Centre County, Pa.*

Fig. 47. *Chalice (left) attributed to William Will, Philadelphia, 1764–1798. Salem Lutheran Church, Aaronsburg, Centre County, Pa.*

Fig. 48. *Quart tankard by John Townsend, London, 1748–1801 (C 4795). H 7 1/4", TD 4 1/8", BD 4 7/8". Flagons by Daniel Heldenreich, Durlach, Germany, 1764, (H v.5, 709). H 14 1/2", TD 4", BD 5 1/2". Chalice by Johann Christoph Heyne, Lancaster, 1752–1781, (L 532, 533). H 9", TD 4", BD 4 1/2". St. Luke's Lutheran Church, Schaefferstown, Lebanon County, Pa.*

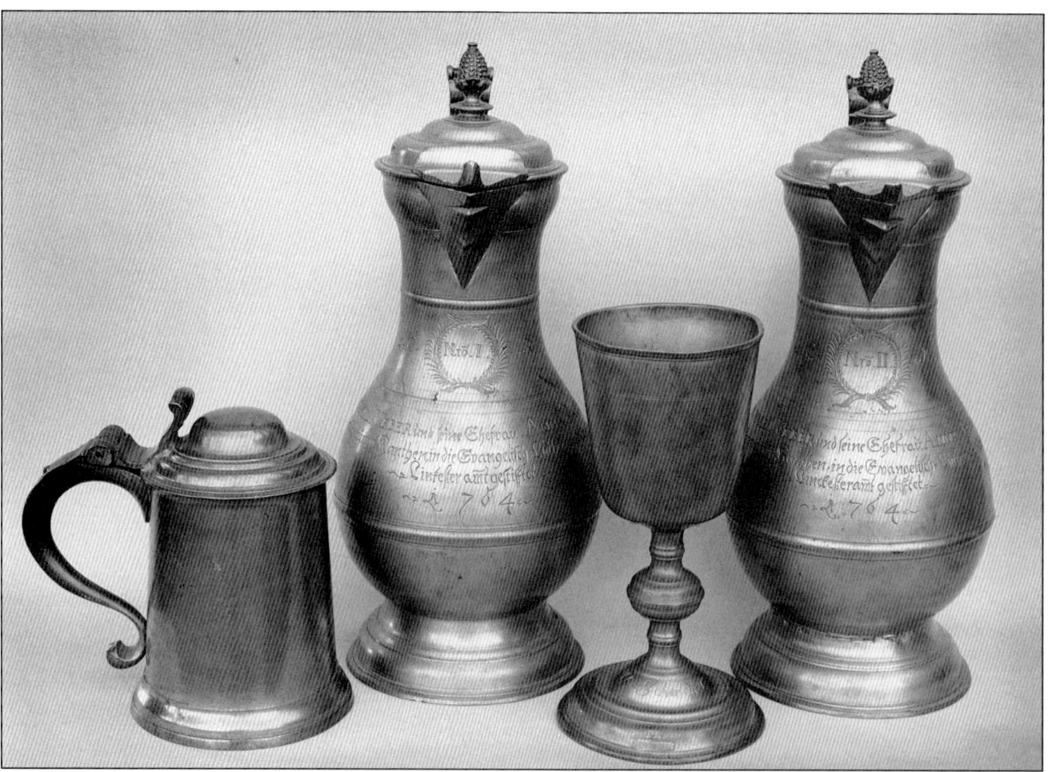

lisch Lutherische Kirche in Heidelberg Linkester ammt gestifftet 1764. [Michael Weber and his wife Anna Barbara have presented these communion flagons to the Evangelical Lutheran Church in Heidelberg, Lancaster County, 1764]. The church is located at Schaefferstown in Lebanon County, Pa.

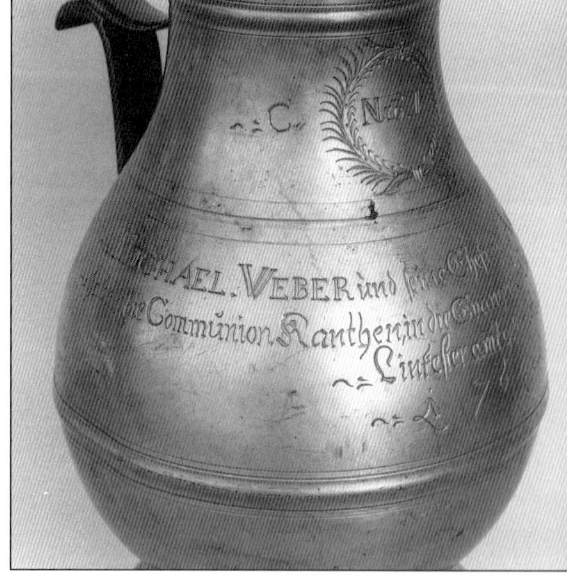

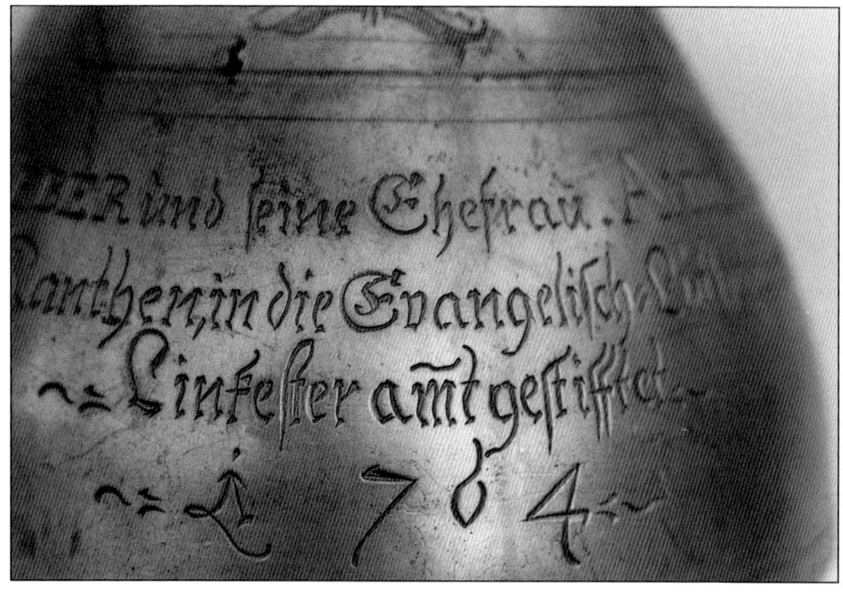

Fig. 49. *Body (above) of flagon given by Michael and Anna Barbara Weber to the Lutheran Church in Heidelberg Township, Lancaster County, in 1764. Lebanon County was formed from Lancaster and Dauphin Counties in 1813. St. Luke's Lutheran Church, Schaefferstown, Lebanon County, Pa.*

Fig. 50. *Detail (left) of inscription on flagon.*

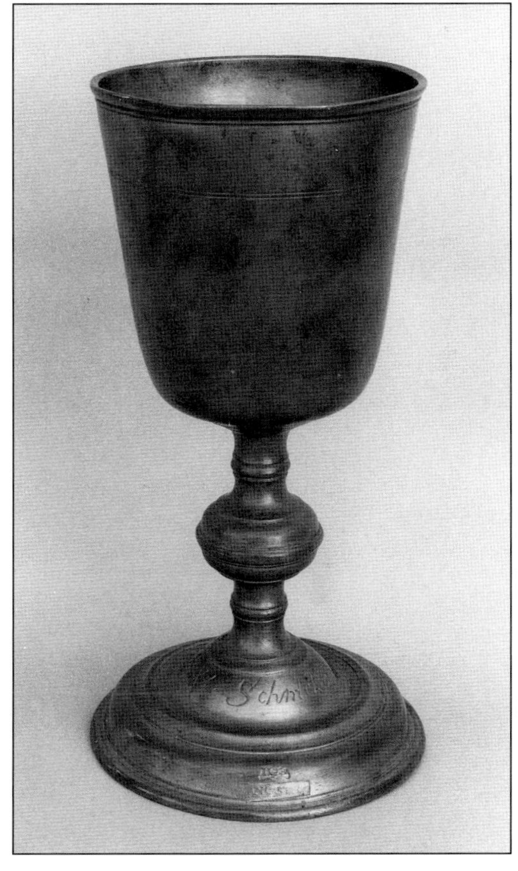

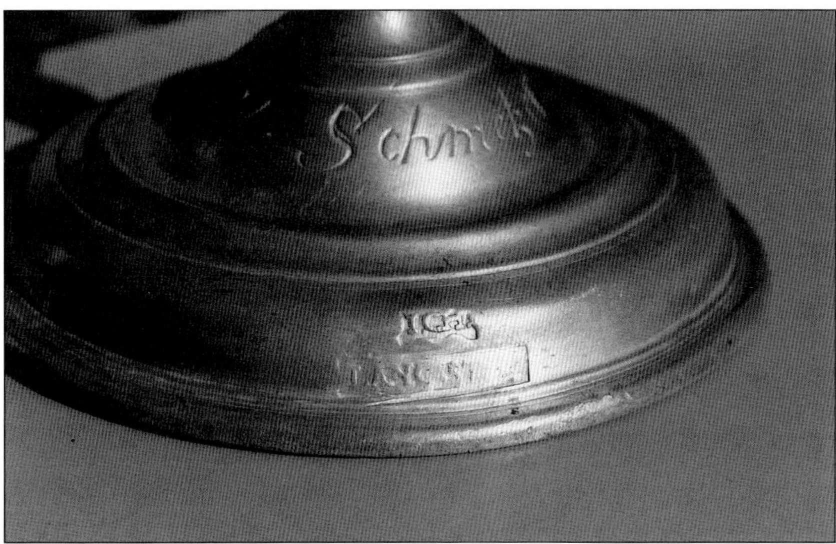

Fig. 51. *Chalice (left) by Johann Christoph Heyne, Lancaster, Pa. St. Luke's Lutheran Church, Schaefferstown, Lebanon County, Pa.*

Fig. 52. *Detail (above) of Heyne chalice engraved "H. W. Schmetzer 1761."*

The chalice by Lancaster pewterer Johann Christoph Heyne is inscribed "H. W. Schmetzer 1761."[11]

Andreas Morr (1727–1801) gave a wonderfully decorated flagon to a Lutheran church near Freeburg in 1795. See Figure 53. It is engraved "Zur ehre Gottes gestifftet Von Andreas Morr in die Evangelisch Lutherische Zion Kirche, in Penns-township Northumberland County Den 29ten july Anno dom. 1795." [To the glory of God, presented by Andreas Morr to the Evangelical Lutheran Zion Church in Penns Township, Northumberland County, the 29th of July, in the year of our Lord, 1795]. Andrew More, Peter Stroup, and Casper Rousch were granted a warrant for fifty acres in Penns Township, Northumberland County, on April 12, 1774, "in trust for a Lutheran Church and School House."[12] The church became known as "Mohrs" and was first called that in the minutes of the Lutheran synod in 1801. Descendants of Andreas Morr and orthographic variations of the name (Mohr and Moore) were associated with the church into the nineteenth century. Philip Moore was one of the trustees who sold the Mohr church property on September 16, 1816. The congregations became part of St. Peter's Lutheran and Reformed Church in Freeburg. Penns Township, Northumberland County, is located in present-day Snyder County, which was formed in 1855.

A companion chalice was given to the congregation by Catharina Elisabetha Morr (1732–1795), wife of Andreas Morr. It is inscribed *"Zur ehre Gottes Gestifftet von Catharina Elisabetha Morrin"* [To the Glory of God, presented by Catharina Elisabetha Morr]. Figure 54.

11. The inscription on the chalice appears to be H. W. Schmetzer, but church records prior to 1800, taken from Brendle's *History of Schaefferstown,* list Schweitzer, Schwertzele, Scheutz, and Scheetze, but no Schmetzer.

12. Charles H. Glatfelter, *Pastors and People: German Lutheran and Reformed Churches in the Pennsylvania Field, 1717–1793,* vol. 1, *Pastors and Congregations* (Breinigsville, Pa.; The Pennsylvania German Society, 1980), 453.

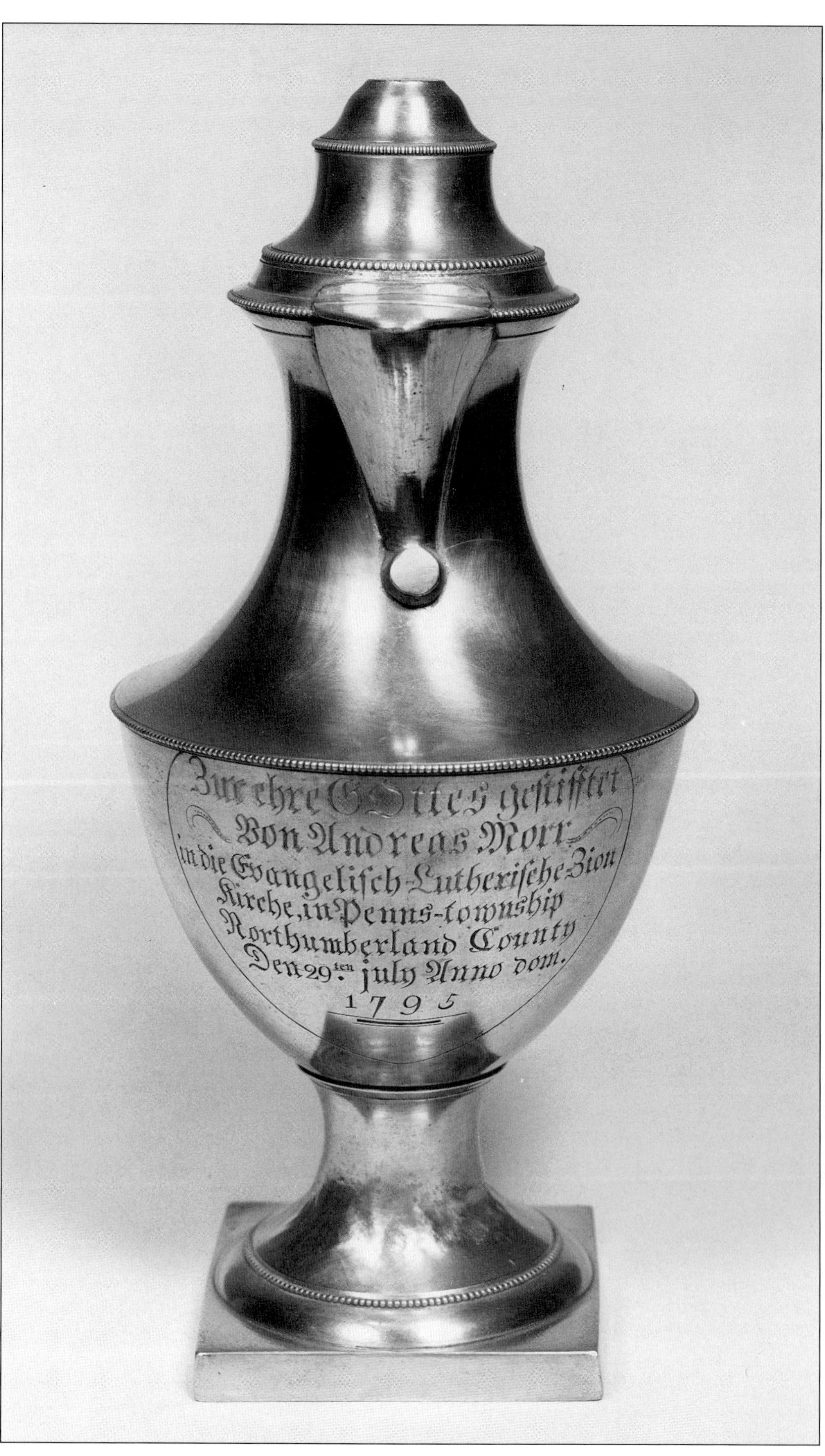

Fig. 53. *Flagon attributed to William Will, Philadelphia, 1764–1798. H 13 3/4", TD 1/4", BD 4 1/4". Formerly in St. Peter's Lutheran Church, Freeburg, Snyder County, Pa. Collection of Charles V. Swain.*

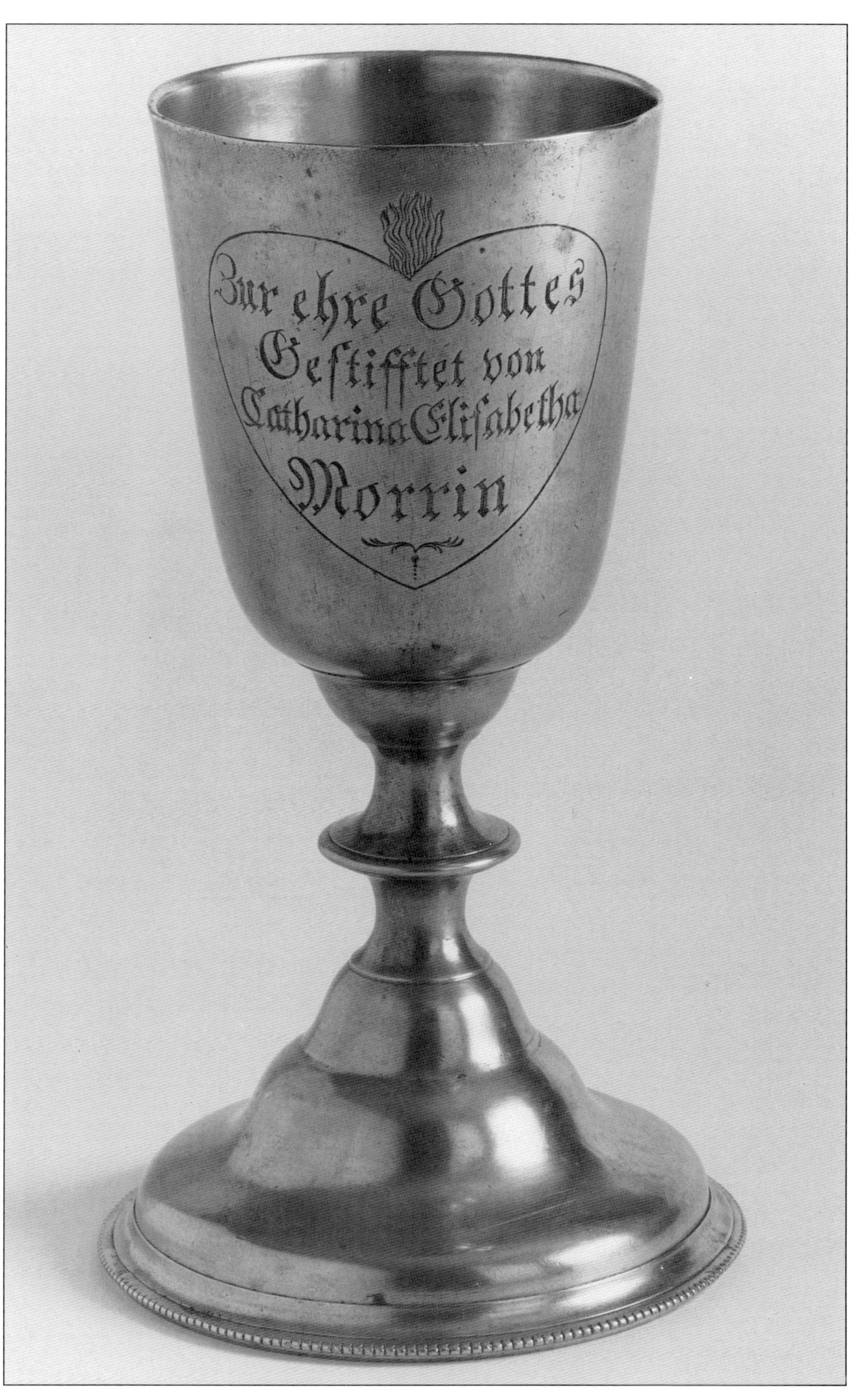

Fig. 54. *Chalice attributed to William Will, Philadelphia, 1764–1798. H 7 7/8″, TD 3 1/2″, BD 4 3/8″. Formerly in St. Peter's Lutheran Church, Freeburg, Snyder County, Pa. Courtesy, Winterthur Museum.*

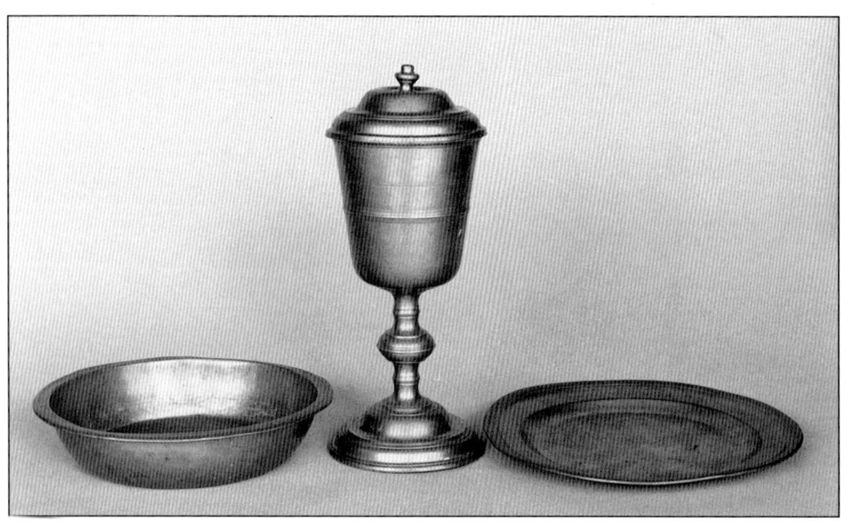

Fig. 55. *Basin, England, 1750–1800. TD 8 1/4″, H 1 3/4″. Chalice with lid attributed to Johann Christoph Heyne, Lancaster, Pa., 1752–1781. H 10 1/2″, TD 4 1/4″, BD 4 3/8″. Plate, probably Birmingham, England, 1750–1800. TD 8 3/4″. St. Peter's Lutheran Church, Freeburg, Snyder County, Pa.*

A covered chalice by Johann Christoph Heyne and a British basin and plate remain in the collection of the congregation. Figure 55.

The records of St. John's Lutheran Church in Maytown, Lancaster County, tell us that

> On May 27, 1771, the officers of the church presented the following gifts as free-will offerings in the presence of the entire congregation:
>
> 1. Frederick Schwartz gave a pewter chalice and plate for the use of the holy communion.
>
> 2. Jacob Wolf gave a pewter baptismal bowl and tankard for the wine....[13]

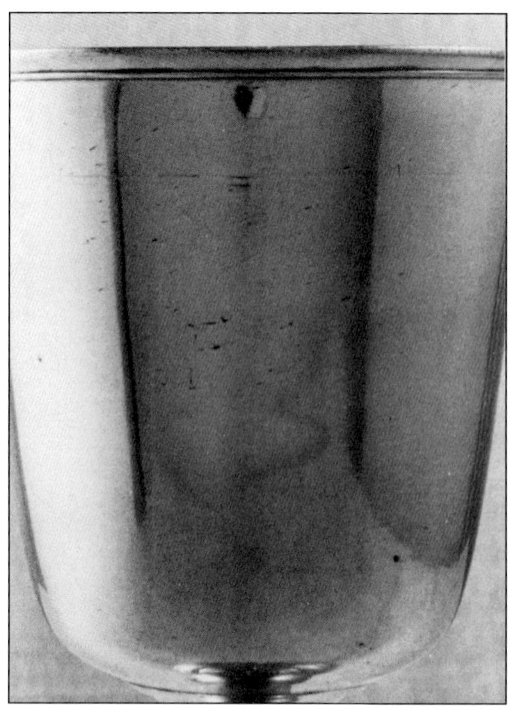

Fig. 56. *The initials FS scratched on body of chalice attributed to Johann Christoph Heyne, Lancaster, Pa., 1752–1781. St. John's Lutheran Church, Lancaster County, Pa.*

The chalice attributed to Johann Christoph Heyne does indeed have an *F S* scratched on the body for its donor, Frederick Schwartz (Figure 56). The whereabouts of the plate is unknown. It has been missing from the congregation for

13. George Philip Goll, *The History of the St. John Evangelical Lutheran Church, Maytown, Lancaster Co. Pa., 1765–1904* (Lancaster, Pa.: Wickersham Printing Co., 1904), 21.

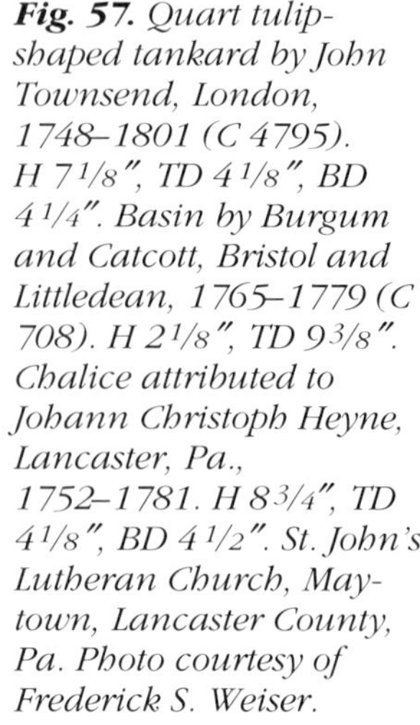

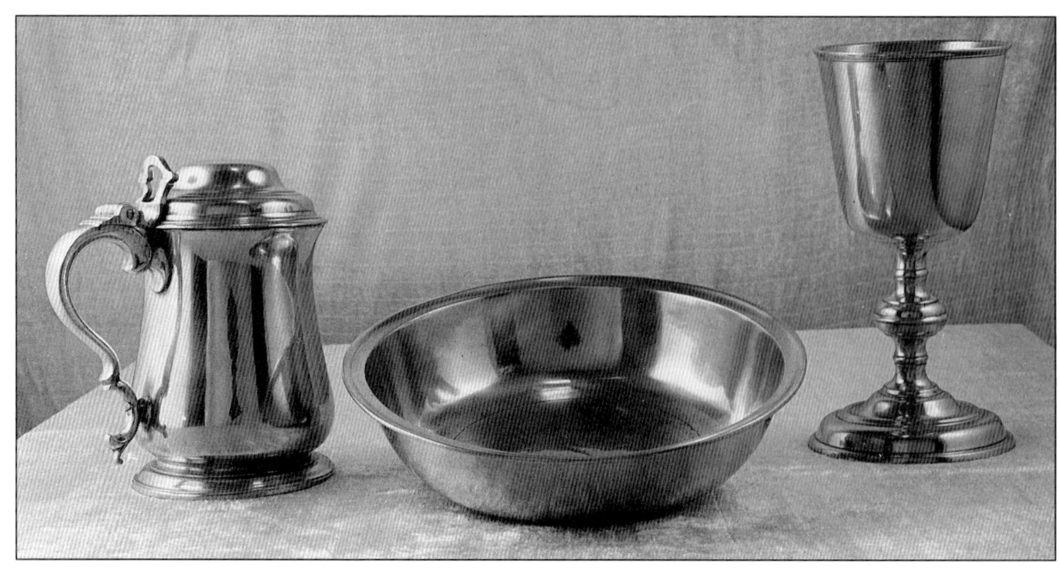

Fig. 57. *Quart tulip-shaped tankard by John Townsend, London, 1748–1801 (C 4795). H 7 1/8″, TD 4 1/8″, BD 4 1/4″. Basin by Burgum and Catcott, Bristol and Littledean, 1765–1779 (C 708). H 2 1/8″, TD 9 3/8″. Chalice attributed to Johann Christoph Heyne, Lancaster, Pa., 1752–1781. H 8 3/4″, TD 4 1/8″, BD 4 1/2″. St. John's Lutheran Church, Maytown, Lancaster County, Pa. Photo courtesy of Frederick S. Weiser.*

more than seventy-five years.[14] Jacob Wolf's initials are scratched on the bottoms of the British tankard and basin (Figure 56).

The initials "H R V" are engraved on the bottom of a beaker owned by the Lower Skippack Mennonite Church of Montgomery County, Pa. (Figure 58). They are very likely those of a donor. Matthias Van Bebber, a Dutch Mennonite land owner from Germantown deeded the congregation 50 acres in 1717 and sold the group another fifty acres. Four families from Germantown formed this early congregation on February 1, 1703.[15] A photograph of the church shows Sally Hallman Dambly and Lavinia Hunsicker Bauer sitting on a fence in front of the meetinghouse. Sally was born in 1885 and appears to be in her teens in the photo, which would date the view of the church to about 1900.[16]

There is evidence that occasionally parishioners signed a subscription list promising to provide financial support for the purchase of a new communion set. A document in the possession of the Wentz's United Church of Christ in Montgomery County, Pennsylvania, written about 1835, notes that "The subscribers pay the respective sums opposite to their names for the purpose of purchasing a new Communion Set, such as a Flagon, Goblet, Plate & Baptismal Bowl to be used at Wentz's Church in the administration of the Sacrament." Fifteen subscribers signed the document for the new communion set. The old communion set, illustrated in the previous chapter, is in the possession of the church. An early account book of Wentz's Reformed Church lacks entries about the acquisition of the old set.[17]

The initials on a piece of pewter need not be that of its donor. Such is the case with a flagon given to the Holy Trinity Lutheran Church in Lancaster, Pennsylvania. An entry written in German script on the front inside cover of the earliest record book in the possession of the

Fig. 58. *Basin (above) by Thomas Swanson, London, 1753–1783 (C 4593). H 2 7/8″, TD 11 3/4″. Beaker by Robert Iles, London, 1695–1735 (C 2522). H 5 1/4″, TD 3 3/8″, BD 3 1/8″. Lower Skippack Mennonite Church, Skippack, Montgomery County, Pa.*

Fig. 59. *The initials "H R V" (left) on outside bottom of beaker.*

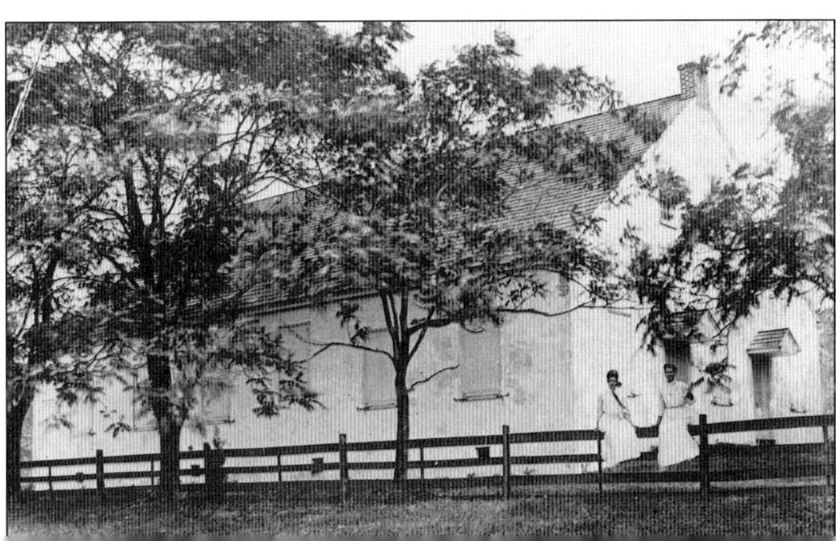

Fig. 60. *Photograph of Lower Skippack Mennonite Church, ca. 1900. Courtesy of Lower Skippack Mennonite Church, Skippack, Montgomery County, Pa.*

14. Frederick S. Weiser, *A Congregation Named Saint John's: Two Hundred Years of Parish Life in Saint John's Evangelical Lutheran Church, Maytown, Pennsylvania 1767–1967* (Maytown, Pa.: St. John's Lutheran Church Council, 1967), 22.

15. Personal communication from Alan G. Keyser, March 13, 1994.

16. Information written on the back of the photograph and information from Helen H. Patterson, September 15, 1992.

17. Reformed Church Records in Pennsylvania, vol. 3, Account Book for Wentz's Reformed Church, Worcester Township, Montgomery County, 1762–1770. In the Evangelical and Reformed Church Archives of the United Church of Christ, Schaff Library, Lancaster Theological Seminary, Lancaster, Pa.

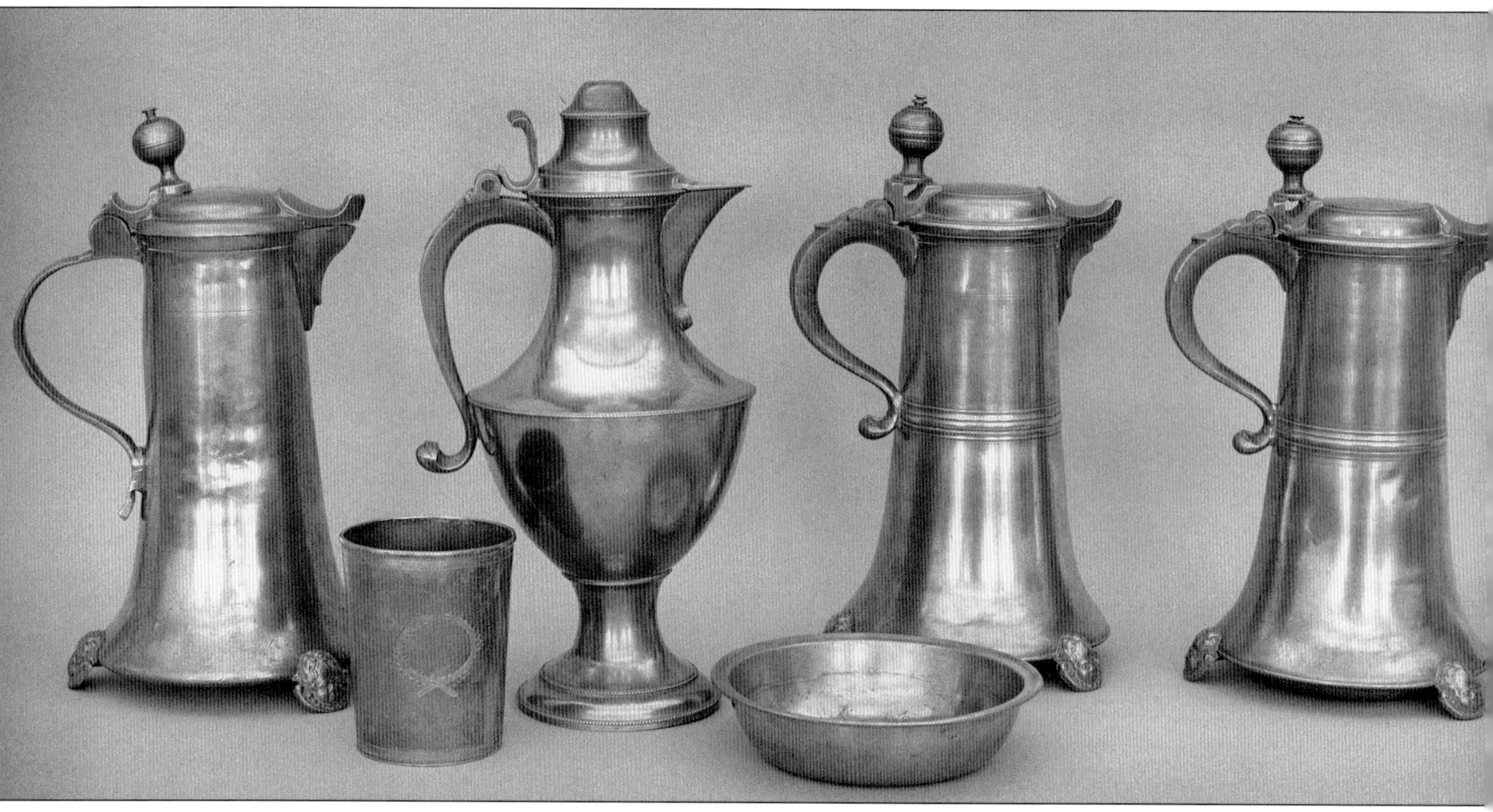

Fig. 61. *Flagon by Heinrich Müller, Rothenburg ob der Tauber, Germany, 1712–1744 (H v.6, 1199). H 12 1/2", TD 3 1/2", BD 6 1/2". Beaker unmarked, seamed on side of body . Dimensions identical to a marked beaker by Broadhead, Gurney, Sporle & Co., Sheffield, England, 1792–1800. H 4 3/8", TD 3 3/8", BD 2 7/8". Flagon attributed to William Will, Philadelphia, 1764–1798. H 13 1/2", TD 3 3/8", BD 4 3/8". Basin by Blakeslee Barnes, Philadelphia, 1812–1817 (L 557) TD 6". Both flagons are by Johann Christoph Heyne, Lancaster, Pa., 1752–1781. They bear the same marks and have the same dimensions (L 530, 531, 532). H 12 1/2", TD 3 1/2", BD 6 1/2". Holy Trinity Lutheran Church, Lancaster, Pa.*

church and in the hand of minister Johann Caspar Stoever reveals that

> Anno 1733, 30 September, Johann Martin Weybrecht donated a pewter flagon with a cover and spout, and below three feet, on each of which an angel's head, holds nearly two quarts. There is a little lamb with a banner on the cross engraved thereupon with three initials I.C.S.
>
> Anno 1734 was purchased by Joh. Martin Weybrecht a pewter chalice holding about a pint. There is a lamb with a banner on the cross engraved thereupon together with three initials I.C.S.
>
> Item. A pewter baptismal flagon and bowl: these three pieces were paid for out of the offering money for 12 shillings for the churchly use of the congregation in Lancaster.
>
> Anno 1735, there was added thereto by Joh. Caspar Stöver, Pastor in Lancaster, a pewter host box as well as a little host plate, which Joh. Christian Schultz, former pastor, had left behind.[18]

The church does own a flagon with the initials *I.C.S.* A lamb with a banner and cross is engraved on its body. It is part of the communion set illustrated in Figure (61).

A closeup of the engraving on the

18. Trinity Lutheran Church Archives. TLC, 100 German and Trans 1729–1743 files. Information from Averil Christman, Archivist, Trinity Lutheran Church, Lancaster, Pa.

body of the Müller flagon is illustrated in Figure 62. The inscription is problematical because the initials of both pastors, Johann Christian Schultz and Johann Caspar Stoever, are I.C.S.

The church no longer has in its possession the similarly engraved pewter chalice that was given by Weybrecht in 1734. An engraved chalice of similar description decorated by the same hand and probably the previously described chalice is owned by the Swamp United Church of Christ at Reinholds, in northern Lancaster County, Pa. (Figure 63). Holy Trinity Lutheran Church of Lancaster provided ministerial and financial support to smaller Lutheran congregations in the surrounding area. It is possible that the chalice was given or loaned to a small group of Lutherans who joined the Swamp Reformed congregation and formed a union church in 1806. This union lasted until 1959, when the Lutherans built a new church nearby.[19] The chalice is now in the possession of the United Church of Christ congregation, where a Pennsylvania German church service is held each year.

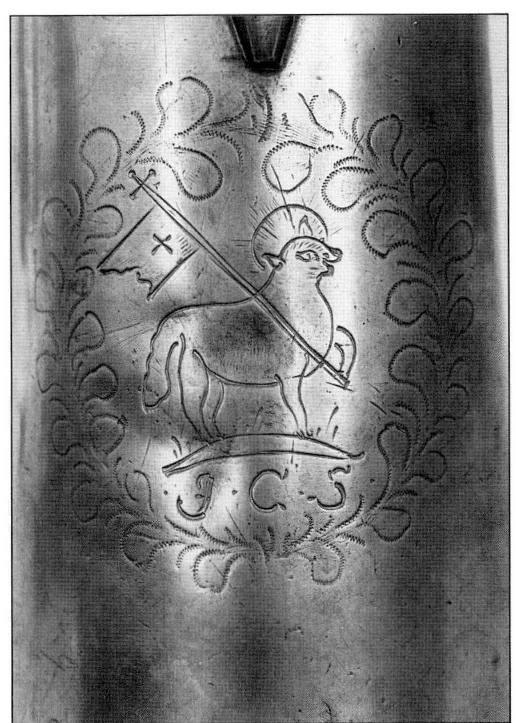

Fig. 62. *Detail of engraving on flagon by Heinrich Müller. Holy Trinity Lutheran Church, Lancaster, Pa.*

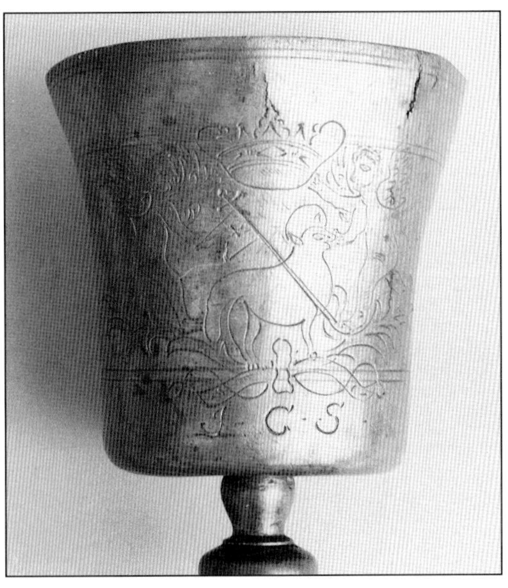

Fig. 63. *Detail of similar engraving on chalice probably Continental or British origin. Eighteenth century. Swamp United Church of Christ, Reinholds, Lancaster County, Pa.*

The other baptismal flagon, basin, host box, and plate of 1735 vintage are no longer in the archives of Holy Trinity Lutheran Church.

SUMMARY OF INITIALED AND DATED PEWTER

One hundred and two (17 percent) of the 606 pewter pieces in this survey were engraved with the initials of donors. Flagons and chalices were found initialed most frequently, suggesting the importance of these vessels in the eyes of the parishioners. Fifty percent of the initialed pewter were flagons and chalices. Twenty-nine flagons, twenty-one chalices, fifteen plates, eight tankards, eight basins, eight beakers, four mugs, three tablespoons, two measures, one ewer, one dish, one pitcher, and one footed paten were inscribed with initials.

The name of the church was found on twenty-two other pieces. Fourteen pieces bore the names or initials of both the donor and the church.

Sixty-six pewter pieces were dated in the survey. Again flagons and chalices were the forms most frequently dated (65 percent). Twenty-seven flagons, sixteen chalices, nine plates, five basins, four tankards, two beakers, one ewer, one mug, and one measure bore dates.

19. Glatfelter, *Pastors and People,* vol. 1, 319.

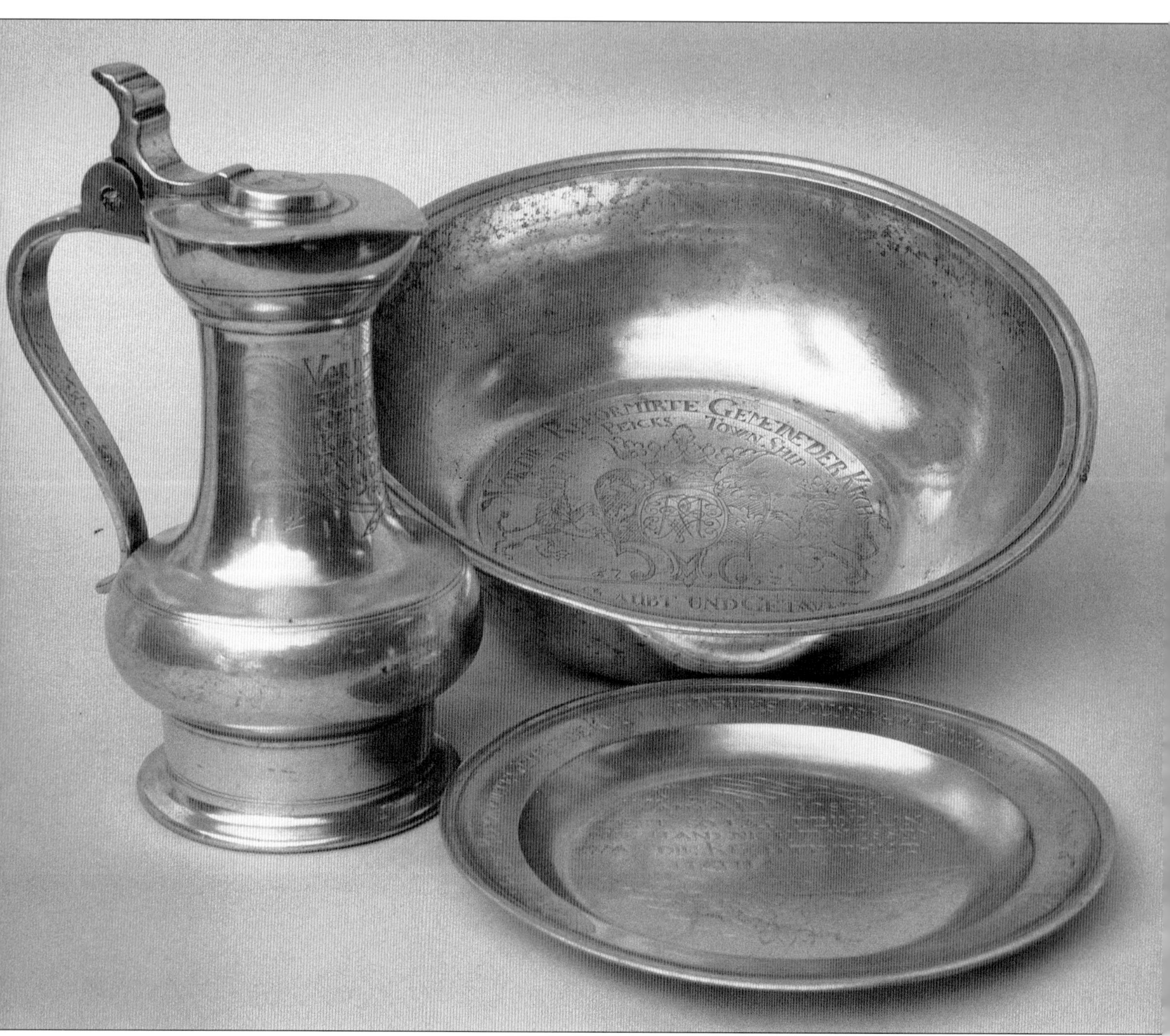

Fig. 64. *Flagon, Cologne, Germany, 1757. H 9 1/8″, TD 3 3/8″, BD 4 1/8″. Basin, John Townsend, London, 1748–1801 (C 4795), H 3 1/4″, TD 11 1/2″. Plate, Cornelius Bradford, New York 1752–1753, 1770–1785, Philadelphia 1753–1770 (L 496, 497), TD 8″. East Vincent United Church of Christ, Spring City, Chester County, Pa.*

CHAPTER 4

Decoration

Most ecclesiastical pewter was not decorated, but some was skillfully ornamented through a variety of techniques. Engraving, both line engraving and wrigglework, painting, hammering, cast decoration designs, and the application of feet and medallions were adornments that decorated and enhanced the simple forms of pewter.

LINE ENGRAVING

Line engraving was achieved with the use of a sharp cutting tool, often hand held, that cut a flowing continuous line.

The vigorously decorated flagon, basin, and plate in Figure 64 are decorated by line engraving. They are from Germany, England, and America, respectively, but appear to have been decorated by the same hand, probably in America. They are

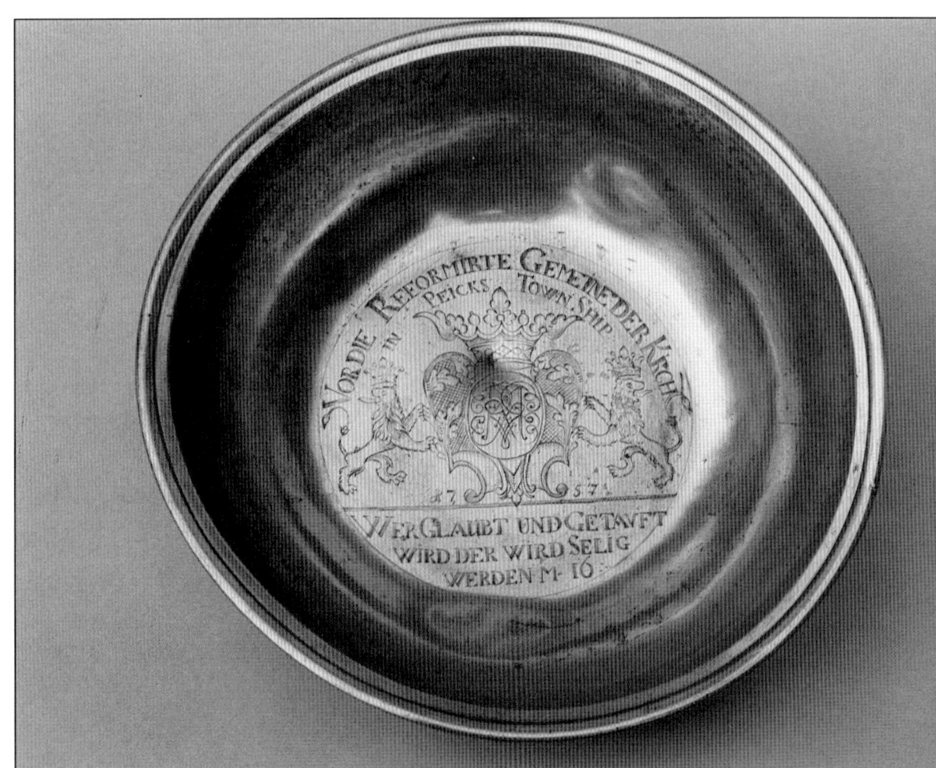

Fig. 66. *This elaborately engraved British basin (above) was made by John Townsend of London. It is similarly inscribed and includes* ***"WER GLAUBT UND GETAUFT / WIRD DER WIRD SELIG / WERDEN M 16"*** *[Whoever believes and is baptized will be saved (but whoever does not believe will be condemned) Matt. 16:16]. A pair of crowned, rampant lions flank a crowned shield in the engraving dated 1757. East Vincent United Church of Christ, Spring City, Chester County, Pa.*

engraved "For the Reformed Congregation Church in Pikes Township, Chester County In the Year of Our Lord 1757." They lack the name or initials of a donor.

The Cologne flagon is inscribed *"VOR DIE RE / FORMIRTE / GEMEINE DE / KIRCH IN PEI / TAUNSCHIP / ANNO 1757"* [For the Reformed congregation church in Pikes Township in the year

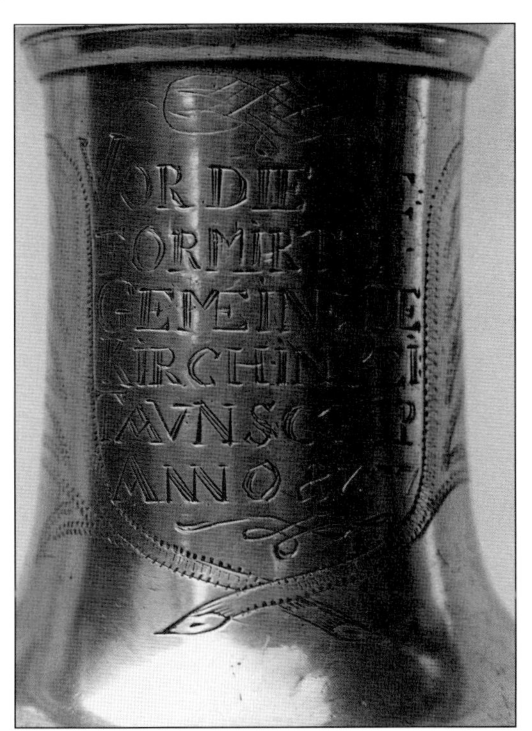

Fig. 65. *Engraving (left) on flagon dated 1757 from Cologne, Germany. East Vincent United Church of Christ, Spring City, Chester County, Pa.*

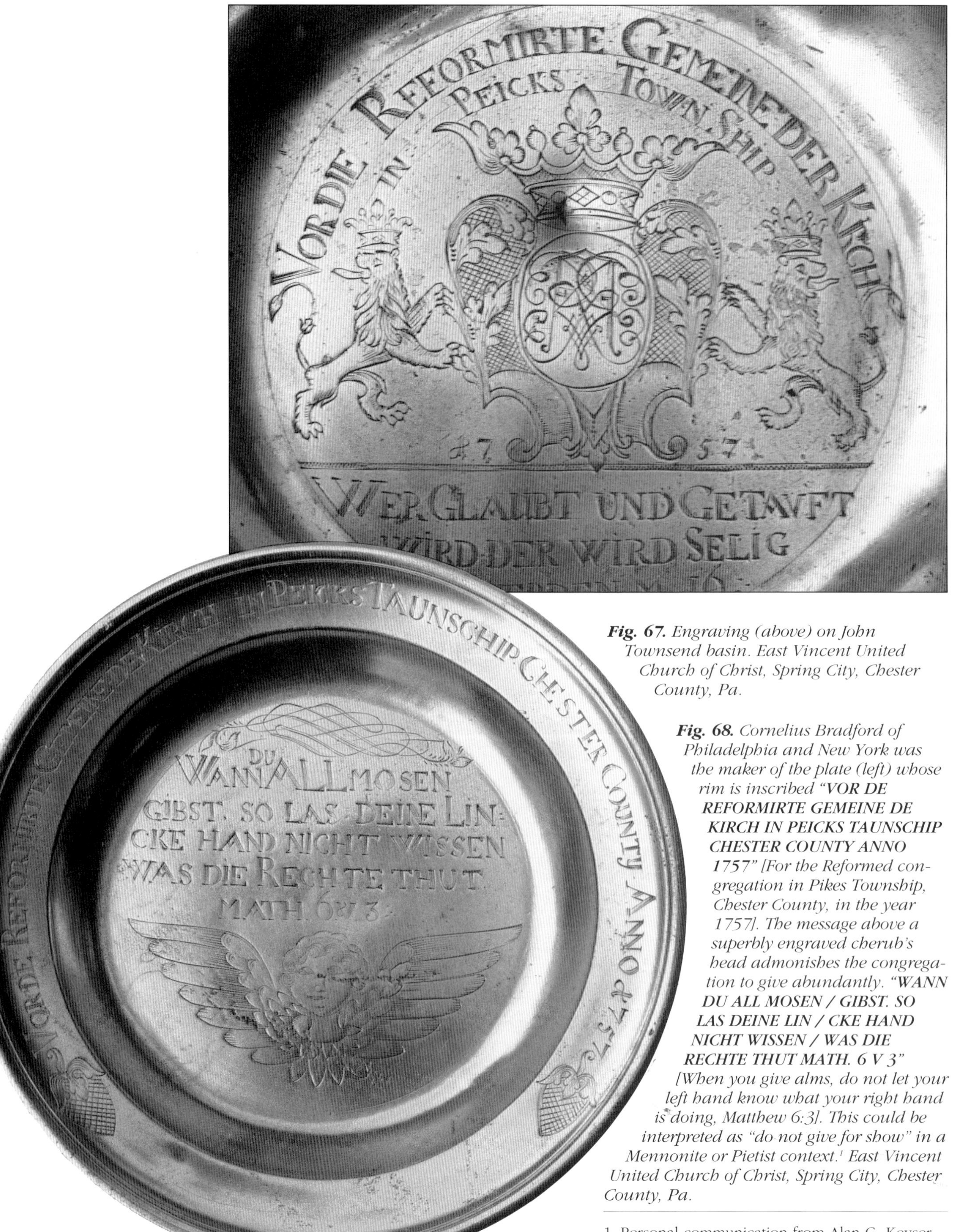

Fig. 67. *Engraving (above) on John Townsend basin. East Vincent United Church of Christ, Spring City, Chester County, Pa.*

Fig. 68. *Cornelius Bradford of Philadelphia and New York was the maker of the plate (left) whose rim is inscribed* ***"VOR DE REFORMIRTE GEMEINE DE KIRCH IN PEICKS TAUNSCHIP CHESTER COUNTY ANNO 1757"*** *[For the Reformed congregation in Pikes Township, Chester County, in the year 1757]. The message above a superbly engraved cherub's head admonishes the congregation to give abundantly.* ***"WANN DU ALL MOSEN / GIBST. SO LAS DEINE LIN / CKE HAND NICHT WISSEN / WAS DIE RECHTE THUT MATH. 6 V 3"*** *[When you give alms, do not let your left hand know what your right hand is doing, Matthew 6:3]. This could be interpreted as "do not give for show" in a Mennonite or Pietist context.*[1] *East Vincent United Church of Christ, Spring City, Chester County, Pa.*

1. Personal communication from Alan G. Keyser, July 10, 1994.

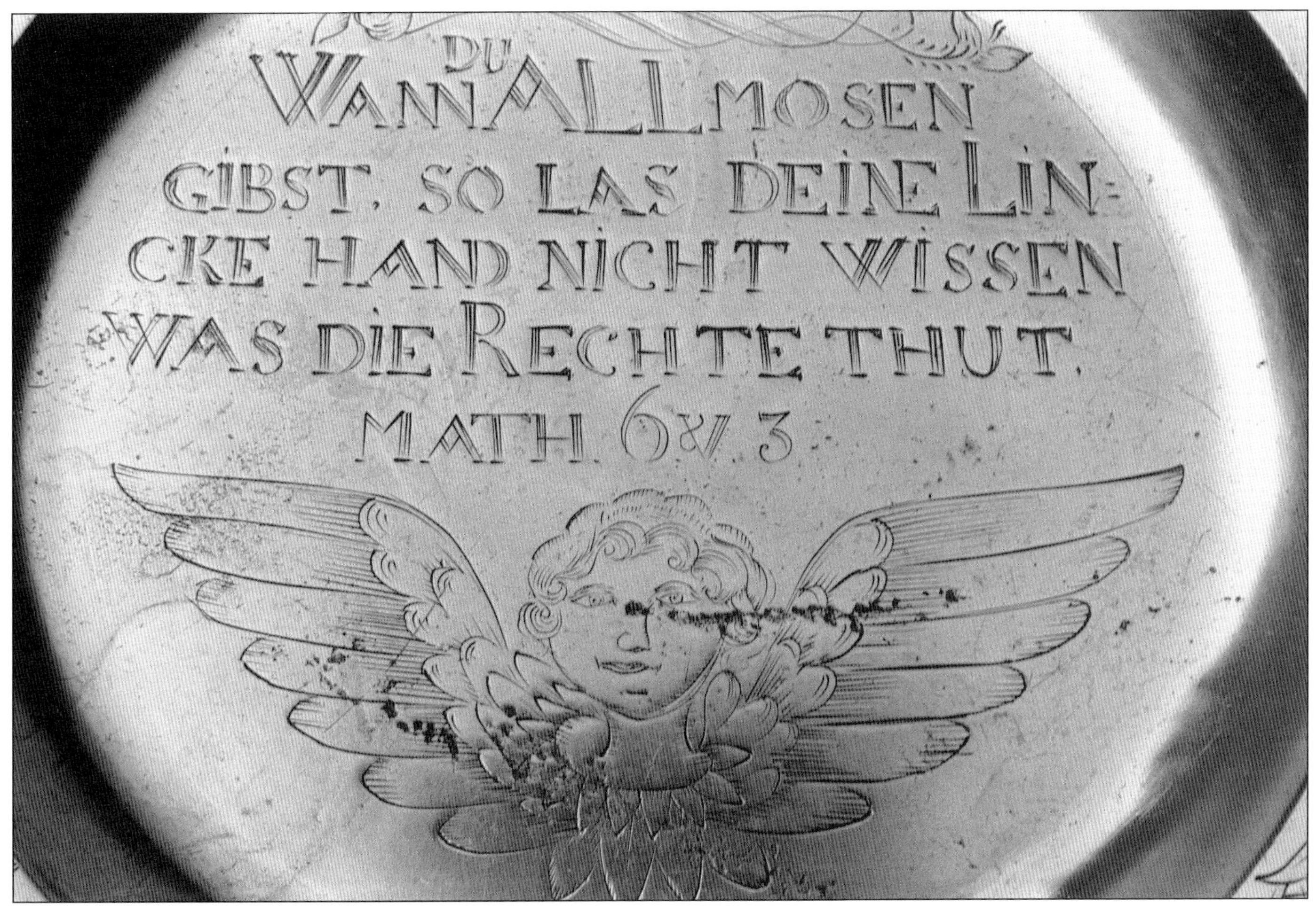

Fig. 69. *Engraving on Cornelius Bradford plate. East Vincent United Church of Christ, Spring City, Chester County, Pa.*

1757]. The initials *WS* engraved on the top of the lid may be that of its donor.

The Reformed congregation in East Vincent Township began as a union church with the Lutherans about 1750. The Reformed congregation moved a mile to the south and dedicated a new church on May 27, 1758.[2] The above pewter is dated 1757, suggesting that it was in existence when the congregation was in Pikes Township, now Pikeland Township, prior to their move, just across the line, to East Vincent township the following year. Pikeland Township is located less than one mile from the site on which the present church building is located.

The New Hanover Lutheran church in Montgomery County, Pennsylvania, has a flagon made by German pewterer Gabriel Syren of Frankfurt am Main. The straight-line decoration on the body of the *Abendmalskanne* [communion flagon], illustrated in Figures 70, 71, and 72, includes a peafowl, a female figure, and the words *ANA MARGEREDA KERAUSSEN / DEN 6 APRIL 1750.* A side view of this flagon is illustrated in the chapter on forms.

2. Charles H. Glatfelter, *Pastors and People: German Lutheran and Reformed Churches in the Pennsylvania Field, 1717–1793,* vol. 1, Pastors and Congregations (Breinigsville, Pa.: The Pennsylvania German Society, 1980), 281.

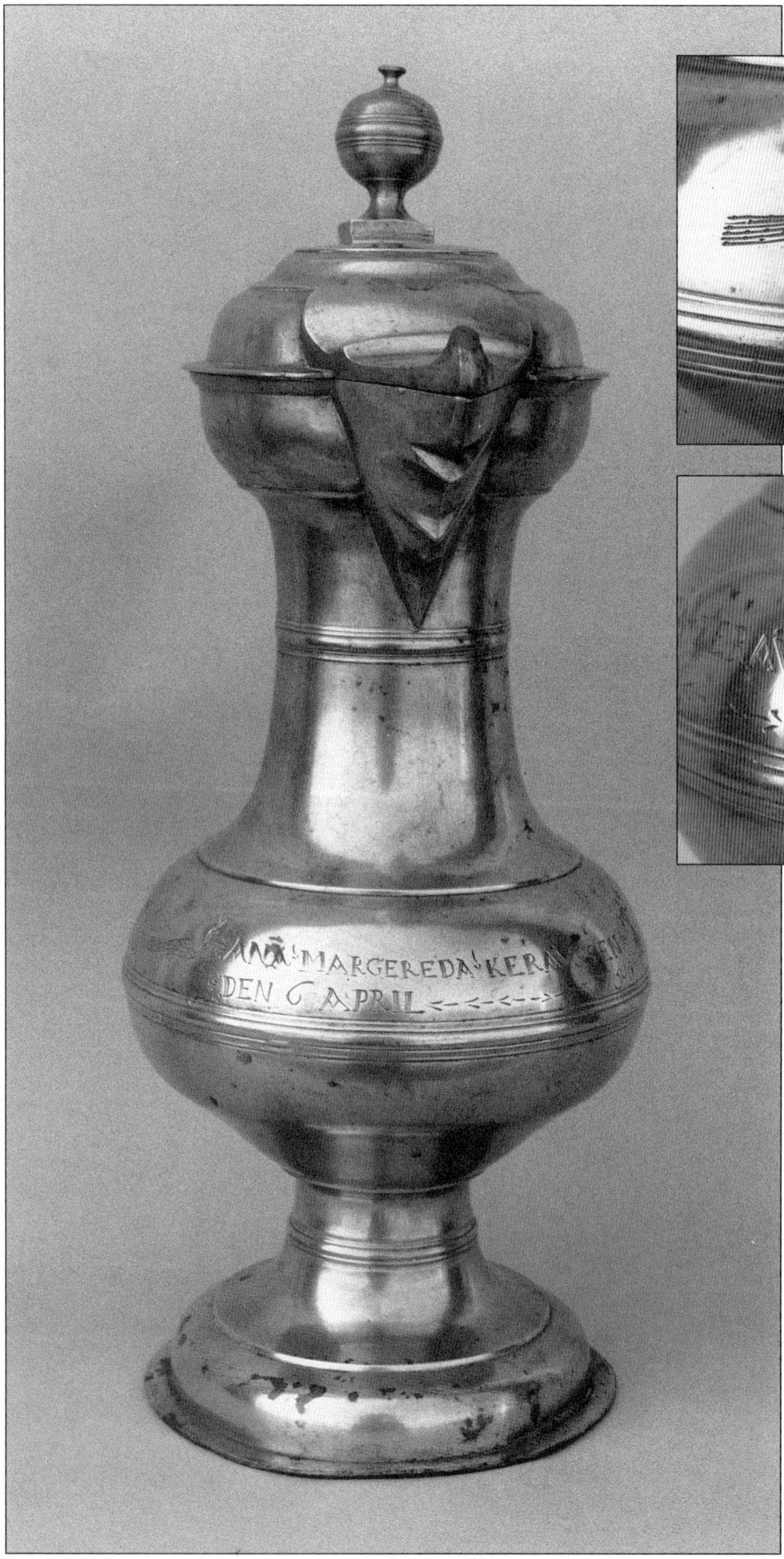

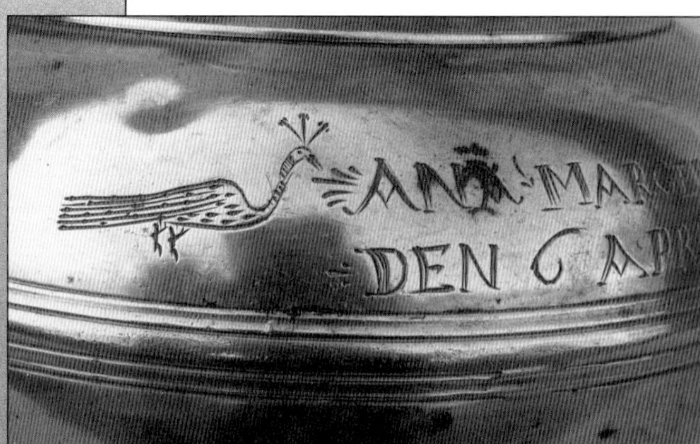

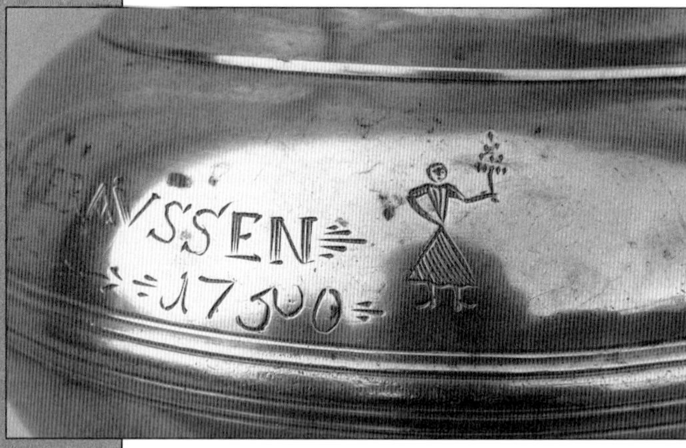

Fig. 70. *Straight-line decoration on the body of a flagon (left) made by Gabriel Syren of Frankfurt am Main, Germany, 1727–1753. H 15″, TD 4 5/8″, BD 5 3/4″. New Hanover Lutheran Church, Gilbertsville, Montgomery County, Pa.*

Fig. 71. *Detail (above top) of the body of the same flagon by Gabriel Syren, showing a straight-line decorated peafowl.*

Fig. 72. *Detail (above) of decoration of a human figure on the body of the same flagon by Gabriel Syren.*

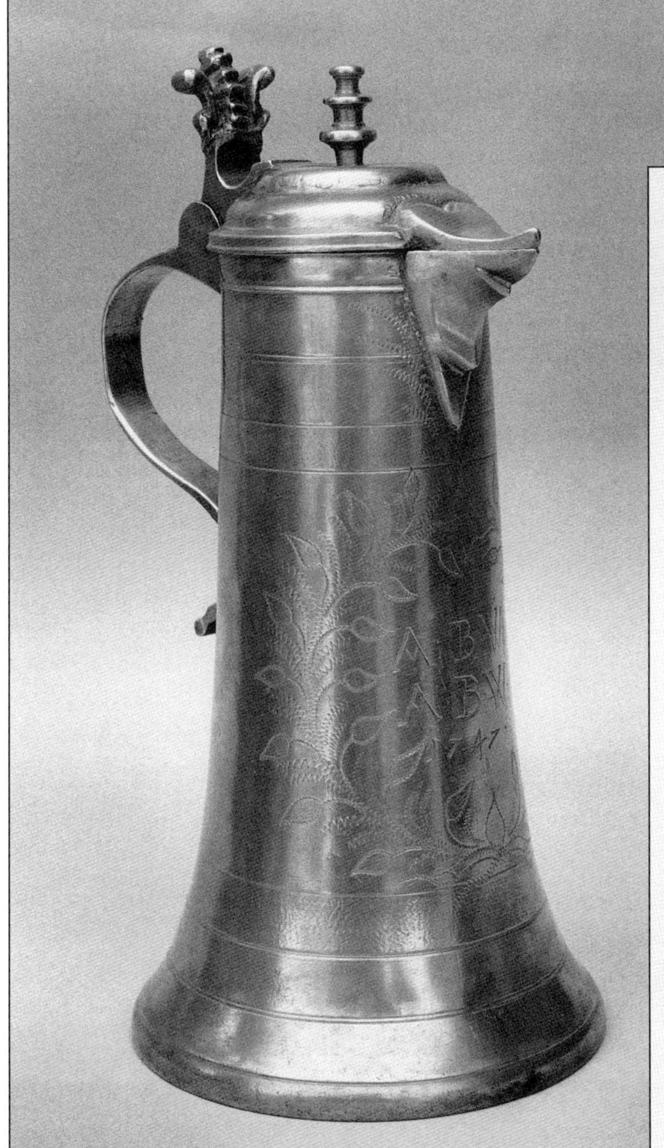

Fig. 73. *Flagon (left). Southern Germany, 1747. H 11 3/4", TD 3 1/4", BD 5 3/8". Trinity Lutheran Church, New Holland, Lancaster County, Pa.*

Fig. 74. *Detail (above) of engraving on flagon from southern Germany. Trinity Lutheran Church, New Holland, Lancaster County, Pa.*

WRIGGLEWORK ENGRAVING

Wrigglework, or *"Flecheltechnik"* as it is called in the German pewter vocabulary, is produced by rotating a sharp point back and forth to produce a zigzag line.[3] It was frequently used by Continental pewterers, less frequently by craftsmen in England and America.

The flagon in Figure 73 is decorated with both fine and coarse examples of wrigglework. Coarse wrigglework is found around the spout. The leaves are finer in size but done in the same rocking-movement technique. The band of decoration below the floral motif is done in a random manner, giving a rippling effect to the surface. The style of the decoration on this flagon is consistent with wrigglework found on pewter made in Germany and Switzerland.

3. Mechthild Wiswe, *Historische Zinngiesserei im südöstlichen Niedersachsen* (Braunschweig: Braunschweigisches Landesmuseum, 1981), 136.

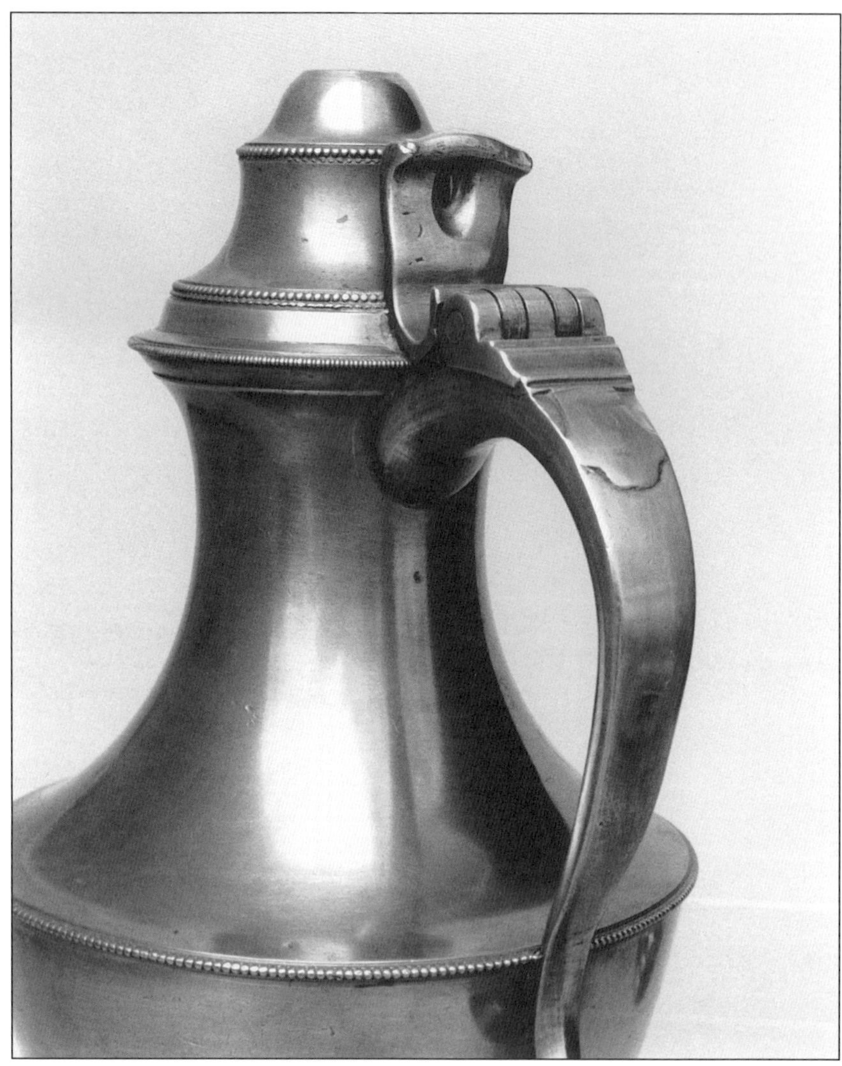

Fig. 75. *Four rows of beading on a flagon attributed to William Will, Philadelphia, 1764–1798. Salem United Church of Christ, Harrisburg, Dauphin County, Pa.*

BEADING

Beading was sometimes used as a decorative device. It was frequently used by Philadelphia pewterers in the Federal period. Two sizes of beading are found on the flagon attributed to William Will, illustrated in Figure 75.

CAST DECORATION

Continental dishes and plates were sometimes cast in molds having designs. The resulting piece is cast in relief as in Figure 76.

Another example of decoration that was part of the mold is the tankard handle thumbrest in Figure 77.

Fig. 76. *Cast relief decoration or gadrooning (below) on a dish made by Johann Dietrich Finck, Bamberg, Germany, ca. 1731. St. Michael's Lutheran Church, Philadelphia, Pa.*

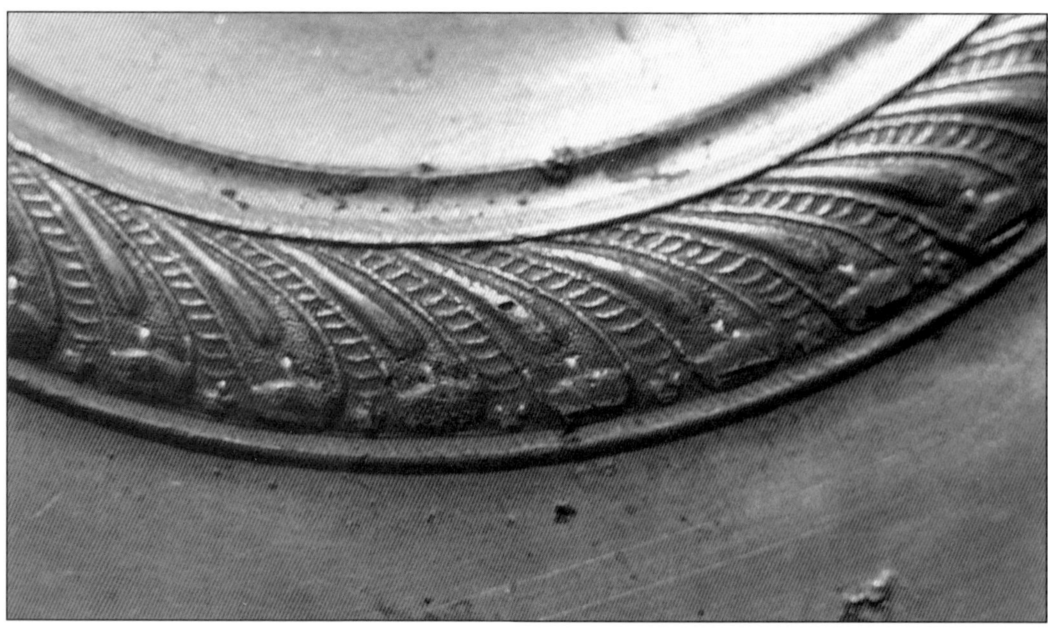

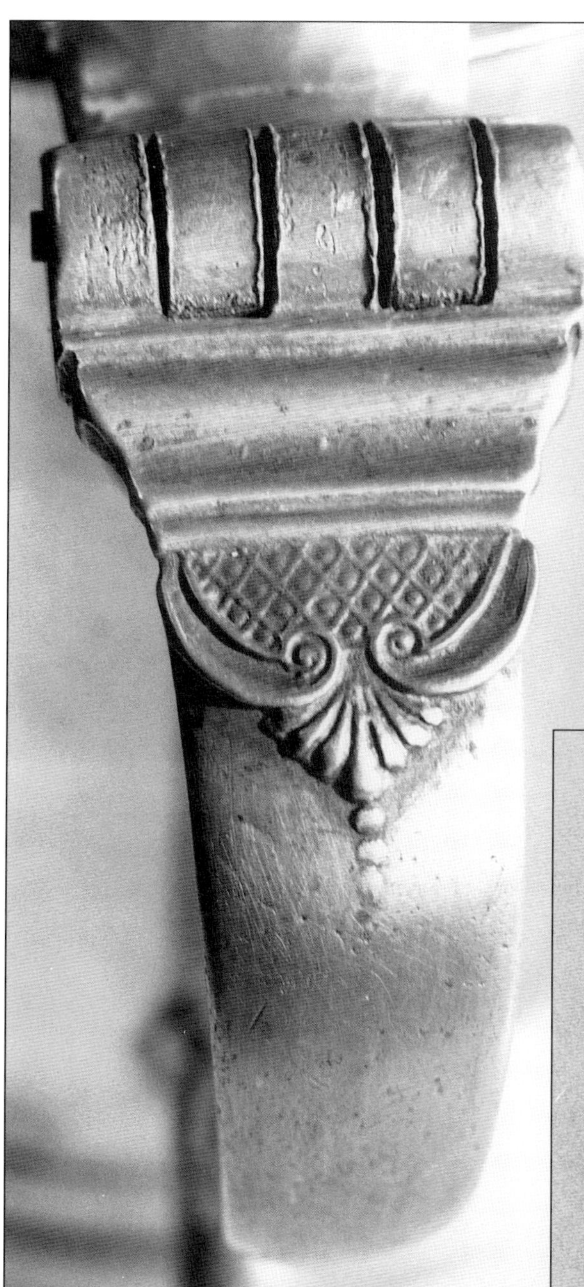

Fig. 77. *Cast relief decoration on a quart tankard handle made by Townsend and Compton, London, 1785–1810. Lutheran Church, Lebanon, Lebanon County, Pa.*

Fig. 78. *Detail (below) of unmarked tablespoon. Probably American, last quarter of the eighteenth century. L 7 3/4″. Pipe Creek Church of the Brethren, Linwood, Carroll County, Md.*

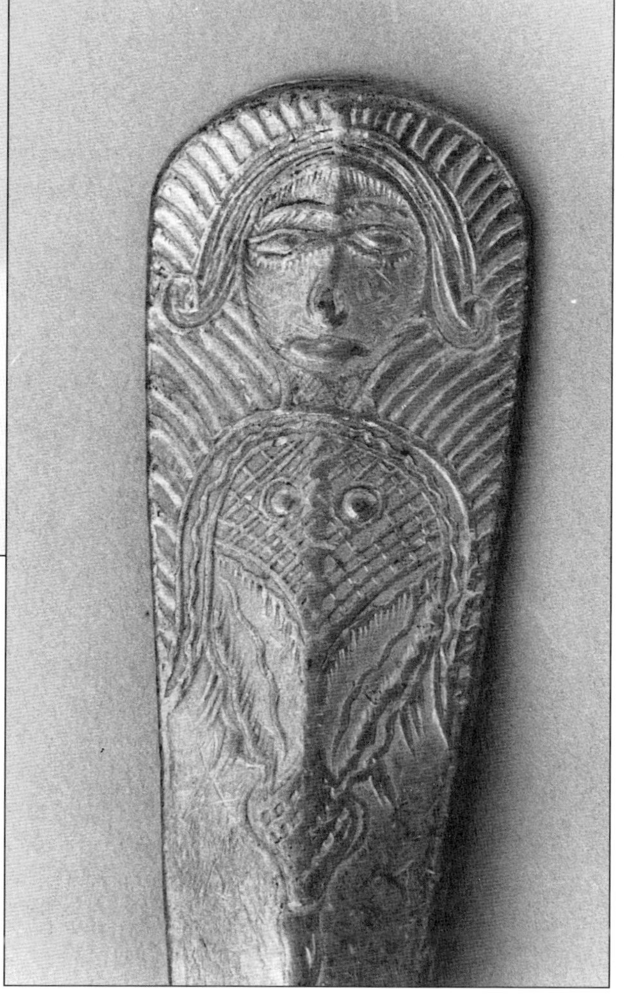

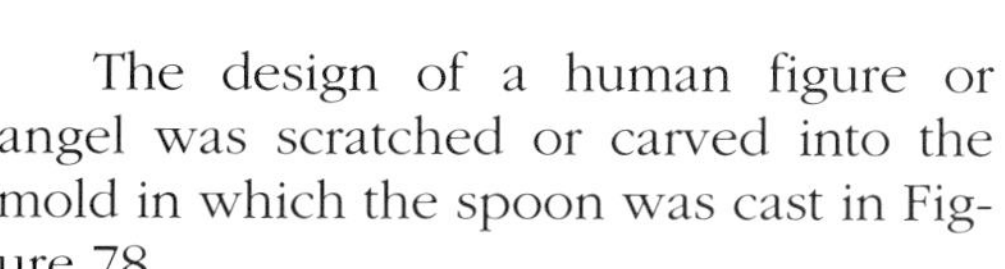

The design of a human figure or angel was scratched or carved into the mold in which the spoon was cast in Figure 78.

Ornate candlesticks were made for use in the church. They have sections that were cast in molds, and the products of the molds were soldered together to complete the candlestick form. Examples of cast-decorated candlesticks are found in the chapter on pewter forms.

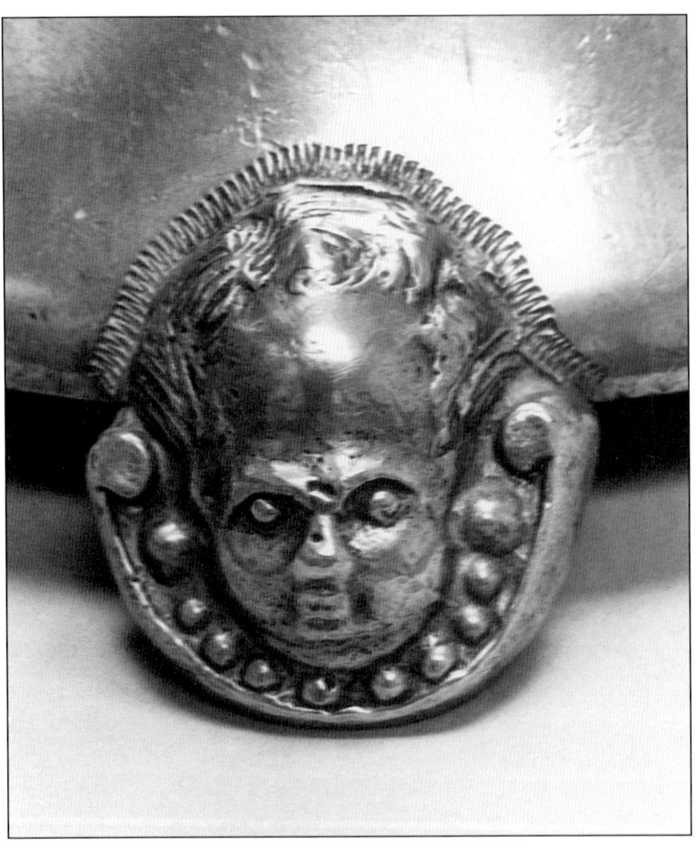

Fig. 79. Cherub's head feet applied to flagon made by Johann Christoph Heyne, Lancaster, Pa. 1752–1781. Brickerville United Lutheran Church, Brickerville, Lancaster County, Pa.

The German tradition of casting feet separately and applying them to the body of a flagon was continued in America by Johann Christoph Heyne. Note the wrigglework decoration above the applied cherub's head in Figure 79. Two Heyne flagons are visible in a nineteenth-century photograph of the interior of Emanuel Lutheran Church in Figure 80. Note the "wine glass" pulpit and sounding board behind the communion table.

The British tankard in fine condition in Figure 81 has a cast decorated portrait medallion applied to its body that says LONG • LIVE • PRINCE • AND • PRINCESS • OF • ORANGE. The medallion commemorates the Prince of Orange (William III) and his wife Mary Stuart, daughter of Charles I of England. William

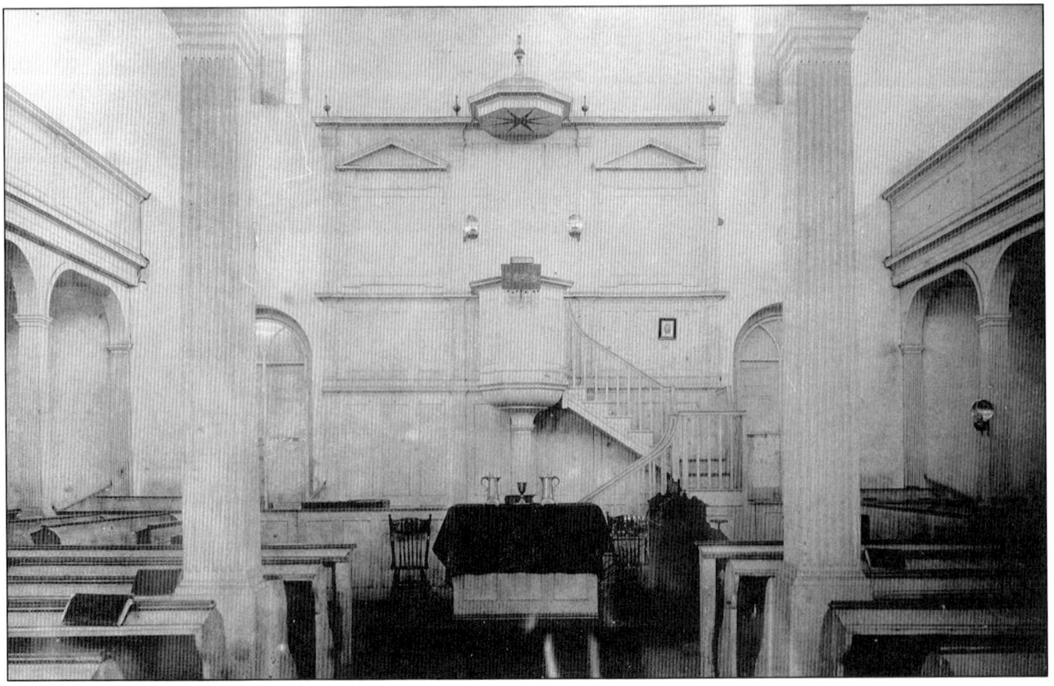

Fig. 80. *Nineteenth-century photograph of the interior of Emanuel Lutheran Church, now Brickerville United Lutheran Church, Brickerville, Lancaster County, Pa. Photograph courtesy of Kenneth L. Weaver.*

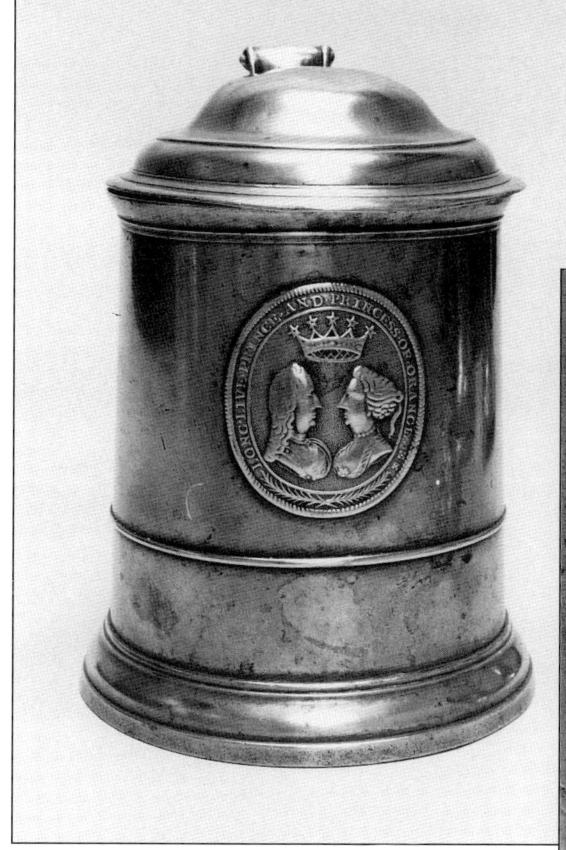

Fig. 81. *Tankard, quart (left). England ca. 1700. H 6 3/4", TD 4", BD 4 3/4". Brickerville United Lutheran Church, Brickerville, Lancaster County, Pa.*

Fig. 82. *Detail (below) of medallion on quart tankard.*

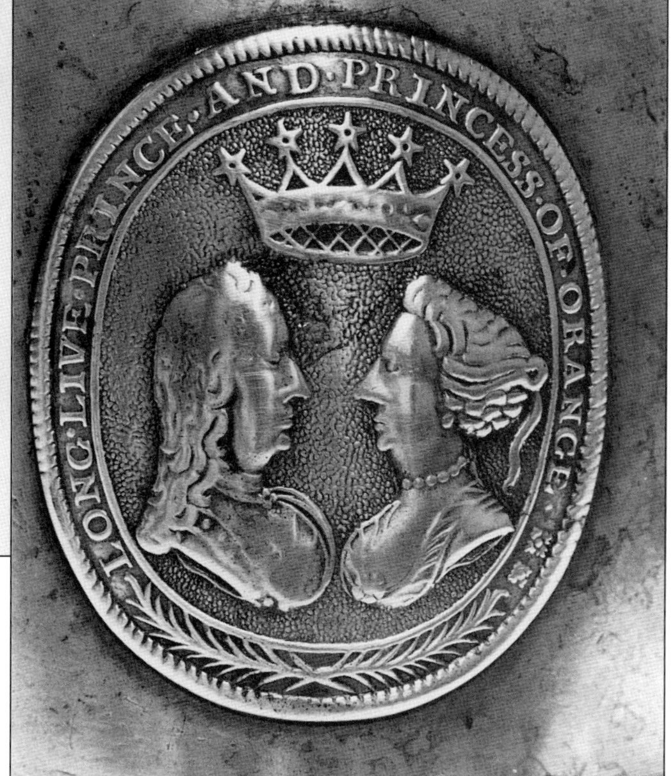

and Mary ruled England as joint sovereigns 1689–1702. A mug with similar applied decoration but in poor condition does exist. Medallions were occasionally applied to lids of tankards—but rarely onto bodies, as in this example.[4]

4 Peter R. G. Hornsby, *Pewter of the Western World, 1600–1850* (Exton, Pa.: Schiffer Publishing Ltd., 1983), 60, fig. 97. The author examined the mug in the Worshipful Company of Pewterers of London collection on April 6, 1993. A label affixed to the bottom of the mug said "Carpenter." The remnant of a mark on this tankard does not appear to be that of John Carpenter (C 810 or P 810).

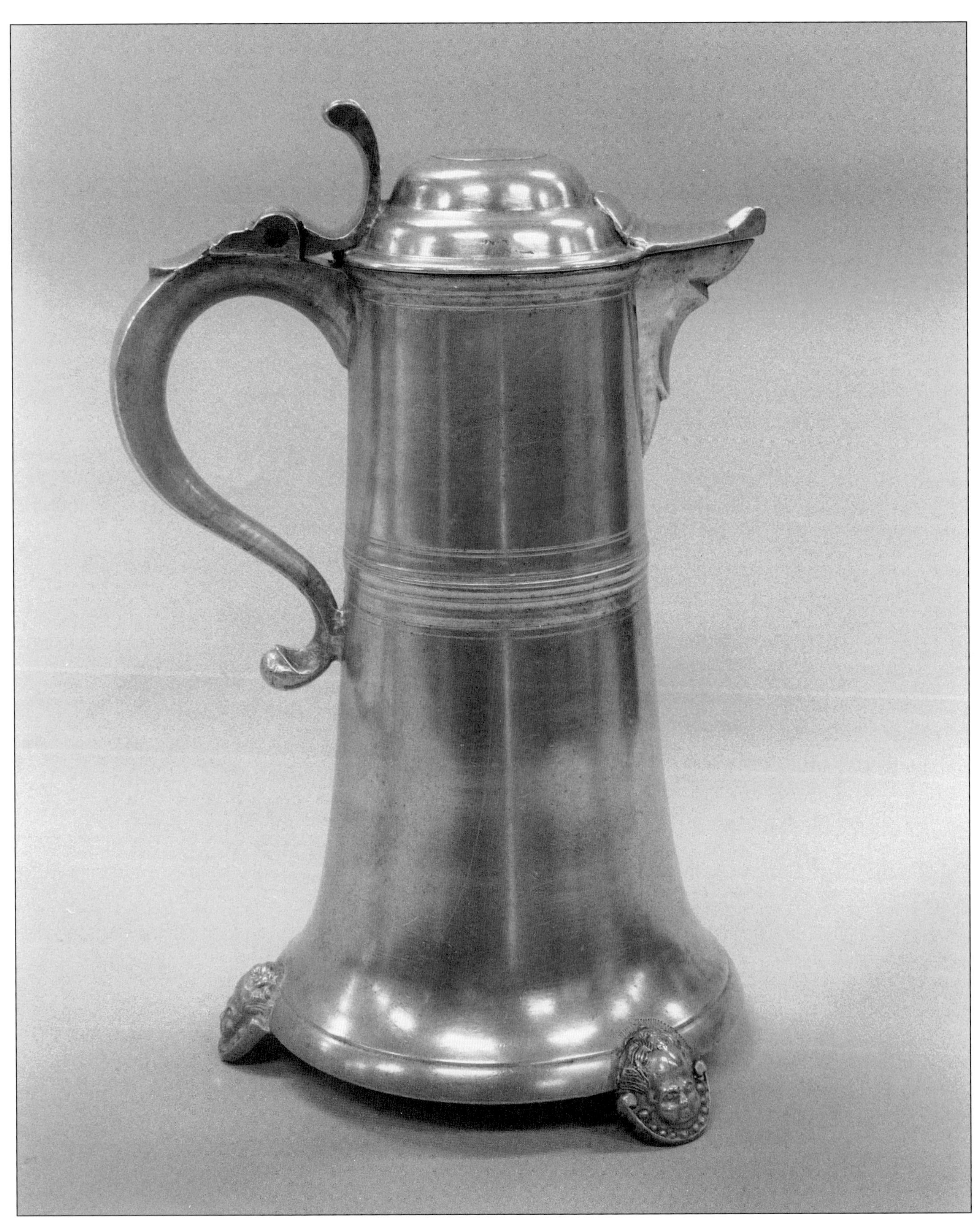

Flagon by Johann Christoph Heyne, Lancaster, Pa., 1752–1781, (L 530, 532). H 11 1/4″, TD 3 1/2″, BD 5 7/8″. Hill Lutheran Church, Cleona, Lebanon County, Pa.

CHAPTER 5

Pewter Forms

Basins

A basin is a bowl-shaped container with a narrow rim. Essentially a food container, it was widely used in the home as tableware. Basins were made in a variety of sizes and in great quantities. Ordinary food or washbasins for domestic use found frequent use in the church in connection with the sacrament of baptism. Footed basins were made for use in the church and occasionally are found in sets accompanied by flagons, chalices, and plates made by the same maker.

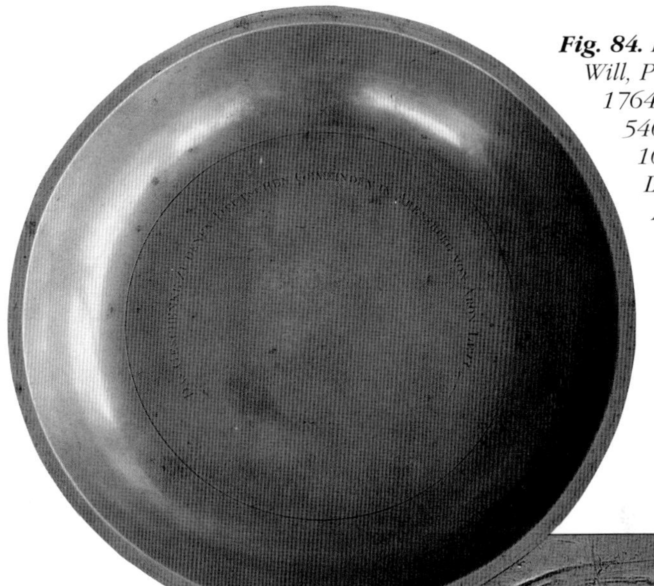

Fig. 84. *Basin by William Will, Philadelphia, 1764–1798 (L 537, 540). H 1 1/2", TD 10 5/8". Salem Lutheran Church, Aaronsburg, Centre County, Pa.*

AMERICA

The basin illustrated in Figure 83 has its booge, the curved part of the basin between the rim and the base, unhammered, as do most American basins. It was made by John Will of New York City, the father of pewterers Henry, Philip, and William Will. (See the chapter on makers for more information about pewterers.) The basin is marked on the inside bottom, a tradition that with American pewterers continued into the nineteenth century with few exceptions. British and Continental makers preferred to mark their wares on the outside bottom.

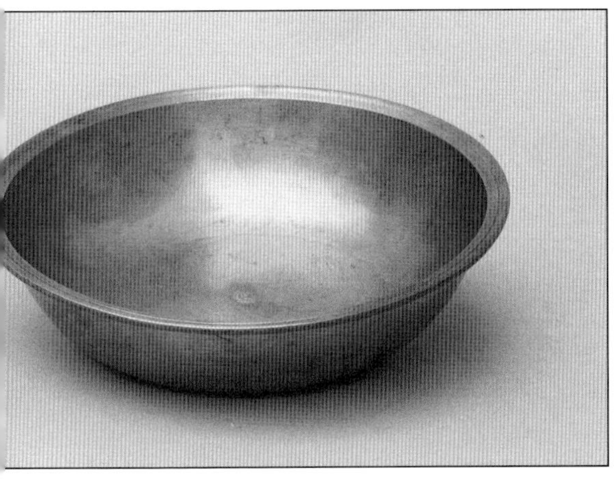

Fig. 83. *Basin by John Will, New York, 1752–1774, (L 481). H 2", TD 7 7/8". Zion's (Stone) United Church of Christ, Northampton, Northampton County, Pa.*

William Will's low and attractive baptismal basin (Figure 84) is enhanced by the addition of a row of beading on its rim, an adornment popular in the Federal period. The basin bears his Philadelphia and Federal eagle marks (Figure 85).

Fig. 85. *Marks on basin by William Will illustrated in Figure 84. Salem Lutheran Church, Aaronsburg, Centre County, Pa.*

Footed basins or baptismal bowls of the form shown in Figure 86 have been

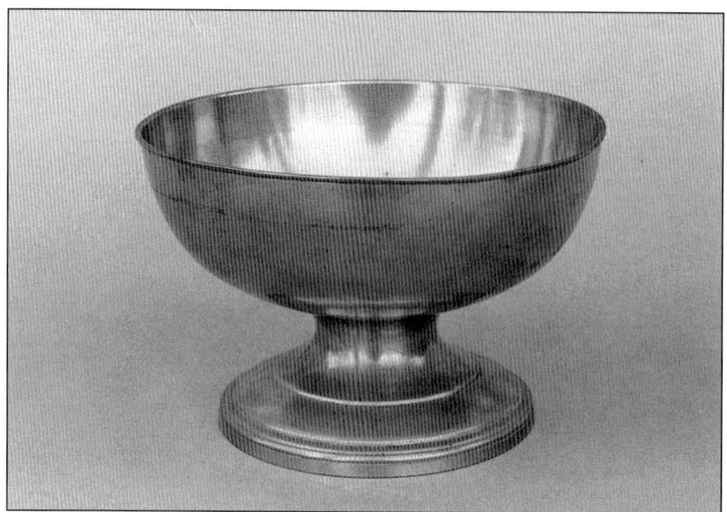

Fig. 86. *Footed basin (top left) attributed to Parks Boyd, Philadelphia, 1795–1819. H 4 7/8″, TD 7 5/8″, BD 5 1/4″. Christ United Church of Christ, New Ringgold, Schuylkill County, Pa.*

Fig. 87. *Footed basin (center left) marked Boardman Warranted made by Boardman & Company, Hartford, Conn., 1825–1827 (L 434). H 4 1/2″, TD 8″. Central Moravian Church, Bethlehem, Northampton County, Pa.*

Fig. 88. *Boardman Warranted mark (lower left) on footed baptismal basin illustrated in Figure 87.*

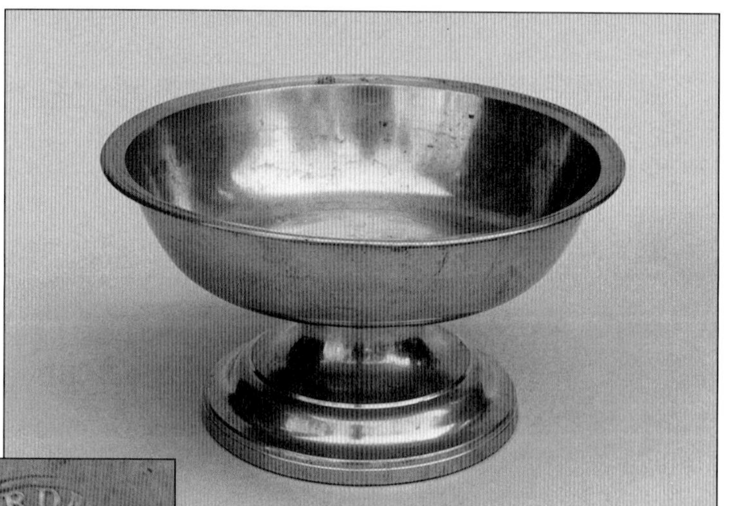

attributed to Philadelphia pewterer Parks Boyd. The design, especially of the foot, is closely related to elements of marked Boyd pieces.

The addition of a foot to a common quart basin elevates the piece into an attractive ecclesiastical form (Figures 87 and 88).

Another form of baptismal basin made by the Boardmans (Figure 89) is stylistically later than the previous example and is typical of American baptismal basins made in the second and third quarters of the nineteenth century.

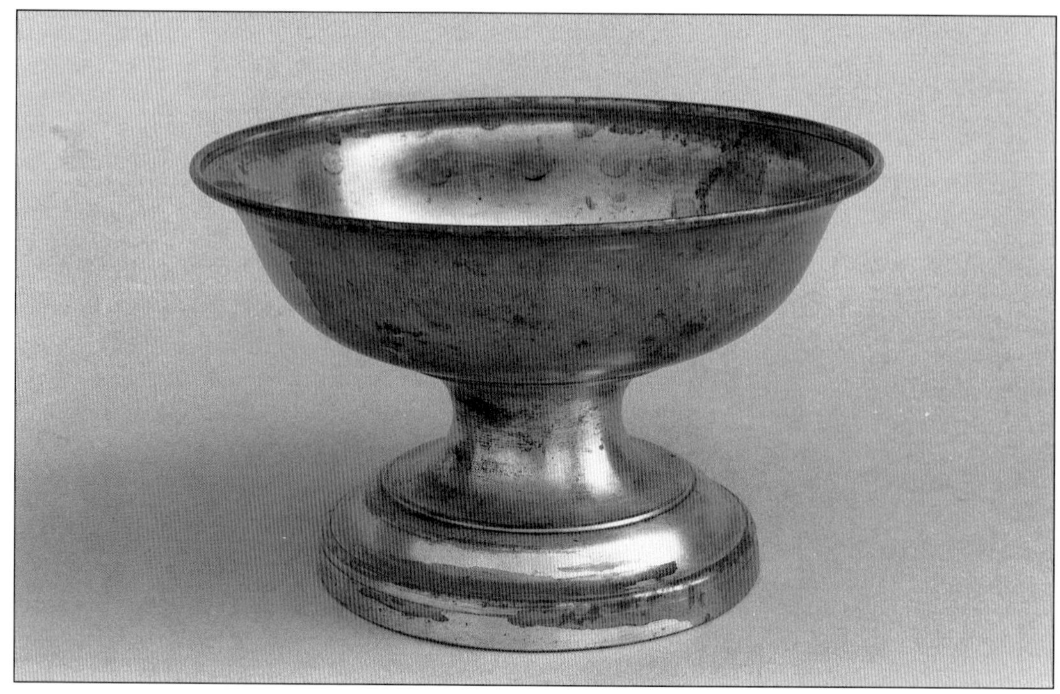

Fig. 89. *Footed basin attributed to the Boardmans, Hartford, Conn., 1804–1873. H 5″, TD 7 3/4″, BD 5 1/8″. Epler's United Church of Christ, Leesport, Berks County, Pa.*

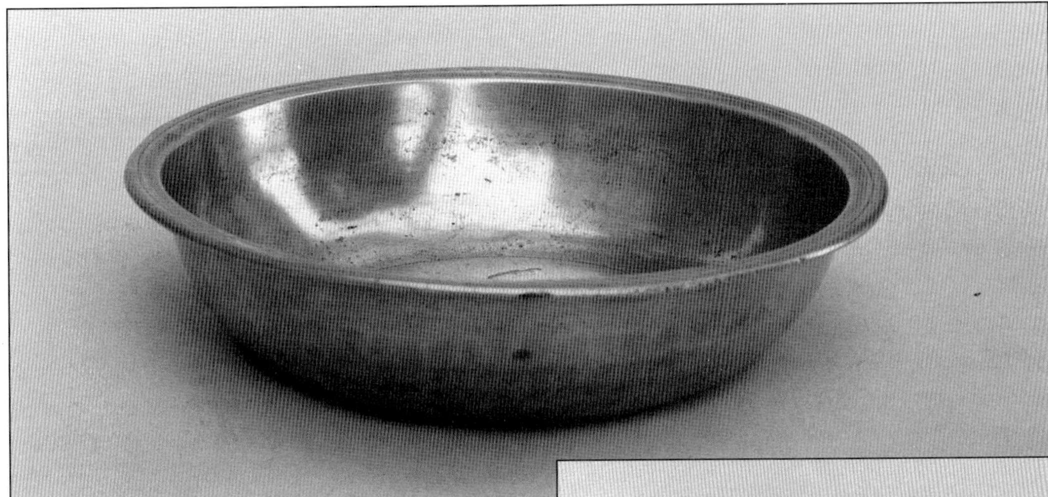

Fig. 90. *Basin (left) by Stynt Duncumb, Wribbenhall, England, 1730–1767, (C 1466). H 2″, TD 8″. Trinity United Church of Christ, Berlin, Somerset County, Pa.*

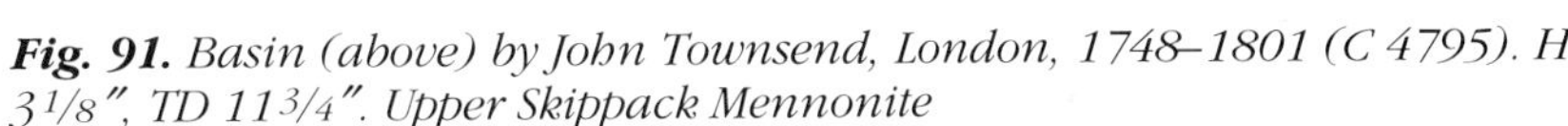

Fig. 91. *Basin (above) by John Townsend, London, 1748–1801 (C 4795). H 3 1/8″, TD 11 3/4″. Upper Skippack Mennonite Church, Skippack, Montgomery County, Pa.*

BRITISH ISLES

The basin made by Stynt Duncumb has its curved surface, or booge, hammered, a practice found in most British pewter of this form (Figure 90).

It is not surprising that flatware (basins, plates, and dishes) by John Townsend and his partnerships with Thomas Giffin and Robert Reynolds and the firm of his daughter Mary and son-in-law Thomas Compton and their son Townsend Compton, are found more frequently in southeastern Pennsylvania than the work of any other British family of pewterers. John Townsend had close ties to Philadelphia Quaker merchants and shipped tremendous quantities of pewter to that city. (For more information about John Townsend, see the chapter on makers.)

CONTINENTAL EUROPE

Germany

A wide brim, unhammered booge, rimmed or footed base, and heavy weight are characteristics of basins from the Continent (Figure 92). *Block Zinn,* or second-grade pewter, had a higher lead content than *fein Zinn*, or fine pewter. *Block Zinn* tended to corrode more readily because of its lead content. Pewterers from Frankfurt and other cities produced great quantities of *Block Zinn* and distributed it widely on the Continent. The basin in Figure 92 was heavily pitted prior to being restored. It was made by Philipp Jacob Schott of Frankfurt am Mein.[1]

Basins made by pewterers from other Continental European countries were not found in the survey.

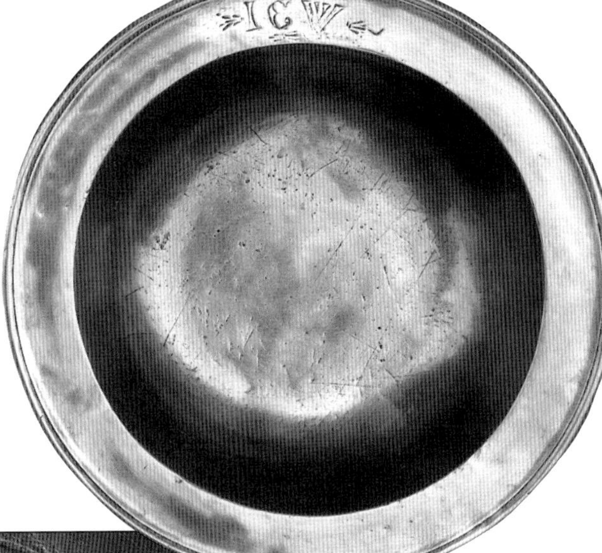

Fig. 92. *Basin (right) by Philipp Jacob Schott, Frankfurt, Germany, 1726–1765. H 1 7/8″, TD 8″. Allegheny Union Church with Lutheran and United Church of Christ congregations, Mohnton, Alleghenyville, Berks County, Pa.*

Fig. 93. *Mark (below) of Philipp Jacob Schott.*

1. Karl Schöppl of Aachen, Germany, identified the maker and commented on the poor quality of block pewter that was mass-produced by Frankfurt pewterers in his letter to the author dated December 17, 1991.

Fig. 94. *Beaker by Simon Edgell, Philadelphia, 1713–1742 (L 526). H 4 3/8″, TD 3 1/2″, BD 3 1/4″. Formerly in the Bowmansville Mennonite Church, Bowmansville, Lancaster County, Pa. Now in a private collection.*

Beakers

A beaker is a flared cylindrical drinking vessel having a body that tapers out toward the top. Handles are found on some beakers. Beakers or cups were used in both home and church. Tall beakers were used in pairs in communion sets of the Church of the Brethren and unpaired, usually, in Mennonite congregations.

The custom of Holy Communion in the Church of the Brethren was to supply one cup for the men and one cup for the women: for that reason, pairs of cups or beakers are found in churches of that denomination.

AMERICA

Fewer than fourteen pewter pieces marked by Simon Edgell (Figure 94) have survived.[2] This is the earliest marked American beaker known to the author. Edgell was working in Philadelphia in 1713, seven years before John Bassett's earliest productions in New York City, and he died nearly two decades before John Bassett. A similar but unmarked example is owned by the Deep Run Mennonite Church East, Perkasie, Bucks County, Pennsylvania.[3]

The outward flare of the body of beakers made by Johann Christoph Heyne reveals the Germanic heritage of the maker (Figure 95). Heyne would have been familiar with this form, for it was used by pewterers on the Continent. Pewterers working in the English tradition often preferred the nearly parallel body form illustrated in the previous example by Edgell. The Heyne beaker is one of a pair. An unmarked pair of beakers with the same dimensions and incised line decoration is owned by the Hanoverdale Church of the Brethren, Dauphin County, Pennsylvania. Similar beakers are owned by the Chiques Church of the Brethren and Middle Creek Church of the Brethren in Lancaster County. Both churches were founded in the nineteenth century which suggests that the beaker mold continued to be used after Heyne's death.

The tall, handsome beaker illustrated in Figure 96 is the only marked beaker by William Will known to the author.[4] Except for the absence of a flared lip, it is similar in form and dimensions to the John Will beakers in the Brooklyn Museum and Currier Gallery of Art. William may have

2. Donald M. Herr, "A Simon Edgell Beaker," *Pewter Collectors' Club of America Bulletin*, no. 76 (March 1978): 274.

3. The beaker is on loan to the Mennonite Historians of Eastern Pennsylvania, Harleysville, Pa.

4. Donald M. Herr, "Marked American Beakers," *Pewter Collectors' Club of America Bulletin*, no. 84 (March 1982): 200.

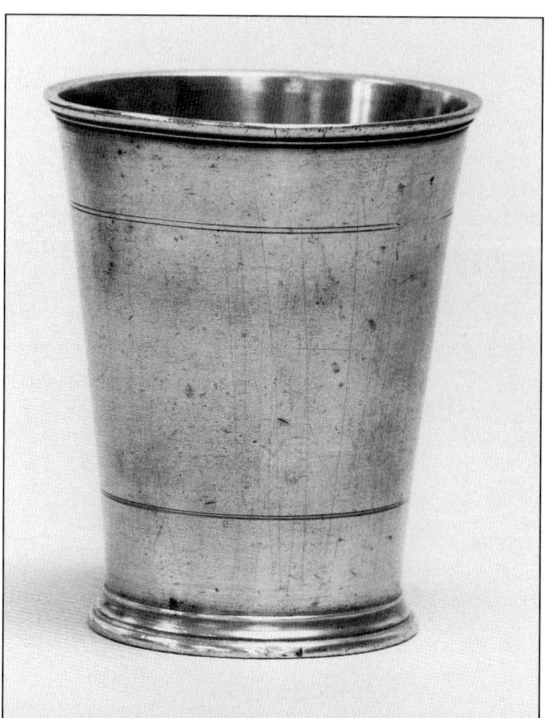

Fig. 95. *Beaker by Johann Christoph Heyne, Lancaster, Pa. 1752–1781 (L 530). H 4 1/8″, TD 3 3/8″, BD 2 5/8″. One of a pair. Two pairs of incised lines decorate the body. Codorus Church of the Brethren, Loganville, York County, Pa.*

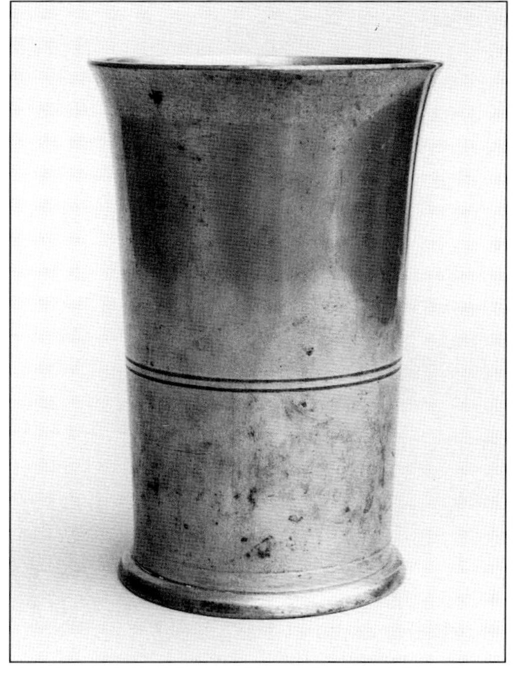

Fig. 97. *Beaker attributed to the Boardmans, Hartford, Conn., 1804–1873. H 5 1/8″, TD 3 1/2″, BD 2 7/8″. One of a pair. Black Rock Church of the Brethren, Brodbecks, York County, Pa.*

obtained the mold from his father, for the beaker appears to be a shortened version of the John Will beaker form.[5] Beakers in the five-inch range were a popular style by American makers in the second half of the eighteenth century.

The piece attributed to the Boardmans and illustrated in Figure 97 is an example of a tall beaker in the 5-inch range that was made by the Boardmans and others during the first half of the nineteenth century. Form and dimensions are similar to marked examples by the Boardmans.[6] Another pair of beakers, similar in form but unmarked, is owned by the Epler's United Church of Christ, Leesport, Berks County, Pennsylvania.

The large, capacious Palethorp beaker (Figure 98) with nearly straight sides is in the style of those produced in the eighteenth century. Larger than most Palethorp beakers, it was probably made in the early years, when Robert Palethorp, Jr., was working alone. It is a new form for this maker. Most other Palethorp beakers are much smaller and have a curve or flare to their rims characteristic of those made in the nineteenth century.

Fig. 98. *Beaker (below) by Robert Palethorp, Jr., Philadelphia, Pa. 1817–1820 (L 560). H 4″, TD 3 1/2″, BD 3 1/2″. Blooming Glen Mennonite Church, Blooming Glen, Bucks County, Pa.*

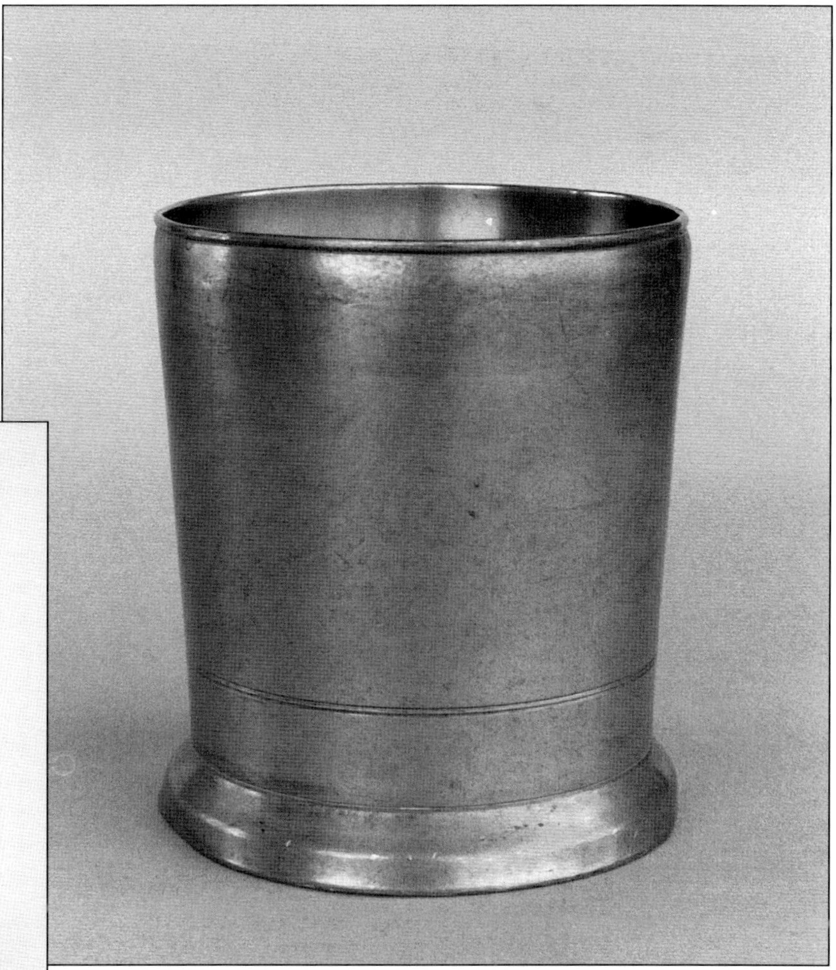

---

5. Donald M. Herr, "A Beaker by William Will," *Pewter Collectors' Club of America Bulletin,* no. 81 (September 1980): 66. The beaker is on loan to the Mennonite Historians of Eastern Pennsylvania, Harleysville, Pa.

6. Charles F. Montgomery, *A History of American Pewter: A Winterthur Book* (New York: Praeger, 1973), 70.

Fig. 96. *Beaker (below) by William Will, Philadelphia, 1764–1798 (L 539). H 5 1/2″, TD 3 5/8″, BD 3 1/4″. Line Lexington Mennonite Church, Line Lexington, Bucks County, Pa.*

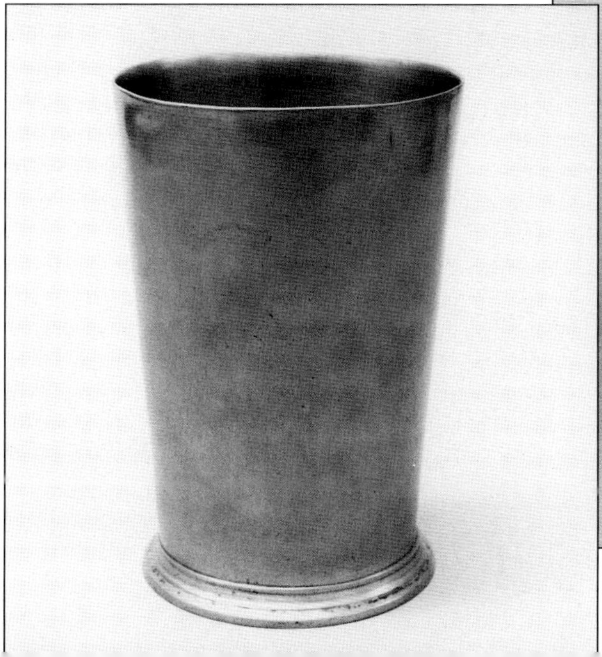

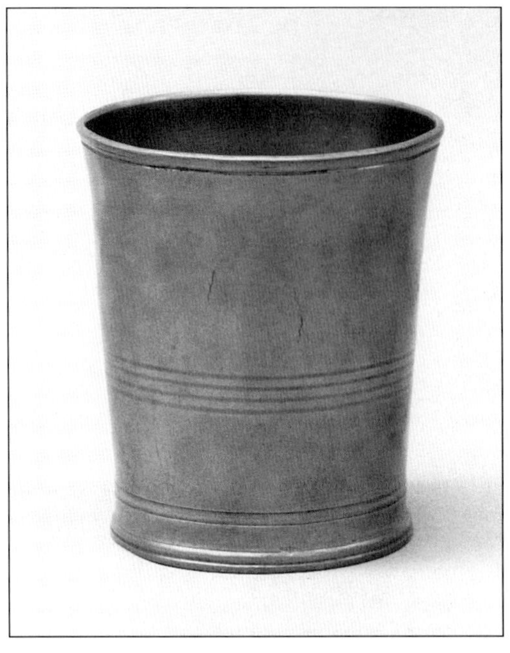

Fig. 99. *Beaker by the Palethorps, Philadelphia, Pa. 1817–1840 (L 2:108). H 4", TD 3 1/2", BD 2 7/8". Salford Mennonite Church, Harleysville, Montgomery County, Pa.*

The commodious Palethorp beaker in Figure 99 has a different foot treatment and gives the appearance of having more flare to its body than the beaker in the previous illustration. It is a previously unrecorded size of this form by the Palethorps. Most Palethorp beakers are smaller in scale and 3 inches in height. A similar beaker is owned by the Plains Mennonite Church, Hatfield, Montgomery County, Pennsylvania.

Many small beakers were made by the Boardman family. Variations in the turning of the foot and body are found on Boardman beakers having similar measurements. Beakers were sold with and without handles. The Boardman beaker illustrated in Figure 100 is marked on the inside bottom with "Hall Boardman & Co." and "Best Britannia Metal." Neither of the marks has been illustrated in most reference books, although the "Hall Boardman & Co." mark has been illustrated in Charles F. Montgomery, *A History of American Pewter*.[7] The majority of Boardman hollowware pieces are marked on the outside bottom.

BRITISH ISLES

The beaker in Figure 102 and another by the same maker in the New Danville Mennonite Church, New Danville, Lancaster County, Pennsylvania, were the only tall British beakers found in the survey. Both are quite early and are not commonly found in their country of origin.

7. Ibid., 222.

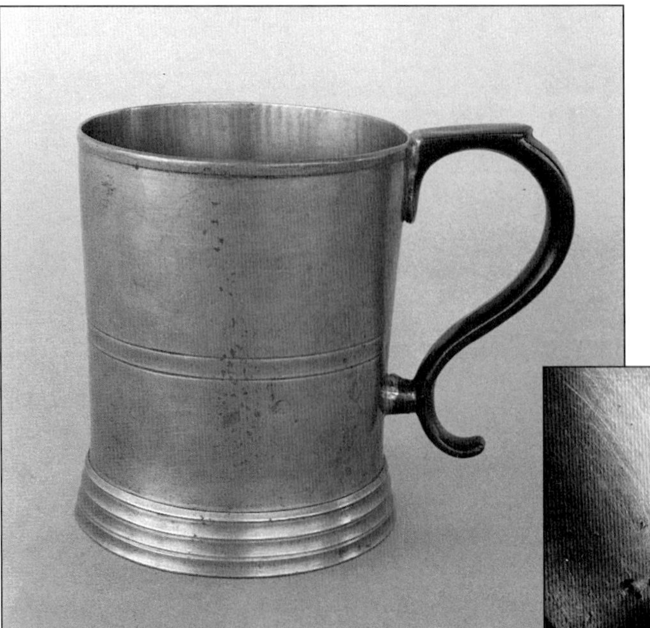

Fig. 100. *Beaker by Hall, Boardman and Company, Hartford, Conn. and Philadelphia, 1842–1857. H 4 1/4", TD 3 3/8", BD 3 1/2". Swamp Mennonite Church, Quakertown, Bucks County, Pa.*

Fig. 101. *"Hall, Boardman & Co." and "Best Britannia Metal" marks on the same beaker.*

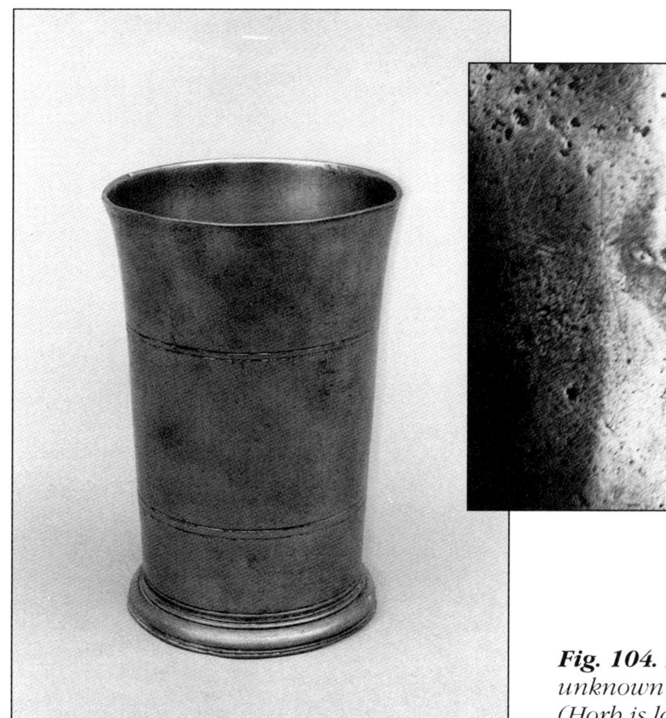

Fig. 102. Beaker (far left) by Robert Iles, London, 1695–1735 (C 2522). H 5 1/4", TD 3 3/8", BD 3 1/8". Lower Skippack Mennonite Church, Skippack, Montgomery County, Pa.

Fig. 103. Mark (near left) of Robert Iles on inside bottom of beaker. The "9" and "5" are visible on either side of the stem of the flower. Iles had leave to strike his mark in 1695 and incorporated the date in his mark.

The initials "H R V" on the outside bottom of the beaker in Fig. 102 are probably those of the donor.

CONTINENTAL EUROPE

Germany

The tall beaker in Figure 104 has a raised rose mark on the inside bottom characteristic of hollowware made in southern Germany and Switzerland.[8]

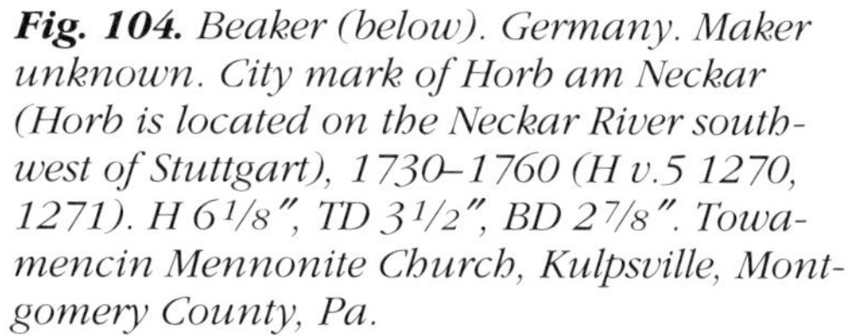

Fig. 104. Beaker (below). Germany. Maker unknown. City mark of Horb am Neckar (Horb is located on the Neckar River southwest of Stuttgart), 1730–1760 (H v.5 1270, 1271). H 6 1/8", TD 3 1/2", BD 2 7/8". Towamencin Mennonite Church, Kulpsville, Montgomery County, Pa.

Fig. 105. City mark (below left) of Horb am Neckar.

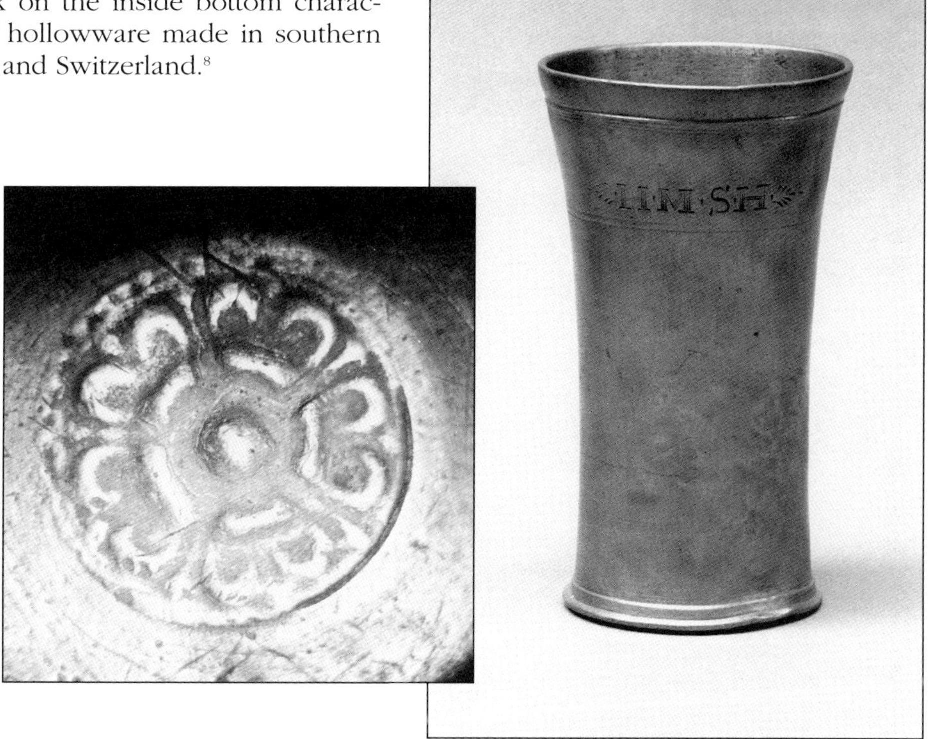

8. Karl Schöppl identified the city mark in a letter to the author dated February 23, 1992.

Netherlands

The outward flare to the top of the beaker in Figure 106, which was used in the Phoenixville Mennonite Church,[9] Chester County, Pa. (congregation no longer in existence), is characteristic of beakers from the Netherlands and Sweden. British and American beakers are usually more parallel.

A paper label on the outside bottom of the beaker reads "Matthias Pennypacker Communion / Cup Mennonite Meeting at / Phoenixville 1794 Bishop / His wife Mary was buried there / . . ." Matthias Pennypacker (1742–1808) was the first official Bishop of the Phoenixville Mennonite Church.[10] His great-grandson was Samuel Whitaker Pennypacker (1843–1916), governor of Pennsylvania from 1903 to 1907.

The Dutch beaker in figure 107 includes the initials of the owner, "I C."[11]

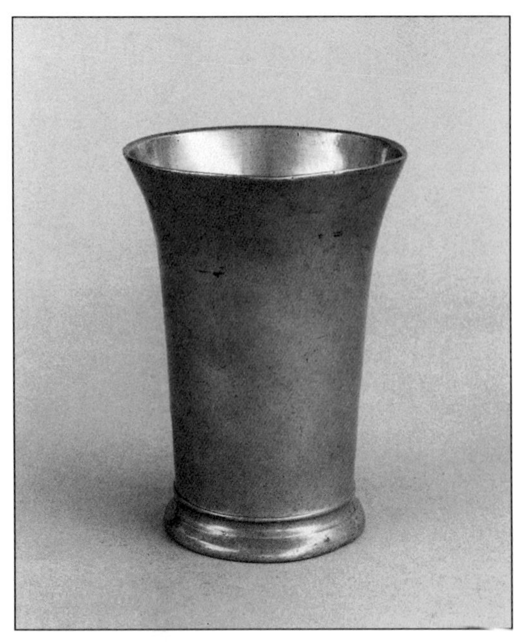

Fig. 107. *Beaker. Netherlands, 1700–1750. H 5 3/8", TD 3 3/4", BD 2 7/8". Bally Mennonite Church, Bally, Berks County, Pa.*

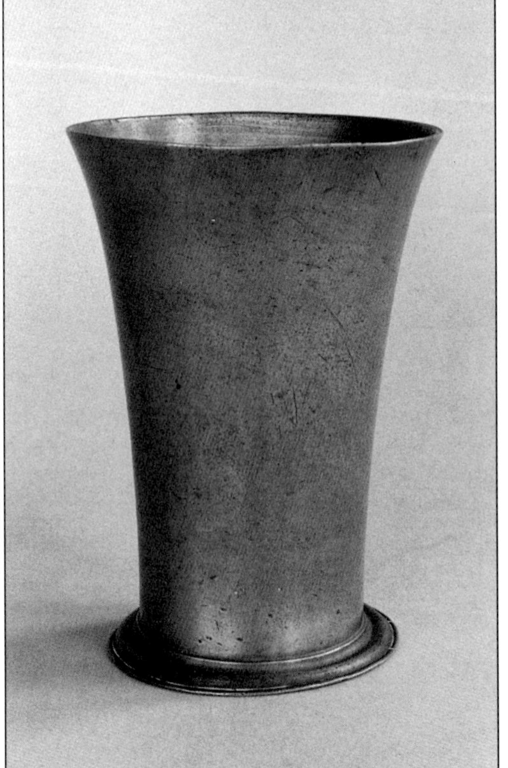

Fig. 106. *Beaker. Netherlands, 1700–1750. H 5 1/2", TD 3 5/8", BD 3 1/8". Pennypacker Mills, Schwenksville, Pa.*

Candlesticks

AMERICA

Candlesticks, or more correctly candlestick holders, were used on the altar table in the Catholic church. Frequently made of brass and other metals, they were occasionally made of pewter as in the following examples (Figure 108). Only four candlesticks, all made by Heyne, were found in this study.

Fig. 108. *Candlesticks (opposite page) made by Johann Christoph Heyne, Lancaster, Pa., 1752–1781 (L 530,533). H 21 1/4", BD 8 3/4". Heyne would have been familiar with altar sticks of this form in his native Saxony. They were produced on the Continent for ecclesiastical use in the seventeenth and eighteenth centuries. Altar sticks frequently were used in sets of six. Two pairs have survived that were once owned by this Catholic church. A recent thorough search of the premises failed to produce the third pair of sticks. Wooden candlesticks, said to predate the pewter sticks, are owned by the congregation. Formerly used in the Most Blessed Sacrament Catholic Church, Bally, Berks County, Pa. (Courtesy, Winterthur Museum).*

9. Personal communication with Harold L. Fly of Towamencin Mennonite Church on January 26, 1990. He reported that the cup was once used by the Phoenixville Mennonite congregation.

10. John C. Wenger, *History of the Mennonites of the Franconia Conference* (Telford, Pa.: Franconia Mennonite Historical Society, 1937), 213.

11. Jan F. H. H. Beekhuizen, president of the "Dutch Pewter Society," said in a letter to the author dated April 24, 1993, that the initials "I C" stamped on the outside bottom of the beaker, are not the initials of the maker but of the owner. He was not able to identify the maker of the beaker but was certain that it was Dutch, early eighteenth century.

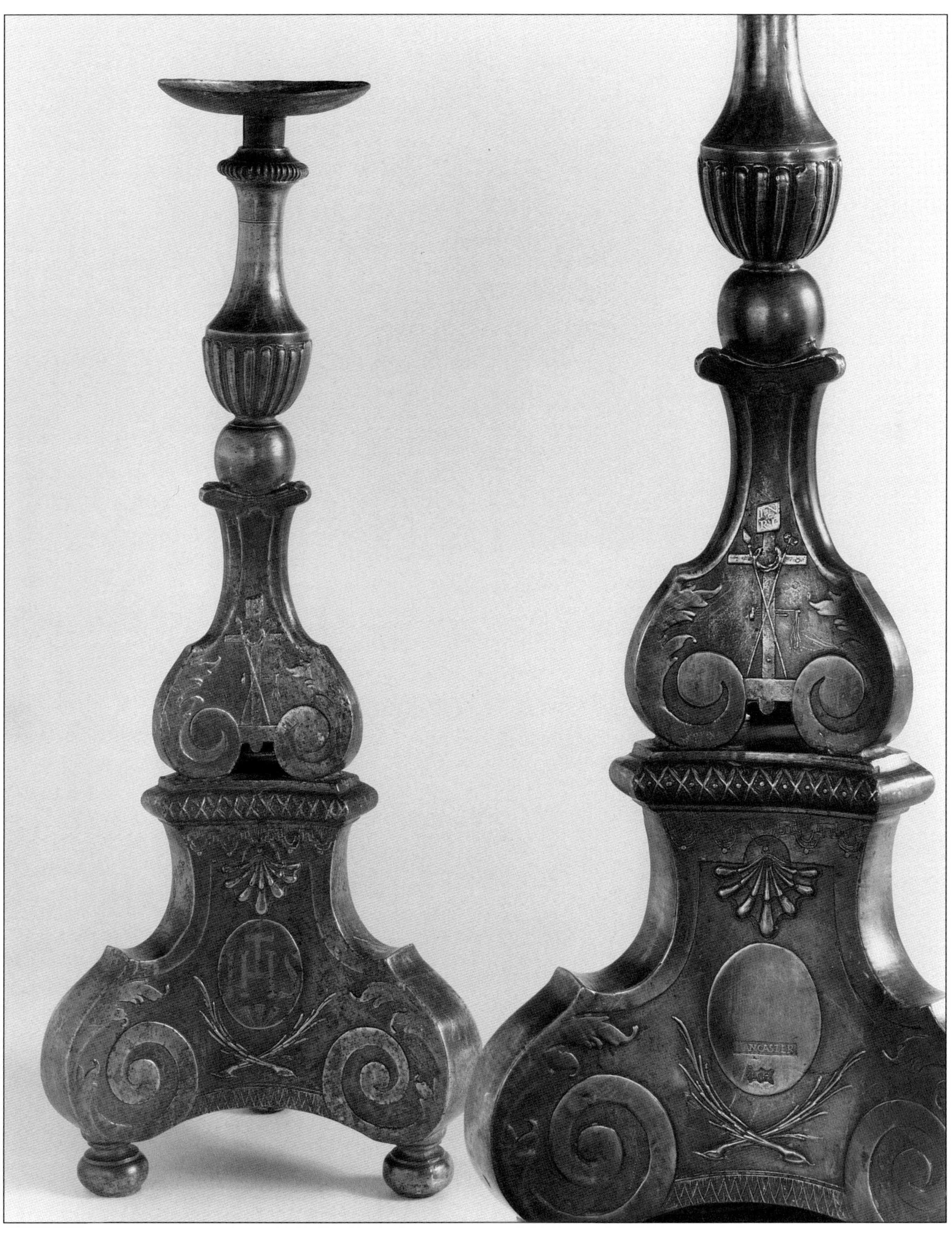

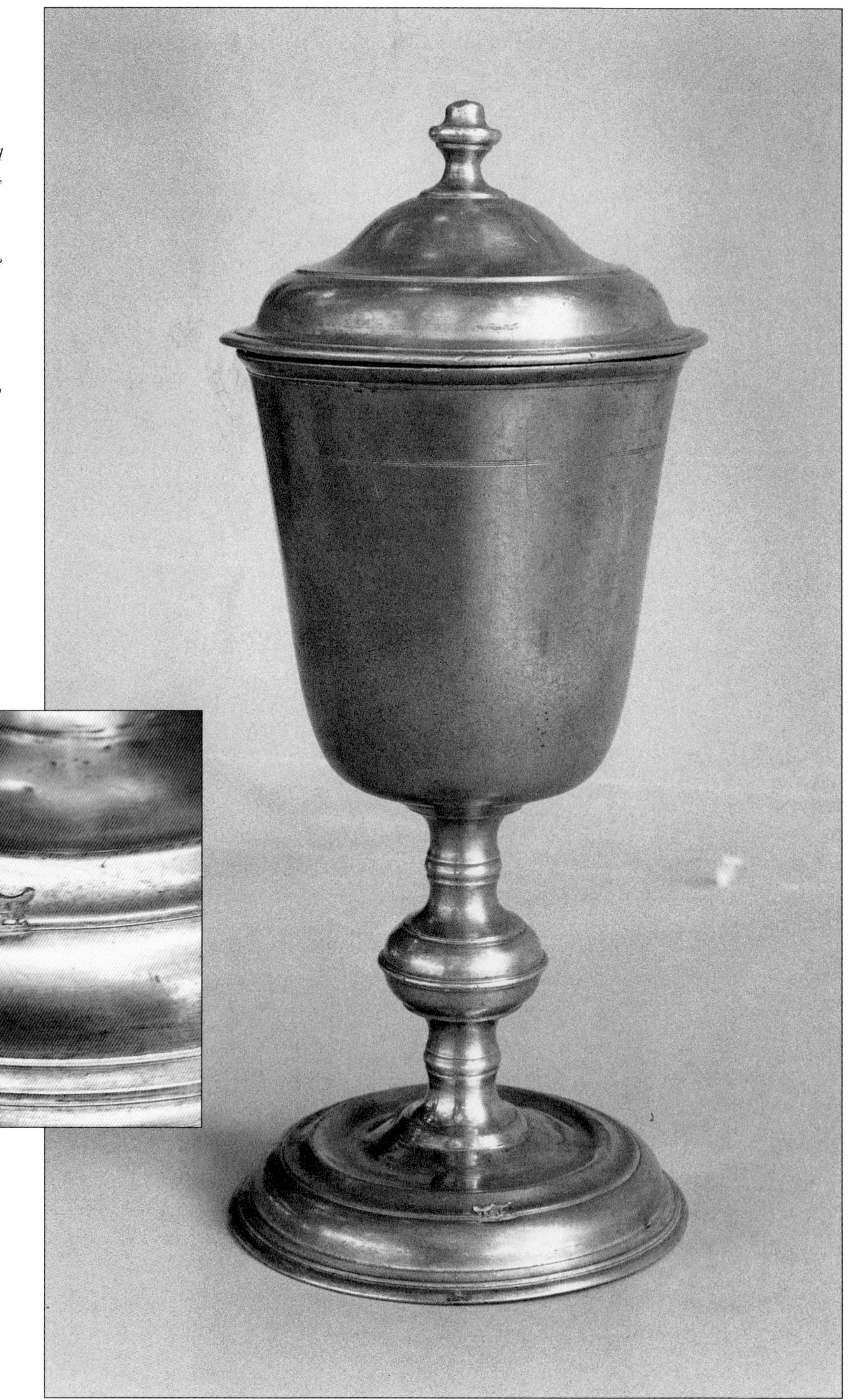

Fig. 109. *Chalice by Johann Christoph Heyne, Lancaster, Pa. 1752–1781 (L 533). H 11 3/4″ with lid, H 8 3/4″ top of body, TD 4 1/8″, BD 4 1/2″. Heyne marked a few of his chalices on the curved surface of the base, as in this example. Occasionally, he marked them on the inside of the lid. Muddy Creek Lutheran Church and Peace United Church of Christ congregations, Denver, Lancaster County, Pa.*

Fig. 110. *Mark (above) on the base of chalice by Johann Christoph Heyne.*

Chalices

Chalices were used as drinking vessels in the celebration of the Eucharist. They represent the cup of the Last Supper. "And he took a cup, and when he had given thanks he gave it to them, saying, 'Drink of it, all of you; for this is my blood of the covenant, which is poured out for many for the forgiveness of sins'." (Matthew 26:27–28, Revised Standard Version). The Lutheran, Reformed, and Moravian denominations used chalices as the communion "cup." The Mennonites and Church of the Brethren preferred beakers.

AMERICA

Chalices were among the finest forms created by American pewterers. A marked example by Johann Christoph Heyne (Figure 109) is such an example. The strong knopped stem, boldness of outline, and ample cup are Germanic influences seen in this stately form. The only marked eighteenth-century lidded chalices of American origin were made by Heyne. His chalices are found infrequently in museums and collections. Twenty-nine Heyne chalices were found in the survey; eight chalices had lids and twenty one did not.

Chalices attributed to John Will (Figure 111) have not been found marked, but they frequently accompany marked pieces by that maker. In this case, the chalice accompanied a marked oval dish and a coffeepot that was used as a flagon. For a chalice similar to those attributed to John Will, see Charles V. Swain, "Three Flagons Attributed to John Will."[12] These chalices frequently have two pairs of line decoration encircling the cup. They are almost nonexistent in museums and private collections, but six chalices of this form were found in the survey.

Illustrated in Figure 112 is a chalice that accompanied a William Will flagon dated 1765 and a footed paten most likely by Will. Stylistically related to the previously mentioned chalice attributed to his father, John Will, it incorporates a tankard lid into the base of the chalice as was done by both men. All three pieces of the Reformed portion of the commu-

Fig. 111. *Chalice attributed to John Will, New York, N.Y., 1752–1774. H 8", TD 4", BD 4¾". Wentz's United Church of Christ, Worcester, Montgomery County, Pa.*

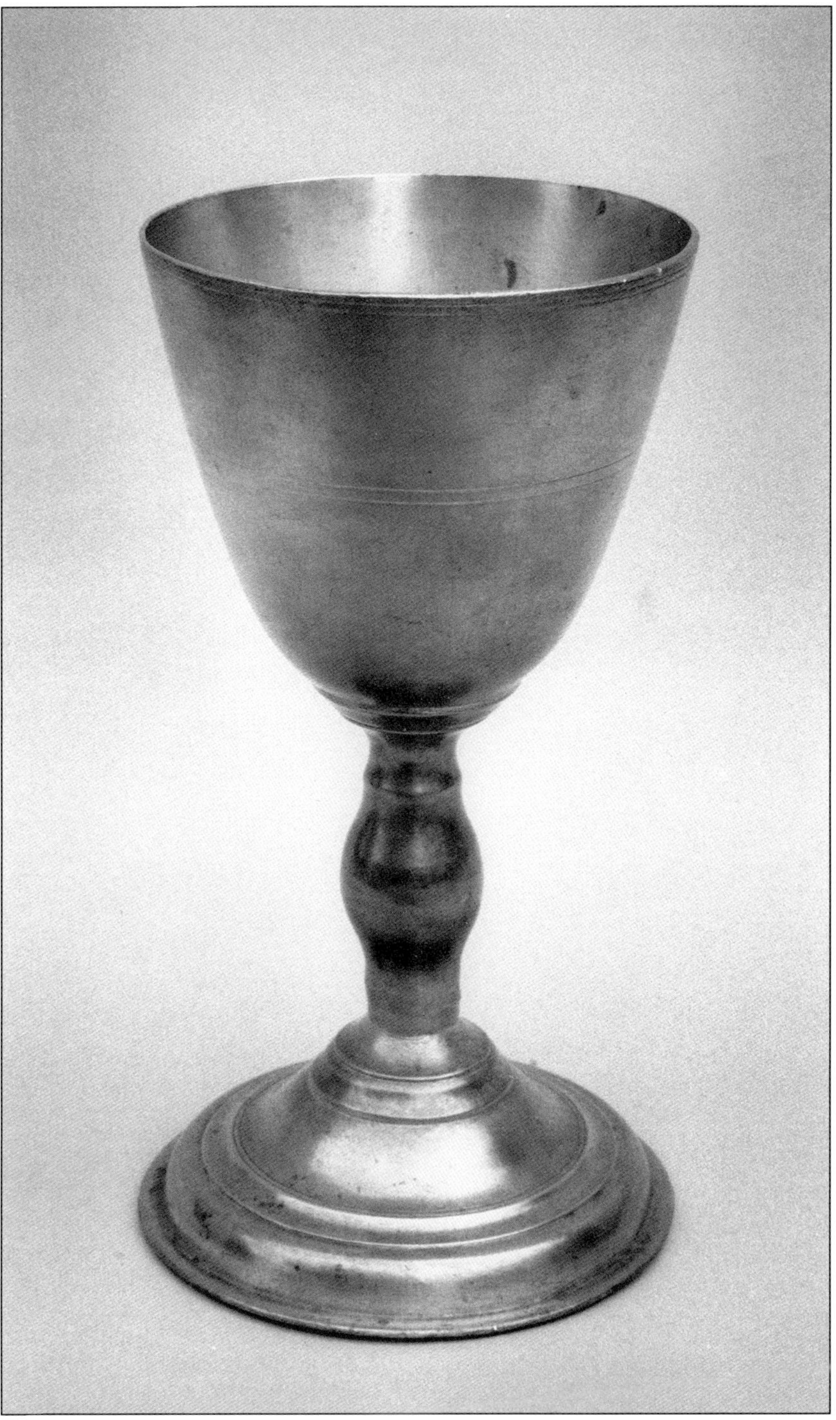

12. Charles V. Swain, "Three Flagons Attributed to John Will," *The Magazine Antiques* (May 1972): 857, Figs. 9–10.

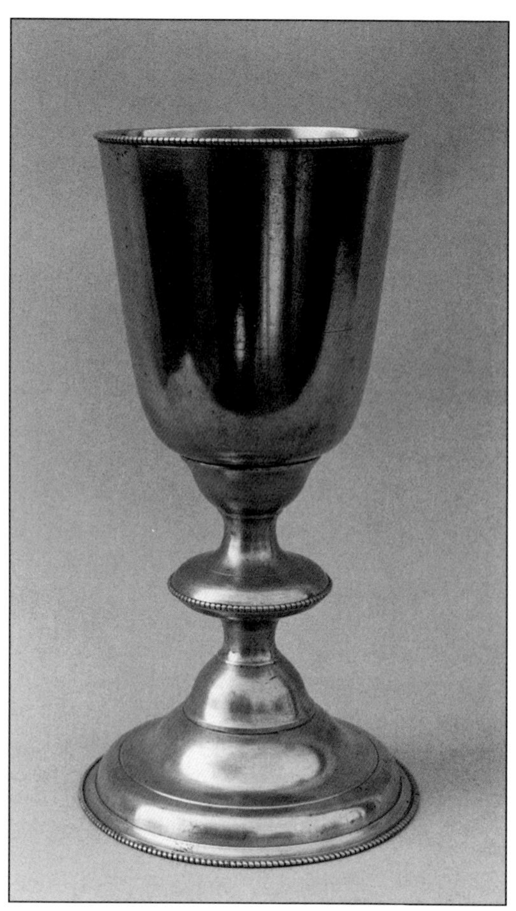

Fig. 113. *Chalice (above) attributed to William Will, Philadelphia, 1764–1798. H 8″, TD 3 5/8″, BD 4 1/4″. Flohr Lutheran Church, McKnightstown, Adams County, Pa.*

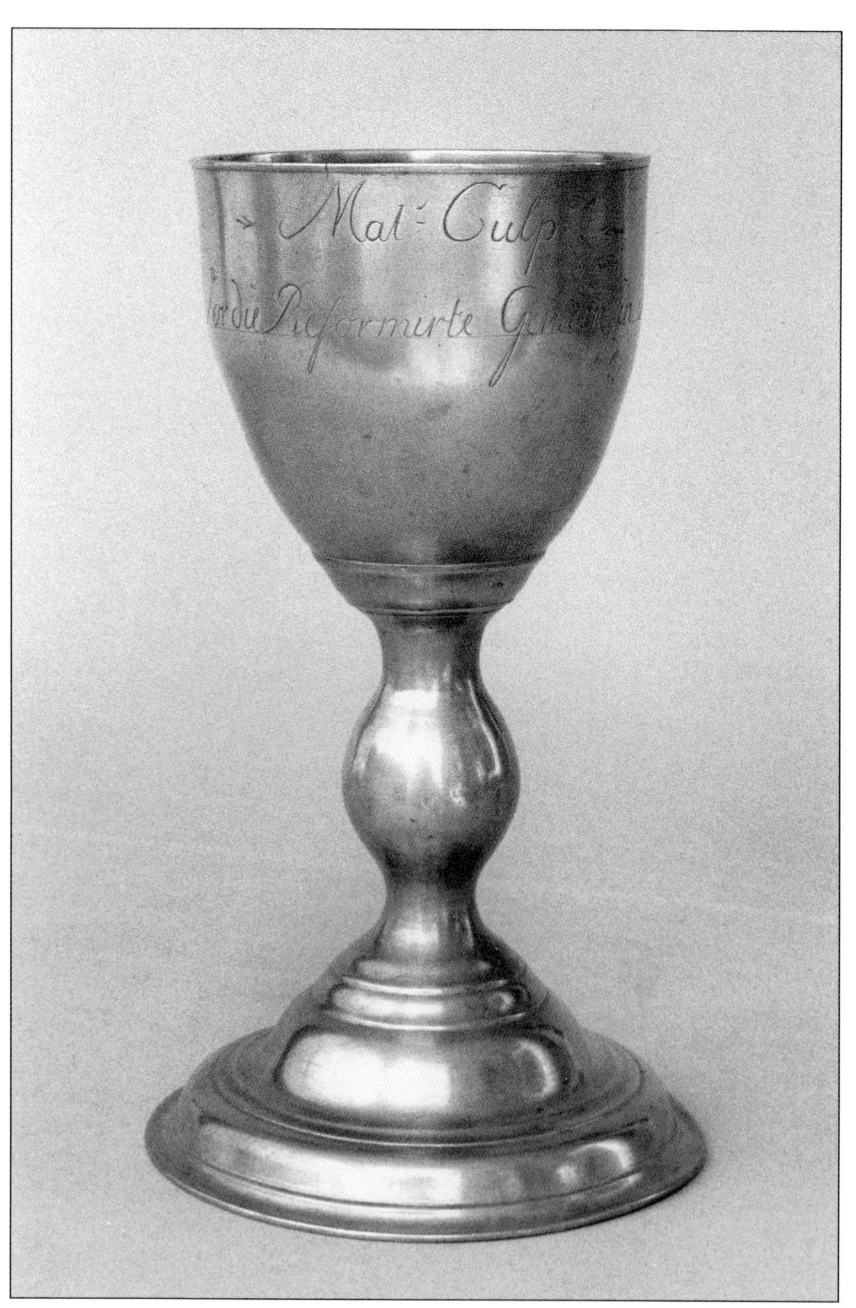

Fig. 112. *Chalice attributed to William Will, Philadelphia, 1764–1798. H 7 3/8″, TD 3 1/4″, BD 4 1/2″. Heidelberg Union Church with Lutheran and United Church of Christ congregations, Slatington, Lehigh County, Pa.*

nion service were engraved by the same hand and probably came from William Will's shop.

The chalice illustrated in Figure 113 is attributed to William Will because of its similar form to a chalice in a set by William Will given by Aaron Levy to the German congregation in Aaronsburg and so inscribed. The stems of a pair of pewter salts were ingeniously used to form the stem of the chalice.[13] Will frequently used a tankard lid for the base of his chalices, as in this example. The success of the form is further enhanced by the addition of beading to the lip, knop, and base of the chalice. Thirteen chalices of this form were found in the survey.

In the chalice illustrated in Figure 114, Will replaced the cup of his more commonly found chalice (as in the preceding example) with the top portion of his beaker form. See the marked beaker by William Will illustrated under beakers (Figure 96). The top diameters of the chalice and the beaker have different measurements. The body, the knop on

13. Charles V. Swain, "Interchangeable parts in Early American Pewter," *The Magazine Antiques* (February 1963); and John C. Thomas, ed., *American and British Pewter: An Historical Survey* (New York: Universe Books, 1976), 106-7.

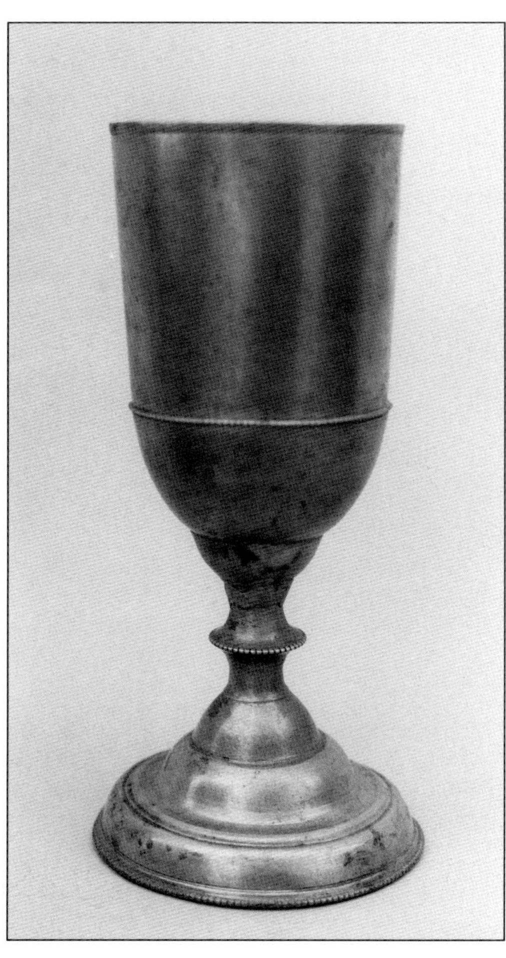

Fig. 114. *Chalice attributed to William Will, Philadelphia, 1764–1798. H 8″, TD 3 1/8″, BD 3 3/4″. Salem (Walmer's) Union Church with Lutheran and United Church of Christ congregations, Annville, Lebanon County, Pa.*

the stem, and the base are ornamented with beading. This form, attributed to William Will, has not been previously pictured.

Another chalice form that has been attributed to William Will because of its association with marked Will flagons is illustrated in Figure 115. Ledlie I. Laughlin stated, "Although unmarked, such chalices are, when they turn up, almost invariably with other William Will forms and are attributed to him with confidence."[14] Again, a tankard lid was used as the base of this chalice. The body of the chalice bears the inscription *"For Reformiet [sic] & Lutherische Gemtn Johan & Barbara Glauser In Bern Taunschip."* Johann and Barbara Glauser may have given the chalice to the Reformed and Lutheran congregations in Bern Township in Berks County and it later was carried to Perry County. There was a significant nineteenth-century migration from the Bern Township area to Perry County. Oral tradition suggests that the chalice was used by Reformed minister Samuel Dubendorff in 1798 in the New Bloomfield church, in whose possession it is today.

In Figure 116, observe that the short cup and the use of a tankard lid for the base are similar characteristics of the pre-

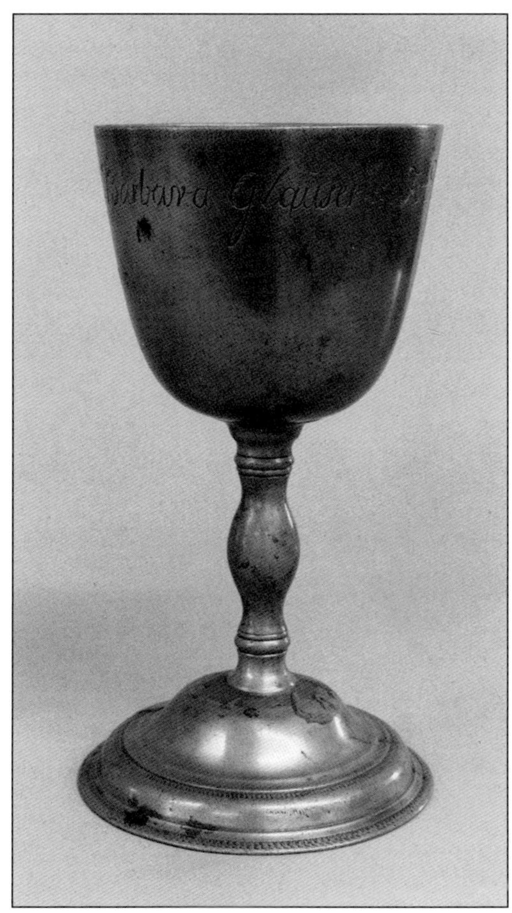

Fig. 115. *Chalice attributed to William Will, Philadelphia, 1764–1798. H 7 3/4″, TD 3 7/8″, BD 4 3/8″. Trinity United Church of Christ, New Bloomfield, Perry County, Pa.*

14. Ledlie I. Laughlin, *Pewter In America Its Makers and Their Marks.* (Barre, Mass: Barre Publishing Co., Inc.) 3: See Plate 97 for examples of similar chalices accompanying a flagon marked by William Will in the communion service of the Presbyterian Church of Oxford, Pa.

Fig. 116. *Chalice (near right) attributed to William Will, Philadelphia, 1764–1798. H 8 1/8", TD 3 7/8", BD 4 1/8". United Church of Christ, Northampton County, Pa.*

Fig. 117. *Chalice (far right) attributed to William Will, Philadelphia, 1764–1798. H 8 1/4", TD 3 1/8", BD 4". Frieden's Peace Church, now St. John's Lutheran and St. Paul's United Church of Christ congregations, Shiremanstown, Cumberland County, Pa.*

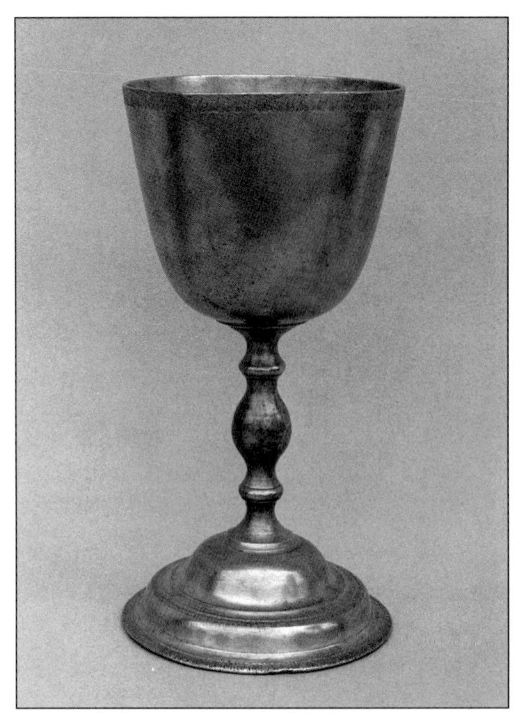

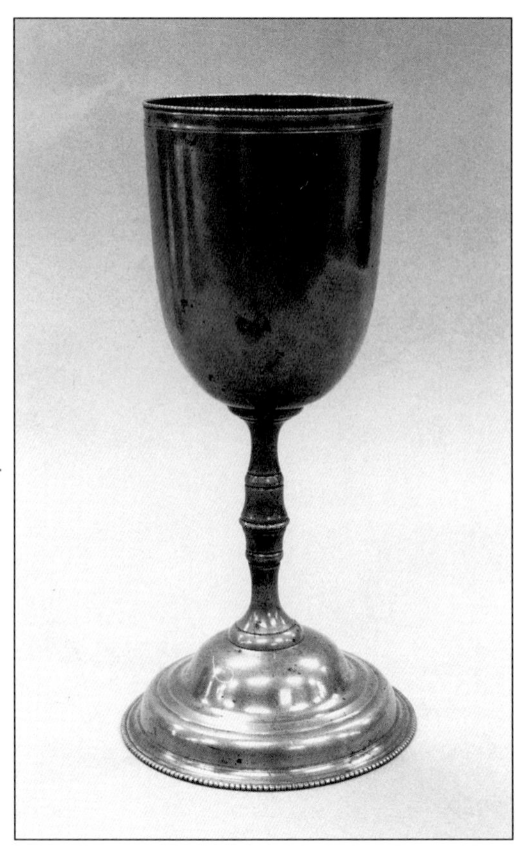

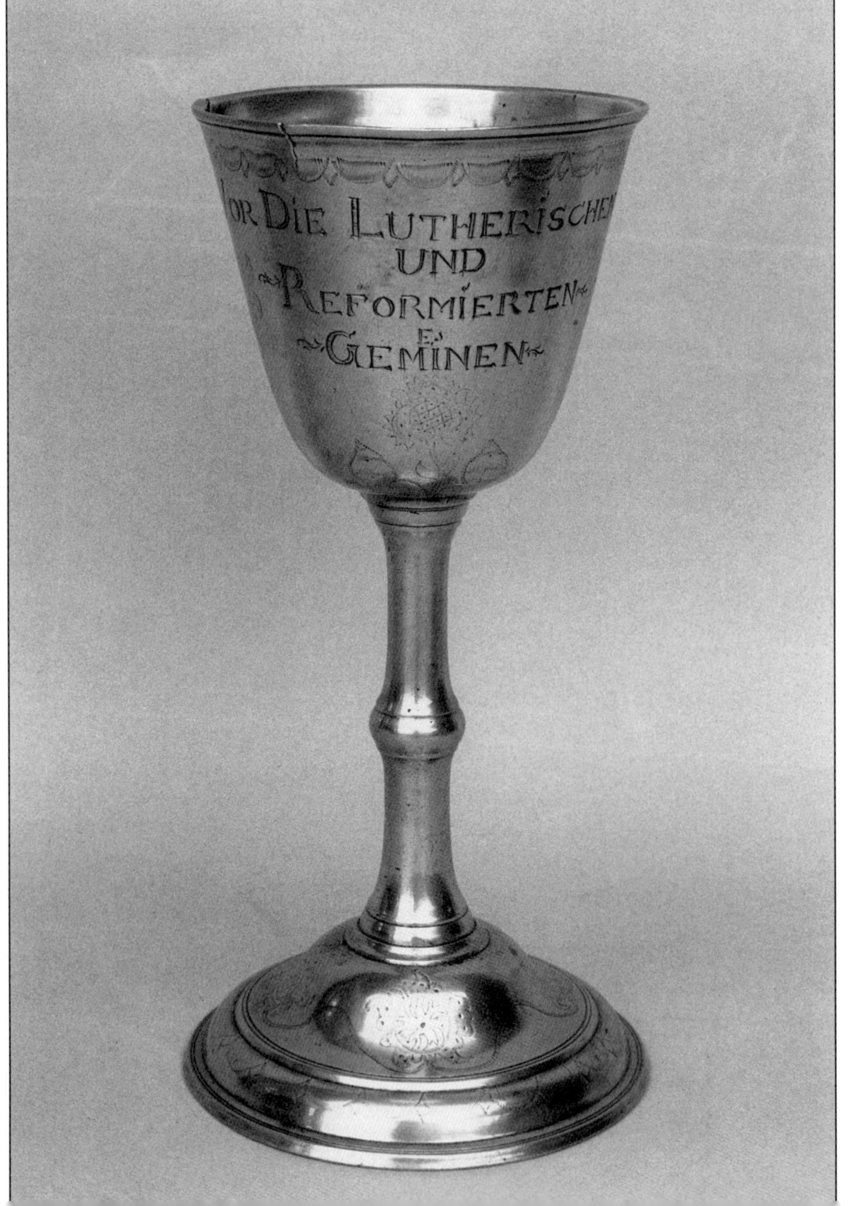

ceding chalice. Note the accentuated turnings, not too different from those found on two other distinct chalice styles. See examples in the First United Church of Christ, Easton, Northampton County, Pennsylvania, and the Bern United Church of Christ Church, Leesport, Berks County, Pennsylvania (Figures 119 and 121).

In Figure 117, as in the preceding examples, a tankard lid was used to form the base of the chalice. Will frequently decorated his pewter with beading. This example has beading on the lip, stem, and base.

The intricately engraved chalice in Figure 118 was given to the Lutheran and Reformed congregations at Stony Run by Johannes Hechler. The swag and diamond decoration around the lip of the chalice has been found on sugar bowls ascribed to William Will. A tulip-shaped

Fig. 118. *Chalice. Probably Philadelphia, possibly William Will, 1764–1798. H 9 1/8", TD 4 1/4", BD 4 1/2". Friedens Lutheran Church, Stony Run, Berks County, Pa.*

quart mug signed by William Will accompanied the chalice.

Eleven chalices of the form shown in Figure 119 were found in the survey. One was engraved with the date 1758 and another in a private collection bears the same date. All the bases appear to have come from the same mold, and they all have a distinctive raised "collar" at the base of the stem. The addition or subtraction of sections to the stems determines the height of the chalices. The short cup on a tall stem gives a sense of gracefulness to these elegant communion chalices. All are unmarked. Six chalices were in sets accompanied by eighteenth-century Philadelphia pewter by William Will and Love. Only one chalice accompanied a Continental flagon.

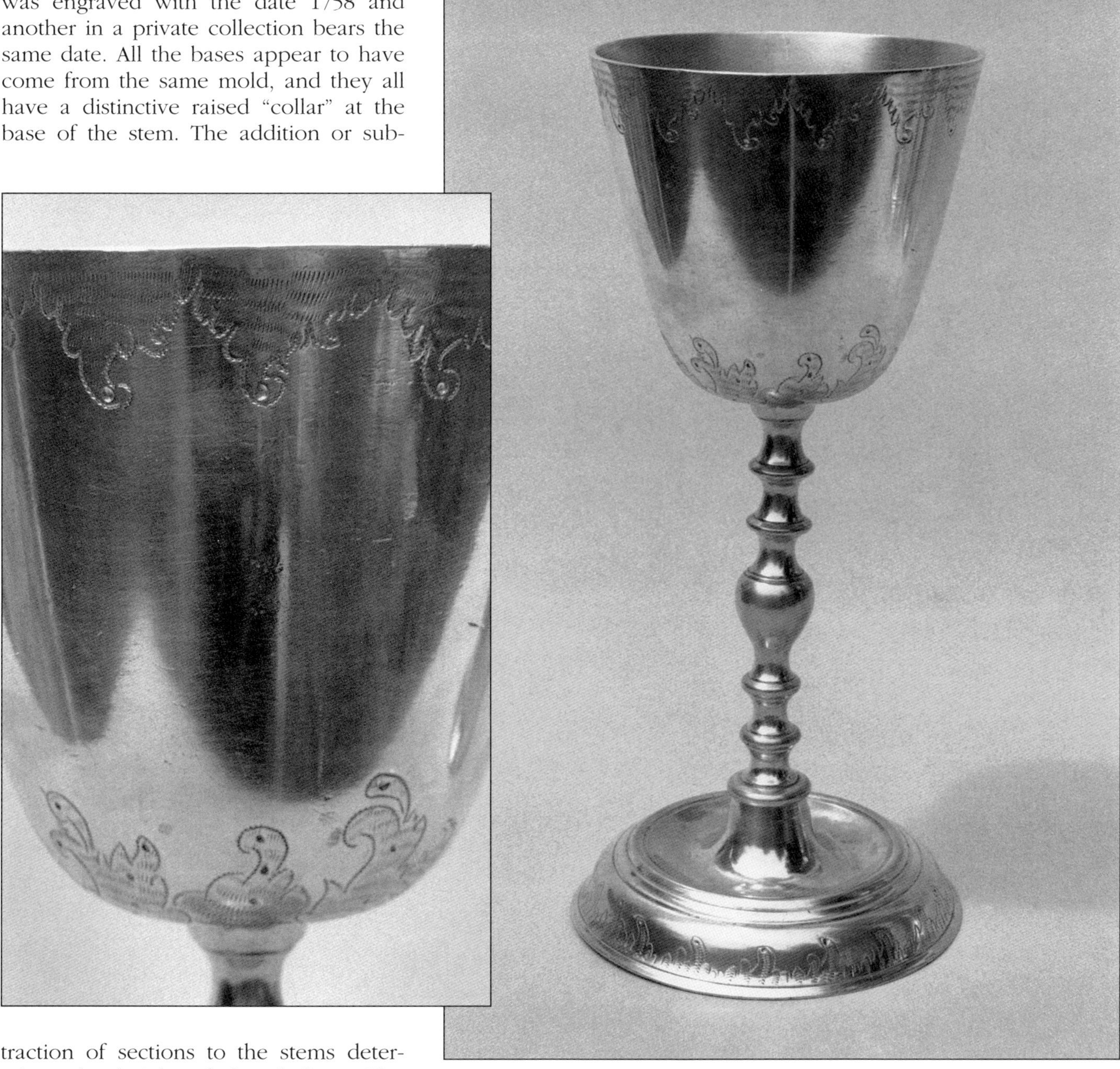

Fig. 119. *Chalice (above). Philadelphia or Continental, 1750–1800. H 9 1/8", TD 4" BD 4 1/4". First United Church of Christ, Easton, Northampton County, Pa.*

Fig. 120. *Engraving (above left) on cup of chalice.*

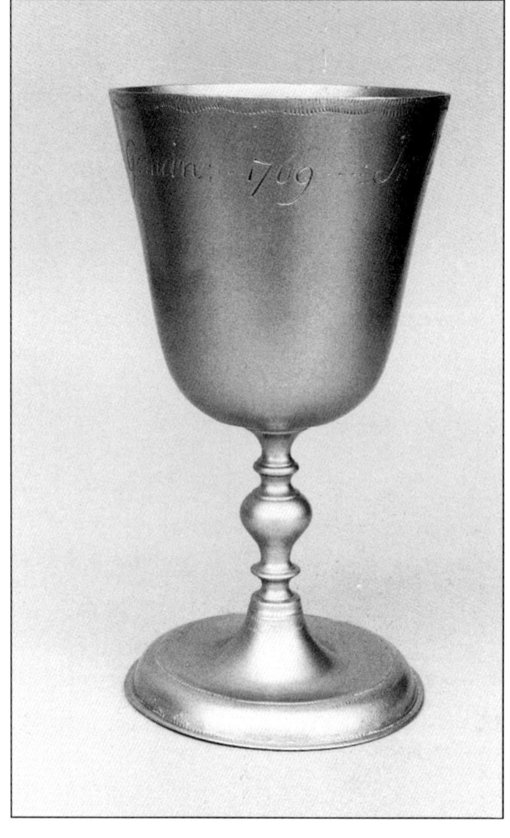

Fig. 121. *Chalice. Philadelphia or Continental, 1750–1800. H 7 5/8", TD 4 1/8", BD 3 7/8". Bern United Church of Christ, Leesport, Berks County, Pa.*

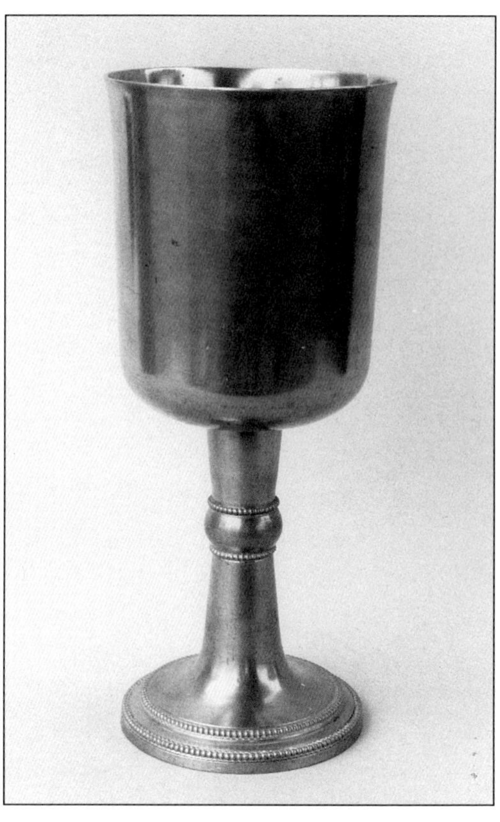

Fig. 123. *Chalice, Philadelphia, 1800–1810. H 8 1/2", TD 3 5/8", BD 3 1/2". Jacob's United Church of Christ, Jacksonville, Lehigh County, Pa.*

Five chalices of the form illustrated in Figure 121 were found in the study. Dates of 1767 and 1769 were engraved on the cups of two of the chalices. The chalice above is engraved *"In die Bernen Kirch Vor Die Reformierte Gemein 1769"* [for the Reformed Congregation in the Bern Church 1769]. Philadelphia pewter accompanied the chalices in each set and included two Edgell tankards, two William Will flagons, and plates by Thomas Byles and Love. None of the chalices was found with Continental flagons. Karl Schöppl, German pewter scholar, states concerning this chalice form and the preceding form (Figure 119), "Chalices in Germany are normally marked (the lead content could not be too high in the case of a drink like wine). I tend to agree with your view, that these chalices were made in America and also engraved there, with the appropriate indications of localities and dates of the institutions."[15]

Always unmarked, chalices with vase-shaped cups, as in Figure 122, have been found with flagons attributed to "Love" and may be by that maker or makers. Stylistically later than the preceding chalices, they were probably made in the early nineteenth century. Two rows of beading encircle the stepped-up base. One chalice of this form was found in the survey.

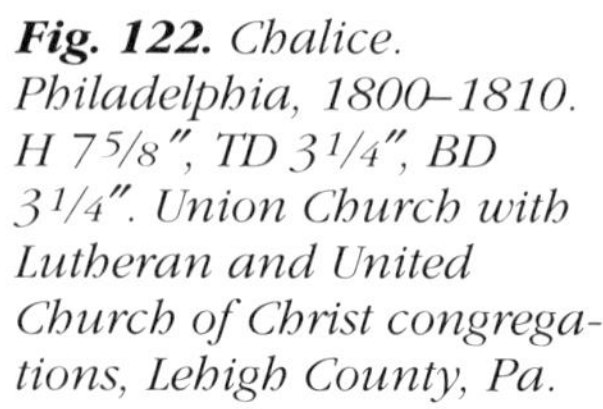

Fig. 122. *Chalice. Philadelphia, 1800–1810. H 7 5/8", TD 3 1/4", BD 3 1/4". Union Church with Lutheran and United Church of Christ congregations, Lehigh County, Pa.*

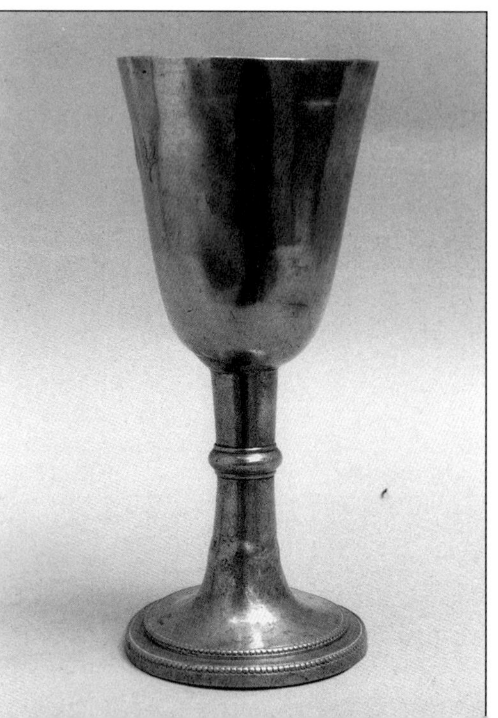

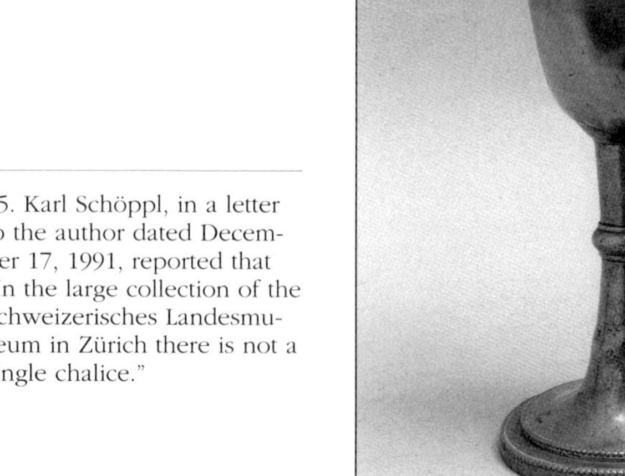

15. Karl Schöppl, in a letter to the author dated December 17, 1991, reported that "In the large collection of the Schweizerisches Landesmuseum in Zürich there is not a single chalice."

With a base similar to that of the previously mentioned chalice, this one has a beaded, knopped stem and a deep cup with nearly parallel sides to produce a pleasing form (Figure 123). Note the beading on this chalice, as well as on the preceding chalice. Seven chalices of this style were found in the survey.

A straight-line mark by the Palethorps is found on the bottom of the chalice in Figure 124. Chalices of similar form were made in the mid-eighteenth century by London pewterer John Jupe.[16]

Boardman chalices are characterized by having an inverted bell-shaped cup.[17] They are usually unmarked. A marked example has been previously recorded.[18] The chalice illustrated in Figure 126 is one of a pair in a set that contained two flagons, a baptismal basin, and two plates by the Boardmans.

Another chalice form of the nineteenth century is the example by Leonard, Reed, and Barton, illustrated in Figure 127.

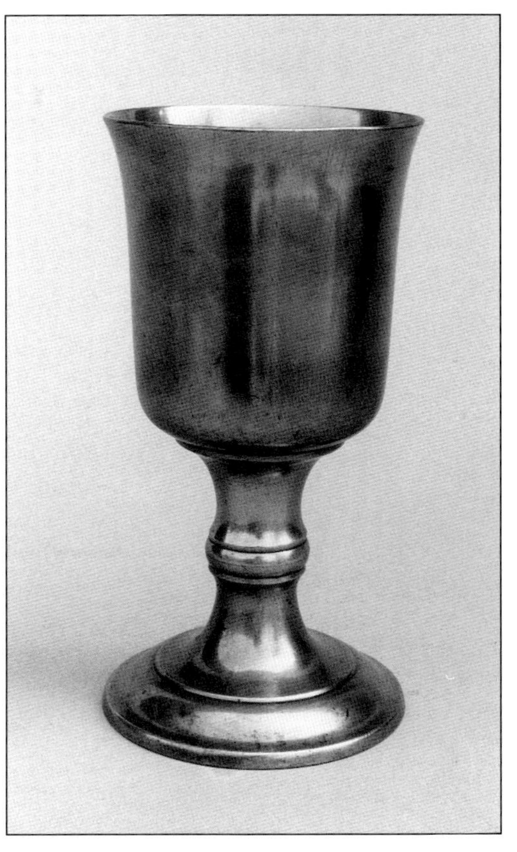

Fig. 126. *Chalice (left) attributed to the Boardmans, Hartford, Conn., 1804–1873. H 7", TD 3 5/8", BD 3 3/4". Epler's United Church of Christ, Leesport, Berks County, Pa.*

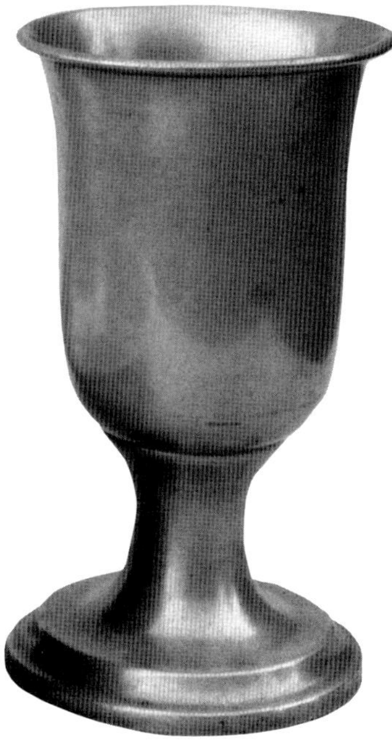

Fig. 127. *Chalice (above) by Leonard, Reed, and Barton, Taunton, Mass., 1835–1840. (L 2:106). H 6 3/4", TD 3 5/8", BD 3 5/8". Upper Skippack Mennonite Church, Skippack, Montgomery County, Pa.*

16. Ronald F. Homer, *The Stanley E. Thomas Collection of Pewter of the Museum of North Devon, Barnstaple with an Account of the Pewterers of Barnstaple* (The Pewter Society, 1993), 86.

17. Melvyn and Bette Wolf, "Nineteenth Century American Chalices," *Pewter Collectors' Club of America Bulletin,* no. 79 (September 1979): 432.

18. John Carl Thomas, "A Marked Boardman Chalice," *Pewter Collectors' Club of America Bulletin,* no. 49 (September 1963):187.

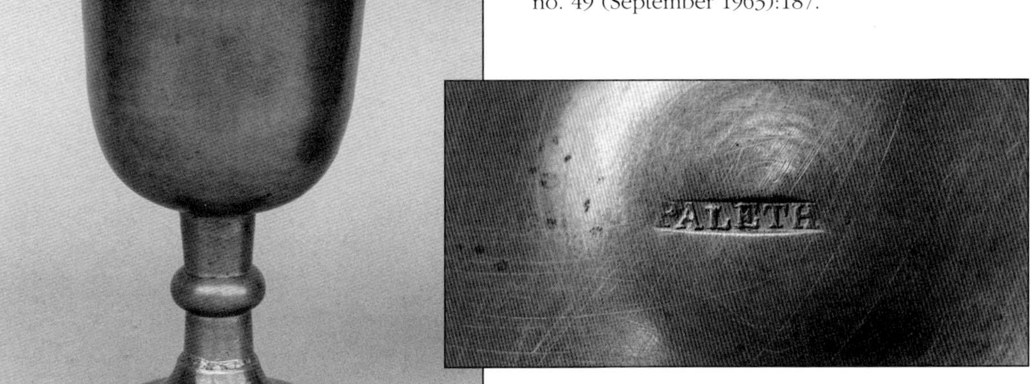

Fig. 124. *Chalice (left) by the Palethorps, Philadelphia, 1817–1845 (L 2:108). H 7 3/4", TD 4 1/8", BD 3 3/8". Emmanuel United Church of Christ, Red Lion, York County, Pa.*

Fig. 125. *Mark (above) on chalice.*

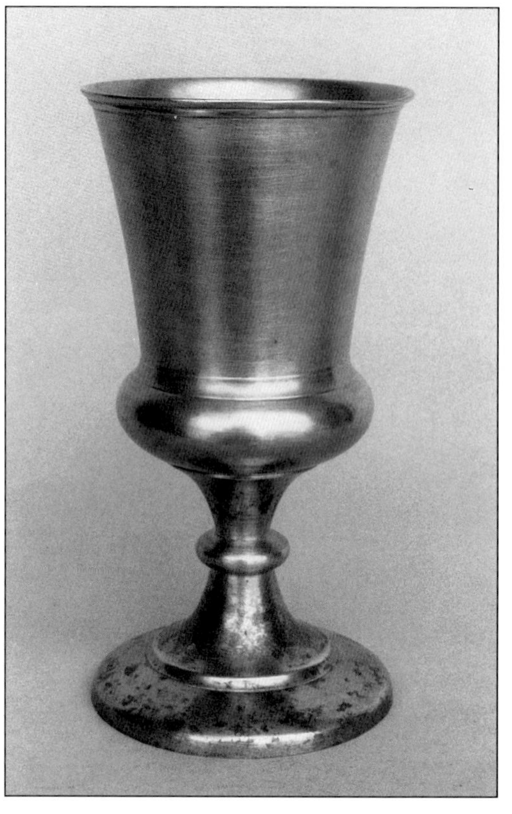

Fig. 128. *Chalice attributed to Smith and Feltman, Albany, N.Y., 1848–1852. H 8", TD 4 1/8", BD 4 1/8". Emanuel Lutheran Church, Bath, Northampton County, Pa.*

Thistle-shaped chalices (Figure 128) were popular in the mid nineteenth century. This was one of a pair in a set that also included a Smith and Feltman flagon and two Sheldon and Feltman dishes.

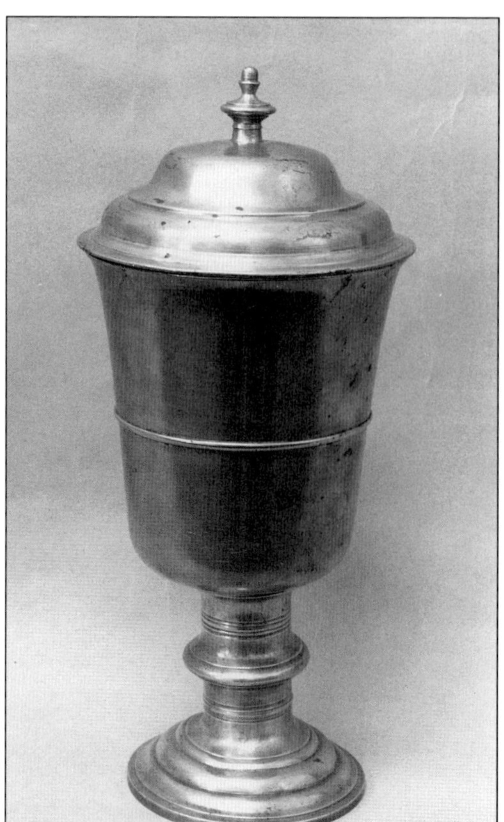

Fig. 129. *Chalice. Unmarked, probably British, second half of the eighteenth century. H 11 3/4", TD 4 3/4", BD 3 7/8". Hill Lutheran Church, Cleona, Lebanon County, Pa.*

BRITISH ISLES

The body of the large lidded chalice in Figure 129 is similar in form to others made in England and Scotland. (See Cotterell, 98–99, for similar vessels dated 1765 and 1790.) The body of this chalice is much deeper than those of American chalices by Heyne. Both British and American chalices had lids.

The lip on the Dixon chalice in Figure 130 has been altered for ease of pouring. This was presumably done after it left the pewterer's shop.

The chalice in Figure 131 and the preceding chalice bear marks that were used by the Dixon firm during the same time period. They differ in style numbers marked on their bases and in form.

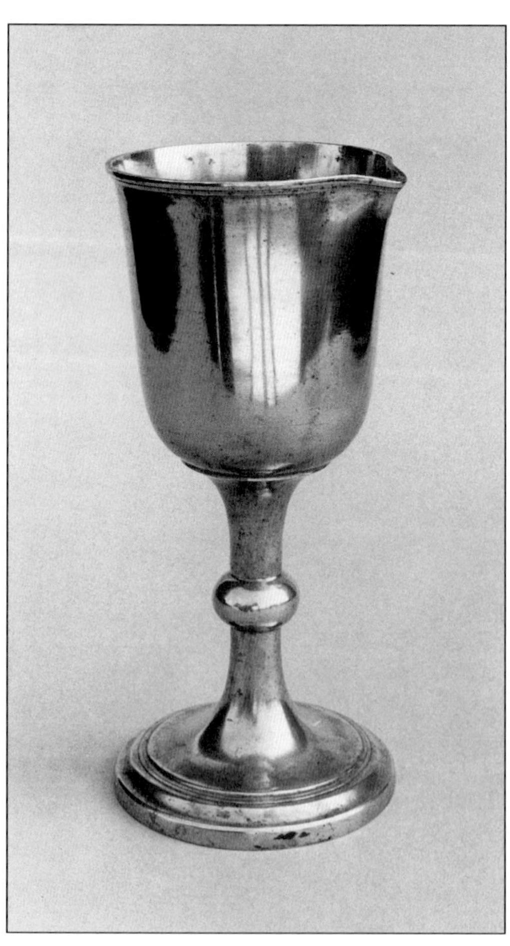

Fig. 130. *Chalice (above) by James Dixon and sons, Sheffield, England, 1842–1851. H 8 3/8", TD 3 1/2", BD 3 3/4". Trinity Lutheran Church, Stephens City, Frederick County, Va.*

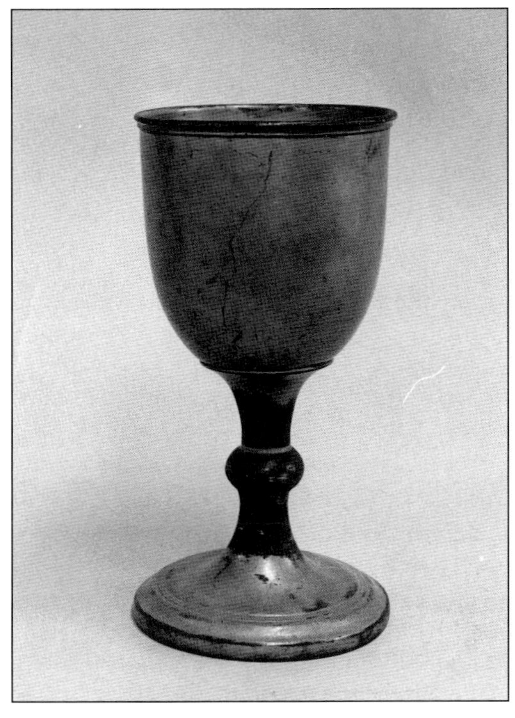

Fig. 131. *Chalice by James Dixon and Sons, Sheffield, England, 1842–1851. H 7 1/2″, TD 3 3/4″, BD 3 3/4″. St. Paul's Lutheran Church, Ardmore, Montgomery County, Pa.*

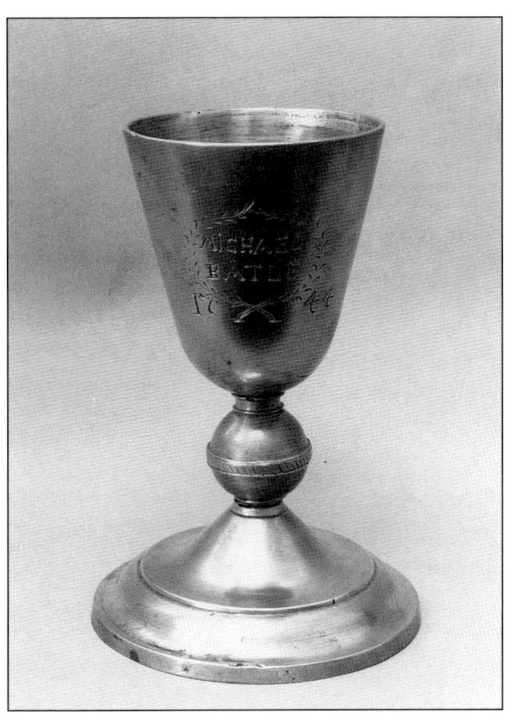

Fig. 132. *Chalice. Unmarked, probably Germany, 1744. H 7″, TD 3 1/2″, BD 4 3/4″. Zion Lutheran Church, Jonestown, Lebanon County, Pa.*

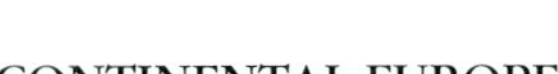

CONTINENTAL EUROPE

Germany

Engraved "MICHAEL BÄTLE 1744," the chalice in Figure 132 has a round knopped stem characteristic of some German chalices. A chalice of similar form and with engraving possibly by the same hand, "ADAM ULRICH 1745," is part of the communion service of the Hill Lutheran Church, Cleona, Lebanon County, Pennsylvania.

In Figure 133, the knopped stem and the proportionally large cup suggest an European or British origin. The contemporary decoration is appropriate for an ecclesiastical piece of pewter. The engraving on the chalice includes a crown and a pair of angels, one feeding a lamb, and the initials "J.C.S." A German flagon similarly engraved with a lamb and a cross with banner has the same initials. The flagon is owned by Trinity Lutheran Church in Lancaster, Pennsylvania. The engraving appears to be by the same hand.

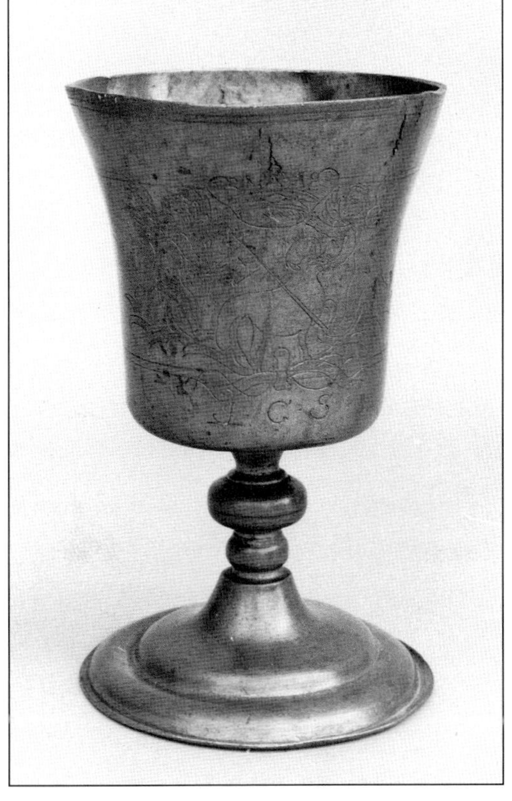

Fig. 133. *Chalice. Unmarked, Continental or British, last half of the eighteenth century. H 7 3/8″, TD 4 3/8″, BD 4 1/2″. Swamp United Church of Christ, Reinholds, Lancaster County, Pa.*

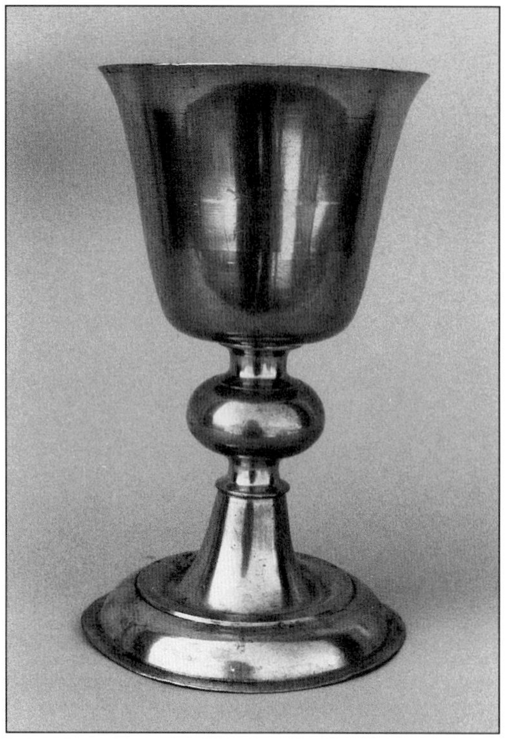

Fig. 134. *Chalice. Unmarked, Continental or British, eighteenth century. H 7 1/2", TD 4 1/8", BD 4 1/4". New Hanover Lutheran Church, Gilbertsville, Montgomery County, Pa.*

The cup of the chalice in Figure 134 can be disassembled, for it has a screw fitting tooled into the base of the body, perhaps for ease of traveling. This method of attachment was done on the Continent and in England but rarely in America in the eighteenth century. A German flagon accompanied the chalice.

Chalices marked by pewterers from the Netherlands and Switzerland were not found in the survey.

Ciboria

A ciborium is a vessel used to hold the eucharistic wafers—the Host—during the sacrament of holy communion.

The ciborium, or sugar bowl, in Figure 135 is the only sugar bowl by Heyne that was found in the survey. This form is called a sugar bowl when used in the home; but because of its ecclesiastical use as a container for the Host, it functioned as a ciborium in the church. American pewterers made the two ciboria found in the survey.

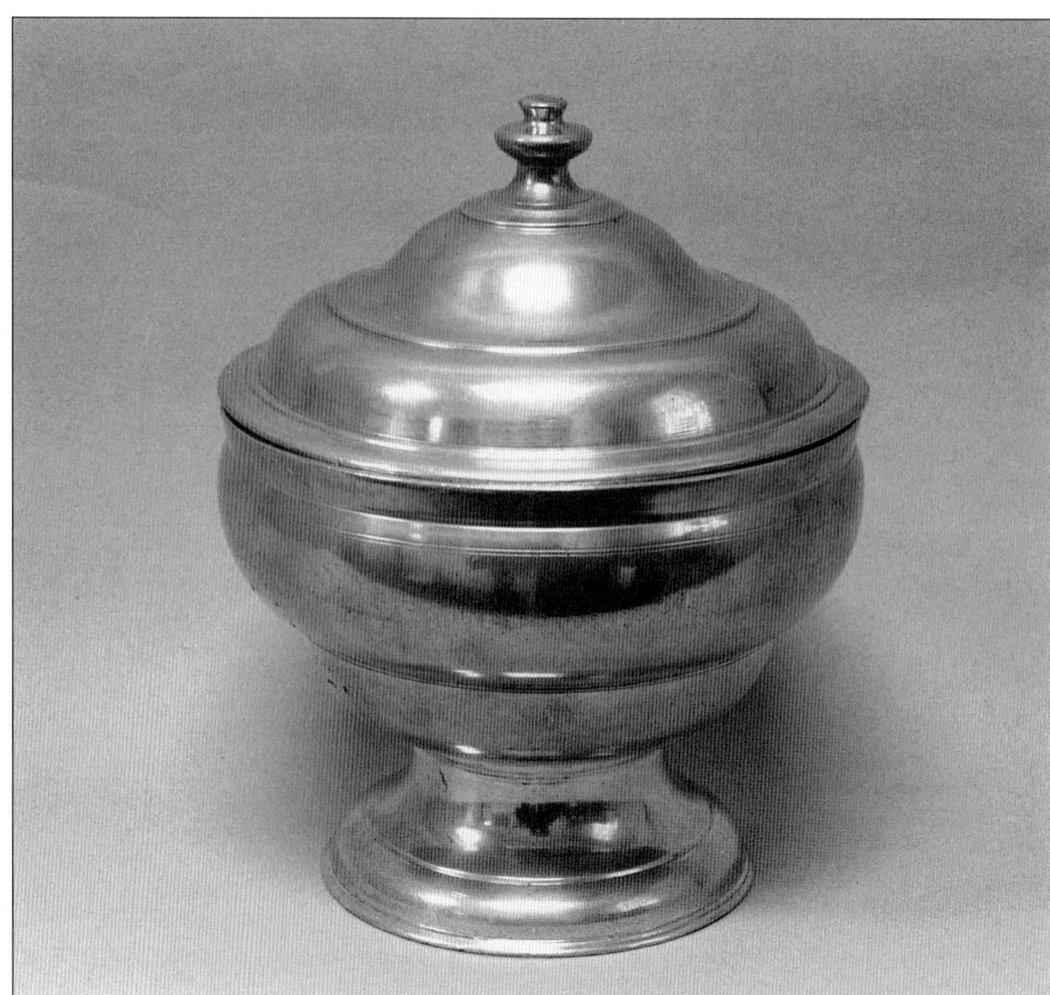

Fig. 135. *Ciborium or sugar bowl by Johann Christoph Heyne, Lancaster Pa., 1752–1781 (L 533). H 5 1/2", TD 4 1/4", BD 3 1/4". Hill Lutheran Church, Cleona, Lebanon County, Pa.*

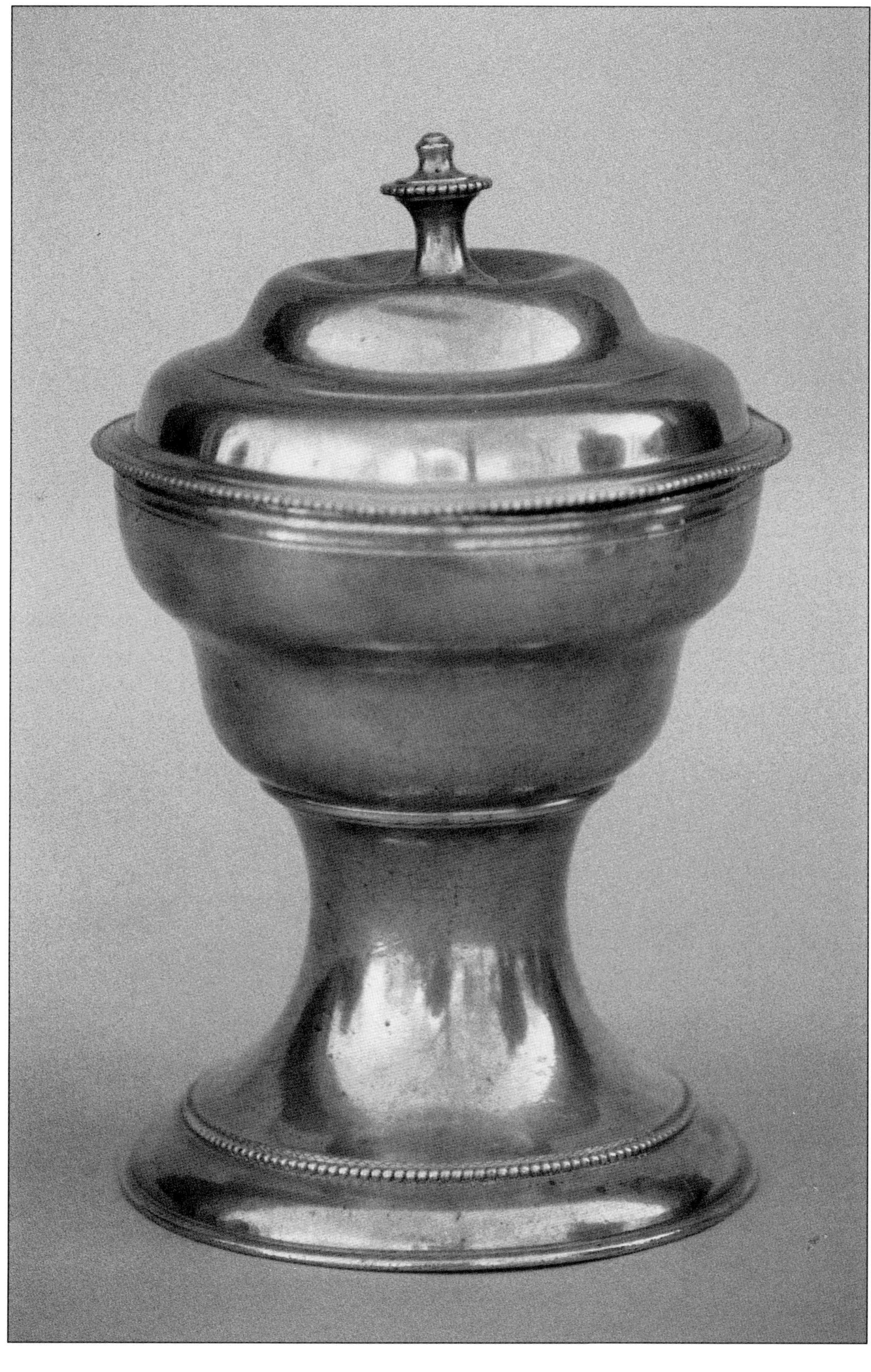

Fig. 136. *Ciborium attributed to William Will, Philadelphia, 1764–1798. H 7 1/8", TD 4 1/4", BD 4 1/8". St. Michael's Lutheran Church, Strasburg, Lancaster County, Pa.*

In the ciborium in Figure 136, the bowl and lid closely resemble the bowls and lids of other pieces that have been attributed to William Will. The attribution is based on a ewer or pitcher having a similar sugar bowl body and marked by William Will.[19] Furthermore the foot of this ciborium matches the feet of a tall pitcher and flagon attributed to Will in the same service.[20]

19. Charles V. Swain, "Varying Forms From One Mold," *Pewter Collectors' Club of America Bulletin,* no. 48 (March 1963):147.

20. Donald M. Herr, "Two More Forms by William Will," *Pewter Collectors' Club of America Bulletin,* no. 67 (December 1972):236, 242.

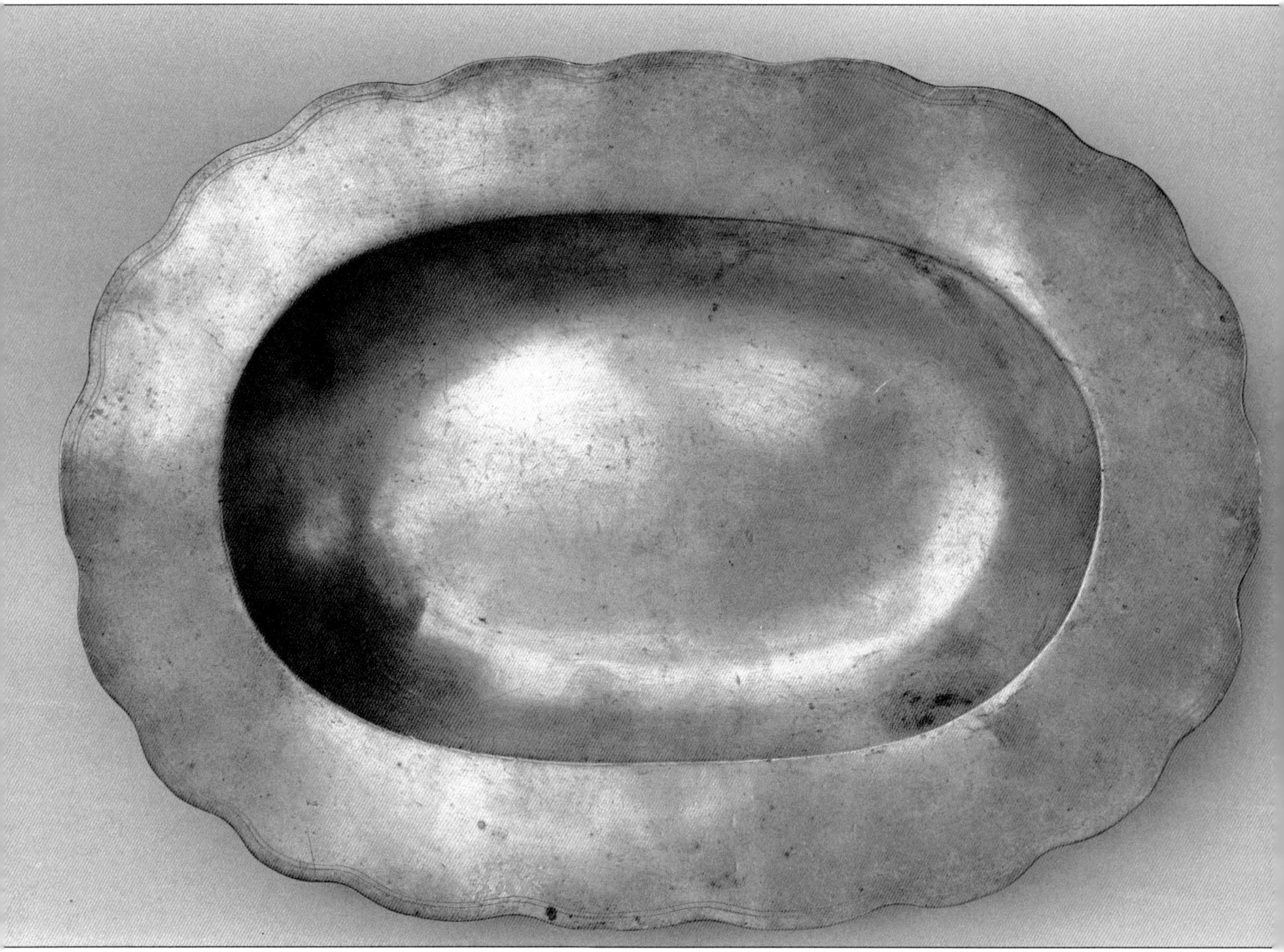

Fig. 137. *Oval dish (above) by John Will, New York, 1752–1774 (L 481,482). H 1 3/8", L 14 1/4", W 10 1/4". Wentz's United Church of Christ, Worcester, Montgomery County, Pa.*

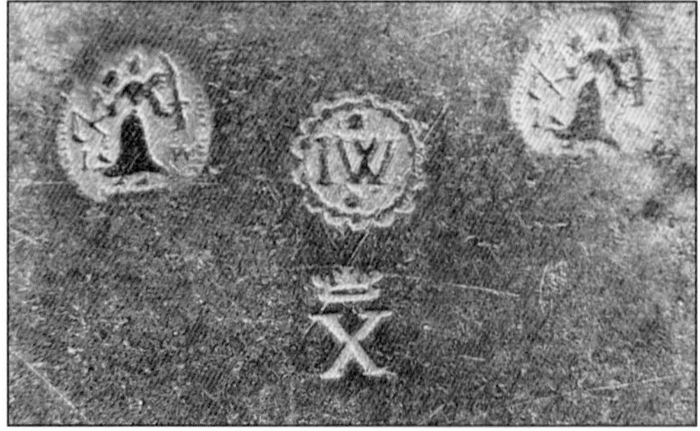

Fig. 138. *John Will's marks (right) struck on the outside bottom of oval dish.*

Dishes and Plates

Dishes and plates were used to hold bread or wafers for the sacrament of communion. Plates larger than ten inches are known as dishes.[21] Deep dishes frequently were used as collection plates and in the absence of basins may have been used to hold water for the sacrament of baptism.

AMERICA

The oval dish by John Will (Figure 137) has a pair of inscribed lines on the top of the rim that follow the contour of the scalloped edge. Its booge is not hammered. The piece is marked on the outside bottom with two IW angel marks and an IW in a circle and his crowned X. This striking oval dish may have been used as a baptismal basin. The church does not own another basin or vessel that may have been used as a baptismal basin. The oval dish also may have been used as a paten or bread plate. Smaller

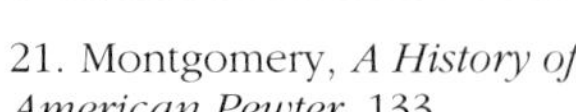

21. Montgomery, *A History of American Pewter*, 133.

plates are owned by the church and were probably used as patens. Published here for the first time, the oval dish is the only known dish of this shape marked by John Will.

The design of the oval dish by William Will (Figure 139) is related to but not the same as the previously mentioned dish by his father, John Will. The scalloped edge and wrigglework decoration of the brim vary from the previous example. William's well-struck mark is located on the top of the brim. The oval dishes appear to be from different forms and were likely special-order items. This oval dish has been previously illustrated.[22] Both oval dishes in the survey were not hammered.

A third oval dish made by an American pewterer does exist. It was formerly in the John W. Poole collection and is now in the Brooklyn Museum. Henry Will of New York City and Albany, a brother of William Will, made the dish. It is 15¼″ in length and 11⅝″ in width. The dimensions of the three oval dishes are dissimilar, and they are not made from the same mold. They may have been special order items.

Oval dishes were made by European pewterers in large quantities and in various sizes. They may have been made on a *"machine a ovale du Potier d'etain"* [pewterer's oval machine] as illustrated in

22. Donald M. Herr, "Communion Services on View at Lancaster," *Pewter Collectors' Club of America Bulletin,* no. 72 (February 1976):83, 95. Also in the Two Hundredth Anniversary and Two Hundred Twenty-Fifth Anniversary publications of the Jerusalem (Red) Church with Lutheran and Reformed congregations, Kempton, Berks County, Pa.

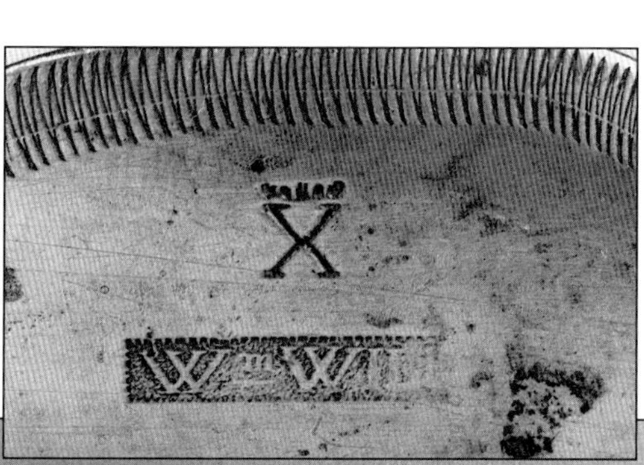

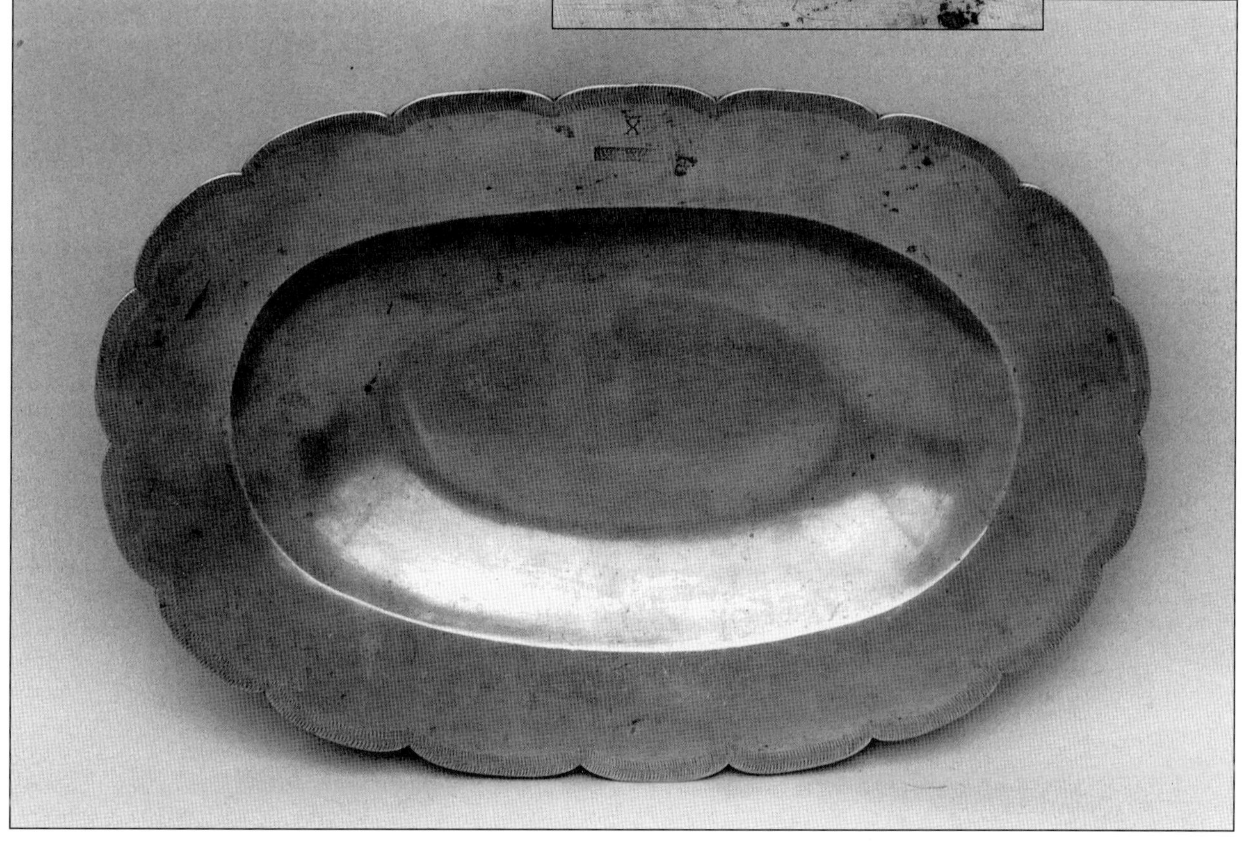

Fig. 139. *Oval dish (bottom) by William Will, Philadelphia, 1764–1798 (L 538, 539). H 1⅝″, L 15½″, W 10½″, Brim 2″. Jerusalem (Red) Union Church with Lutheran and United Church of Christ congregations, Kempton, Berks County, Pa.*

Fig. 140. *William Will's mark (left) on upper brim of dish. Note the wrigglework engraving used as a decorative treatment near the edge of dish.*

eighteenth-century French publications by Diderot and Plumier.[23]

The unusual form of the footed plate that is embellished with an applied edge in Figure 141 further attests to the design capabilities and craftsmanship of William Will. The three ball-and-claw feet on this footed plate, or paten, are similar to those found on teapots marked by William Will. Will is the only American pewterer known to have used the ball-and-claw foot design. The footed plate was probably used as a paten. It is inscribed *"Mat. Culp Vor den Gebrauch der Reformirten Gemein in Heitelberg"* [Matthias Culp for the use of the Reformed congregation in Heidelberg].

Unmarked but definitely attributed to William Will, the paten in Figure 142 has four ball-and-claw feet from the same

23. Roland G. Cortelyou, Jr., "The Pewterers' Oval Machine," *Pewter Collectors' Club of America Bulletin*, no. 103 (December 1991):73. See Denis Diderot et al., *Encyclopedia, Dictionaire des Sciences, Recueil des Planches sur les Sciences, les Arts Libereaux, et les Arts Mechaniques*. Paris, Briasson, et al. (1762-1777), Plate 31, fig. 15; Charles Plumier, and Paul H. Ferraglio, ed. and trans., L'Art De Tourner (Brooklyn, N.Y.: Ferraglio, 1975) from original work published at Paris by Jombert in 1749.

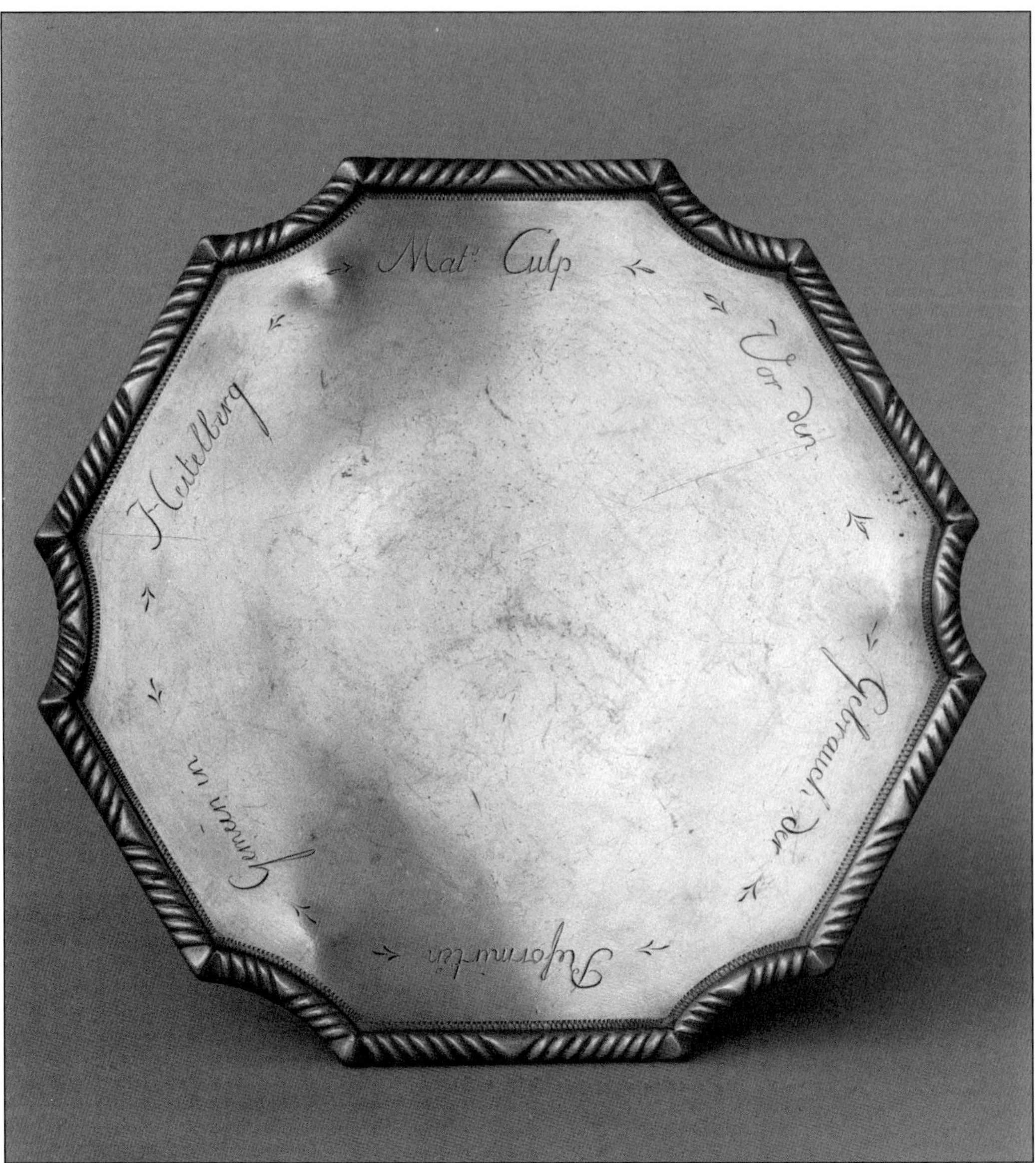

Fig. 141. *Footed plate attributed to William Will, Philadelphia, 1764–1798. H5/8", TD 9". Heidelberg Union Church with Lutheran and United Church of Christ congregations, Slatington, Lehigh County, Pa.*

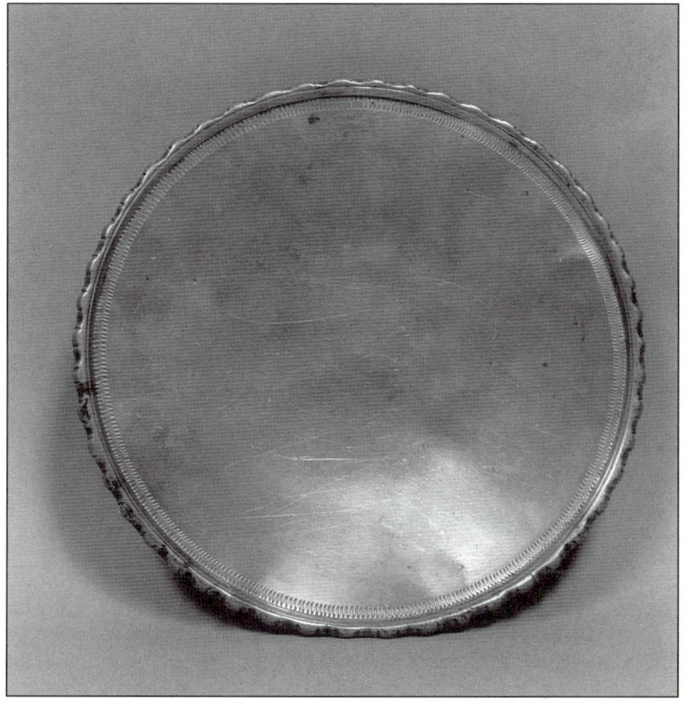

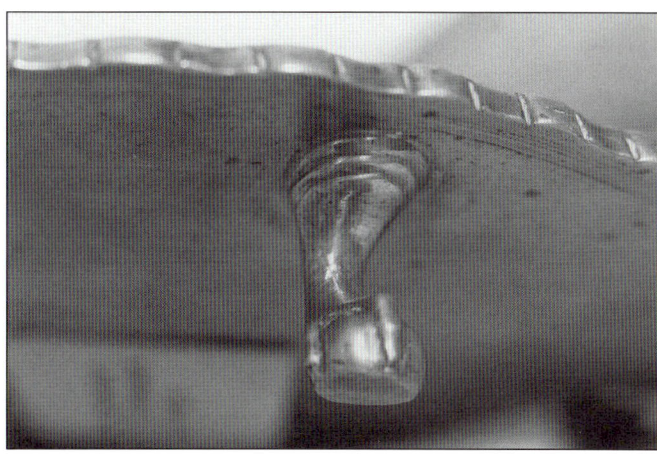

Fig. 142. *Footed plate (left) attributed to William Will, Philadelphia, 1764–1798. H 1 1/4″, TD 9 1/2″. Zion Evangelical and Reformed United Church of Christ, Hagerstown, Washington County, Md.*

Fig. 143. *Detail (above) of ball-and-claw foot on plate.*

mold as the previous example. The scalloped edge appears to be applied and the paten probably was a special-order item. Note the zigzag engraving around the top of the plate, a type of decoration that Will frequently used.

The plate in Figure 144 has four ball-and-claw feet similar to the previous examples. It is attributed to William Will and accompanies a flagon attributed to Will. Both are inscribed *"Vor Die Revormierte Gemein in Weisenburg & Lowhill"* [For the Reformed Congregation in Weisenburg and Lowhill]. The multiple-reeded edge of the plate is beaded and joins the profuse wrigglework and straight-line engraving.

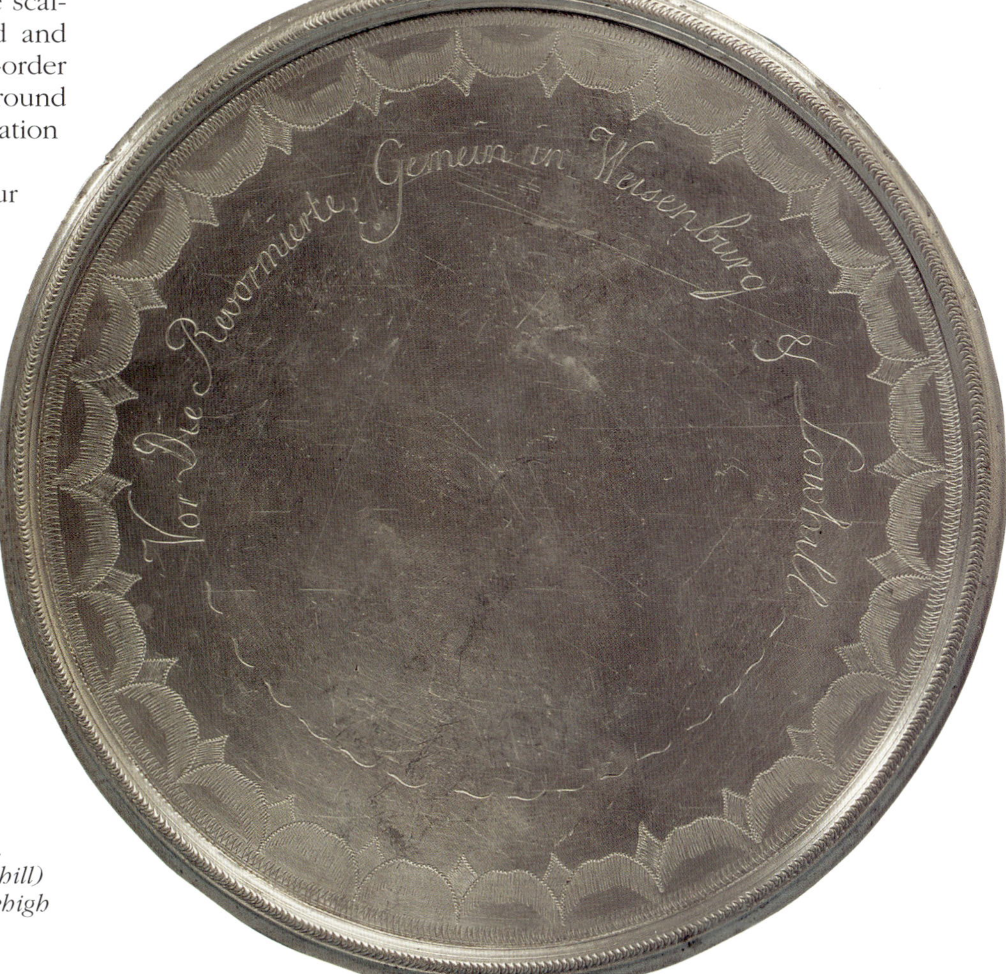

Fig. 144. *Footed plate attributed to William Will, Philadelphia, 1764–1798. H 1 1/8″, TD 9 3/4″. Christ's Church (Lowhill) United Church of Christ, New Tripoli, Lehigh County, Pa.*

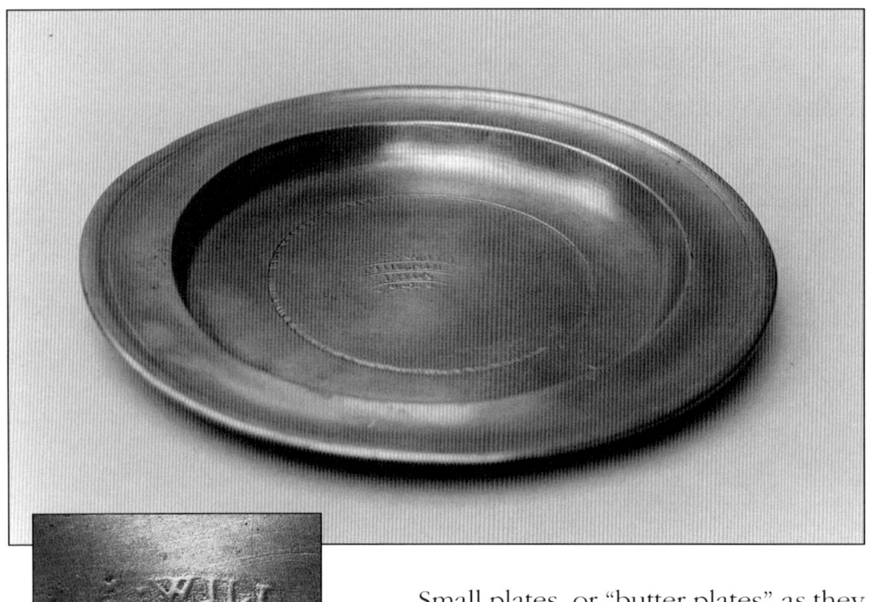

Fig. 145. *Plate (above top) by William Will, Philadelphia, 1764–1798 (L 534). TD 6 1/4″. Zion's (Stone) United Church of Christ, Northampton, Northampton County, Pa.*

Fig. 146. *William Will, Philadelphia mark (above) on plate.*

Small plates, or "butter plates" as they were called in early advertisements, were frequently used as patens. In *The Pennsylvania Gazette* for November 25, 1772, Lancaster pewterer Johann Christoph Heyne advertised, "He also makes himself many sorts of Pewterer's work such as small butter-plates. . . ." The small plate in Figure 145 is marked by William Will.

Domestic plates and dishes of various sizes were used as patens in Pennsylvania German churches. The most popular size made by American pewterers was in the eight-inch range. An example by Blakeslee Barnes is illustrated in Figure 147.

BRITISH ISLES

Smooth-brim or flat-rim plates, as in the British example by Francis Piggott in Figure 148, were not as frequently found in the survey as the more commonly found single-reeded plate.

CONTINENTAL EUROPE

Germany

The dish by German pewterer Johann Dietrich Finck in Figure 150 has two rows of cast decoration. The raised gadrooning on the rim and inside bottom was a product of the design in the mold. This type of decoration was favored by pewterers on the Continent. The dish may have been used as a baptismal basin. The church also owns an unmarked small plate that probably was used as a paten.

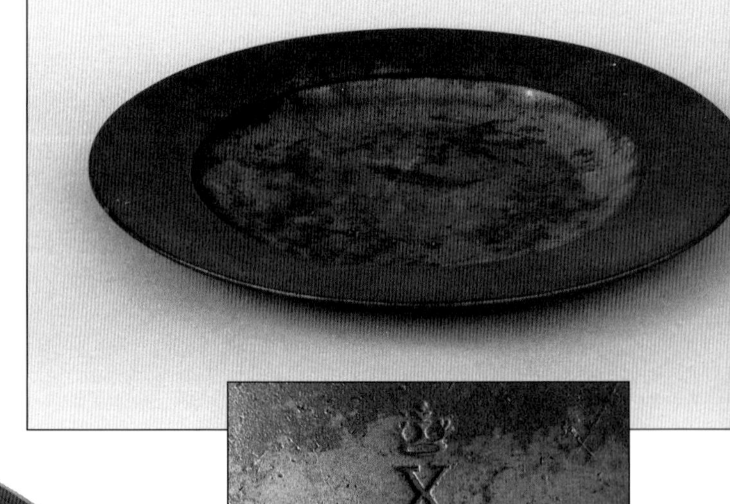

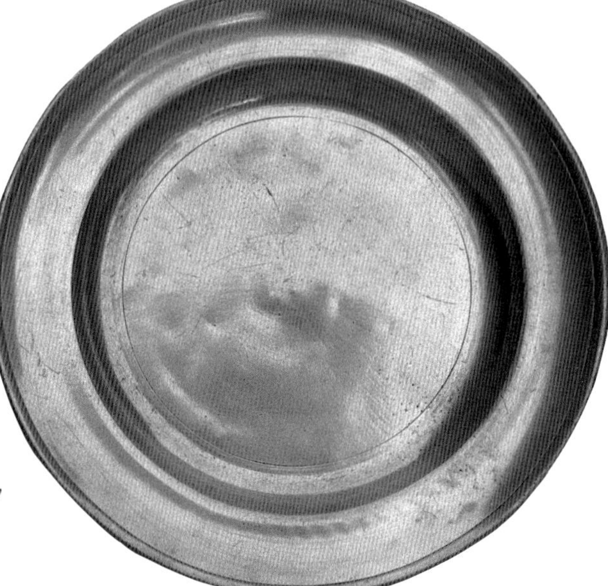

Fig. 147. *Plate by Blakeslee Barnes, Philadelphia, 1812–1817 (L 556). TD 7 7/8″. Emmanuel Lutheran Church, Pottstown, Montgomery County, Pa.*

Fig. 148. *Plate (above top) by Francis Piggott, London, 1738–1773 (C 3682). TD 9 3/4″. Jordan Lutheran Church, Orefield, Lehigh County, Pa.*

Fig. 149. *Mark (above) of Francis Piggott.*

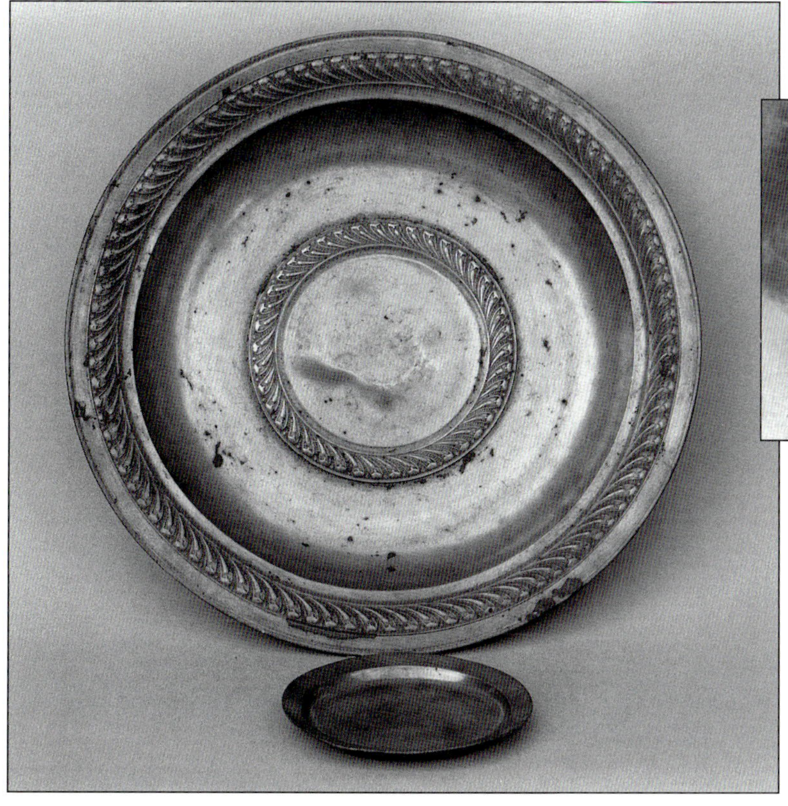

Fig. 150. Dish (left) by Johann Dietrich Finck, Bamberg, Germany, circa 1731 (H 5, fig. 387). TD 12 5/8″. Unmarked plate 4 3/8″. St. Michael's Lutheran Church, Germantown, Philadelphia Co., Pa.

Fig. 151. Mark (above) of Johann Dietrich Finck.

Fig. 152. Ewer (below) attributed to John Will, New York, 1752–1774. H 9 1/8″, TD 3 3/8″, BD 3 3/8″. Wentz's United Church of Christ, Worcester, Montgomery County, Pa.

Dishes and plates marked by pewterers from the Netherlands and Switzerland were not found in the survey.

Ewers and Pitchers

A ewer is a vessel for holding liquid. It has a handle and a lip or spout with a wide mouth. A pitcher frequently has a narrow spout. The terms "ewer" and "pitcher" are interchangeable. Both vessels could accommodate wine or water. Only American ewers and pitchers were found in the survey.

AMERICA

John Will used a low beaker mold with flared foot to form the upper portion of the body of his ewer illustrated in Figure 152. An example of a beaker of this form is in the collection of the Yale University Art Gallery, New Haven, Connecticut.[24] John Will elongated the lip of his beaker and made a spout for ease of pouring. He also added a strap handle to its body. This ewer, found in a set with three other John Will pieces, is the only ewer known to the author that can be attributed to John Will with confidence.

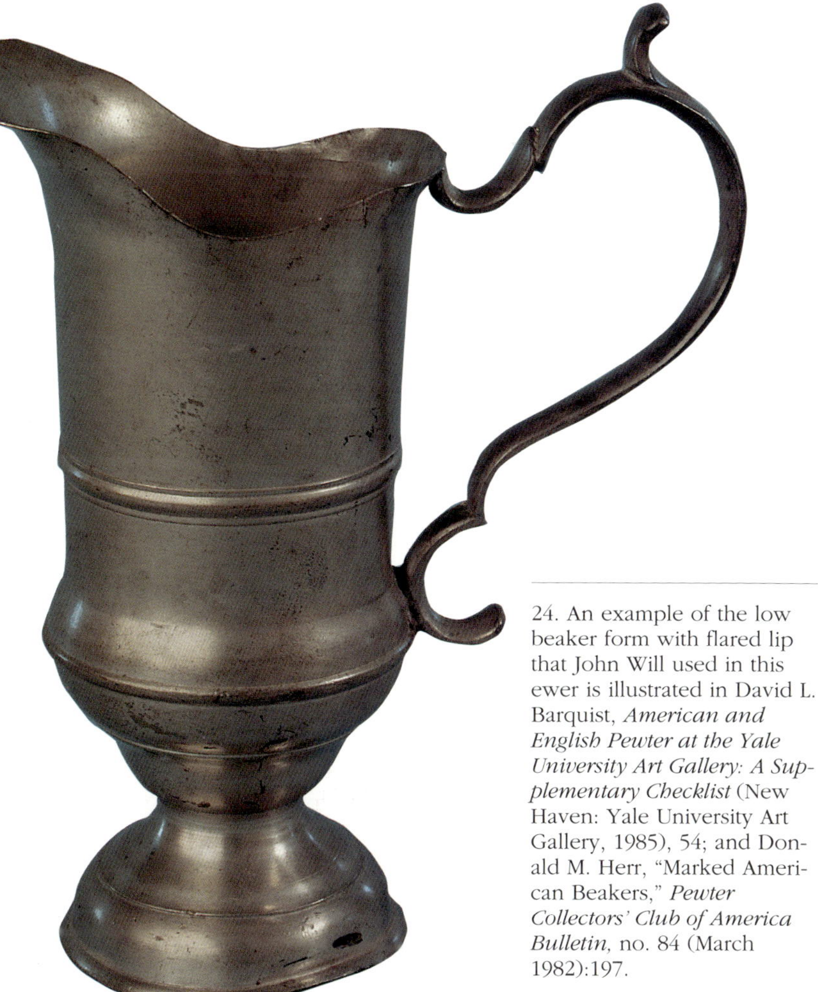

24. An example of the low beaker form with flared lip that John Will used in this ewer is illustrated in David L. Barquist, *American and English Pewter at the Yale University Art Gallery: A Supplementary Checklist* (New Haven: Yale University Art Gallery, 1985), 54; and Donald M. Herr, "Marked American Beakers," *Pewter Collectors' Club of America Bulletin,* no. 84 (March 1982):197.

Fig. 153. *Pitcher attributed to Johann Philip Alberti, Philadelphia, 1754–1780. H 6 1/2″, TD 3 1/2″, BD 5″. Boehms Reformed United Church of Christ, Blue Bell, Montgomery County, Pa.*

The addition of a spout of Germanic design to a quart mug of English fashion (Figure 153) provides an example of the assimilation of cultures in this unusual form. The spout design appears to be an abbreviation of the spout used on Alberti's flagon found in the survey (Figure 166). It is strongly Germanic in form and would have been familiar to pewterers working on the Continent. The handle design with hooded bud terminal, the low body fillet, and the shape of the foot

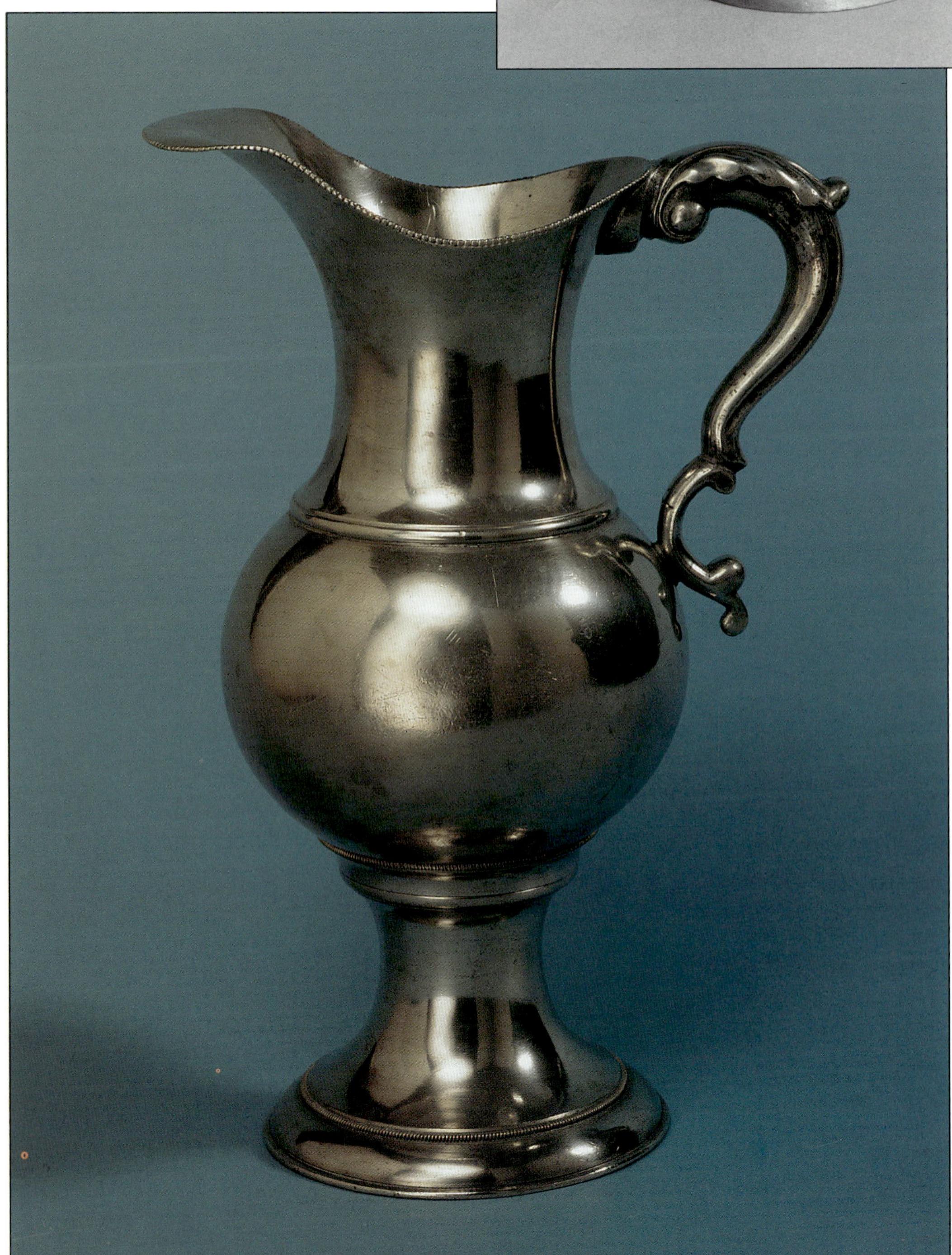

Fig. 154. *Ewer attributed to William Will, Philadelphia, 1764–1798. H 10 3/4″, TD 3 1/4″, BD 4 1/4″. Egypt United Church of Christ, Whitehall, Lehigh County, Pa.*

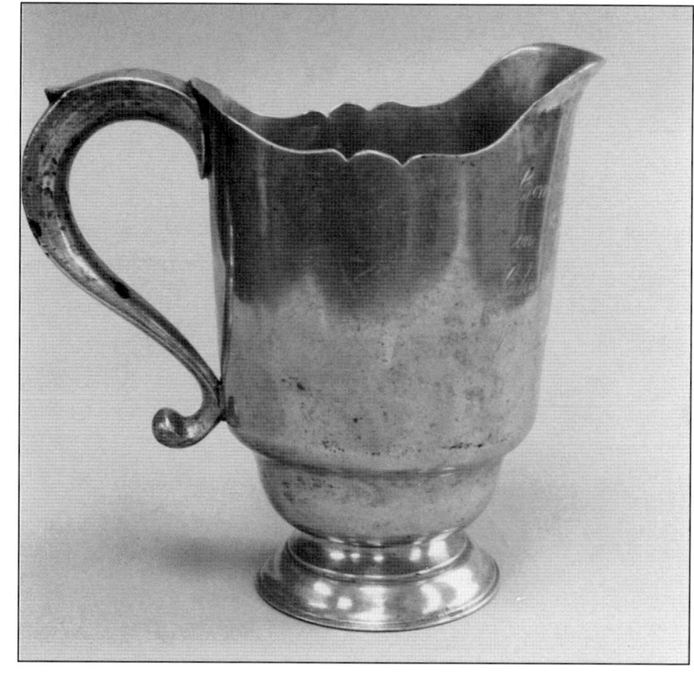

are similar to those on the marked Alberti pint mug found in the survey (Figure 217). These English design elements were popular with Philadelphia pewterers working in the second half of the eighteenth century.

The acanthus-leaf decoration on the double-C scrolled handle and beading on the lip, body, and base enhance the clean symmetry of the ewer in Figure 154. It is one of the most attractive forms of American pewter. Four ewers, or pitchers, of this style were found in the survey; this doubles the number of previously known ewers of this form made by William Will.[25] All four ewers are owned by Pennsylvania German congregations, three ewers by Lutheran congregations, the fourth by a United Church of Christ congregation.

In Figure 155, Will added a spout to the lip of a quart tulip-shaped mug to form a vessel that poured more easily. Note the crenated edge treatment of the lip of the pitcher. Wrigglework ornamentation around the top, base, and handle attachment is similar to that on the oval dish marked by William Will and owned by the same church.

A sugar bowl was used to form the base of the ewer illustrated in Figure 157. The body has been extended and the lip received the undulating treatment similar to the previous ewer. The ewer has been attributed to William Will because he used a similar edge treatment on a few creamers that bear his marks. The bowl is a form that has been attributed to Will. A quart mug handle was used on this version of the ewer.

Fig. 157. *Pitcher attributed to William Will, Philadelphia, 1764–1798. H 7″, TD 4 1/4″, BD 3 1/4″. Blaser's Reformed (now Christ Church United Church of Christ), Elizabethtown, Lancaster County, Pa. The pitcher is at the Evangelical and Reformed Historical Society of the United Church of Christ, Lancaster, Pa.*

25. Two ewers of this form attributed to William Will were exhibited at the October 14, 1972, Pennsylvania Regional Group meeting of the Pewter Collectors' Club of America held at Trinity Lutheran Church in Lancaster, Pa. See *Pewter Collectors' Club of America Bulletin* no. 8 (December 1972):235, 238.

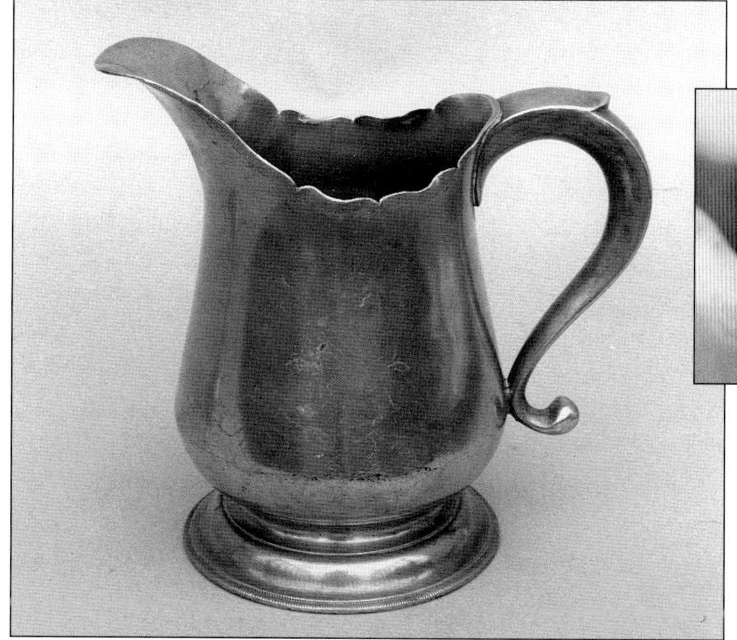

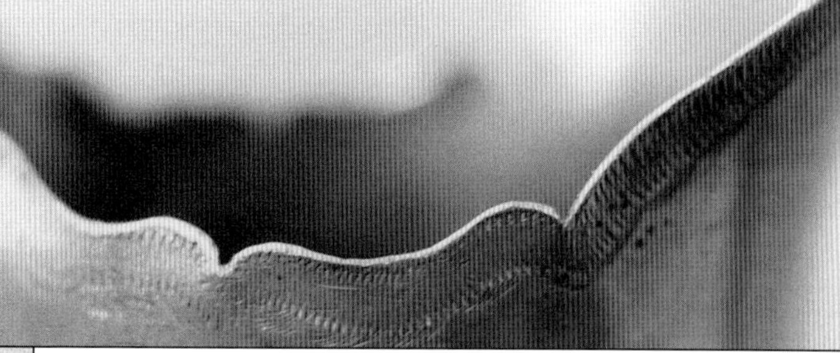

Fig. 155. *Ewer (left) attributed to William Will, Philadelphia, 1764–1798. H 7″, TD 3 3/8″, BD 4 1/4″. Jerusalem (Red) Union Church with Lutheran and United Church of Christ congregations, Kempton, Berks County, Pa.*

Fig. 156. *Detail (above) of wrigglework engraving on lip of ewer.*

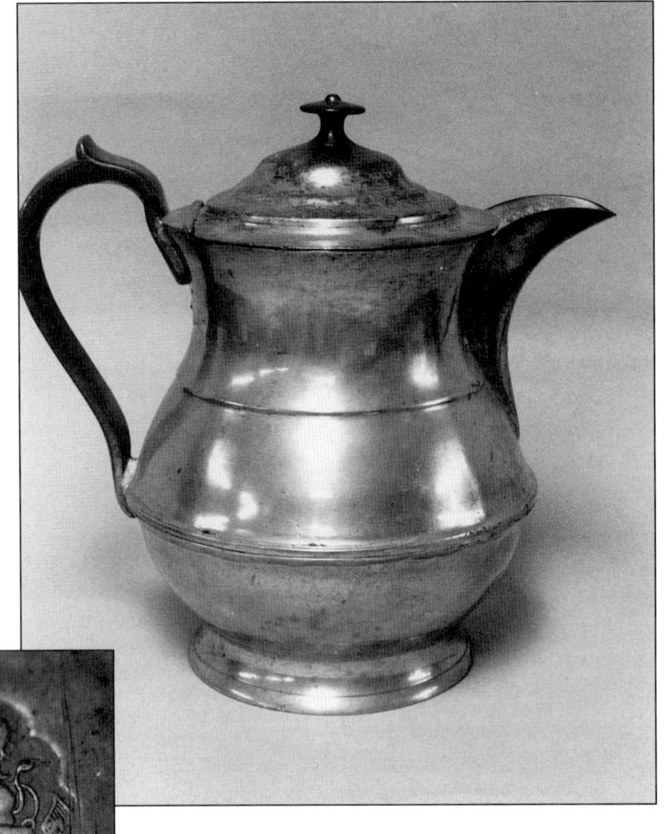

Fig. 158. *Pitcher (above right) by the Boardmans, Hartford, Conn., 1804–1873 (L 435). H 10 1/4″, TD 5 7/8″, BD 5 1/2″. Salem (Heller's) United Church of Christ, Leola, Lancaster County, Pa.*

Fig. 159. *Boardman lion mark (above) on covered pitcher.*

Commonly used in the home, pitchers of nineteenth-century form occasionally found use in the church. The Boardman lion mark is found on the outside bottom of the covered gallon pitcher in Figure 158.

Flagons

Flagons are frequently listed in seventeenth-century inventories. In paintings of that period, they are found being used in the home. They were presumably used to bring liquids to the table. Engravings and prints of the same period likewise confirm their use in the church. The vessels were used to hold unconsecrated wine that filled chalices or cups at the communion table. Home and church use was the norm on both the Continent and in the British Isles. In the early years of the next century, the use of flagons appears to have been increasingly restricted to church usage. Most flagons made in the eighteenth century by American pewterers have a history of church usage.

AMERICA

The extraordinary piece of pewter in Figure 160 functioned as a flagon in a church. Its body is distinctly Continental in form. A flagon with the same body form but having a spout and lid has been found marked by John Will.[26] Upon his arrival in New York City, Will probably continued to make those shapes with which he had been familiar in his native Herborn, Germany. But he was quick to adapt to current tastes and styles. His foliate finial and his swan-neck spout rising from a rococo cartouche and capped by a leaf relate directly to coffeepots made by New York silversmiths such as Myer Myers, ca. 1750–1760 (Figure 161).[27] The foliate finial design is found on British and Philadelphia silver coffeepots. The finial and distinctive handle design were likewise used by John Will's pewterer sons William and Philip. John Will's coffeepot is the earliest surviving eighteenth-century coffeepot of American origin and, so far as the author knows, the only surviving example made by a New York pewterer.

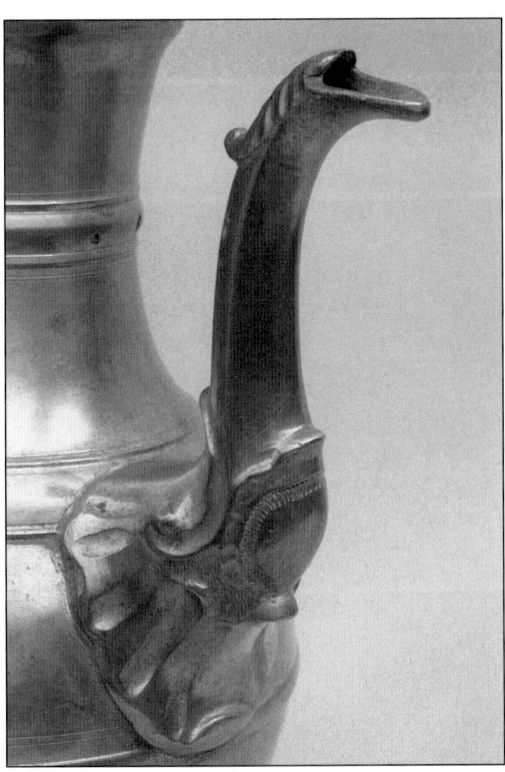

Fig. 161. *Detail of rococo design and cartouche on spout, an unusual treatment for an eighteenth-century American pewter tea or coffeepot. Wentz's United Church of Christ, Worcester, Montgomery County, Pa.*

26. Charles V. Swain, "Three Flagons Attributed to John Will," in *American and British Pewter: An Historic Survey*, ed. John Carl Thomas (N.Y.: Universe Books, 1976), 89. Reprinted from *The Magazine Antiques*, May 1972.

27. Sotheby's auction catalogue for June 23, 1988, item 244, illustrates a silver coffeepot by Myer Meyers with similar design elements.

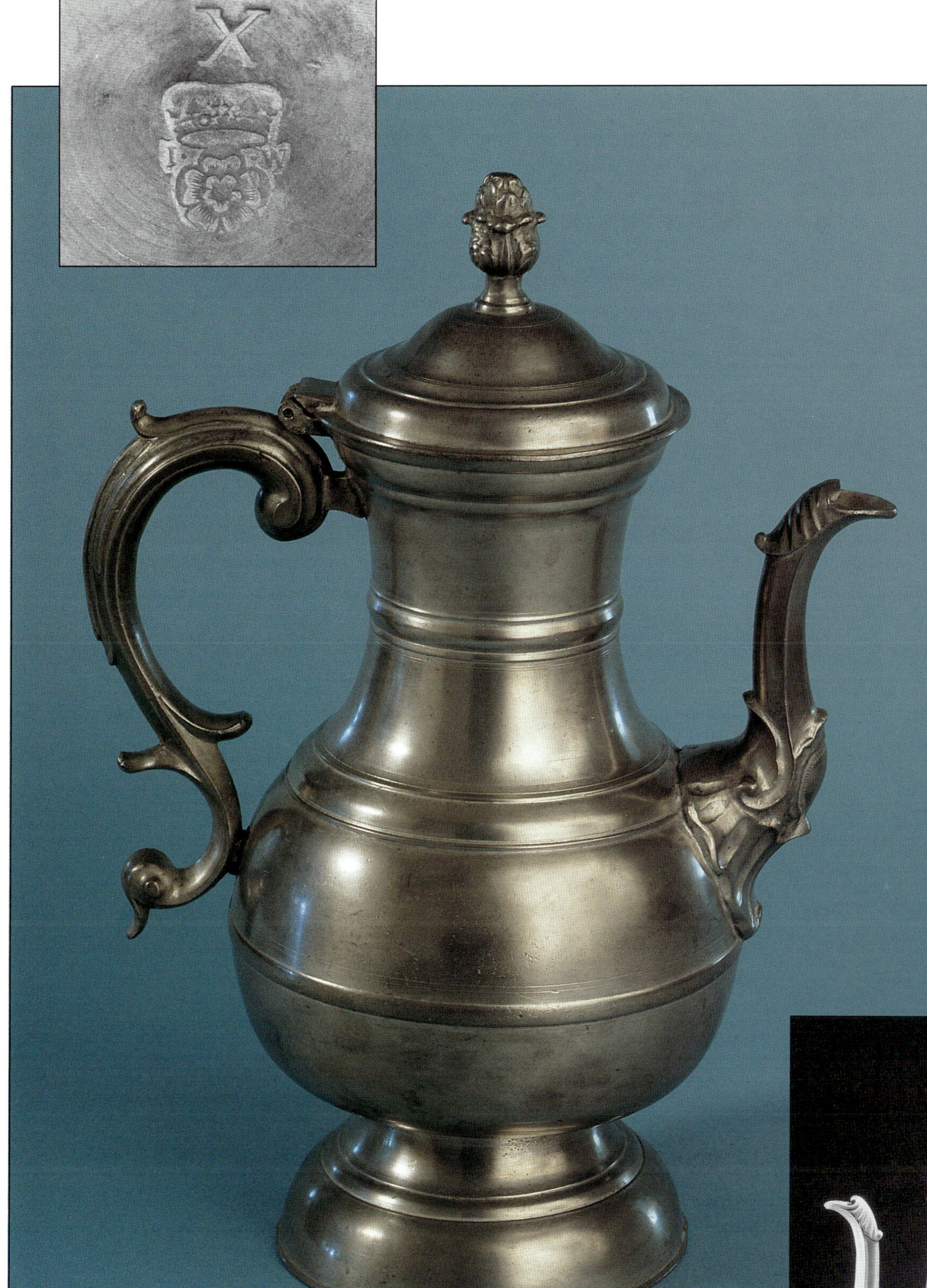

Fig. 163. *Silver coffeepot (below) by Myer Myers, New York, ca. 1750–1760. Photo courtesy of Sotheby's, New York City.*

Fig. 160. *Flagon or coffeepot (above) by John Will, New York, 1752–1774 (L 479). H 13$\frac{3}{8}$″, TD 4$\frac{1}{8}$″, BD 5″. Wentz's United Church of Christ, Worcester, Montgomery County, Pa.*

Fig. 162. *John Will's well-struck marks (top) on outside bottom of coffeepot used as a flagon.*

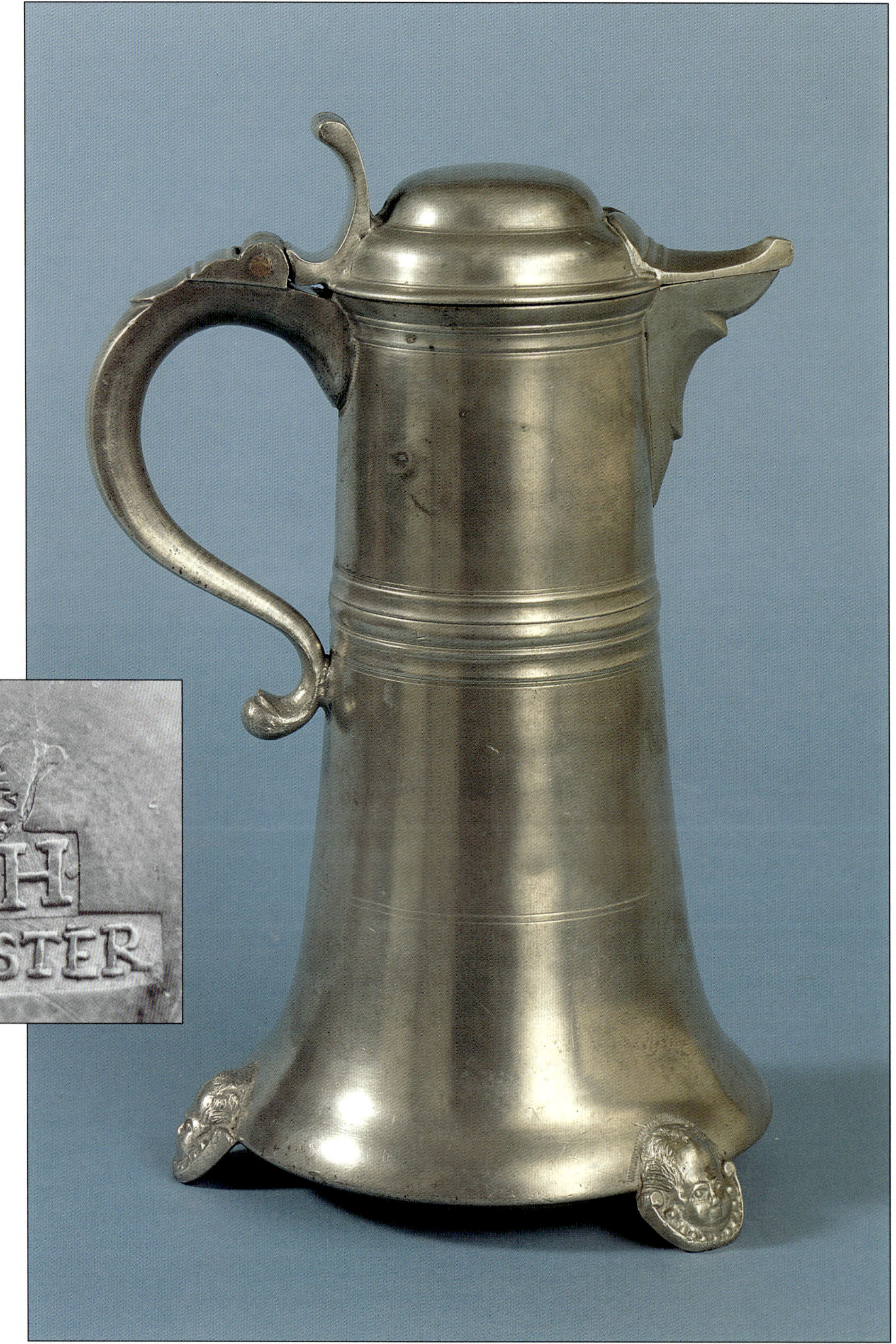

Fig. 164. *Flagon by Johann Christoph Heyne, Lancaster, Pa., 1752–1781 (L 530,532). H 11 3/8", TD 3 1/2", BD 6". Zion Lutheran Church, Hummelstown, Dauphin County, Pa.*

Fig. 165. *Johann Christoph Heyne's marks on the outside bottom of the above flagon. Zion Lutheran Church, Hummelstown, Dauphin County, Pa.*

Heyne's splendid flagons with their strongly Germanic elements of cherub's head feet, flaring base, and upturned lid and spout, combined with cast hollow English handles, are pointed examples of the cultural assimilation of styles (Figure 164). A few Heyne flagons can be seen in museums but they are rare in private collections. Fourteen Heyne flagons were found in the survey.

The Germanic elements of a ball-shaped thumbpiece, heavy lidded spout, and bulbous body, combined with such English features as a double-C scrolled handle with hooded terminal, are found in the flagon illustrated in Figure 166. A sugar bowl body is incorporated in the lower portion of the belly. A mark with a lamb and the letters ALB appear in the inside bottom of the flagon. The mark is that of Johann Philip Alberti.[28] The flagon is the only known flagon marked by this maker. Alberti arrived in Philadelphia on a ship from Hamburg but his flagon belies his background. He may have added a handle of English design to satisfy his Philadelphia customers.

Fig. 168. *Mark on inside bottom of Alberti flagon.*

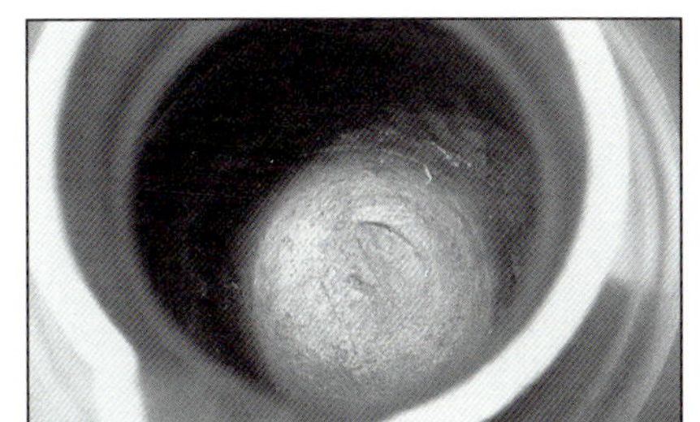

28. The mark on the flagon is not the same mark illustrated in Melvyn D. Wolf, "A Tankard by Johann Philip Alberti," in *Pewter Collectors' Club of America Bulletin,* no. 94-95 (March-September 1987):107. It is not the mark illustrated in Bette and Melvyn D. Wolf, "Johann Philip Alberti," in Bulletin no. 84 (March 1982):178.

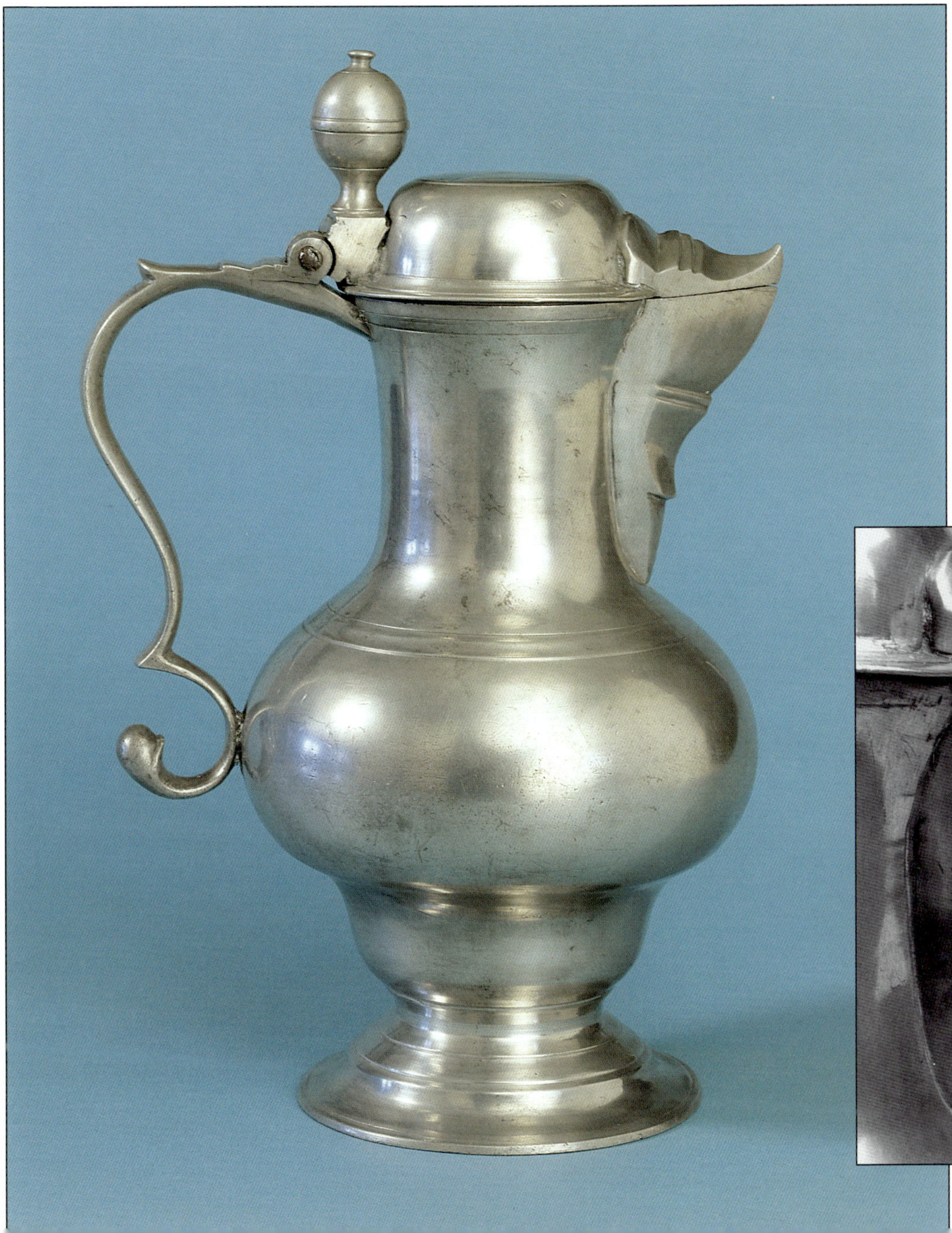

Fig. 166. *Flagon (left) by Johann Philip Alberti, Philadelphia, 1754–1780. H 13", TD 3¾", BD 5". Emmanuel Lutheran Church, Pottstown, Montgomery County, Pa.*

Fig. 167. *Detail (below) of spout of Germanic design on Alberti flagon. Alberti used the same spout design on his pitcher (Fig. 153).*

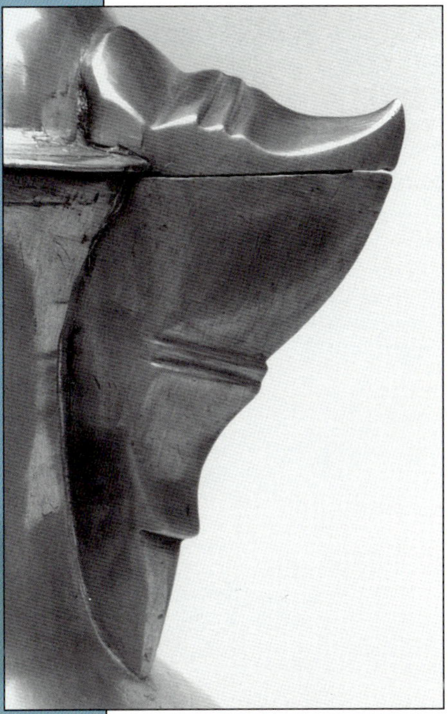

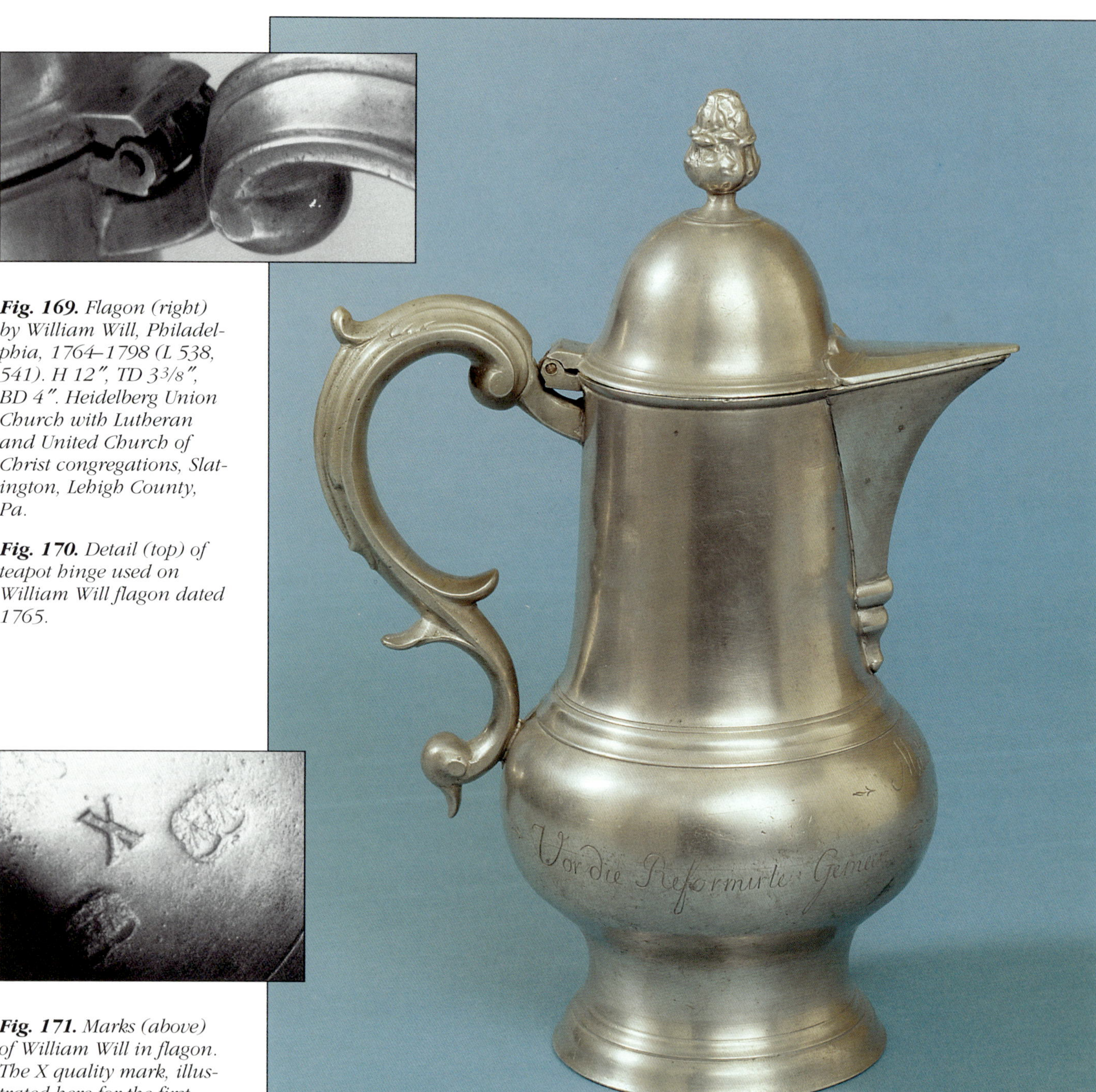

Fig. 169. *Flagon (right) by William Will, Philadelphia, 1764–1798 (L 538, 541). H 12", TD 3³/8", BD 4". Heidelberg Union Church with Lutheran and United Church of Christ congregations, Slatington, Lehigh County, Pa.*

Fig. 170. *Detail (top) of teapot hinge used on William Will flagon dated 1765.*

Fig. 171. *Marks (above) of William Will in flagon. The X quality mark, illustrated here for the first time, probably was used early in Will's career. It is not the same mark as his more frequently found X quality mark with a crown.*

Without question, no Colonial American pewterer equaled the variety of forms or had greater ability to make new designs from existing molds than the Pennsylvania German pewterer William Will. The following nine flagons attest to the ingenuity of this master craftsman. Arranged according to engraved dates, they allow us to study the evolution of his flagon form. Six of the flagons are published here for the first time.

The use of a pint mug for the body and a chalice cup for the lid is a testament to the originality of William Will (Figure 169). Used on this flagon was a teapot hinge, much like his father, John Will, used on a coffeepot/flagon and at least one other flagon.[29] The foliate finial and ornate handle design were used by his brother Philip and father John—they must have shared the same molds. Dated 1765, the flagon was made early in his career. He was working in Philadelphia in 1764 and died there in 1798.

29. In a telephone conversation with the author, March 11, 1994, John Carl Thomas reported having seen a John Will flagon with a teapot hinge.

In an apparent embellishing of the preceding flagon in Figure 169, William Will added a chair-back thumbpiece that appears to have little function, substituted an English-style handle, and enlarged the body and flare of the foot of this version (Figure 172). It bears the inscription R. B. 1765.

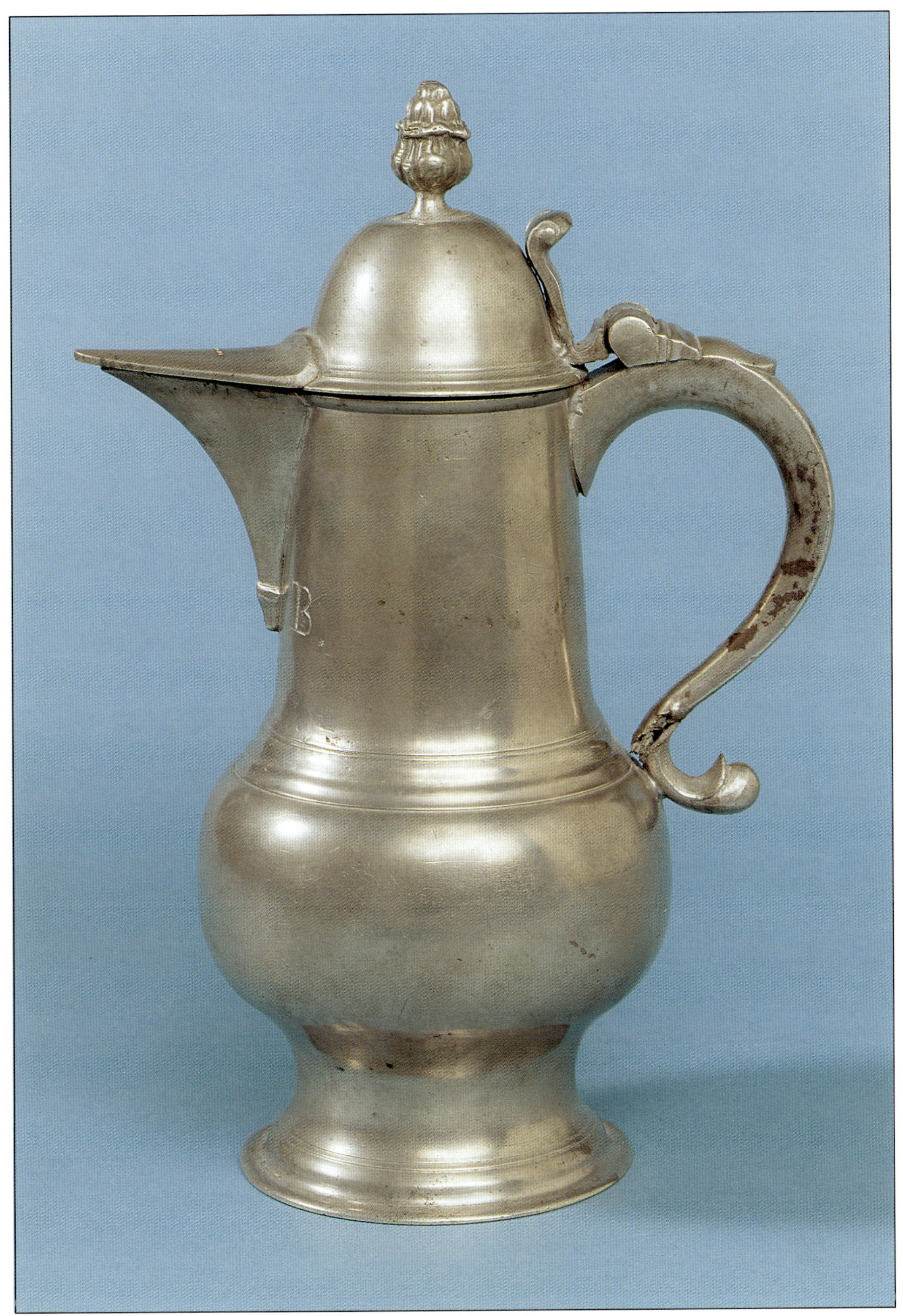

Fig. 172. *Flagon by William Will, Philadelphia, 1764–1798 (L 539). H 12 1/2", TD 3 3/8". BD 4 3/8". Bergstrasse Lutheran Church, Ephrata, Lancaster County, Pa.*

In the example in Figure 173, William Will used a similar spout design, elongated the English-style handle, rounded the middle, and used a quart tankard for the top portion and lid of the flagon. The flagon is taller than the previous example (Figure 172), though it is missing its finial.

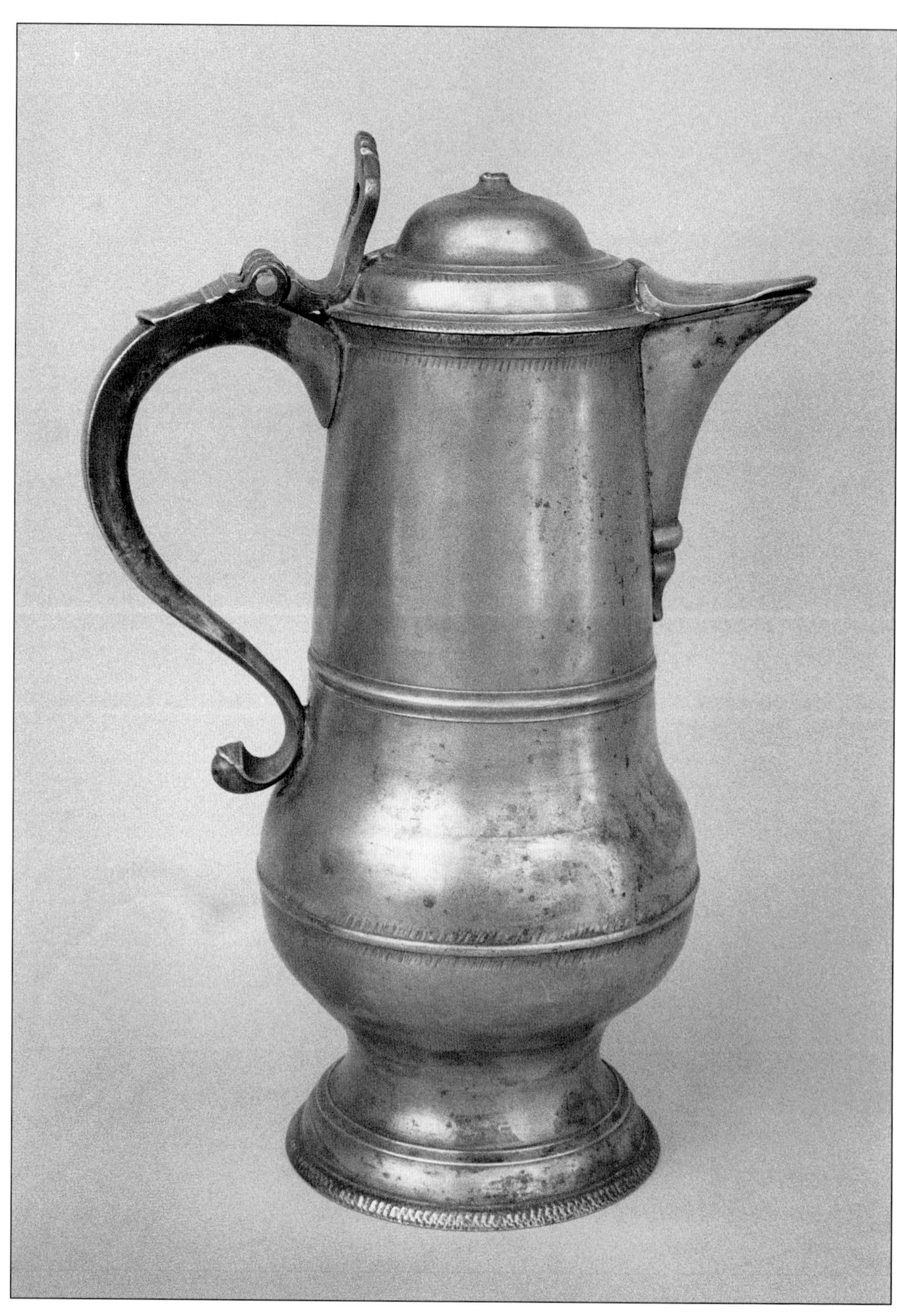

Fig. 173. *Flagon by William Will, Philadelphia, 1764–1798 (L 541). H 12¾", TD 3⅞", BD 4¾". St. Peter's Lutheran Church, North Wales, Montgomery County, Pa.*

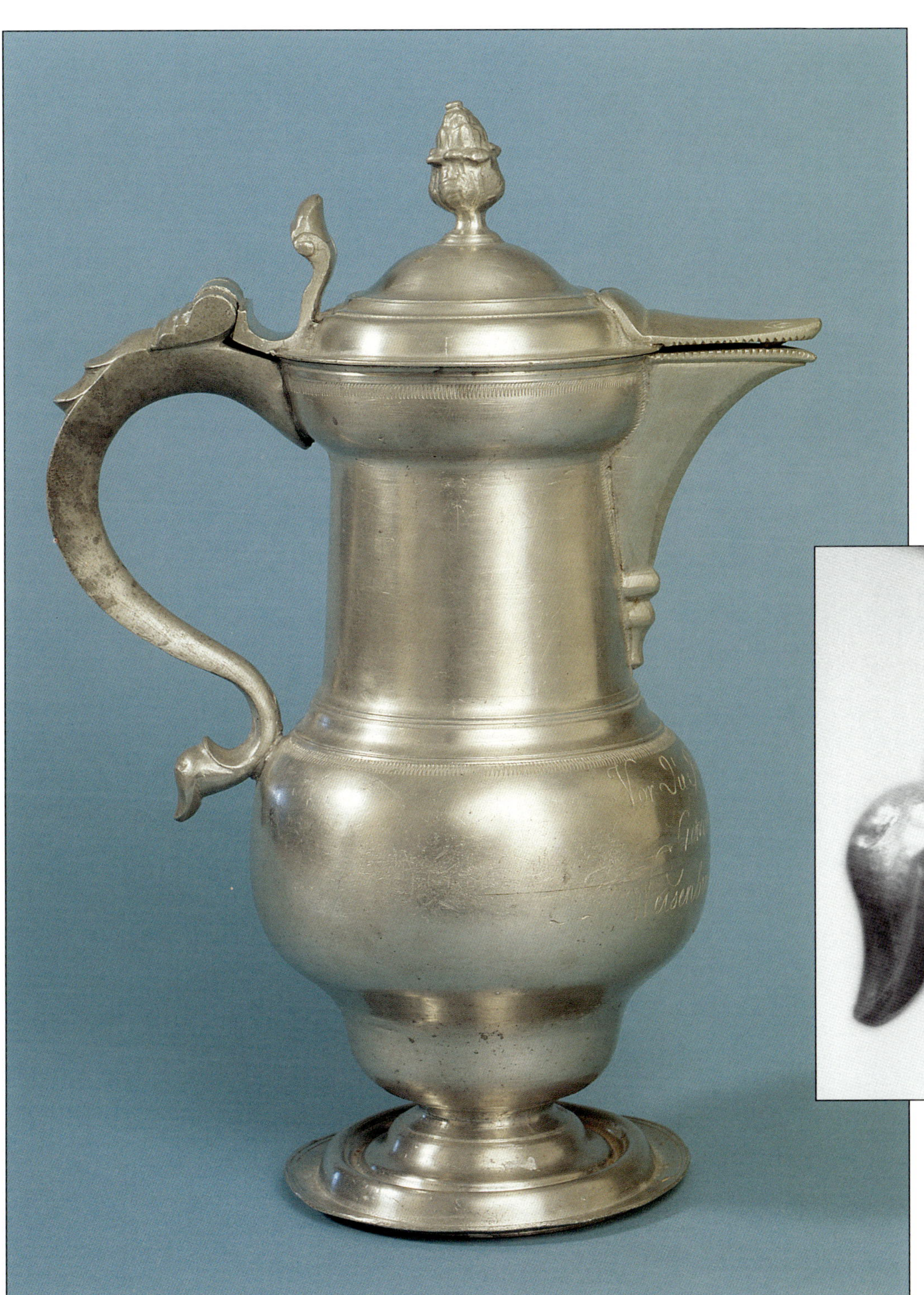

Fig. 174. *Flagon attributed to William Will, Philadelphia, 1764–1798. H 12³/₈", TD 4³/₈", BD 4⁵/₈". Christ's Church (Lowhill) United Church of Christ, New Tripoli, Lehigh County, Pa.*

Fig. 175. *Detail: "Duck's head" handle terminal.*

In Figure 174, William Will made the upper belly by using the inverted mold technique that included a pair of six-inch basins. A sugar bowl body was used to complete the lower belly, and a sugar bowl lid is the foot of the flagon. Will embellished the thumbpiece, handle, and handle terminal more than in Figure 172. The flagon is undated but is stylistically related to the following examples.

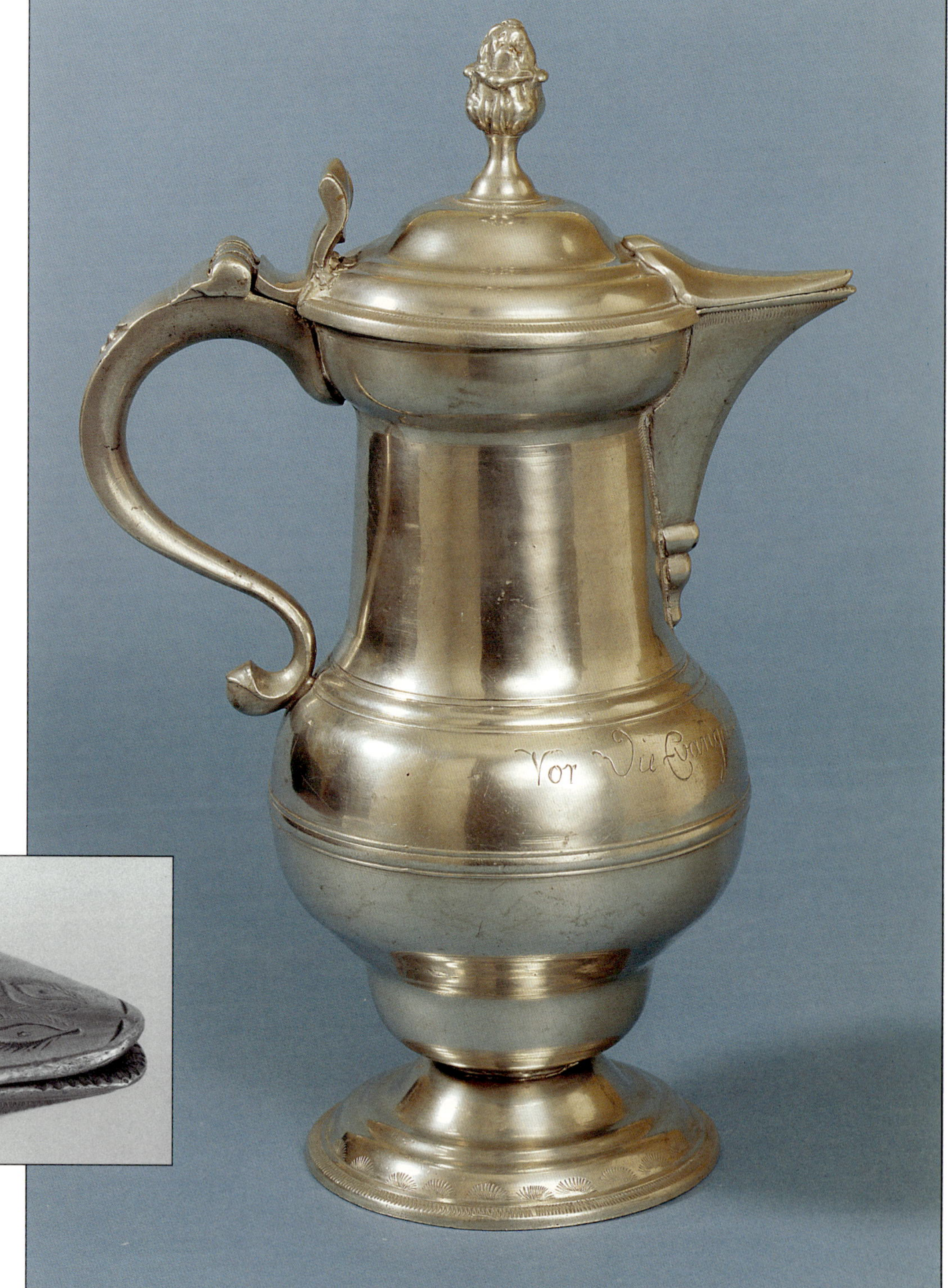

Fig. 176. *Flagon attributed to William Will, Philadelphia, 1764–1798. H 12 7/8″, TD 4 1/2″. BD 4 5/8″. Heidelberg Union Church with Lutheran and United Church of Christ congregations, Slatington, Lehigh County, Pa.*

Fig. 177. *Serpent's head (below) engraved on spout.*

Another flagon made by William Will is engraved *"Vor Die Evangelische Gemein in Heidelberg 1767"* [For the evangelical congregation in Heidelberg 1767]. It is illustrated in Figure 176. Wrigglework decoration on the lid at the base of finial, lid, rim, spout, and base is similar to that on other Will pewter. A beaker may have been used to form the top portion of the body of this and other flagons. Surprisingly, a wonderful serpent's head complete with teeth is engraved on the spout of this flagon, as on the previous flagon.

Will incorporated a straight-sided quart tankard lid and body into the upper portion of the flagon illustrated in Figure 178. The erect, open-chair thumbpiece, the design of the handle and hooded bud terminal are all elements found on William Will tankards. A nearly identical flagon with a slightly elongated handle is in a private collection.[30] The sugar bowl lid that forms the foot of that flagon retains its antiskid rim and in fact fits nicely onto a sugar bowl body attributed to Will. The lid of the flagon is interchangeable with the lid of a marked tankard. The flagon is dated 1769.

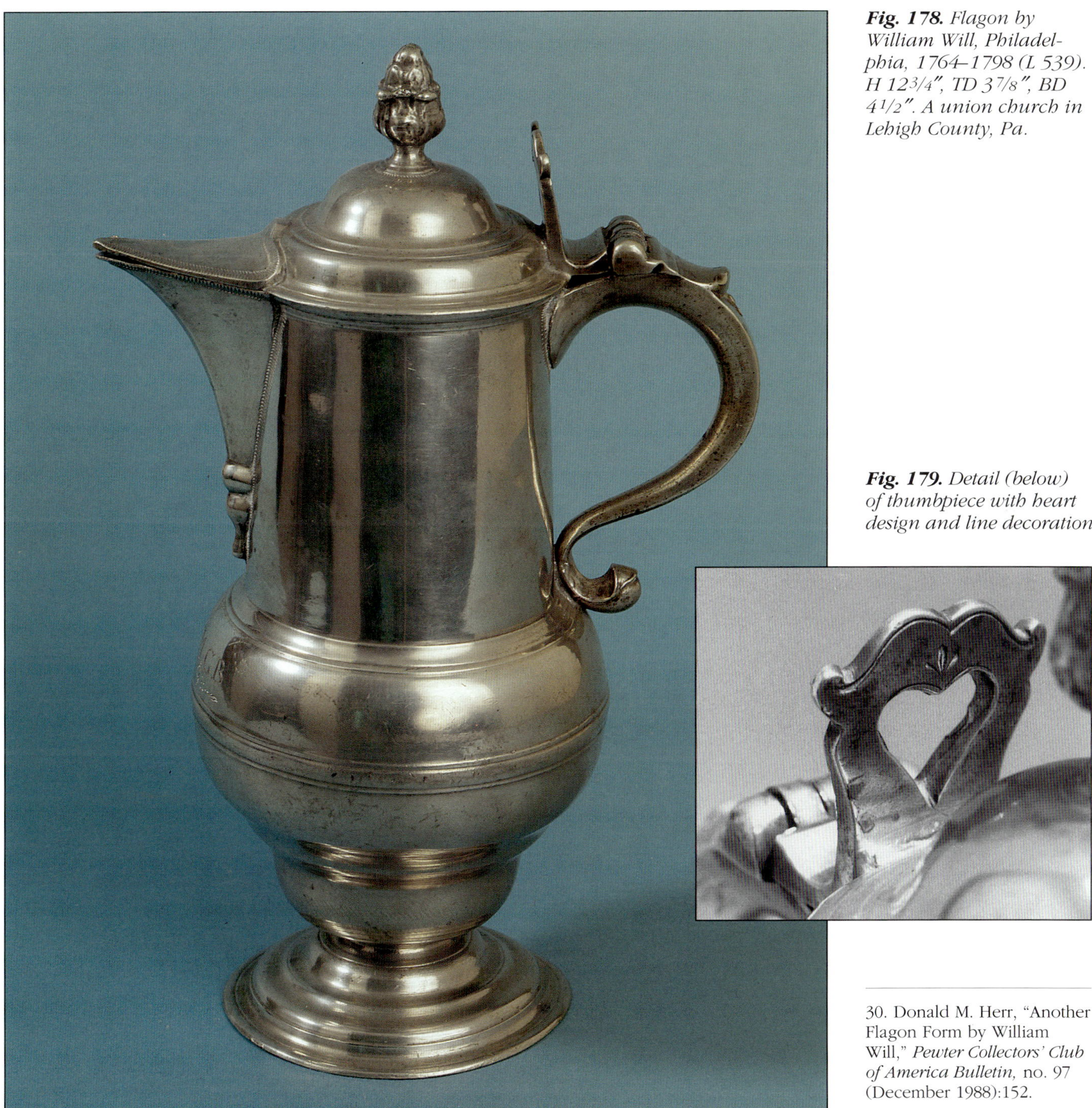

Fig. 178. *Flagon by William Will, Philadelphia, 1764–1798 (L 539). H 12 3/4", TD 3 7/8", BD 4 1/2". A union church in Lehigh County, Pa.*

Fig. 179. *Detail (below) of thumbpiece with heart design and line decoration.*

30. Donald M. Herr, "Another Flagon Form by William Will," *Pewter Collectors' Club of America Bulletin,* no. 97 (December 1988):152.

The evolution of Will's flagon styles continues in Figure 180 with the use of a measure for the top of the body of this communion vessel. Measures are listed in Will's inventory in the gill, half-pint, quart, and half-gallon sizes. A quart measure was used in this flagon. The solid finial is similar to, but larger than his teapot finials and is scaled according to the size of the piece. Will elongated the handle and attached it lower on the body to further accentuate the lines of the flagon. This is the only flagon of American manufacture known to the author that incorporates a measure into its body. The flagon is dated 1775.

Fig. 180. *Flagon by William Will, Philadelphia, 1764–1798 (L 539). H 12 3/4", TD 4 1/4", BD 3 7/8". Zion Moselem Lutheran Church, Kutztown, Berks County, Pa.*

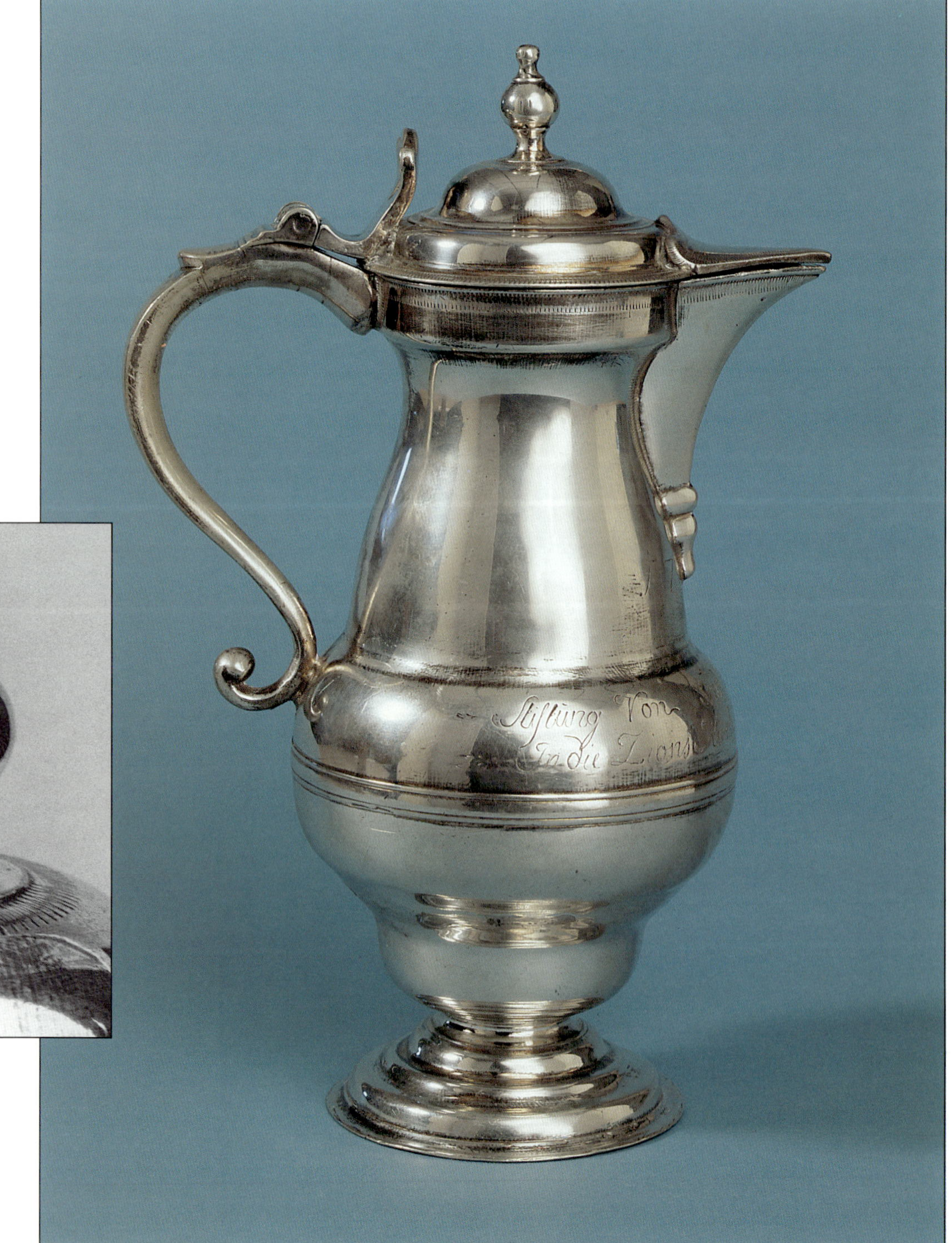

Fig. 181. *The finial (above) on the flagon is an enlarged version of a finial that Will used on some of his teapots.*

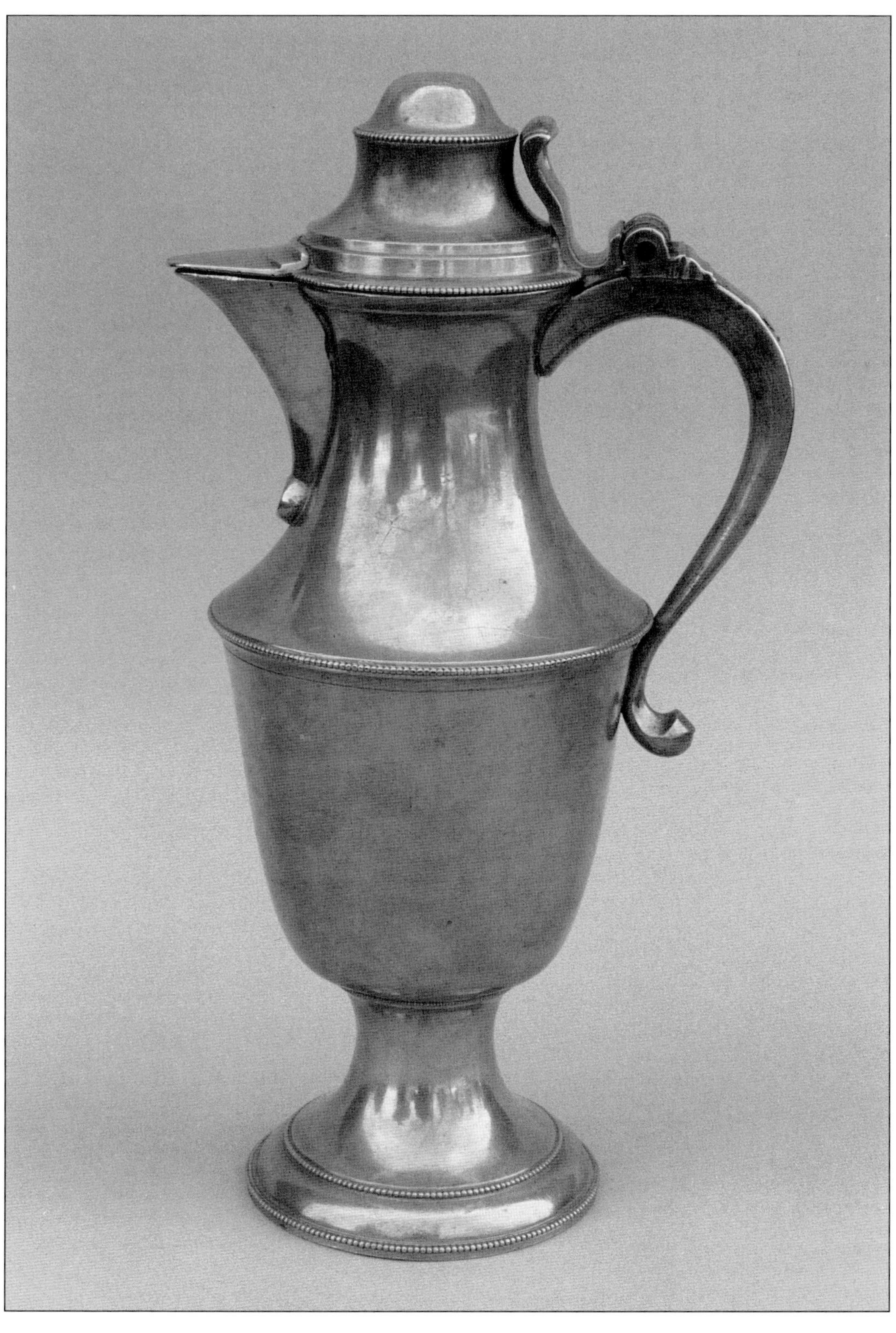

Fig. 182. *Flagon attributed to William Will, Philadelphia, 1764–1798. H 13 7/8", TD 3 3/8", BD 4 1/4". St. Michael's Lutheran Church, Strasburg, Lancaster County, Pa.*

The flagon of Federal design in Figure 182 is one of four known pieces of that form. Though they are unmarked, all are undoubtedly made by William Will. Three of these flagons are still owned by Lutheran congregations. Five rows of beading embellish the flagon. Its body is smaller than the following example.

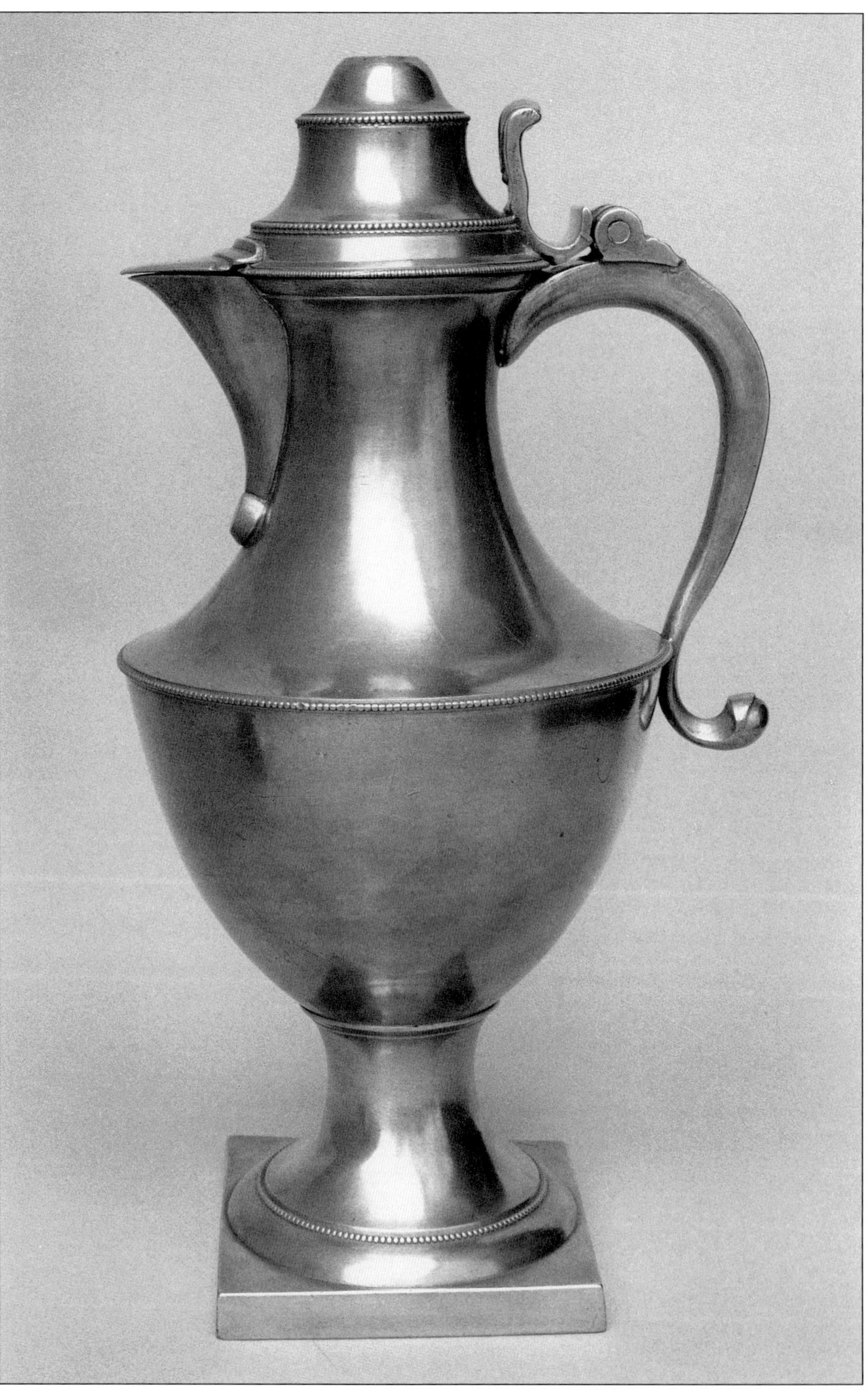

Fig. 183. *Flagon attributed to William Will, Philadelphia, 1764–1798. H 14", TD 3³/₈", BD 4³/₈" Salem United Church of Christ, Harrisburg, Dauphin County, Pa.*

Will used his coffeepot body to make a few large flagons. An example of the result is shown in his flagon in Figure 183. It is one of his most successful flagon styles. Note that five rows of beading enhance the simplicity and beauty of the form. Six flagons of this style were found in the survey.

The flat dome lid on the flagon in Figure 184 is an example of the Swedish influence on some Philadelphia tankards by Love, Parks Boyd, and later Robert Palethorp, Jr. This flagon shares a distinctive handle design that has been found on a Love tankard in a private collection.[31] The urn-shaped body, foot, and square plinth appear to have come from the same mold as an unmarked coffeepot undoubtedly of Philadelphia origin and stylistically related to silver pots of the same period.[32] The spout is similar to those on quart flagons by Boyd. The lid is a tankard lid and is a style made by Philadelphia pewterers.

The addition of a spout to a tankard resulted in a vessel that is classified as a flagon by pewter scholars. In Figure 186, a spout has been added by the pewterer to a tulip-shaped tankard of quart capacity. Tankards of this form have been found with the Love touchmark. Such an example is illustrated in Figure 249.

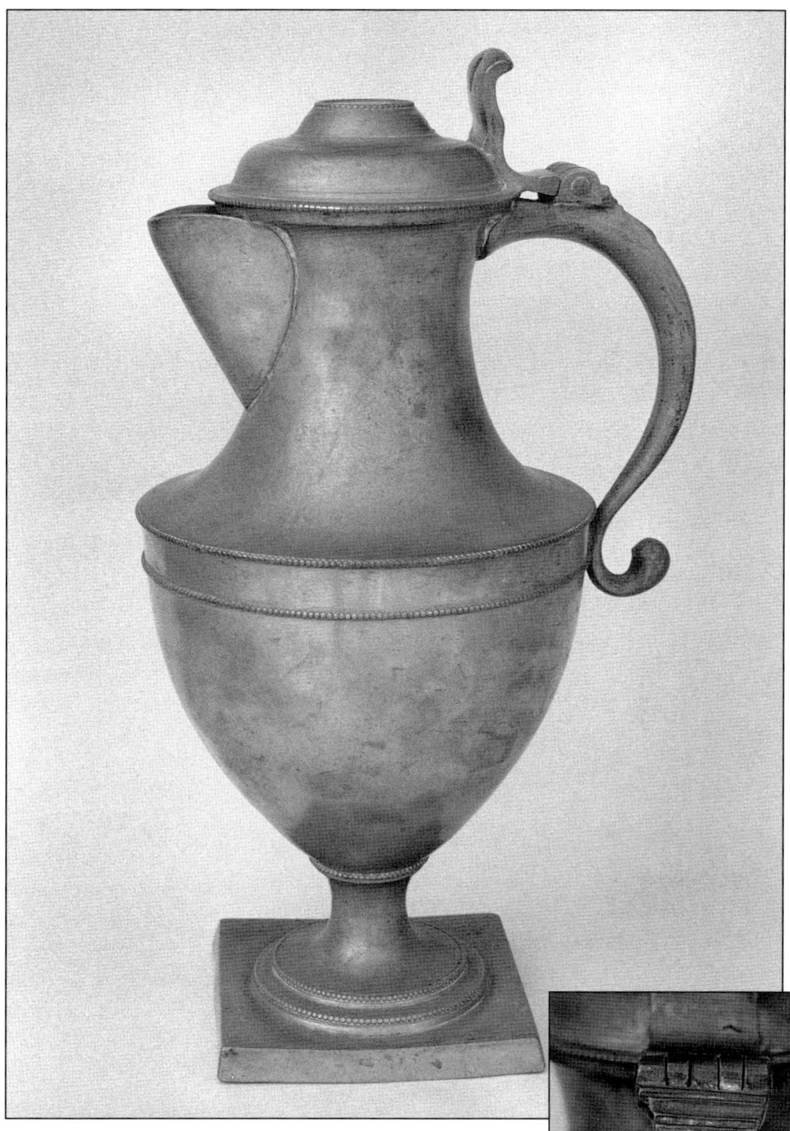

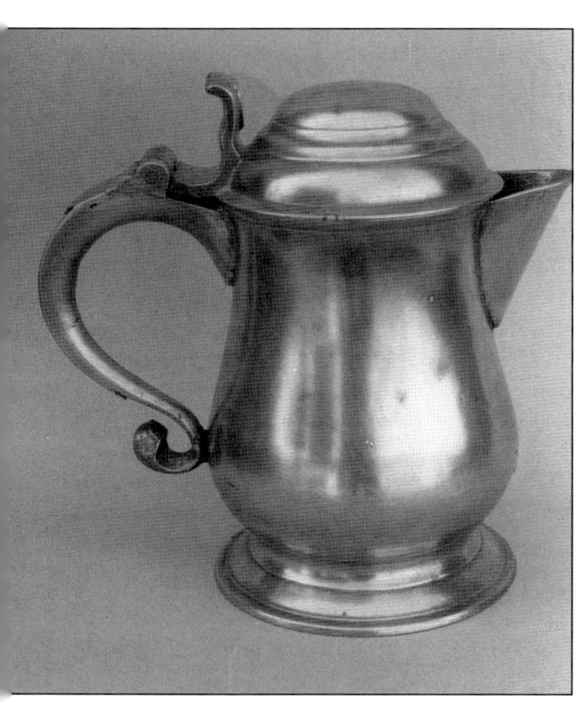

Fig. 184. *Flagon (above) attributed to Love, Philadelphia, 1775–1800. H 13″, TD 3 7/8″, BD 4 3/8″. St. Michael's Lutheran Church, Germantown, Philadelphia, Pa. The flagon is at the Lutheran Archives Center, Lutheran Theological Seminary, Mt. Airy, Philadelphia, Pa.*

Fig. 185. *Handle design (right) of above flagon.*

Fig. 186. *Flagon (left) attributed to Love, Philadelphia, 1750–1825. H 7 1/2″, TD 3 3/8″, BD 4 5/8″. Christ Lutheran Church, Spangsville, Berks County, Pa.*

31. A Love tankard in the collection of Charles V. Swain, Jr., shares the same irregular design on the top of the handle near the hinge attachment as is on this flagon.

32. A coffeepot with the same body and base shape is illustrated in Bernard Esner, "The Cause of a Skipped Heartbeat (Almost)!," *Pewter Collectors' Club of America Bulletin,* No. 7 (March 1979), p. 390. The coffeepot is in the collection of George W. Wolfe, Jr.

Modeling their work after British "spire" flagons of the previous century, the Boardmans continued to make two-quart flagons well into the third quarter of the nineteenth century. See Figure 187.

The addition of a spout to a one-quart tankard enhanced the ease of pouring of wine or water (Figure 188).

Two plates by Massachusetts pewterer Roswell Gleason accompany the flagon depicted in Figure 189.

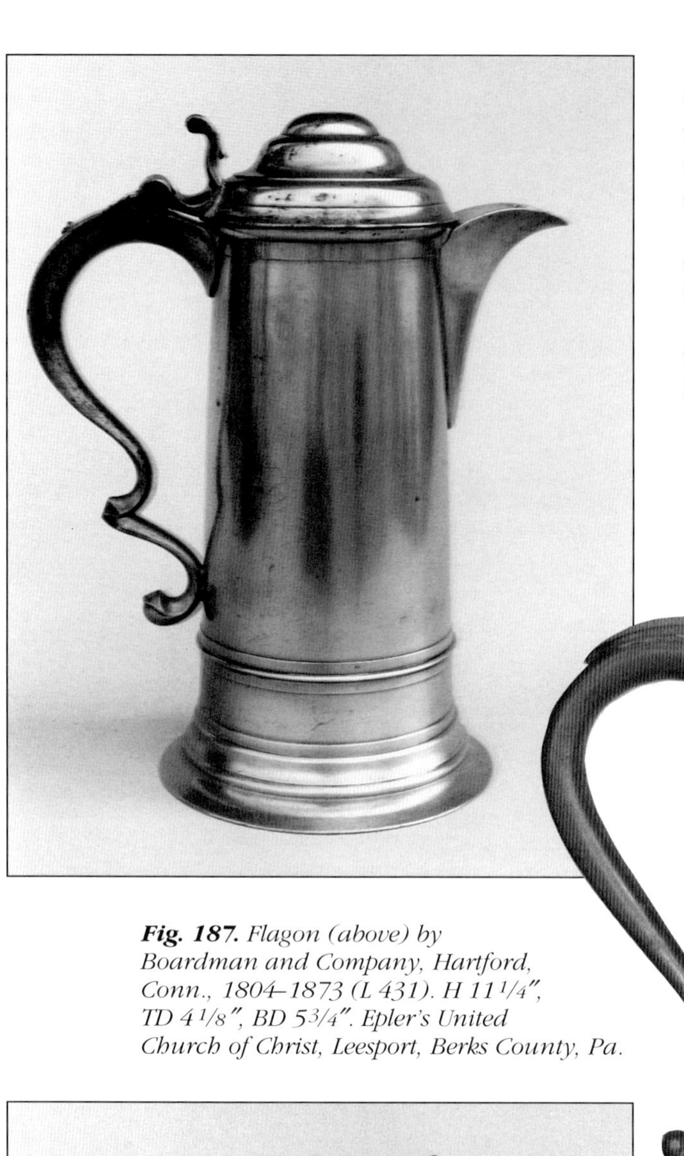

Fig. 187. *Flagon (above) by Boardman and Company, Hartford, Conn., 1804–1873 (L 431). H 11 1/4", TD 4 1/8", BD 5 3/4". Epler's United Church of Christ, Leesport, Berks County, Pa.*

Fig. 189. *Flagon (above) by Roswell Gleason, Dorchester, Mass., 1821–1871 (L 2:102). H 9 7/8", TD 4 3/8", BD 5 7/8". Christ United Lutheran Church, Stroudsburg, Monroe County, Pa.*

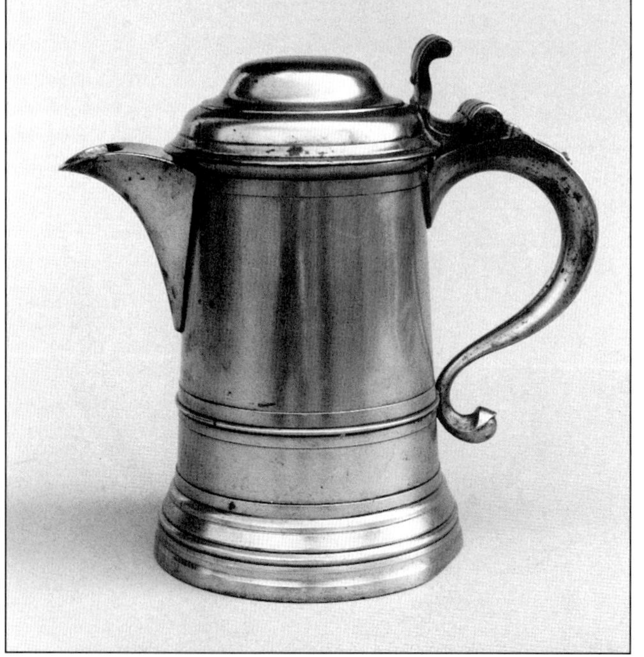

Fig. 188. *Flagon (left) by Boardman and Company, Hartford, Conn., 1804–1873 (L431). H 7 1/2", TD 4 1/8", BD 5". Epler's United Church of Christ, Leesport, Berks County, Pa.*

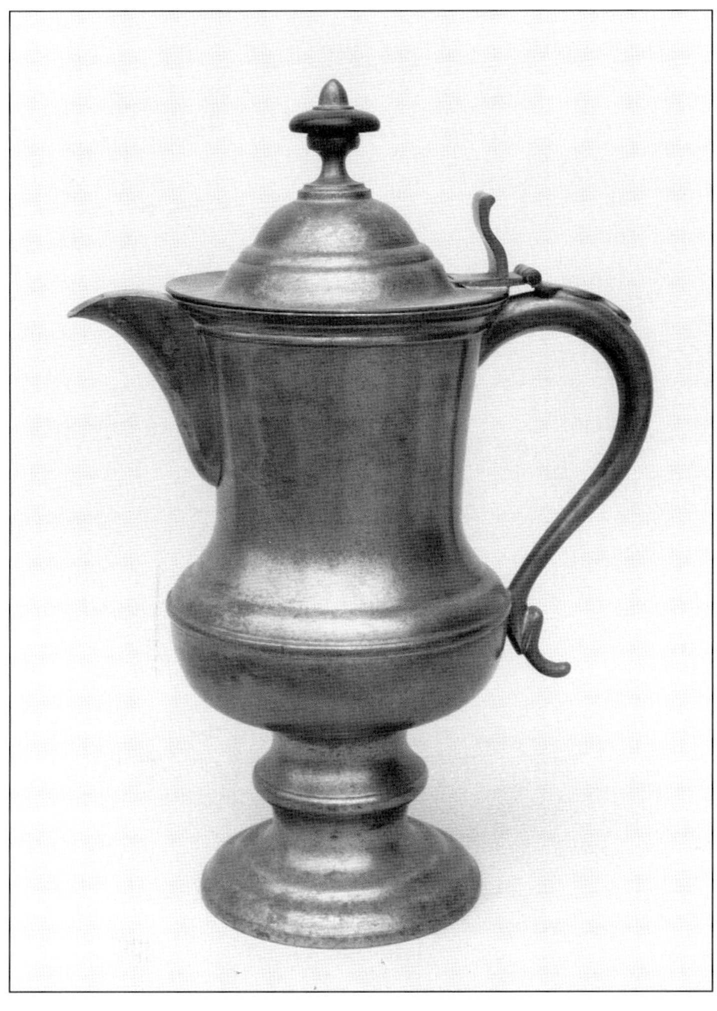

Fig. 190. *Flagon (left) by Hiram Yale and Company, Wallingford, Conn., 1824–1835 (L 445). H 14 1/4″, TD 5 1/2″, BD 5″. St. Paul's Lutheran Church, Red Hill, Montgomery County, Pa.*

Fig. 191. *Flagon (below) attributed to Leonard, Reed, and Barton, Taunton, Mass., 1835–1840. H 10 1/8″, TD 4″, BD 5 1/4″. Centenary United Church of Christ, Winchester, Frederick County, Va.*

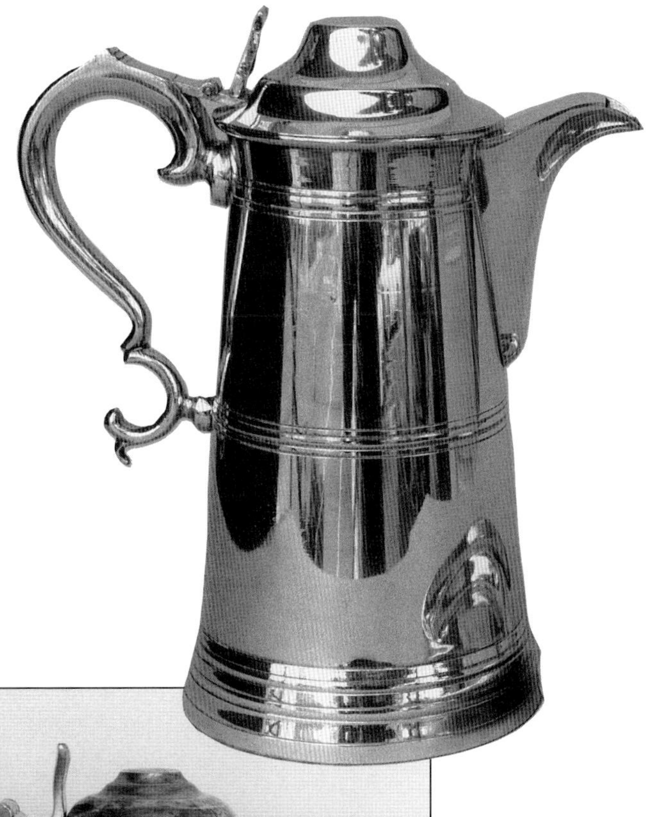

Wallingford, Connecticut, makers Hiram and Charles Yale made flagons that were unusually tall. See Figure 190.

The flagon in Figure 191 is accompanied by a dish marked Leonard, Reed and Barton. Production of the same form was continued by the firm of Reed and Barton.

The flagon marked "Smith and Feltman Albany" in Figure 192 is a style that was fashionable in the mid-nineteenth century.

BRITISH ISLES

No British flagons were found in the survey.

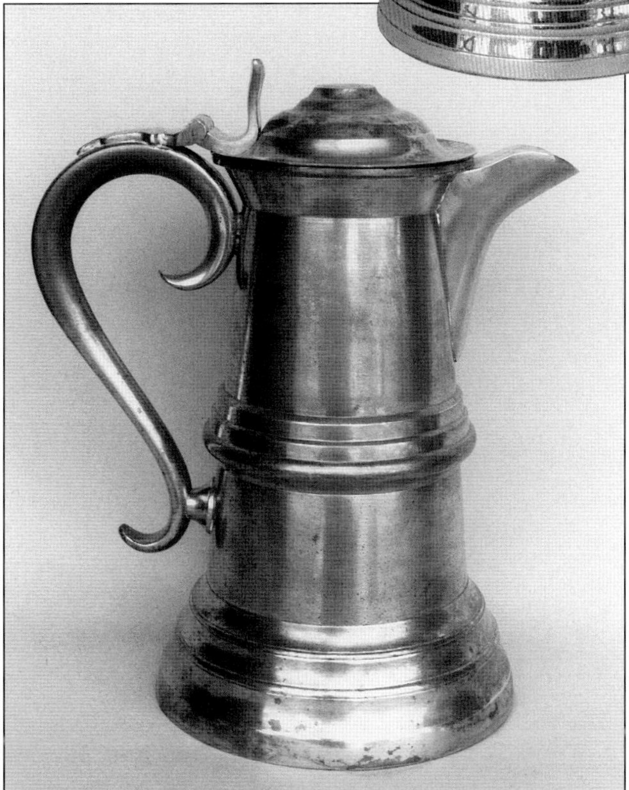

Fig. 192. *Flagon by Smith and Feltman, Albany, N.Y., 1849–1852 (L 2:113). H 12″, TD 4 3/4″, BD 7″. Emanuel Lutheran Church, Bath, Northampton County, Pa.*

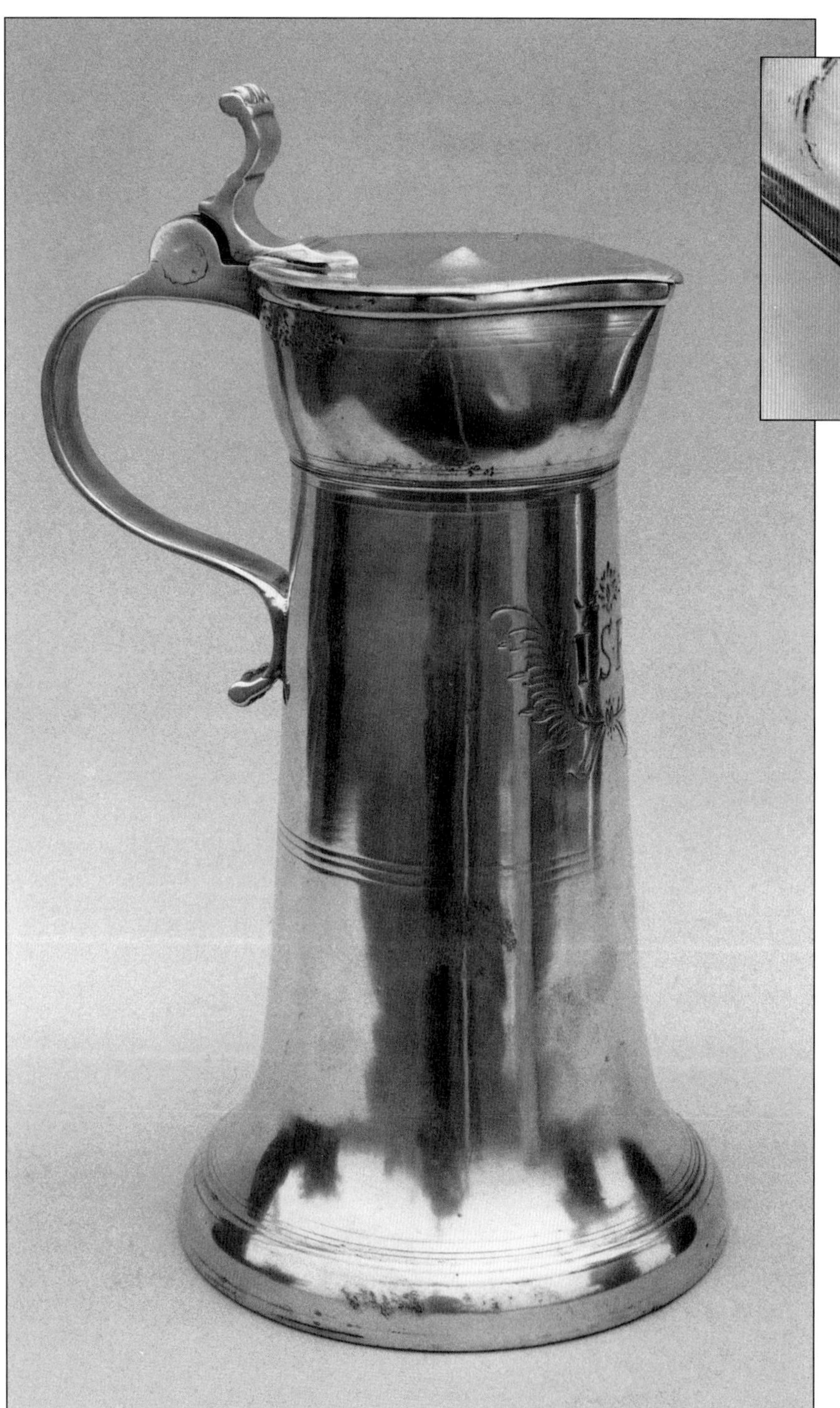

Fig. 193. *Flagon by Johann Jacob Bühler, Heilbronn and Karlsruhe, 1702–1733, and probably later (H 5:1184, 1340). H 10 1/2", TD 3 5/8", BD 5 1/8". New Goshenhoppen Reformed United Church of Christ, East Greenville, Montgomery County, Pa.*

Fig. 194. *Mark on top of spout of flagon.*

CONTINENTAL EUROPE

Germany

Johann Jacob Bühler made the flagon in Figure 193. The body form is typical of those made in Heilbronn. The lid, however, has a raised or pointed elevation in its center, characteristic of flagons made in Karlsruhe. Bühler probably made this flagon while in Karlsruhe.[33] He moved there in 1733 from Heilbronn. Hintze mentions that Bühler began working "about 1712" but has no examples of his mark. The mark on the top of the lid of this flagon clearly includes the date 1702 and enables us to be more precise about when he first struck his mark. A pewterer often incorporated into his mark the year in which he was admitted as a pewterer. Bühler probably began his career in 1702 and not 1712 as is listed by Hintze. The initials ISF are engraved on the body of the flagon, possibly for Jacob Fischer, whose name was entered in the church register by Pastor John Henry Goetschy sometime between 1736-1739.[34]

33. In a letter to the author dated November 11, 1991, Karl Schöppl identified the maker.

34. See "List of the Heads of Families Belonging to the Congregation of New Goshenhoppen Reformed Members: Entered in Church Register by John Henry Goetschy sometime between 1736-1739," in *Two Hundred Twenty-five Years at New Goshenhoppen 1727–1952*. Published by the congregation, 1952.

The form of the flagon made by Heinrich Müller (Figure 195) was used by pewterers in southern Germany, including Bavaria and Switzerland. The ball thumbpiece, pointed spout, strap handle, body form, and cherub's head feet are indigenous to this region. Lancaster pewterer Johann Christoph Heyne used this flagon style with its ball thumbpiece as a prototype for similar vessels he made that are owned by the same congregation. The mark on the handle of the Müller flagon (Figure 196) clearly shows the date (1)712 and includes castles that were the secondary city mark used by makers in Rothenburg ob der Tauber. The date in the mark suggests that Müller began his career as a pewterer in 1712. Hintze lists 1721 as the beginning of Müller's working period but does not illustrate a mark. Ludwig Schnurrer's *Das Zinngiesserhandwerk in Rothenburg ob der Tauber* lists Müller but found no marked examples.[35]

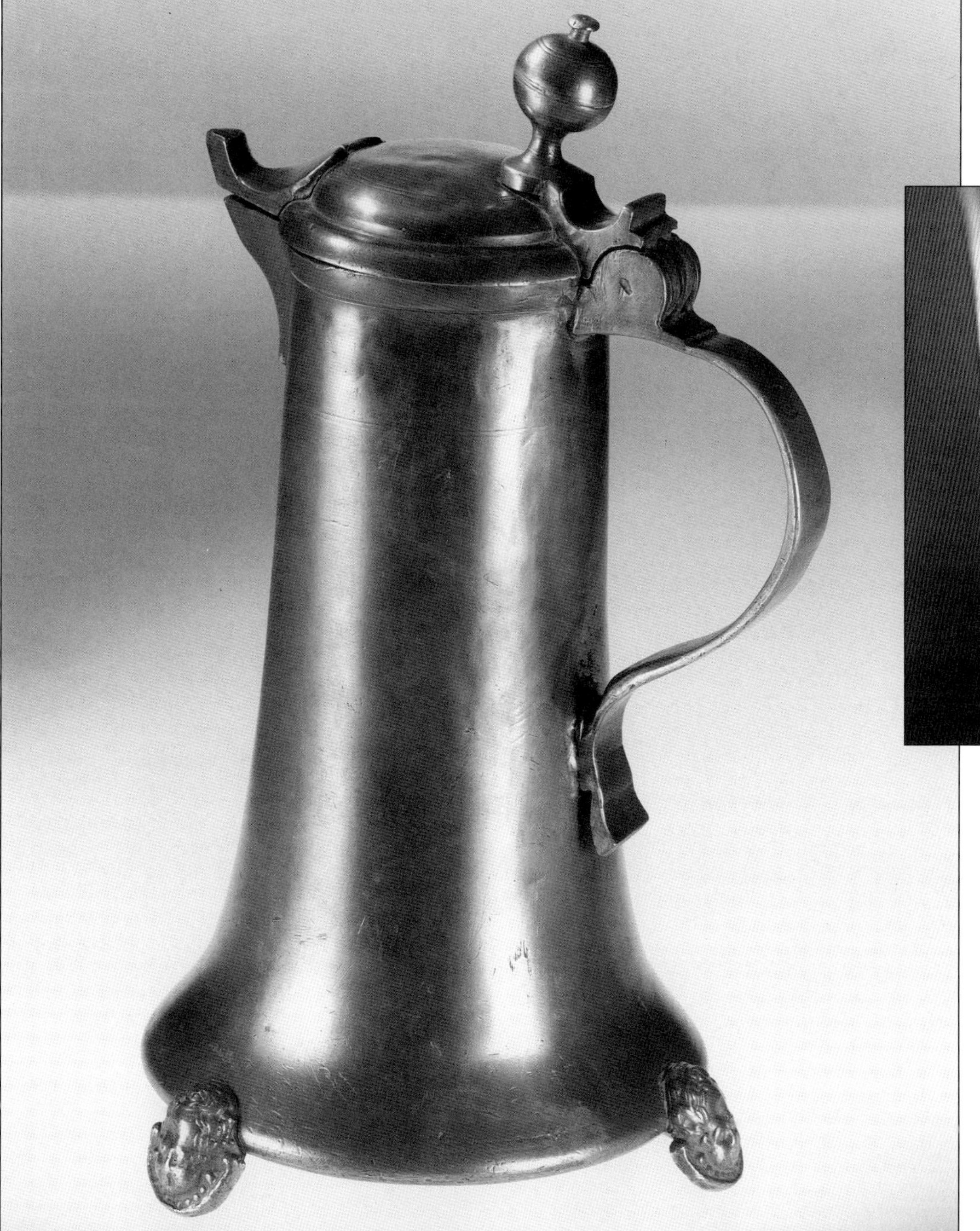

Fig. 195. *Flagon by Heinrich Müller, Rothenburg ob der Tauber, Germany, 1712–1744 (H 6: fig. 1199). Holy Trinity Lutheran Church, Lancaster, Pa.*

Fig. 196. *Date of 1712 in mark (below) of Heinrich Müller on handle of flagon.*

35. Ludwig Schnurrer, *Das Zinngiesserhandwerk in Rothenburg ob der Tauber* (Rothenburg ob der Tauber: Verlag des Vereins Alt-Rothenburg, 1981), 96. Letter from Karl Schöppl dated February 2, 1993. Erwin Hintze incorrectly read the date as 1719, in a postscript to John J. Evans, Jr.'s "I.C.H., Lancaster Pewterer," in *The Magazine Antiques,* September 1931.

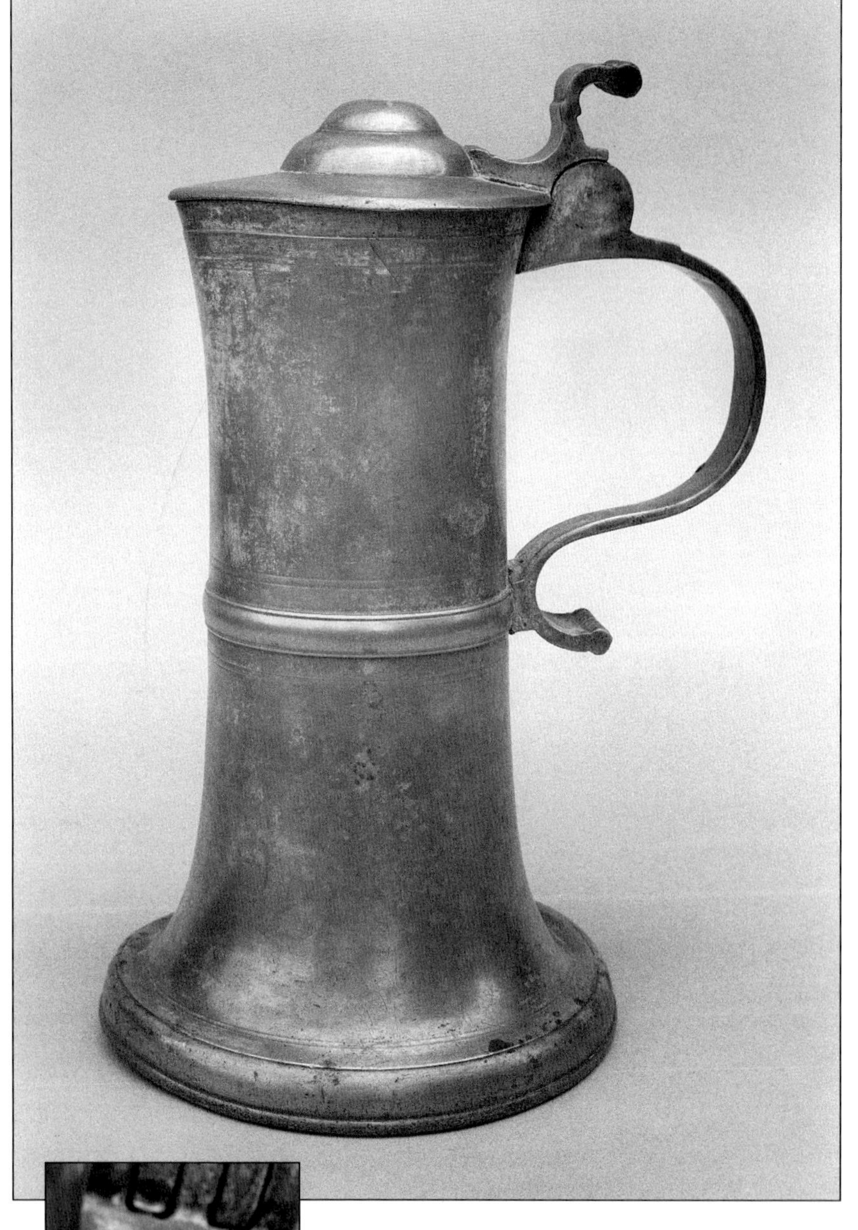

Figure 197 illustrates a flagon made by German pewterer Frantz Kurtz. The flagon is marked on the top of the handle with the initials of the maker and a secondary city mark of Reutlingen in Figure 198.

The flagon illustrated in Figure 199 with its *"Federbusch"* [plumed thumbpiece], strap handle, and pointed spout exemplifies a style that was popular in southern Germany, especially in Franconia, a district in northern Bavaria, in the second quarter of the eighteenth century.[36] It is dated 1747. Other flagons of similar form found in the survey were dated 1743, 1746, 1747, and 1775.

36. See Ludwig Mory, *Schönes Zinn* (Munich: Bruckman, 1972), 279, for examples of the *Federbusch* [bunch of feathers] thumbpiece. Also see Vetter and Wacha, *Linzer Zinngiesser* (Vienna: Schroll, 1967), for a related example dated 1727 by Jacob Mansrieder of Linz, Austria.

Fig. 197. *Flagon (above) by Frantz Kurtz, Reutlingen, Germany, 1734–1798 (H 6: fig. 1146). H 9″, TD 3″, BD 5″. Allegheny Union Church with Lutheran and United Church of Christ congregations, Alleghenyville, Berks County, Pa.*

Fig. 198. *Mark (left) of Frantz Kurtz on handle of flagon.*

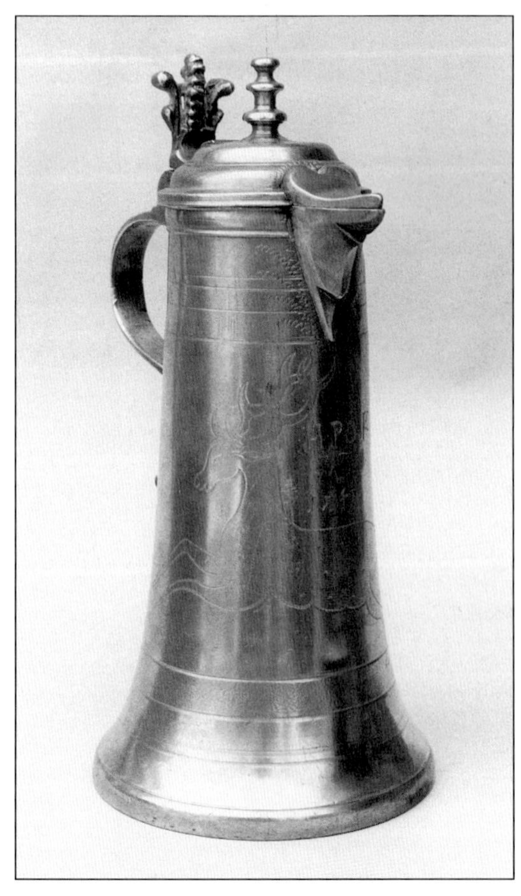

Fig. 199. *Flagon (right). Southern Germany, 1747. H 11¾″, TD 3¼″, BD 5⅝″. Trinity Lutheran Church, New Holland, Lancaster County, Pa.*

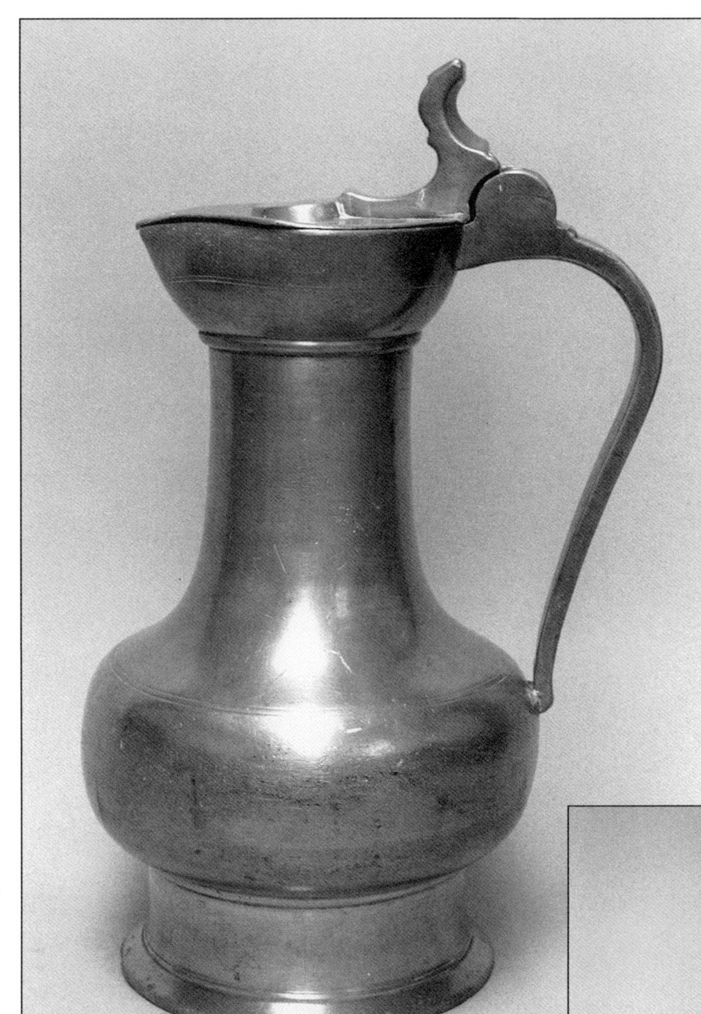

Fig. 200. *Flagon, Cologne, Germany, mid-eighteenth century. H 12″, TD 4″, BD 5″. Trinity Lutheran Church, Bethlehem, Northampton County, Pa.*

Fig. 201. *Flagon, Cologne, Germany, 1757. H 9 1/8″, TD 3 3/8″, BD 4 1/8″. East Vincent United Church of Christ, Spring City, Chester County, Pa.*

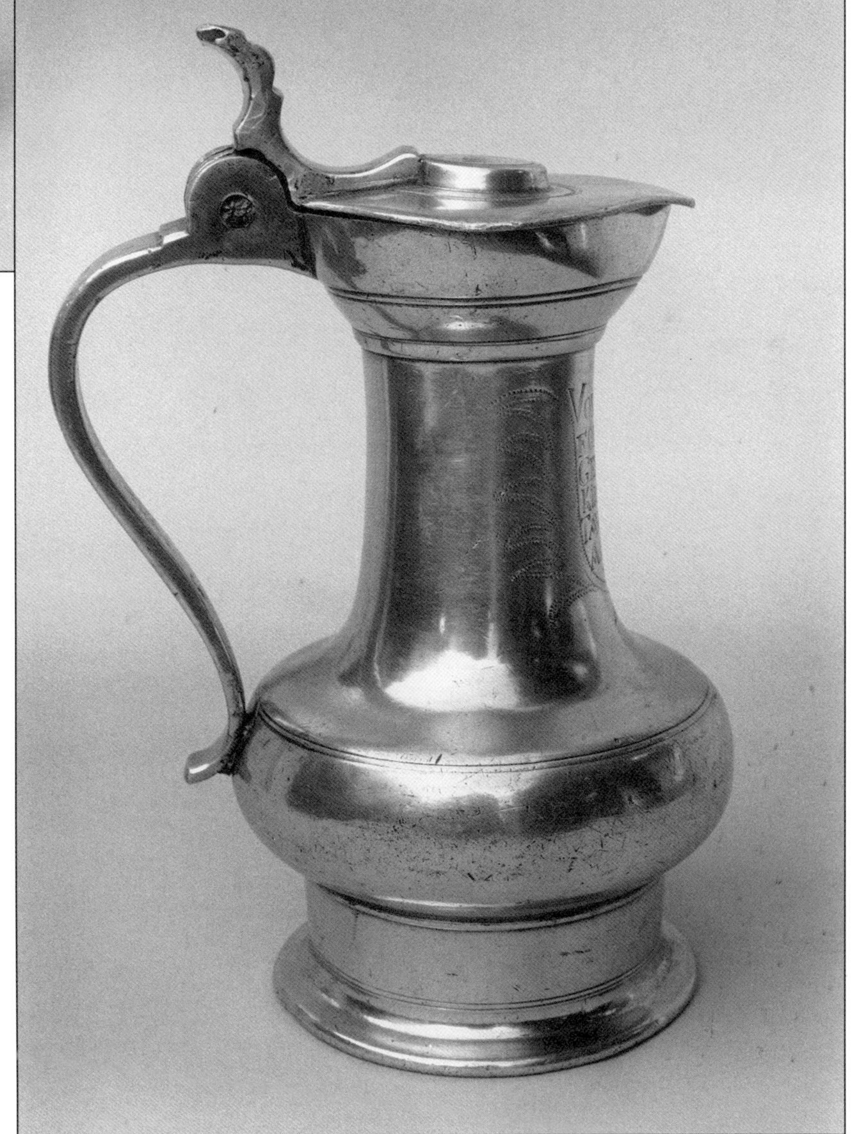

Vessels having a narrow neck and bulbous footed body of the form in Figure 200 were made in the region of the city of Cologne, and they are called Cologne flagons. The raised center of the heart-shaped lid and the erect thumbpiece are other characteristics of flagons made in the region of Cologne.[37]

Another Cologne flagon is illustrated in Figure 201. The neck of the flagon is engraved *"VOR DIE REFORMIRTE GEMEINE DE KIRCH IN PEI TAUNSCHIP ANNO 1757"* [For the Reformed congregation in Pikes Township, in the year 1757].

37. See H. H. Cotterell, A. Riff, and R. M. Vetter, *National Types of Old Pewter* (Princeton, N.J.: The Pyne Press, 1972), 64, Fig. 72, for a flagon of similar form from Cologne. Reprinted in the January 1927 issue of Antiques.

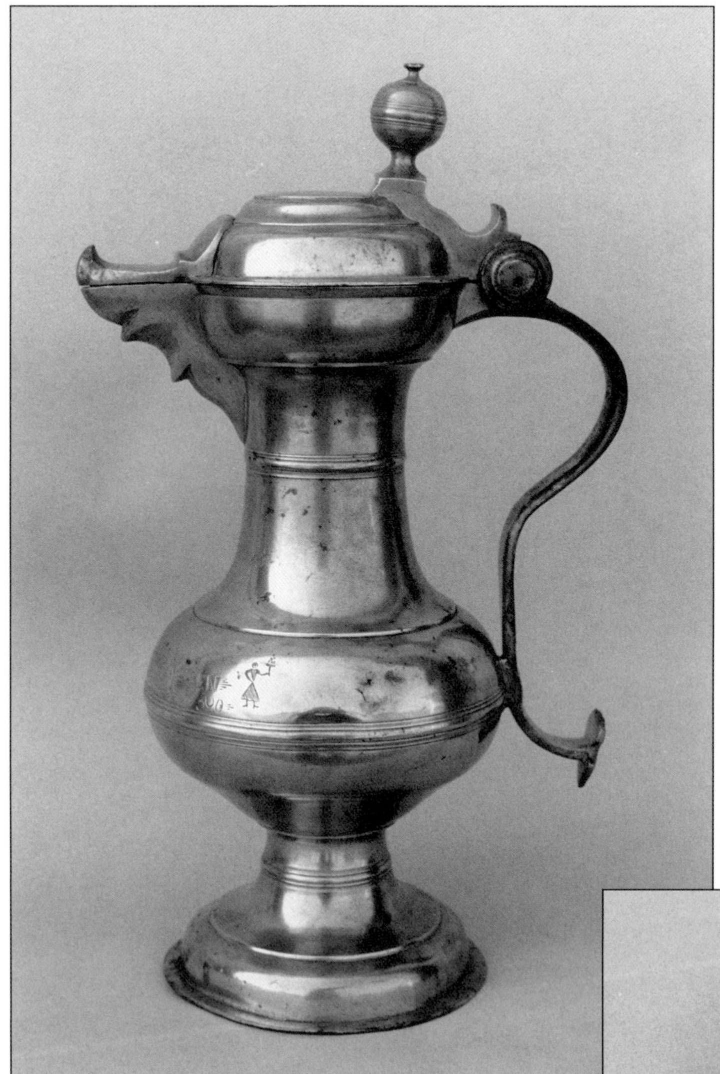

The "Abendmahlskanne" [communion flagon] in Figure 202 was a form made in Frankfurt am Main, Hessen, Worms, and Württemberg.[38] It was made by Gabriel Syren. He became a master in 1727 and worked until about 1753. The flagon is engraved *"ANA MARGEREDA KERAUASSEN [sic] DEN 6 APRIL 1750."*

The flagon in Figure 203 is one of a pair owned by the congregation. Both flagons are engraved with the names of the donors. Michael Weber and his wife Anna Barbara gave a pair of flagons to the Lutheran Church in Heidelberg Township, Lancaster County, in 1764.

38. A similar flagon by Gabriel Syren is owned by Evangelical (Lutheran) churches in Bellnhausen and Fronhausen—Information in a letter from Karl Schöppl, October 1, 1991. See Hanns-Ulrich Haedeke, *Zinn* (München: Klinkhardt and Bierman, 1983), 243, Fig. 331, for a similar flagon by Frantz Nicolaus Scharff of Worms.

Fig. 202. *Flagon (above) by Gabriel Syren, Frankfurt am Main, Germany, 1727–1753. H 15", TD 4 5/8", BD 5 3/4". New Hanover Lutheran Church, Gilbertsville, Montgomery County, Pa.*

Fig. 203. *Flagon (right) by Daniel Heldenreich, Durlach, Germany, 1764. (H v.5, 709). H 14 1/2", TD 4", BD 5 1/2". St. Luke's Lutheran Church, Schaefferstown, Lebanon County, Pa.*

Fig. 204. *Mark (below) on inside of lid of flagon at right.*

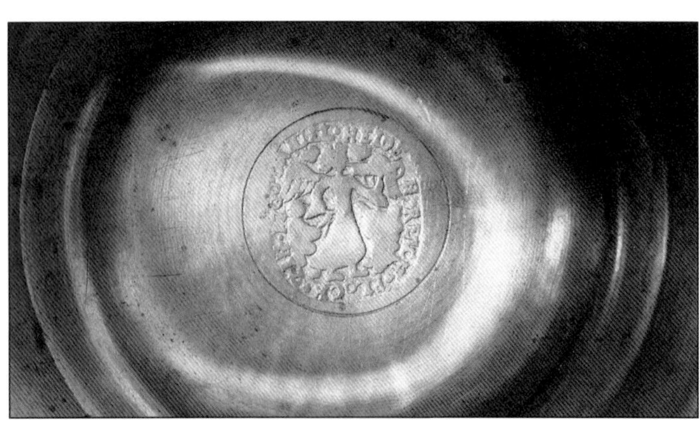

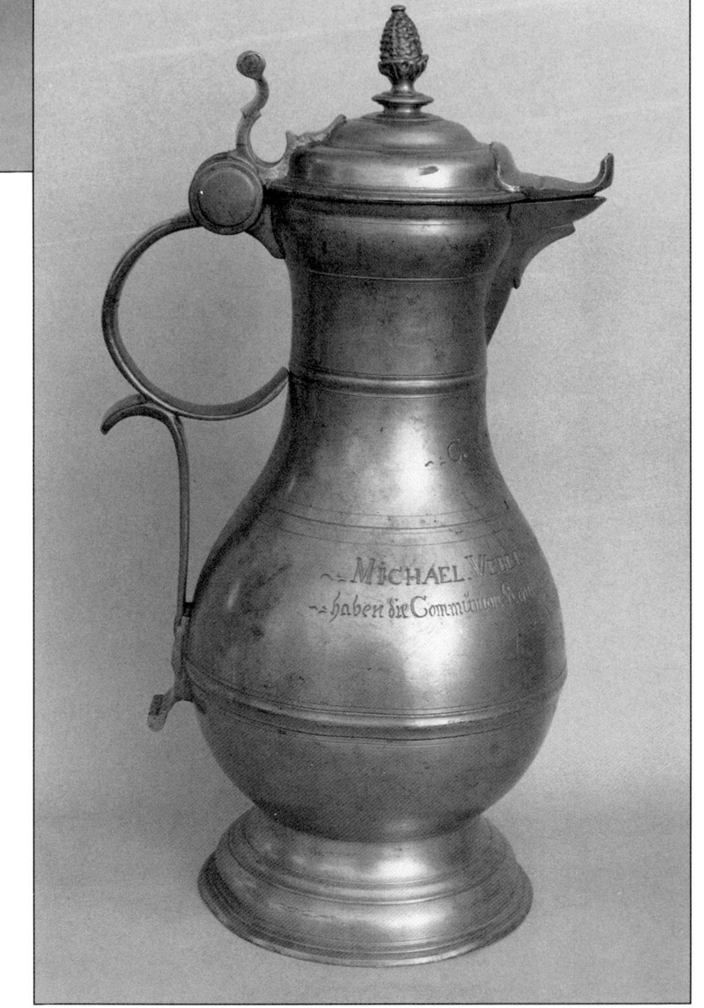

This flagon (Figure 205) and a slightly larger one, both made by Johann Martin Kaller of Heilbronn, are engraved *"John Jacob Blanck 1773"* on their bodies and *"in Wilmsburg"* on their lid shields. Note the cherub's head feet, a device frequently found on German pewter.

Netherlands
The shell thumbpiece, egg-shaped body, and double-C scrolled handle style are found on church flagons from Holland (Figure 207). This is one of a pair; both are engraved "Henrich Andonius Doewler 1769."

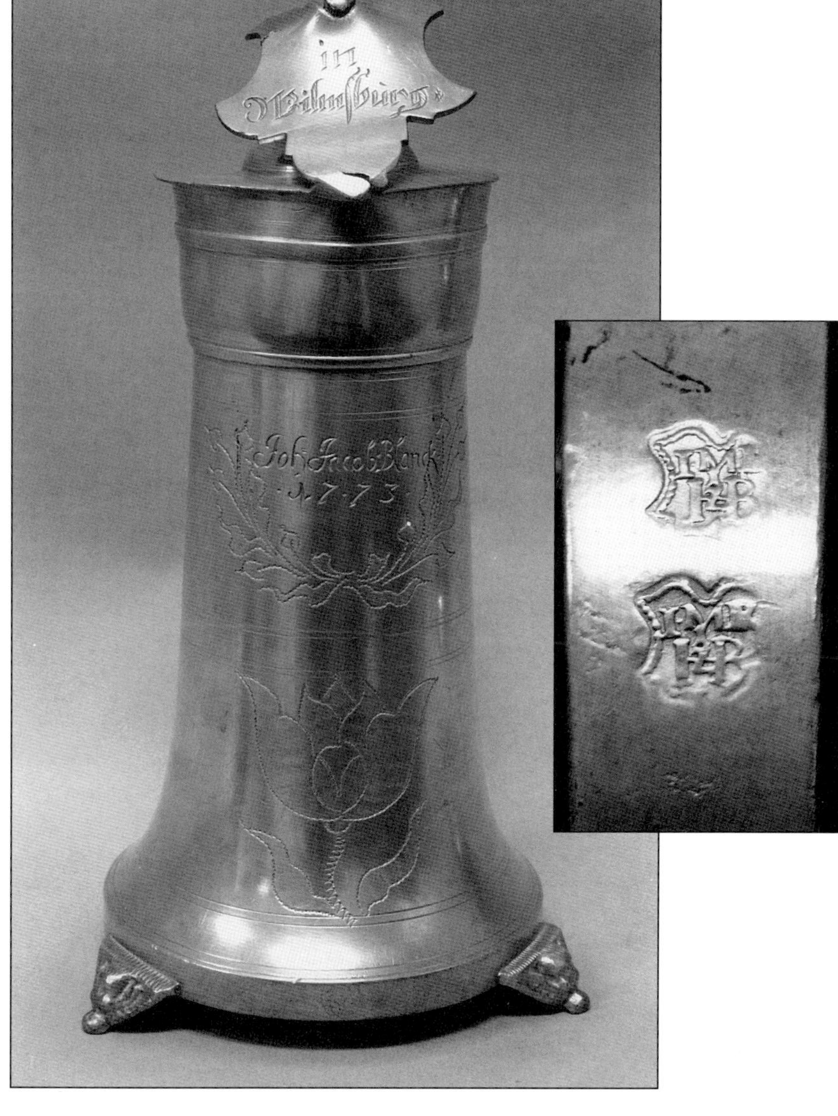

Fig. 205. *Flagon (above) by Johann Martin Kaller, Heilbronn, Germany, 1757–1784 (H 5: fig. 1194). H 10 1/4", TD 3 1/8", BD 4 3/4". Zion Lutheran Church, Jonestown, Lebanon County, Pa.*

Fig. 206. *Mark (above right) of Johann Martin Kaller of Heilbronn on handle.*

Fig. 207. *Flagon (below) by Hendrick Kock, Rotterdam, Netherlands, 1752–1787 (D 519). H 13 3/4", TD 3", BD 5 1/2". Salem Lutheran Church, Lebanon, Pa.*

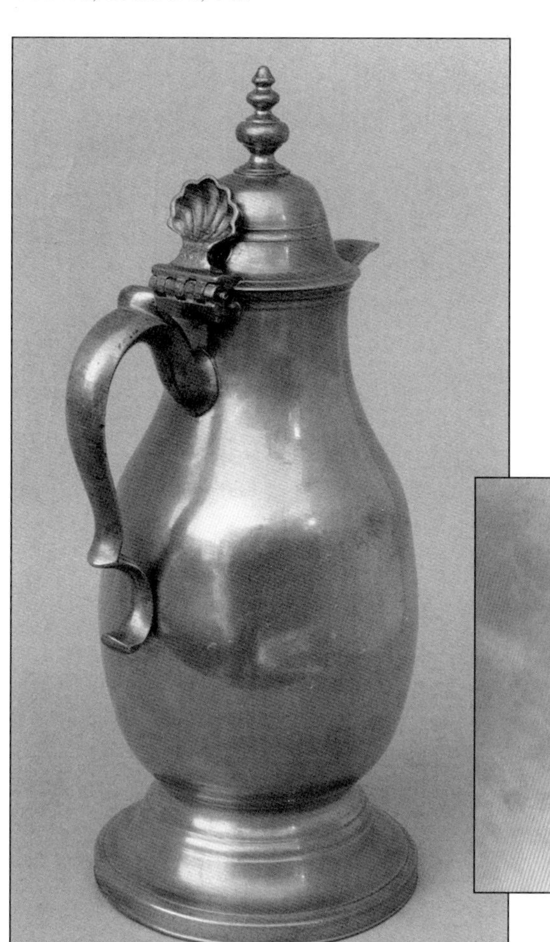

Fig. 208. *Marks (above) of Hendrick Kock on outside bottom of flagon on left.*

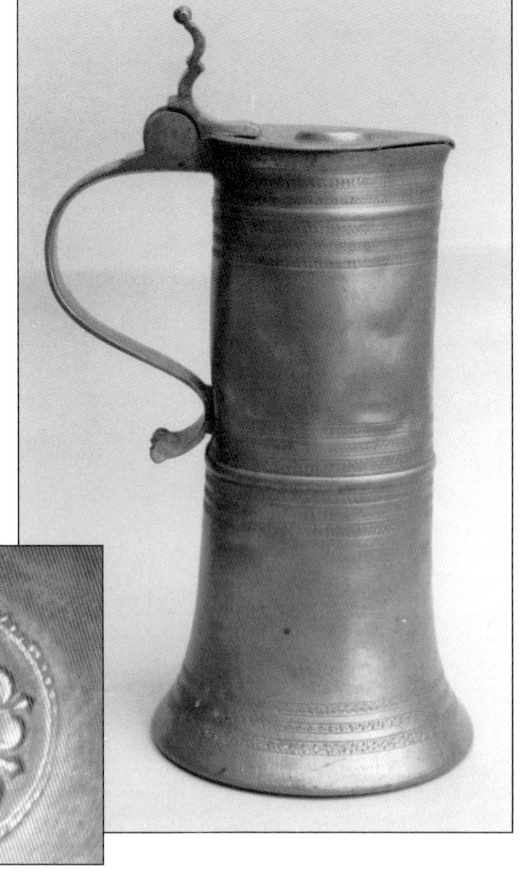

Fig. 209. *Flagon by Jakob Laufer, Zofingen, Switzerland, 1712–1746 (S 3: fig. 1603). H 12 3/4", TD 4", BD 5 3/4". Schwarzwald United Church of Christ, Berks County, Pa.*

Fig. 210. *Mark of Jakob Laufer on inside bottom of flagon.*

Switzerland
This early Swiss flagon from Zofingen (Figure 209) is similar in form to others made in Luzern and Basel. It is dated 1744.

Measures

Measures are domestic forms that are used for measuring dry or liquid goods in the marketplace, tavern, or home. Occasionally they were used in the church. The only measures found in the survey were of British origin and of a shape called baluster. Two unmarked measures bear initials suggesting they were given to the church by donors.

BRITISH ISLES

The name W. Bancks is cast in reverse on the inside of the lid of the baluster measure in Figure 211. It is unusual to find in British pewter a mark that is cast and placed in this position.[39] This lidded quart baluster measure with bud thumbpiece and strap handle is similar to other British measures made in the first decade of the eighteenth century.

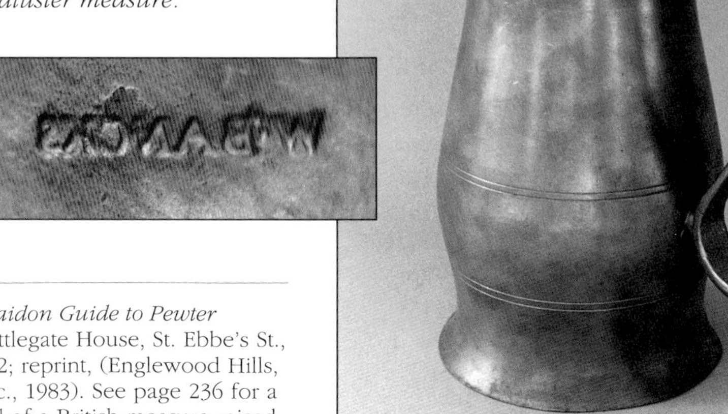

Fig. 211. *Measure. Quart. Probably by William Bancks, England, 1700–1710 (C 240; P 240). H 8 1/4", TD 3 7/8", BD 4 1/8". Trinity (Roth's) United Church of Christ, Spring Grove, York County, Pa.*

Fig. 212. *Mark of W. Bancks cast in reverse on inside of lid of baluster measure.*

39. Vanessa Brett, *Phaidon Guide to Pewter* Phaidon Press Ltd., Littlegate House, St. Ebbe's St., Oxford, England, 1982; reprint, (Englewood Hills, N. J.: Prentice-Hall Inc., 1983). See page 236 for a mark on the inside lid of a British measure raised in relief.

The quart baluster measure in Figure 213 has a solid strap handle and bud thumbpiece and perhaps a slightly later body form. The initials F H are scratched on the outside bottom.

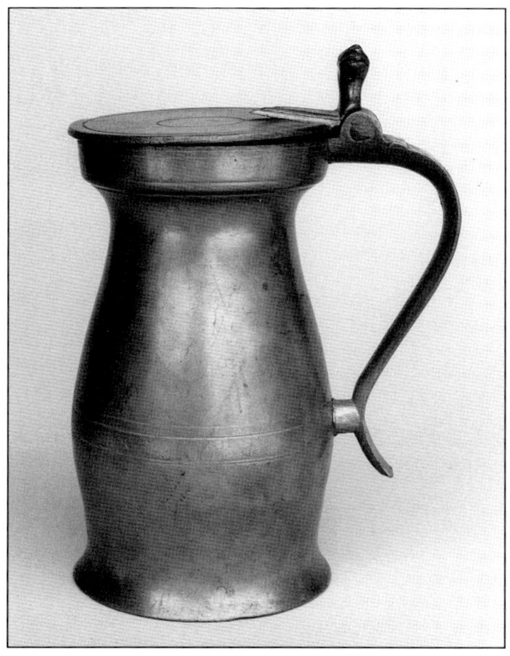

Fig. 213. *Measure. Quart. Unmarked, England, 1700–1710. H 8 1/4″, TD 3 3/4″, BD 4″. Zion Lutheran Church, Hummelstown, Dauphin County, Pa.*

The baluster measure illustrated in Figure 214 has a double volute thumbpiece and solid handle with hooded bud terminal. The initials G H I S and 1765 are pricked into the outside bottom of the measure.

Mugs

Mugs were commonly used in the home and tavern. They frequently found their way into the church where they functioned as containers for baptismal water and communion wine.

AMERICA

The high raised band or fillet on the body of the pint mug in Figure 216 frequently was used by New York pewterers such as John Will.

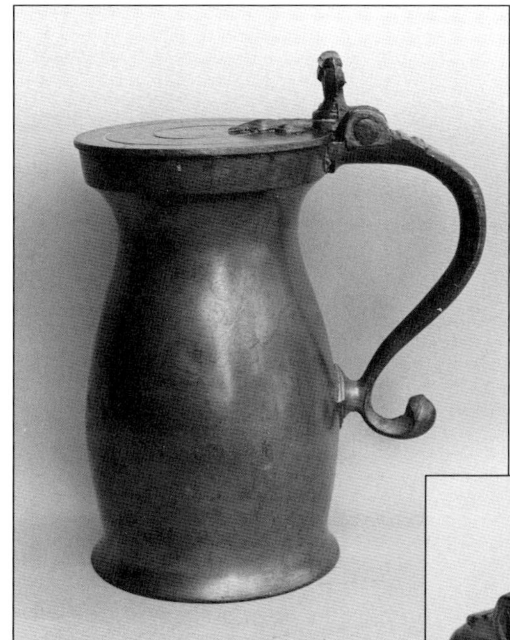

Fig. 214. *Measure. Quart. Unmarked, England, dated 1765. H 8″, TD 3 7/8″, BD 4″. St. Paul's (Wolf's) United Church of Christ, near York, York County, Pa.*

Fig. 215. *Detail (below) of double volute thumbpiece on measure.*

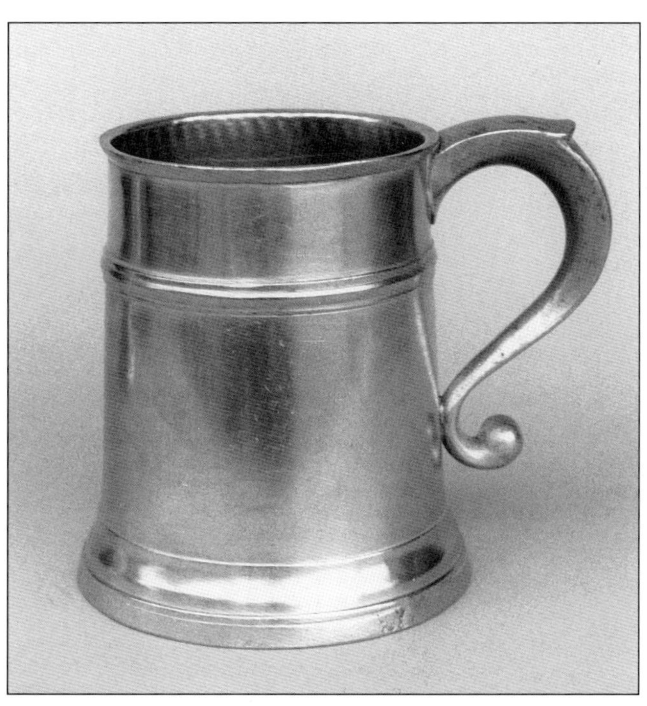

Fig. 216. *Pint mug. John Will, New York, 1752– 1774 (L 481). H 4 5/8″, TD 3 1/4″, BD 4″. Neffs Union Church with Lutheran and United Church of Christ congregations, Neffs, Lehigh County, Pa.*

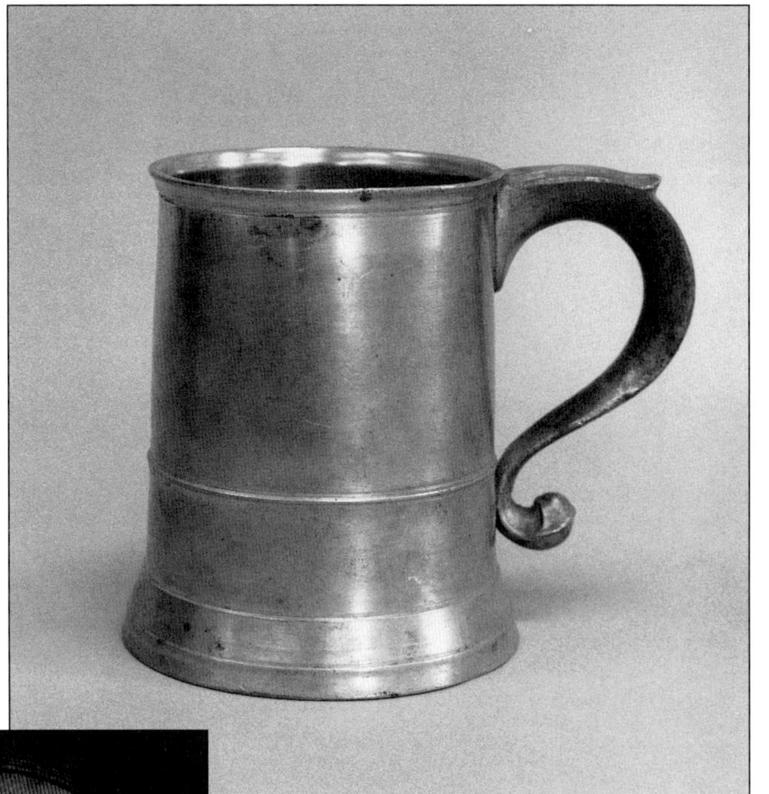

This rare pint mug by Johann Philip Alberti (Figure 217) has a mark that is better struck than another recorded previously.[40] It is the only known pint mug by Alberti and is illustrated here for the first time. At least six other marked Alberti pieces are known, including the flagon previously illustrated in this book.

Only one marked piece with the DS angel mark was found in the survey (Figure 219). The mug is one of two straight-sided mugs of pint capacity that are known to the author. Tulip-shaped pint mugs, straight-sided quart mugs, basins, plates, dishes, and a sugar bowl are forms on which DS marks have been found.

40. The mark on this pint mug is the same mark illustrated in Melvyn D. Wolf, "A Tankard by Johann Philip Alberti," *Pewter Collectors' Club of America Bulletin,* nos. 94-95 (March-September 1987):107.

***Fig. 219.** Pint mug (right). DS, Philadelphia, probably 1750–1790 (L 888). H 4", TD 3 1/4", BD 3 7/8". Good Mennonite Church, Bainbridge, Lancaster County, Pa.*

***Fig. 220.** DS mark (below) on inside bottom of pint mug.*

***Fig. 217.** Pint mug (above right). Johann Philip Alberti, Philadelphia, 1754–1780. H 4 5/8", TD 3 1/2", BD 3 5/8". Christ's Church (Lowhill) United Church of Christ, New Tripoli, Lehigh County, Pa.*

***Fig. 218.** Mark (above) of Johann Philip Alberti in pint mug. Christ's Church at Lowhill United Church of Christ, New Tripoli, Lehigh County, Pa.*

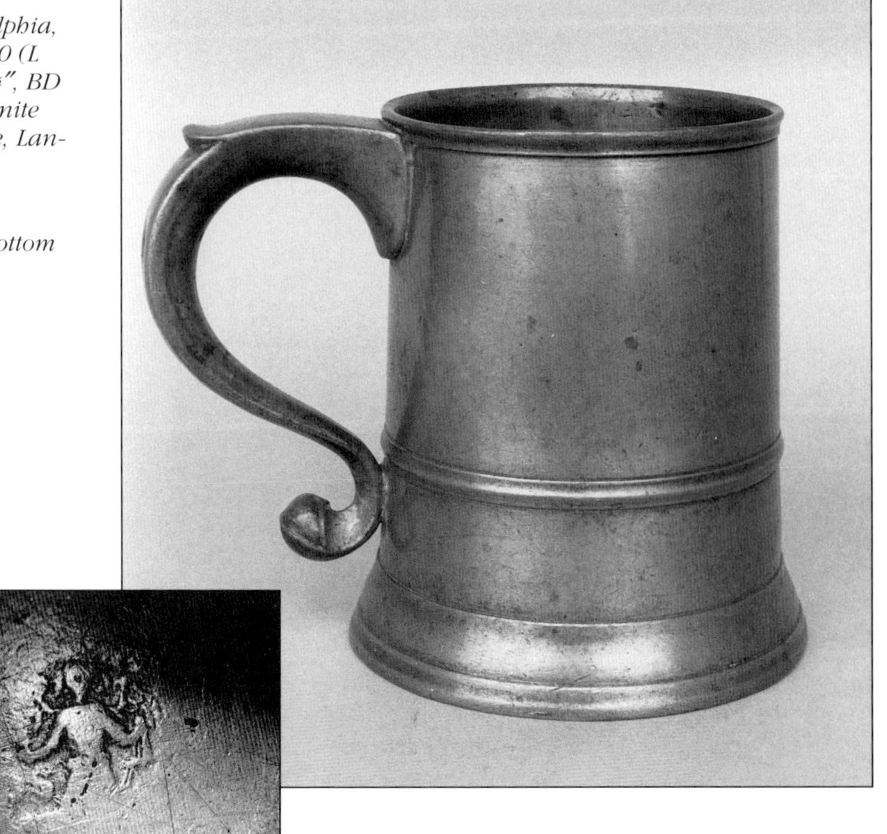

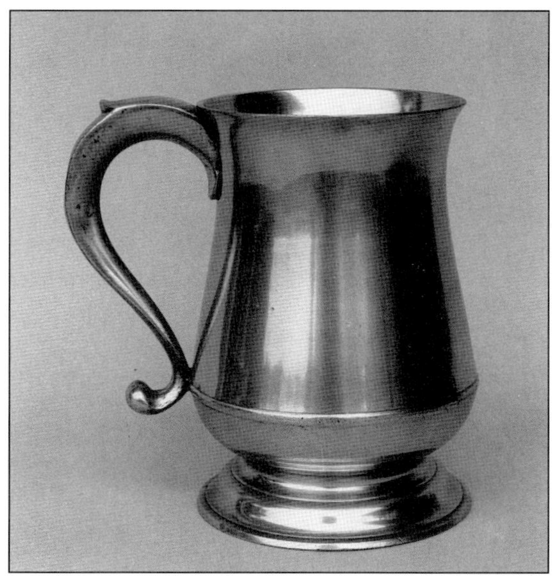

Fig. 221. *Quart mug (left). William Will, Philadelphia, 1764–1798 (L 535). H 6 3/8", TD 4 1/8", BD 4 3/8". Friedens Lutheran Church, Stony Run, Berks County, Pa.*

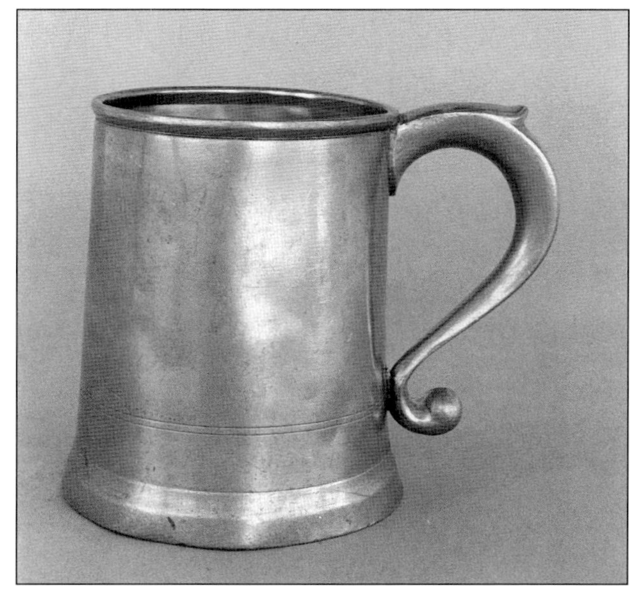

Marked on the inside bottom with William Will's early lamb and dove mark, the tulip-shaped quart mug in Figure 221 exemplifies the superior quality of metal used by William Will and his consistently fine workmanship.

The ball terminal on the handle of the William Will pint mug in Figure 222 is a design frequently used by pewterers from the Philadelphia area.

Raised bands gave way to incised lines on the bodies of mugs made in America during the first quarter of the nineteenth century. The example, in Figure 223, is attributed to the Palethorps. The concentric circles on the inside bottom have been found on mugs made by the Palethorps. The incised circles have been found on mugs of Philadelphia and New York origin.

Fig. 223. *Pint mug (above). Attributed to the Palethorps, Philadelphia, 1817–1840. H 4 1/4", TD 3 1/8", BD 3 3/4". Landisville Mennonite Church, Lancaster County, Pa.*

Diminutive and uncommon, a half-pint mug by Boardman and Hart (Figure 224) is marked on the outside bottom, as were most nineteenth century American mugs.

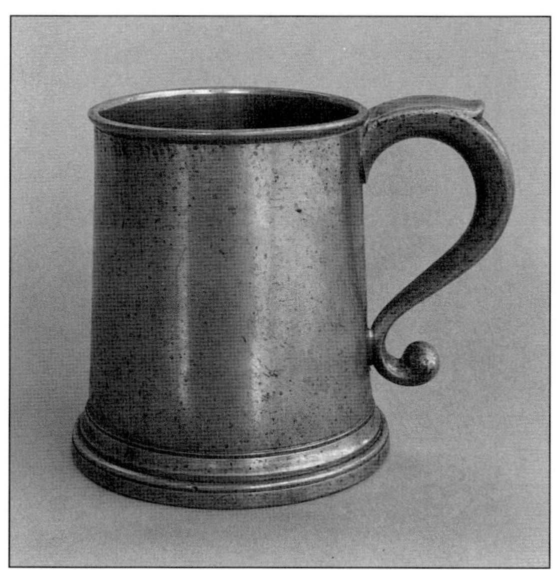

Fig. 222. *Pint mug (above). William Will, Philadelphia, 1764–1798 (L 537). H 4 5/8", TD 3 1/4", BD 4". Chestnut Hill Mennonite Church, Landisvllle, Lancaster County, Pa.*

Fig. 224. *Half-pint mug (below). Boardman and Hart, Hartford, Conn. and New York, N.Y., 1828–1853 (L 437,438). H 3 1/4", TD 2 3/4", BD 3". East Petersburg Mennonite Church, Lancaster County, Pa.*

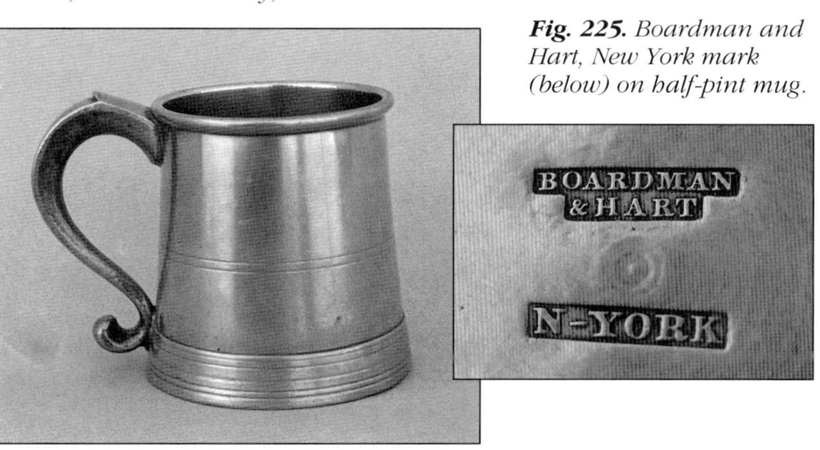

Fig. 225. *Boardman and Hart, New York mark (below) on half-pint mug.*

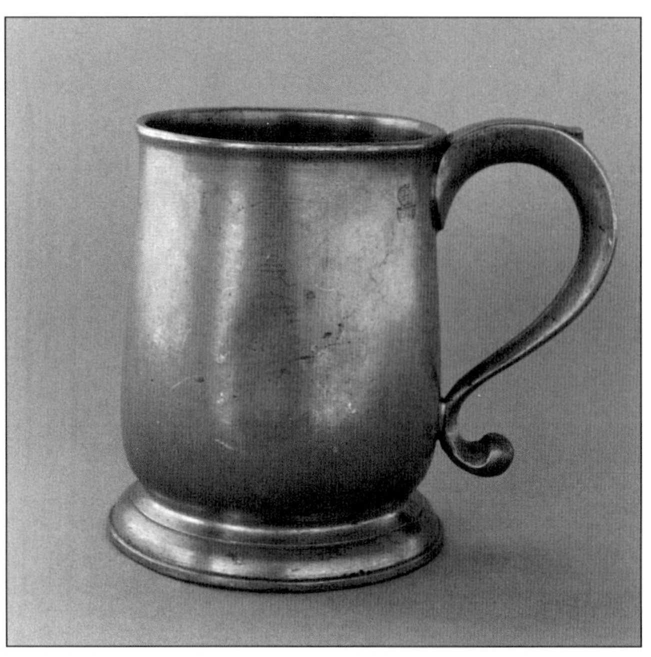

Fig. 226. *Pint mug (above). Philip Matthews, London, 1736–1743 (C 3135). H 4 1/2", TD 3 5/8", BD 3 3/4". Pint capacity. Risser's Mennonite Church, Mt. Joy, Lancaster County, Pa.*

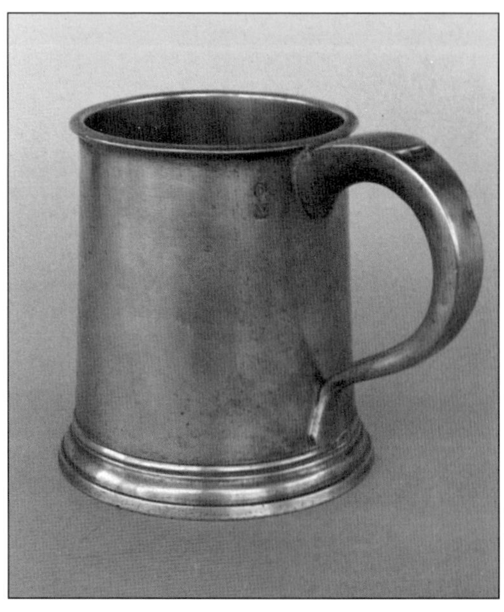

Fig. 227. *Pint mug (above). Richard Pawson, London, ca. 1753 (C 3562). H 4 3/4", TD 3 1/2", BD 4 3/8". Mellinger Mennonite Church, Lancaster, Lancaster County, Pa.*

BRITISH ISLES

The early pint mug in Figure 226 has been called a lidless tankard by Cotterell: more recently, Michaelis has considered it a tavern mug.[41] The entasis of the body is characteristic of some British mugs and tankards made in the second quarter of the eighteenth century. This mug and a similar piece were shared with the neighboring Stauffer's Mennonite Church.

The early pint mug in Figure 227 has a large handle in proportion to the mug itself. The flat handle terminal was frequently used by British makers. Note the nearly parallel sides of the body.

The tulip-shaped pint mugs in Figures 228 and 229 are by British makers John Townsend and Richard Yates.[42]

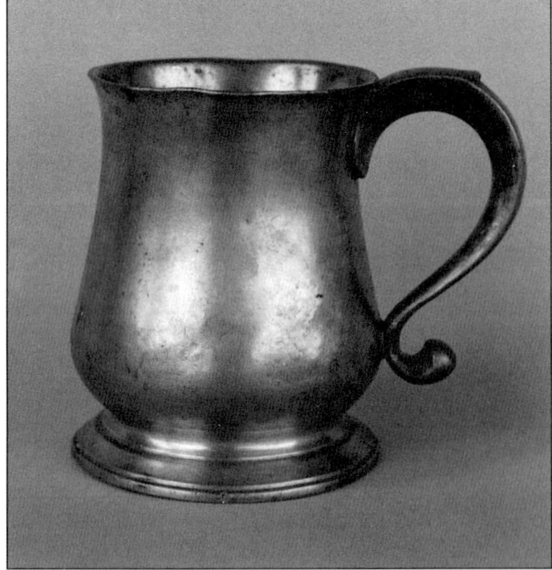

Fig. 228. *Pint mug (above). John Townsend, London, 1748–1801 (C 4795). H 4 3/4", TD 3 1/2", BD 3 3/4". Hope Lutheran Church, Cherryville, Northampton County, Pa.*

41. Ronald F. Michaelis, *British Pewter* (London: Cox and Wyman Ltd., 1969), 57.

42. Ronald F. Homer identified the maker of the pint tulip-shaped mug as Richard Yates of London in a letter to the author dated April 5, 1993. He suggested that the straight line YATES mark on the inside bottom of the mug was a mark used on export wares. This mark is not found in Cotterell or Peal.

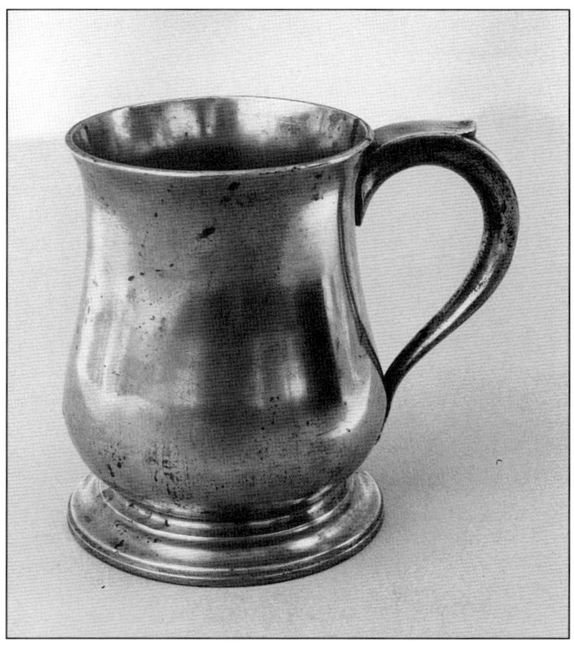

Fig. 229. *Pint mug (above). Richard Yates, London, 1772–1807 (C 5344). H 4 5/8″, TD 3 1/2″, BD 3 3/4″. The handle terminal appears to be altered. It may originally have had a ball terminal. Zion Lutheran Church, Edinburg, Shenandoah County, Va.*

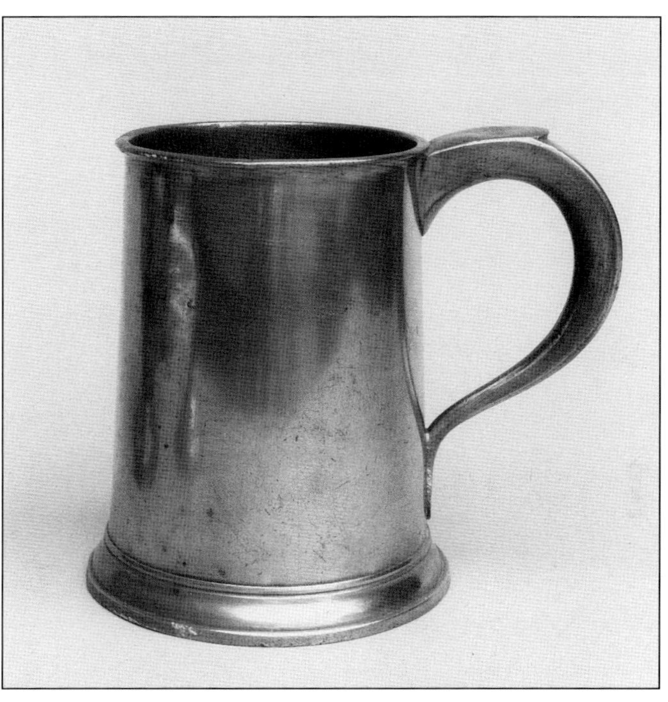

Fig. 230. *Quart mug (above). Townsend and Compton, London, 1785–1810 (C 4800). H 6 1/8″, TD 4″, BD 4 7/8″. Emmanuel Lutheran Church, Pottstown, Montgomery County, Pa.*

Quart mugs, as in this example, and pint mugs made by John Townsend and his various partnerships and descendants, lack handle terminals (Figure 230).

The Bristol quart mug in Figure 231 has a raised fillet on its body and an attractive handle design.

The survey revealed no mugs of Continental European origin. Pewter mugs were used on the Continent, but they were never common.

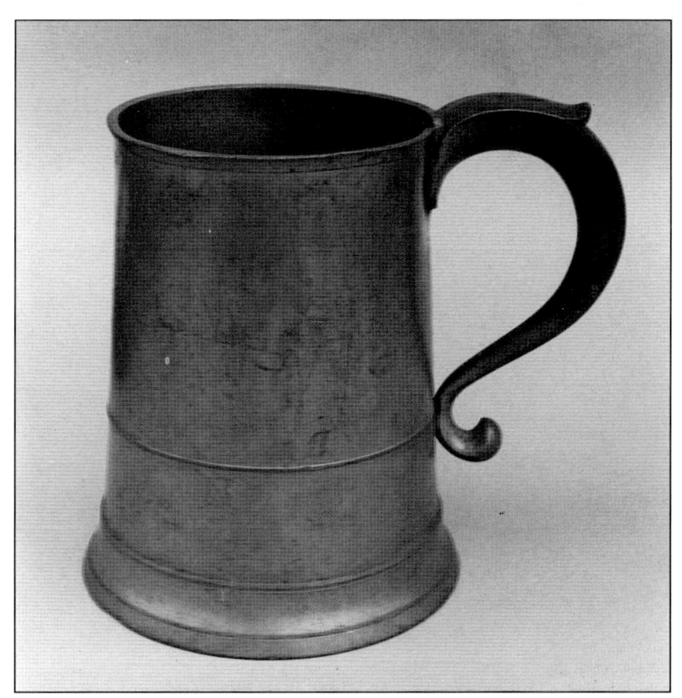

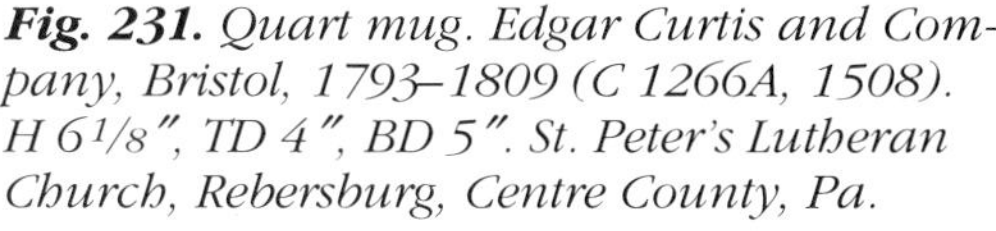

Fig. 231. *Quart mug. Edgar Curtis and Company, Bristol, 1793–1809 (C 1266A, 1508). H 6 1/8″, TD 4″, BD 5″. St. Peter's Lutheran Church, Rebersburg, Centre County, Pa.*

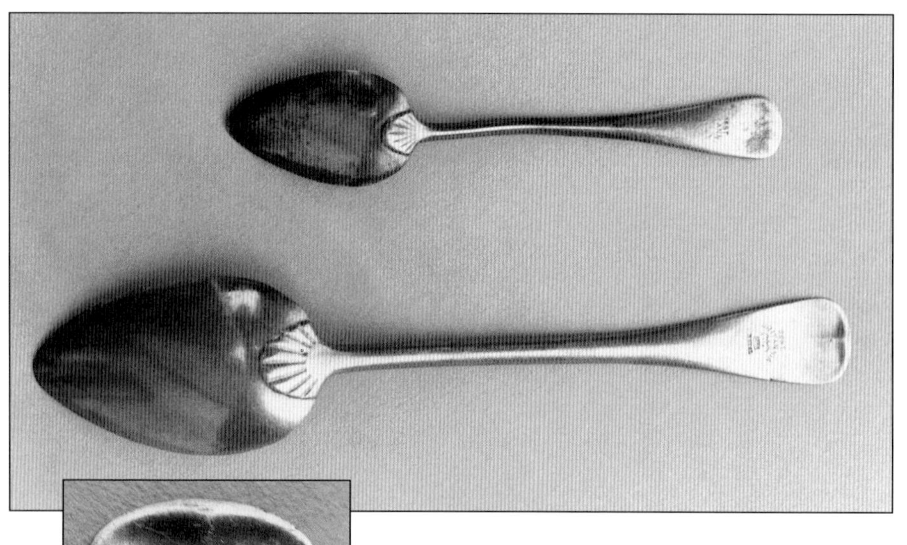

Fig. 232. Tablespoon (above). Boardmans, Hartford, Conn., 1804–1873. L 7 3/4". Teaspoon. L 5 1/4". Black Rock Church of the Brethren, Brodbecks, York County, Pa.

Fig. 233. Detail of BEST BRITANNIA METAL mark on tablespoon.

Spoons

AMERICA

Although many other forms by Thomas Boardman and his brother Sherman have survived, probably fewer than a dozen marked spoons, including both teaspoons and tablespoons, are currently known.[43] A tablespoon and teaspoon, owned by the Black Rock Church of the Brethren in York County, with Thomas Danforth Boardman and his brother Sherman's BEST BRITANNIA METAL mark, are illustrated in Figure 232. Two unmarked beakers of a form frequently marked by the Boardmans also are owned by this congregation.

BRITISH ISLES

The two British tablespoons marked LONDON in Figure 234 have oval bowls. The backs of the bowls were scraped, as was frequently done by pewterers in the eighteenth century. The bottom spoon has a more pointed tip, its bowl is not scraped, and it is slightly later in style.

John Yates from Birmingham, England, produced many teaspoons and tablespoons. An example of his ware is illustrated in Figure 236.

Spoons marked by Continental European pewterers were not found in the survey.

Fig. 234. Tablespoons. Top marked LONDON, maker unknown, England, eighteenth century. L 7 1/2". Middle marked W.H. LONDON, maker unknown, England, eighteenth century. L 7 7/8". Bottom unmarked, maker unknown, probably American, 1780–1825. L 7 3/4". The top surface has a raised human figure or angel and J L in script is raised on the underside of spoon. Pipe Creek Church of the Brethren, Linwood, Carroll County, Md.

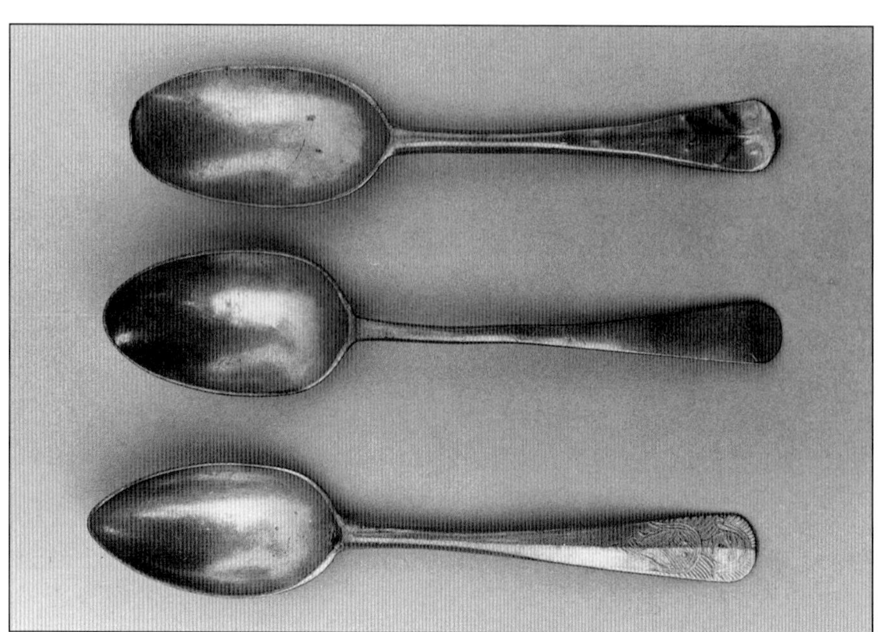

43. Luther Boardman, not of the same firm, was essentially a spoon maker, and by 1860 his production of spoons had increased to 18,000 gross per year! Many spoons marked LB have survived.

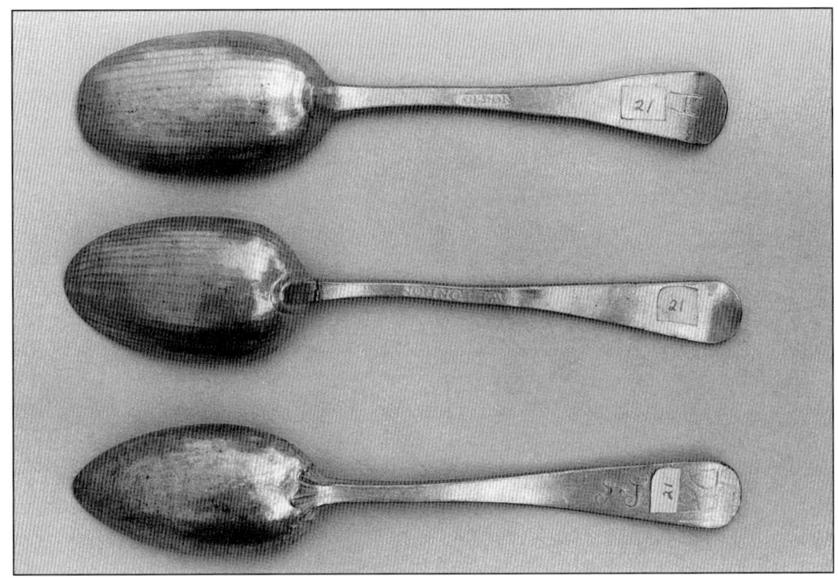

Fig. 235. *Reverse of spoons (left). Pipe Creek Church of the Brethren, Carroll County, Md.*

Fig. 236. *Teaspoon (detail below) by John Yates, Birmingham, England, 1805–1852 (C 5340A). L 5 3/8". Black Rock Church of the Brethren, Brodbecks, York County, Pa.*

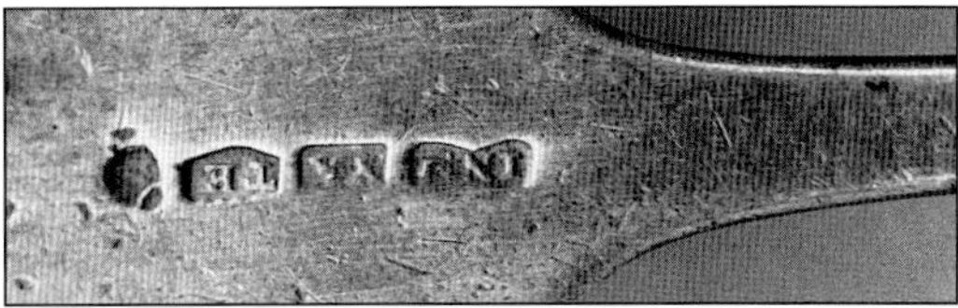

Tankards

AMERICA

The ram's horn thumbpiece and boot-heel handle terminal are early design elements in this rare and early quart tankard by Simon Edgell (Figure 237). A similar but unmarked tankard was found a few miles away in Zion—St. John's (Reed's) Lutheran Church in Stouchsburg, Berks County, Pa. Edgell is the earliest Philadelphia pewterer whose marked pewter has survived.

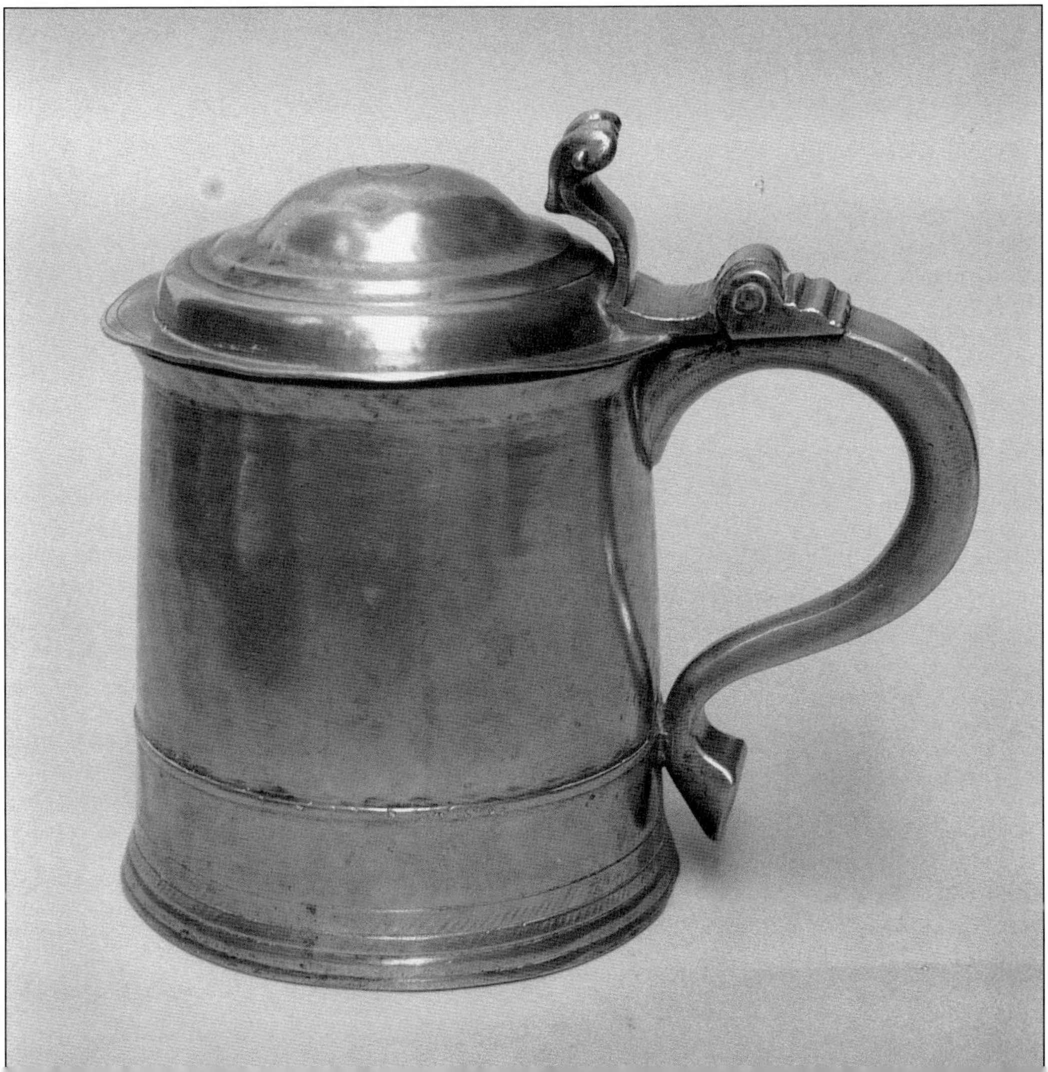

Fig. 237. *Quart tankard. Simon Edgell, Philadelphia, 1713–1742, (L 526). H 6 1/2", TD 4 3/8", BD 4 3/4". St. John's (Hain's) United Church of Christ, Wernersville, Berks County, Pa.*

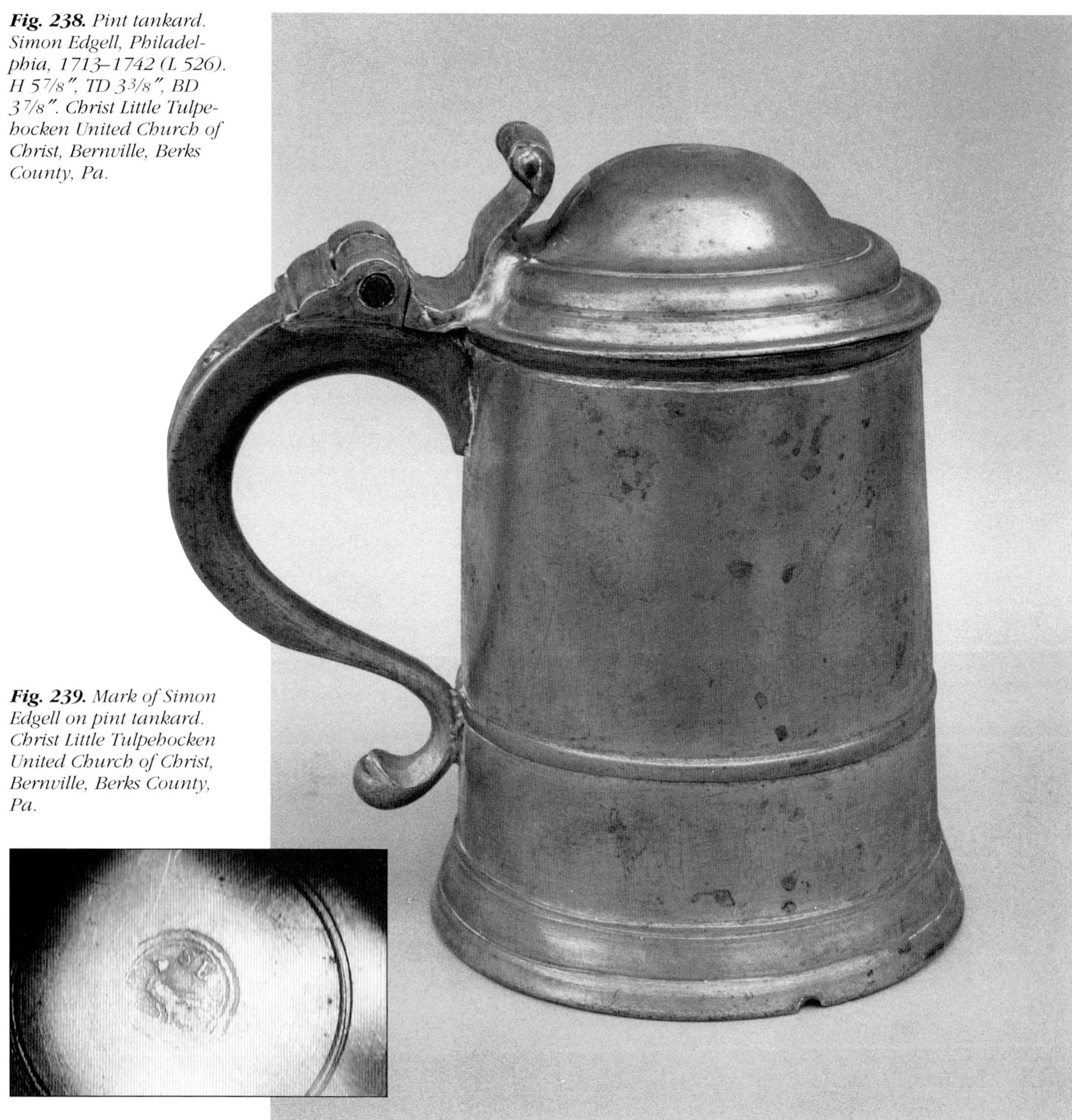

Fig. 238. *Pint tankard. Simon Edgell, Philadelphia, 1713–1742 (L 526). H 5 7/8″, TD 3 3/8″, BD 3 7/8″. Christ Little Tulpehocken United Church of Christ, Bernville, Berks County, Pa.*

Fig. 239. *Mark of Simon Edgell on pint tankard. Christ Little Tulpehocken United Church of Christ, Bernville, Berks County, Pa.*

The rare piece in Figure 238 is likely the earliest known pint tankard made by an American pewterer. It is almost identical to a pint tankard by Cornelius Bradford, who apparently acquired Simon Edgell's molds and continued to make the same form. Pint tankards must not have been a popular item, for very few American pint tankards have survived.

Quart tankards of this form were made in the British Isles and in America (Figure 240).

The body, thumbpiece, and handle with fish-tail terminal of the quart tankard

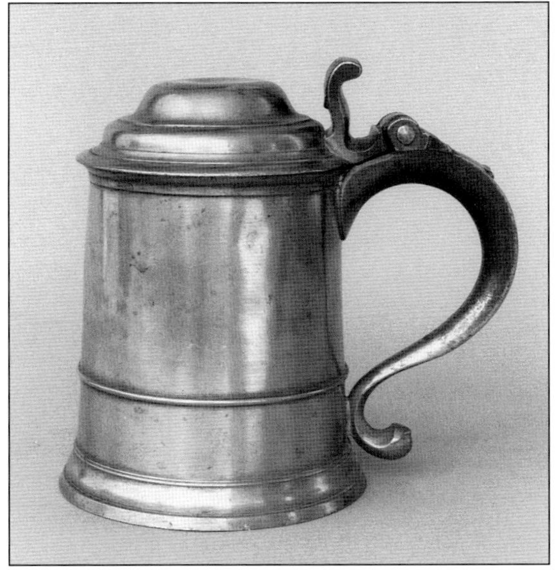

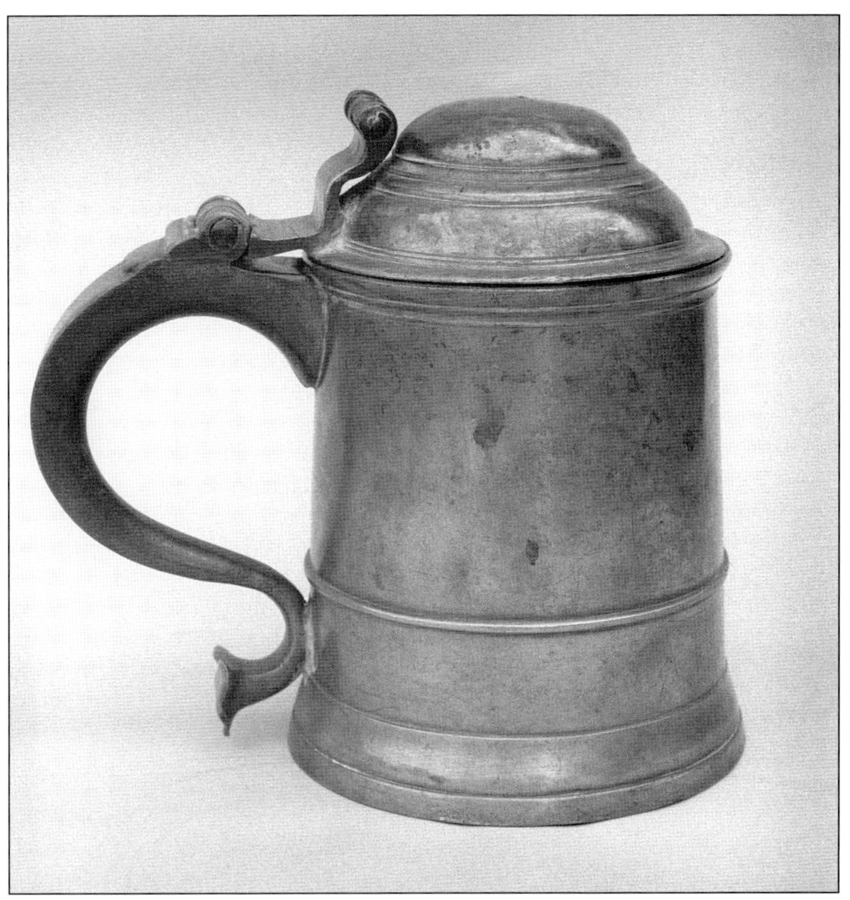

Fig. 240. *Quart tankard (above). John Bassett, New York, 1720–1761 (L 458). H 6 3/4", TD 4", BD 4 7/8". Heidelberg Union Church with Lutheran and United Church of Christ congregations, Slatington, Lehigh County, Pa.*

Fig. 241. *Quart tankard (right). Love, Philadelphia, 1750–1800 (L 869). H 7", TD 4 1/4", BD 5". Allegheny Union Church with Lutheran and United Church of Christ congregations, Alleghenyville, Berks County, Pa.*

in Figure 241 are similar to one with a touchmark attributed to Thomas Byles of Newport and Philadelphia.[44] Byles purchased property in Philadelphia in 1738 and died there in 1770. Straight quart tankards are listed in Byle's inventory. He may have been one of the users of the Love touchmark. A straight-sided tankard with ram's horn thumbpiece and fish-tail handle terminal marked by Love is illustrated here for the first time.

William Will made the quart tankard illustrated in Figure 242. It is engraved on the outside bottom "Used in the Religious Ceremonies of the Community at Ephrata, Pa." The engraving is not contemporary with the piece.

44 See Ledlie I. Laughlin, *Pewter in America,* 3, Fig. 712.

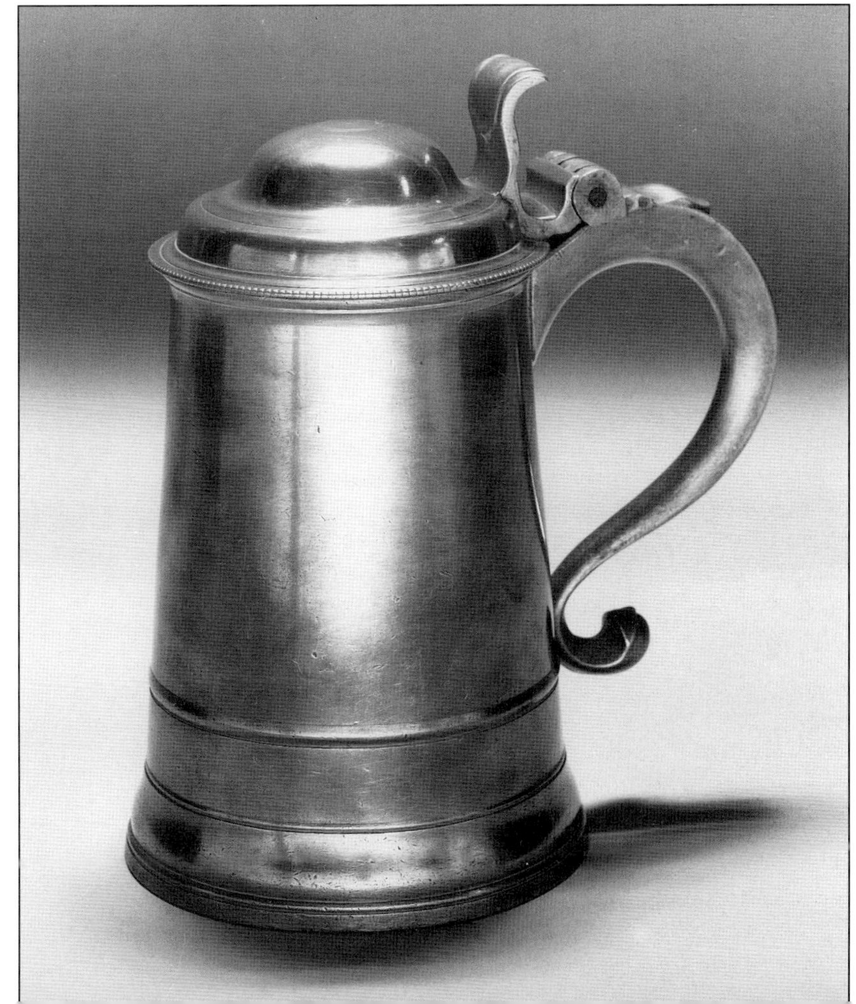

Fig. 242. *Quart tankard. William Will, Philadelphia, 1764–1798 (L 541). H 7 3/4", TD 3 3/4", BD 4 5/8". Possibly used at the Ephrata Cloister, Lancaster County, Pa. (In the collection of and photograph courtesy of the Historical Society of Pennsylvania).*

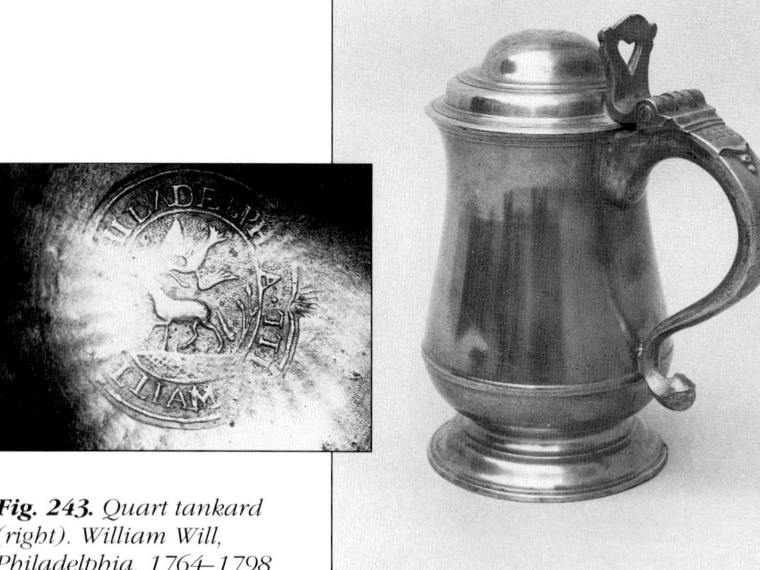

Fig. 243. *Quart tankard (right). William Will, Philadelphia, 1764–1798 (L 535). H 8 1/2″, TD 4 1/8″, BD 4 3/8″. Zion's (Stone) United Church of Christ, Northampton, Northampton County, Pa.*

Fig. 244. *Lamb-and-dove mark (above) of William Will on inside of tulip quart tankard.*

The raised decorative band on the lower body enhances the beauty of Will's quart tulip tankard (Figure 243). It is marked on the inside bottom with his lamb-and-dove mark. The design of the touch is related to British marks such as those used by importers John Townsend and his various partnerships.

The handle design of the tankard in Figure 245, with its indentation and lower raised drop has been found on marked tankards (as in the preceding example) by William Will. Will also used the same handle design on a few of his flagons. The unmarked quart tankard shares the same foot, body, and handle designs of the tankard in Figure 243. The lid and thumbpiece forms are found on other marked Will tankards.

The tankard in Figure 246 has a pair of incised concentric circles on the inside bottom, common on tankards made in Philadelphia. Also, it shares a handle design of indentations and a single drop that William Will used on both marked tankards and flagons. The chair-back thumbpiece was likewise used by Will.

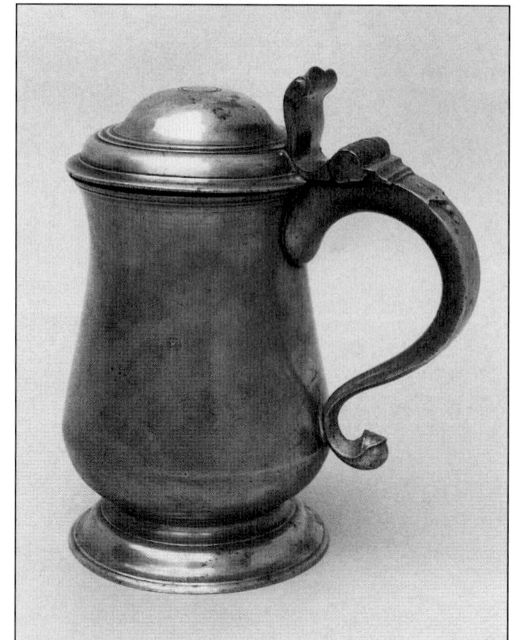

Fig. 245. *Quart tankard (right). Attributed to William Will, Philadelphia, 1764–1798. H 8 1/8″, TD 4 1/8″, BD 4 3/8″. Zion's (Stone) United Church of Christ, Northampton, Northampton County, Pa.*

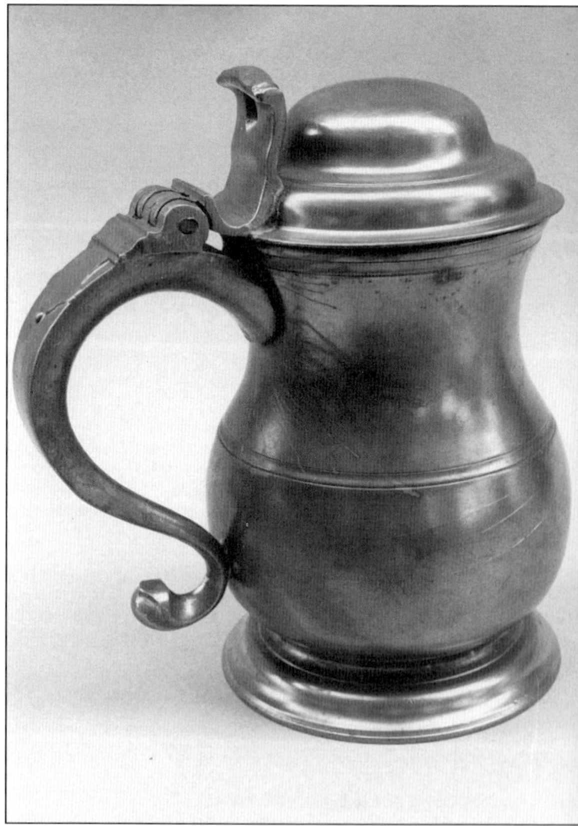

Fig. 246. *Quart tankard (above). Philadelphia, second half of the eighteenth century, probably William Will. H 8″, TD 4″, BD 4 33/43″. Paradise-Holzschwamm Union Church, with Lutheran and United Church of Christ congregations, Thomasville, York County, Pa.*

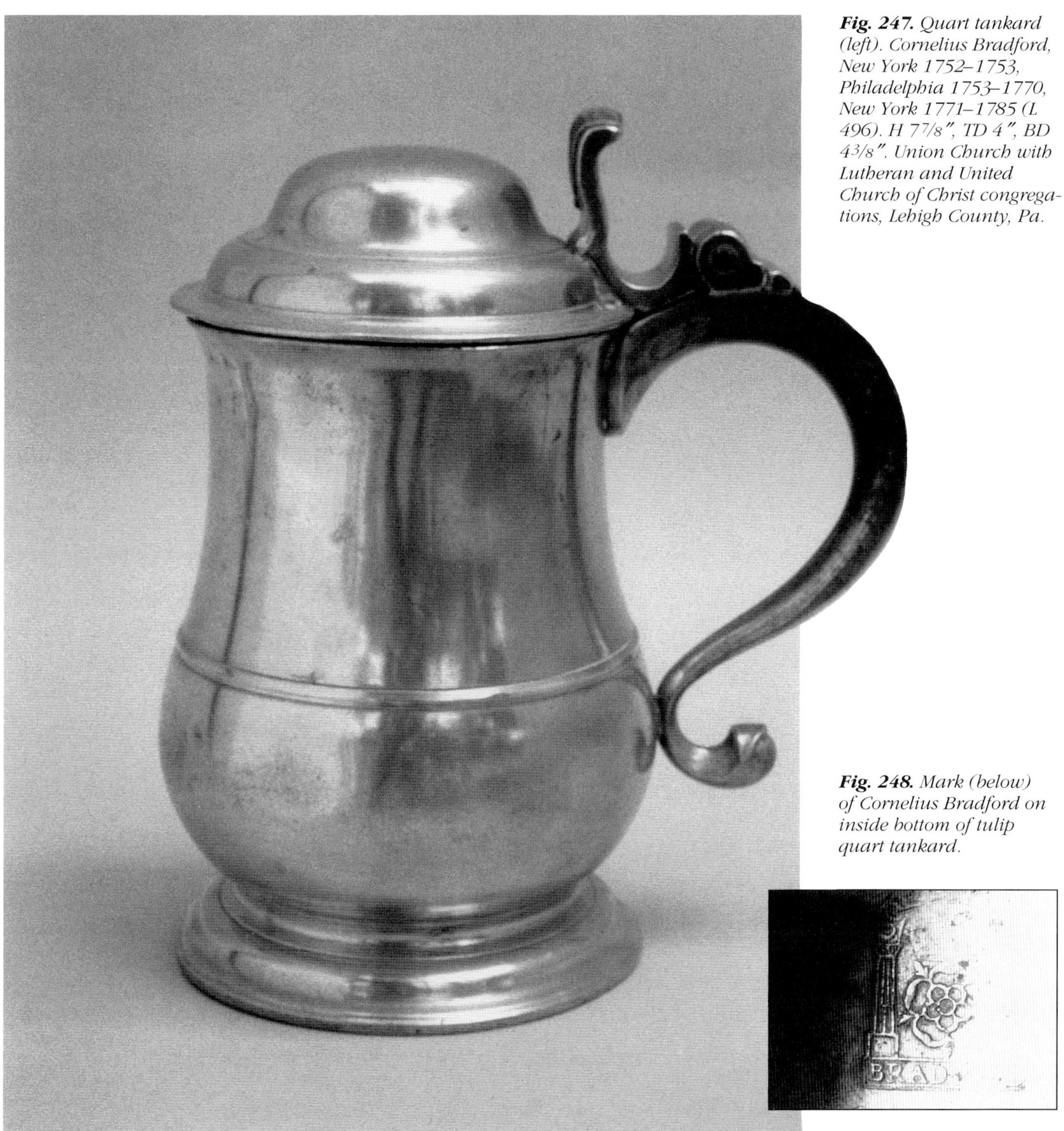

Fig. 247. *Quart tankard (left). Cornelius Bradford, New York 1752–1753, Philadelphia 1753–1770, New York 1771–1785 (L 496). H 7 7/8", TD 4", BD 4 3/8". Union Church with Lutheran and United Church of Christ congregations, Lehigh County, Pa.*

Fig. 248. *Mark (below) of Cornelius Bradford on inside bottom of tulip quart tankard.*

American tulip tankards appear to have been made only in New York City and Philadelphia. The low fillet on the body was popular with Philadelphia makers. The rise to the base of the thumbpiece as it attaches to the handle articulation is found on other Philadelphia tankards, including a few made by William Will. This piece (Figure 247) is one of two tulip-shaped tankards made by Cornelius Bradford that are known to the author.

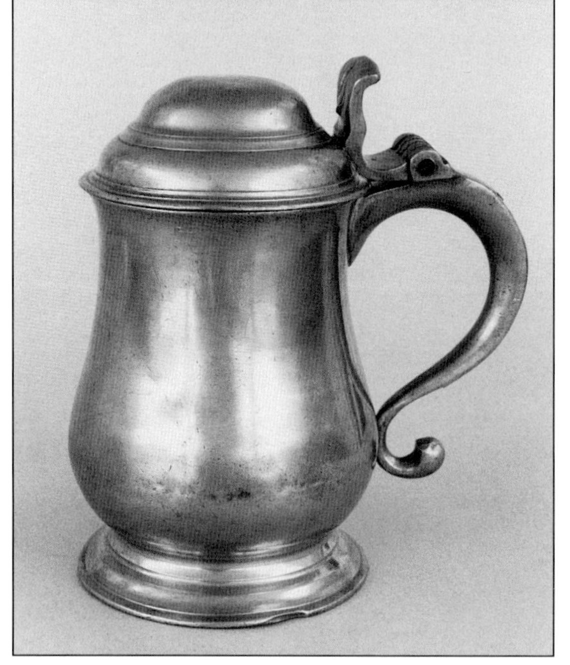

Fig. 249. *Quart tankard. Love, Philadelphia, 1750–1800 (L 869). H 7 1/4", TD 4" BD 4 1/2". Bally Mennonite Church, Berks County, Pa.*

Marked on the inside bottom with the Lovebird touch, the tulip quart tankard has the distinctive high double-domed lid characteristic of other marked Love tankards (Fig. 249). Compare this marked Love tankard with the unmarked spouted flagon illustrated in Figure 186.

The flat dome of the lid and raised bands decorating the body suggest Swedish influence on the Love tankard in

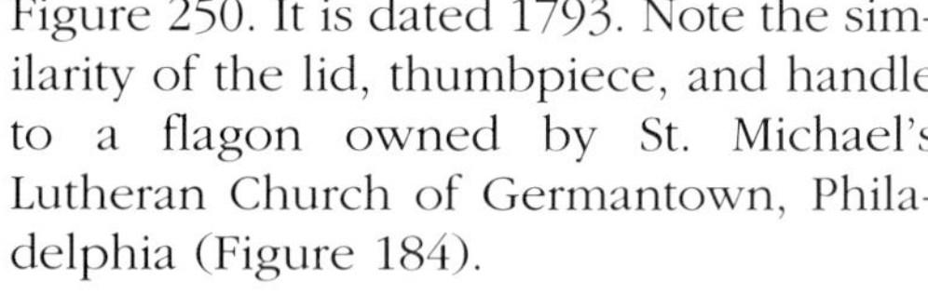

Figure 250. It is dated 1793. Note the similarity of the lid, thumbpiece, and handle to a flagon owned by St. Michael's Lutheran Church of Germantown, Philadelphia (Figure 184).

BRITISH ISLES

William Eddon's straight-sided quart tankard is an attractive balanced form (Fig. 252). The style was made in England during the first half of the eighteenth century. The same form continued to be made in America a half century later.

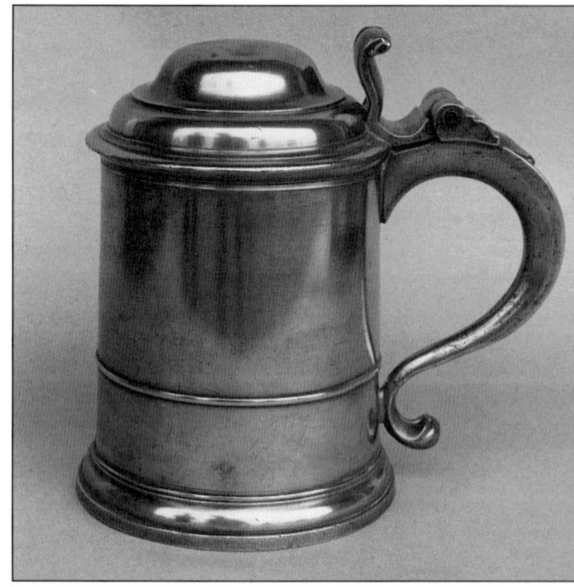

Fig. 252. *Quart tankard (above). William Eddon, London, 1690–1745 (C 1503). H 7 1/4" TD 4 1/4", BD 5". Canadochly Lutheran Church, Delroy, York County, Pa.*

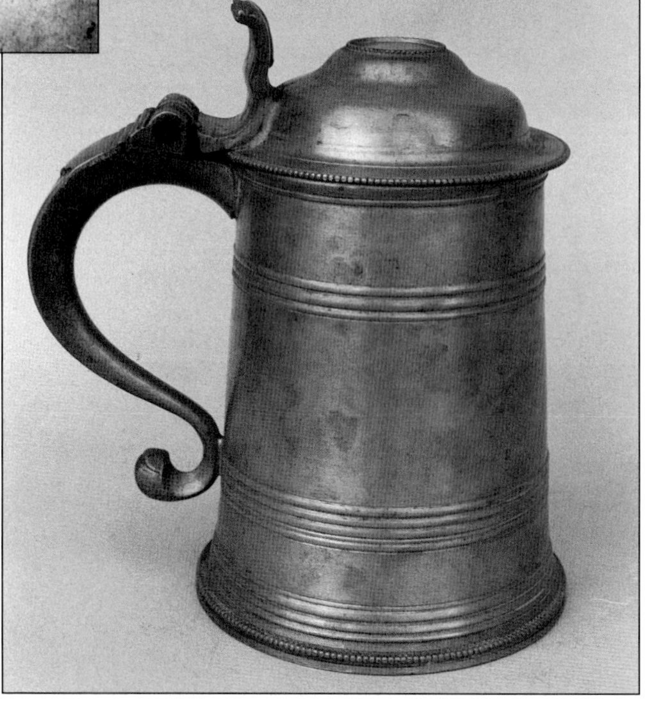

Fig. 250. *Quart tankard (left). Love, Philadelphia, 1750–1800 (L 869). H 7 1/2", TD 4", BD 4 3/4". Formerly owned by Zion Lutheran Church, Middle Smithfield Township, Monroe County, Pa. The congregation no longer exists. In the collection of the Lutheran Archives Center, Lutheran Theological Seminary, Mt. Airy, Philadelphia, Pa.*

Fig. 251. *Love touchmarks (far left) on inside bottom of quart tankard.*

The TS in a square mark on the tankard in Figure 253 is an unrecorded mark. The handle and thumbpiece combination suggest the 1705 to 1750 period. The lack of the mark on the London touch plates and the absence of the "WR crown" verification stamp support an origin other than London. It may have been made in Bristol, since pewterers Going, Cox, and Bush, Sr., used this handle/thumbpiece combination.[45] The quart tankard has a pint tankard handle with a fish-tail terminal. The use of a small handle on a quart body makes the tankard appear larger than it really is.

The diminutive straight-sided tankard in Figure 255 has a capacity of one pint. The mark on the inside bottom is illustrated in Peal's *More Pewter Marks*. It is not listed in Cotterell's *Old Pewter*.

Figure 257 bears the mark of R. King. Three Richard Kings were working in London at the same time, and it is not clear which pewterer used which mark.

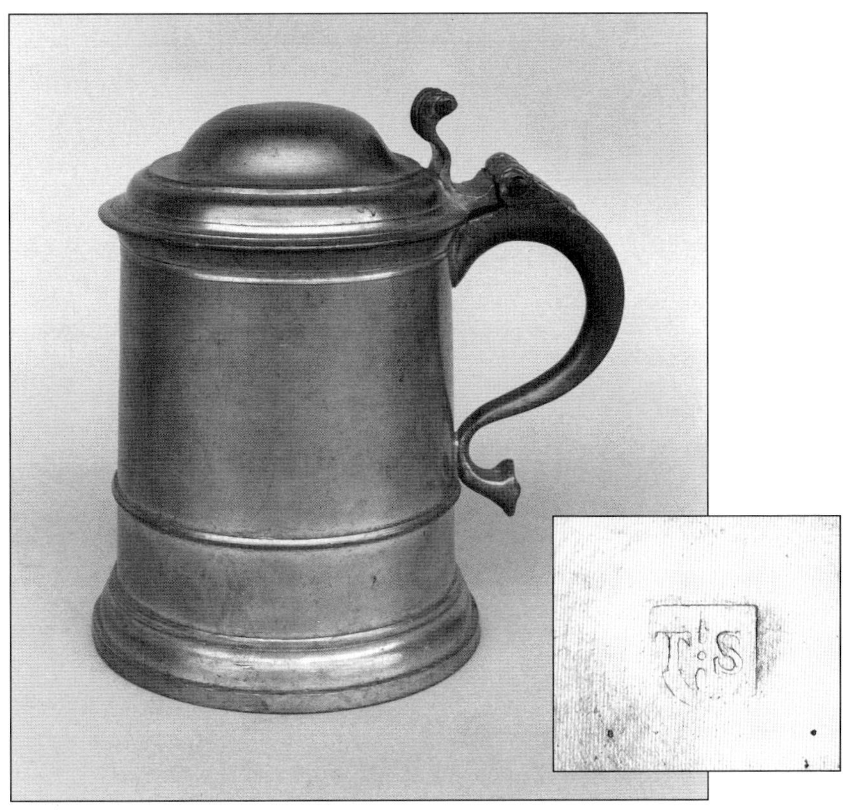

Fig. 253. *Quart tankard (above). Unknown British maker. Probably Bristol, 1705–1750. H 6 3/4", TD 4 1/8", BD 4 7/8". Emmanuel United Church of Christ, Freysville, York County, Pa.*

Fig. 254. *TS mark (below) in quart tankard. Emmanuel United Church of Christ, Freysville, York County, Pa.*

45. Ian D. Robinson reported the information to the author in a conversation May 2, 1993.

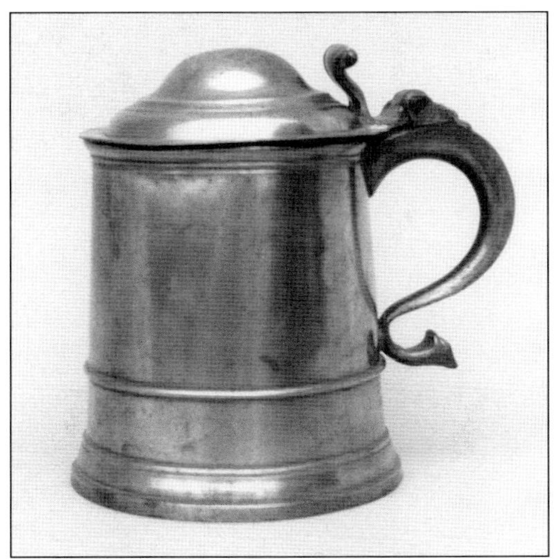

Fig. 257. *Quart tankard (above). Richard King, London, 1745–1798 (C 2748, 2749, 2750). H 6 1/4", TD 4 1/4", BD 4 3/4". St. John's (Schuetz's) Lutheran Church, Spinnerstown, Bucks County, Pa.*

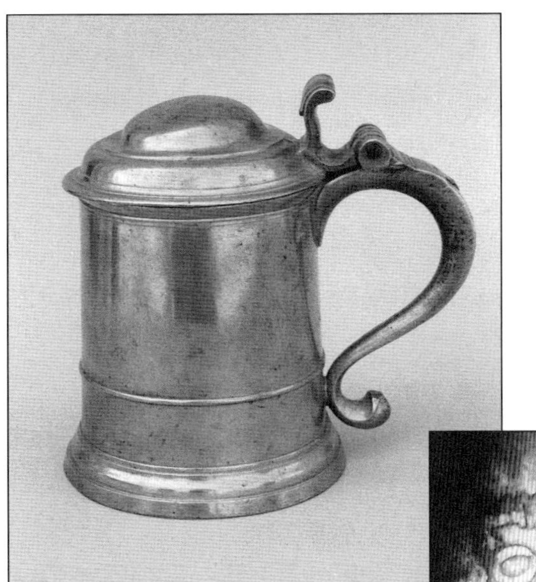

Fig. 255. *Pint tankard (left). Philip Matthews, London, 1736–1755 (P 3135). H 5 5/8", TD 3 1/8", BD 4 1/8". Weisenberg Lutheran Church, New Tripoli, Lehigh County, Pa.*

Fig. 256. *Philip Matthews mark (below) on pint tankard.*

Fig. 258. *Three and one-half-pint tankard (right). Richard King, London, 1745–1798. H 7⁷⁄₈", TD 4⁵⁄₈", BD 5⁵⁄₈". Muddy Creek Lutheran Church and Peace United Church of Christ, Denver, Lancaster County, Pa.*

Fig. 259. *R. King mark (below) in three and one half-pint tankard.*

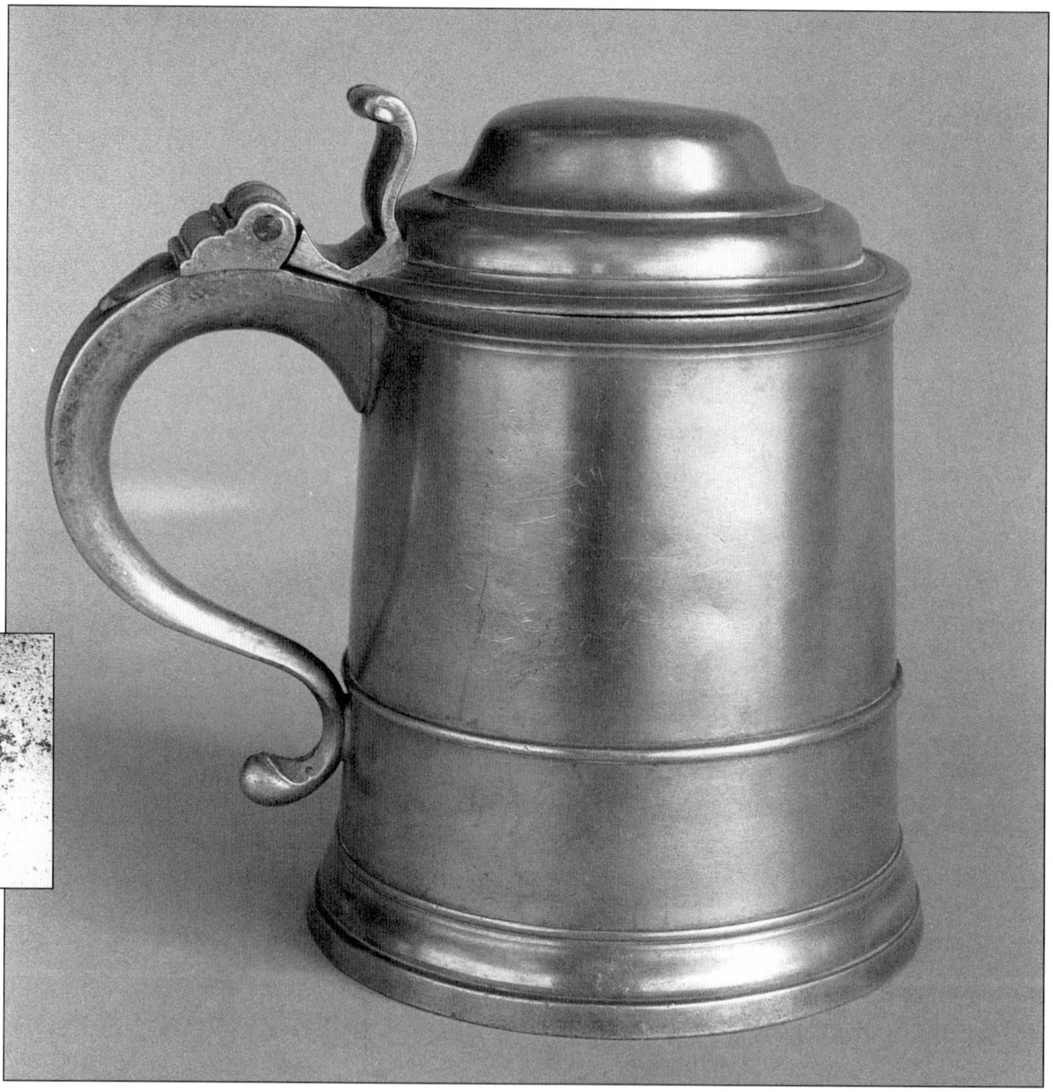

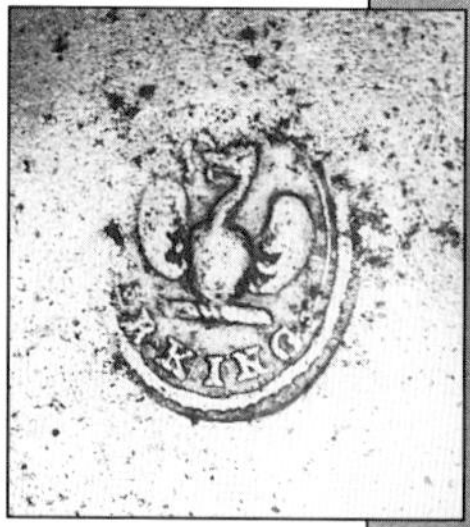

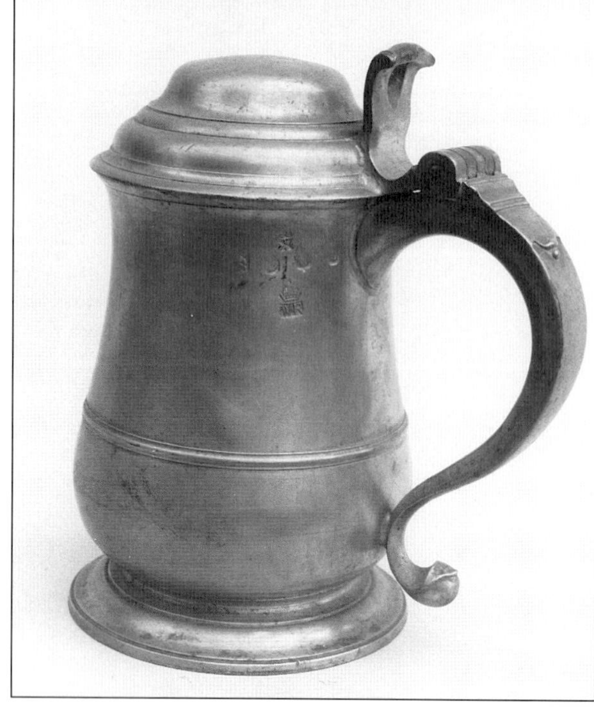

Fig. 260. *Quart tankard. Richard King, London, 1745–1798 (C 2750). H 8", TD 4¹⁄₄", BD 4³⁄₄". Egypt United Church of Christ, Whitehall, Lehigh County, Pa.*

The R. King in an oval mark on the inside bottom of the large tankard in Figure 258 is not recorded in Cotterell or Peal and may be that of a Richard King who worked in London from 1729 to 1745. H 7⁷⁄₈", TD 4⁵⁄₈", BD 5⁵⁄₈". This massive tankard has a capacity of over three and a half pints. Tankards of similar size were made by another London pewterer, William Eddon, who worked from 1689 to 1745, and by American pewterers John and Frederick Bassett.

The tulip-shaped quart tankard in Figure 260 is marked on the inside bottom by Richard King. The set of hallmarks on the outside of the body are those used by Thomas Carpenter and Carpenter and Hamberger, London pewterers working about the same time as King. Occasionally pewterers purchased pewterware made by others and added their marks prior to resale.

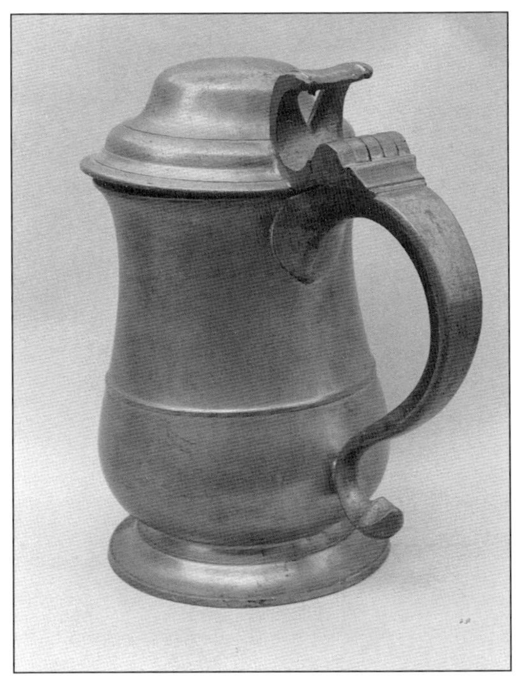

Fig. 261. *Quart tankard (above). Ash and Hutton, Bristol, 1741–1768 (C 118). H 7 1/2", TD 4", BD 4 1/4". Millcreek Lutheran Church, Newmanstown, Lebanon County, Pa.*

The heart-shaped opening on the thumbpiece of the Ash and Hutton tankard illustrated in Figure 261 is occasionally found on mid-to-late eighteenth century British and American tankards.

The quart tankard in Figure 262, by Robert Bush, Sr., has a ram's horn thumbpiece and fish-tail handle.

Bristol pewterers Burgum and Catcott made the quart tankard of early design in Figure 263. It has a ram's horn thumbpiece and fish-tail handle terminal.

Fig. 263. *Quart tankard (left). Burgum and Catcott, Bristol, 1765–1779 (C 708). H 6 3/4", TD 4 1/8", BD 4 3/4". A United Church of Christ congregation in Northampton County, Pa.*

The quart tankard in Figure 264 has an earlier handle design than the one illustrated in Figure 265. This was the only quart tankard made by John Townsend with this handle style found in the survey.

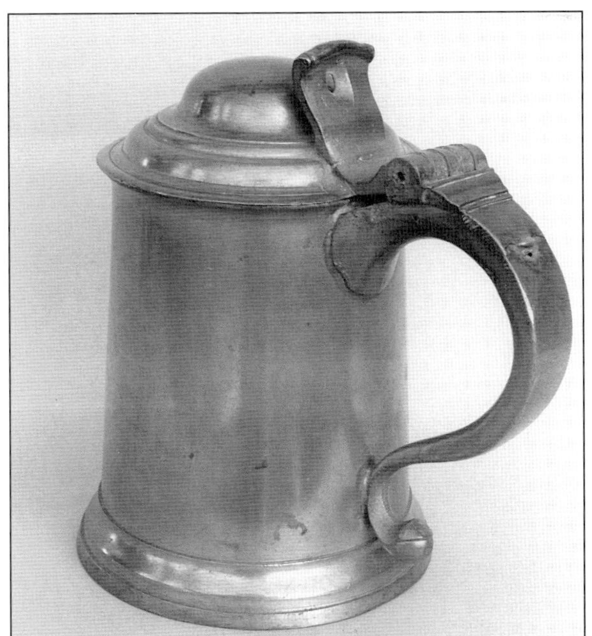

Fig. 264. *Quart tankard. John Townsend, London, 1748–1801 (C 4795). H 7 1/4", TD 4 1/8", BD 4 7/8". St. Luke's Lutheran Church, Schaefferstown, Lebanon County, Pa.*

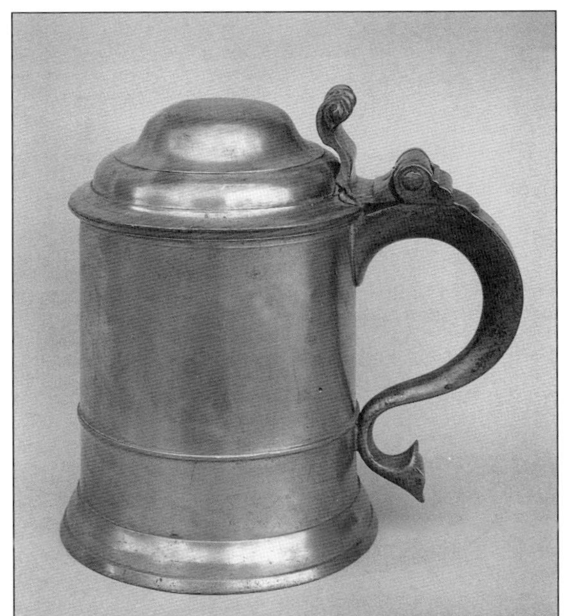

Fig. 262. *Quart tankard (left). Robert Bush, Sr., Bristol, 1755–1801 (C 737). H 7 1/4", TD 4 1/4", BD 5 1/8". St. Peter's (Lischy's) United Church of Christ, Spring Grove, York County, Pa.*

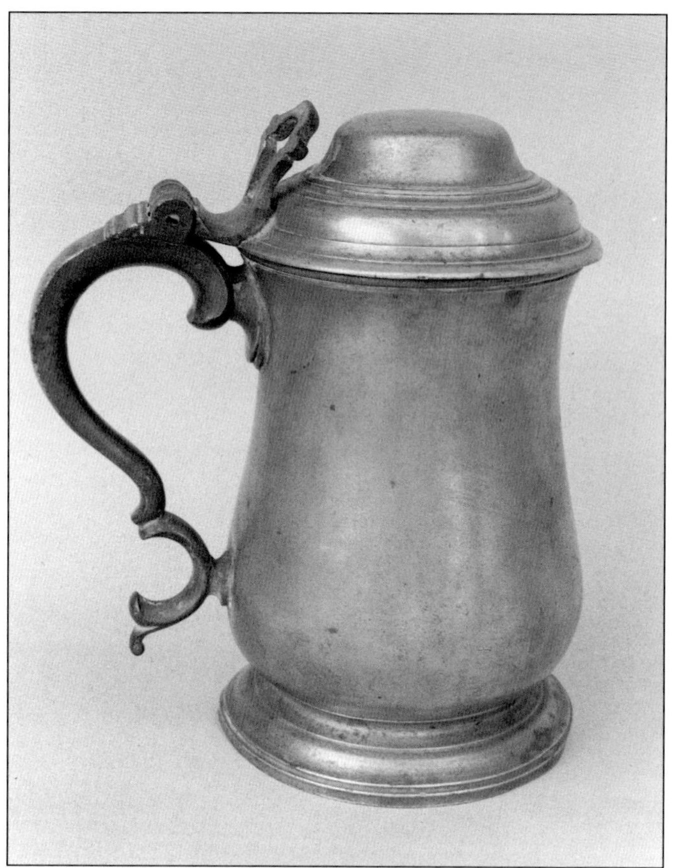

Fig. 265. *Quart tankard (above). John Townsend, London, 1748–1801 (C 4795). H 8″, TD 4 1/4″, BD 4 1/2″. St. Peter's Lutheran Church, North Wales, Montgomery County, Pa.*

A tulip-shaped quart tankard with open-chair thumbpiece and double-C scroll handle design was made by John Townsend (Figure 265).

A straight-sided quart tankard with open-chair thumbpiece and double-C scroll handle made by Townsend and Compton is illustrated in Figure 266. Note the same handle design as in the previous example. John Townsend's molds continued to be used by his various partnerships and by his daughter Mary and son-in-law Thomas Compton.

Another Townsend and Compton tankard of quart capacity has an open chair thumbpiece and double-C scroll handle (Figure 267). Note the interesting decoration at the top of handle. The design was incorporated into the handle mold prior to pouring the alloy.

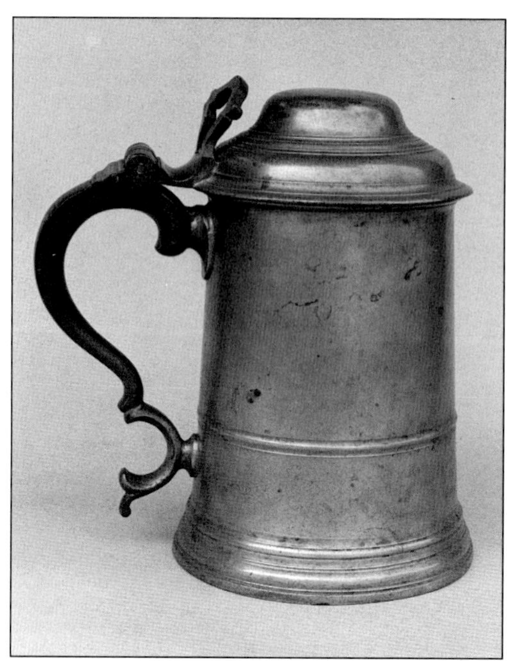

Fig. 266. *Quart tankard (right). Townsend and Compton, London, 1785–1810 (C 4800). H 7 3/4″, TD 4 1/4″, BD 4 7/8″. Holy Trinity Lutheran Church, Berlin, Somerset County, Pa.*

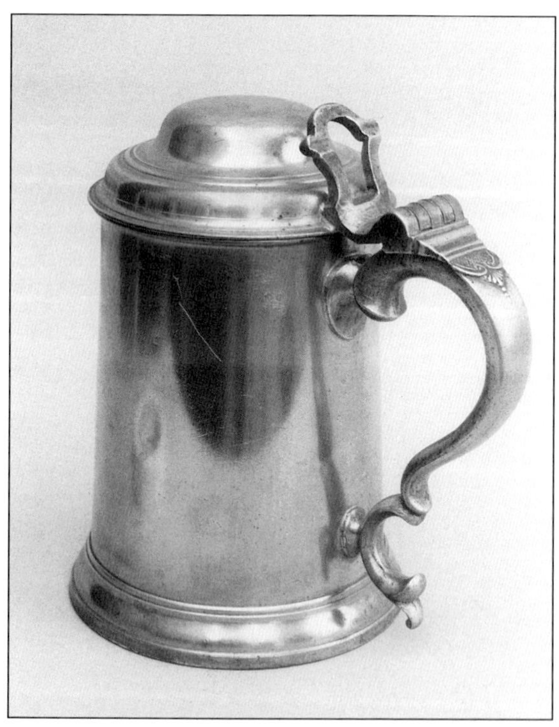

Fig. 267. *Quart tankard (above). Townsend and Compton, London, 1785–1810 (C 4800). H 7 1/4″, TD 4″, BD 4 7/8″. Lutheran Church, Lebanon County, Pa.*

The tulip-shaped quart tankard by Robert Bush and Company illustrated in Figure 268 has a handle design that is found frequently on British tankards made in the last quarter of the eighteenth century.[46]

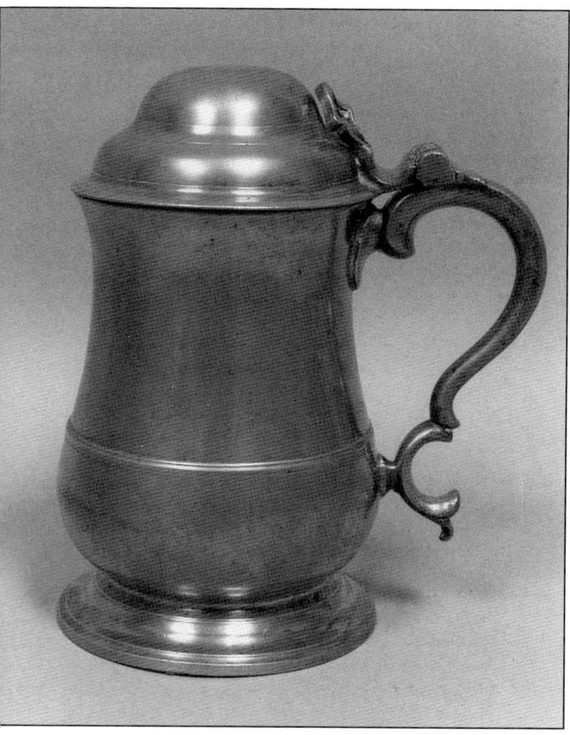

Fig. 268. *Quart tankard. Robert Bush and Company, Bristol, 1787–1795 (C 739). H 7 3/4", TD 5", BD 4 1/2". Zion Evangelical and Reformed United Church of Christ, Hagerstown, Washington County, Md.*

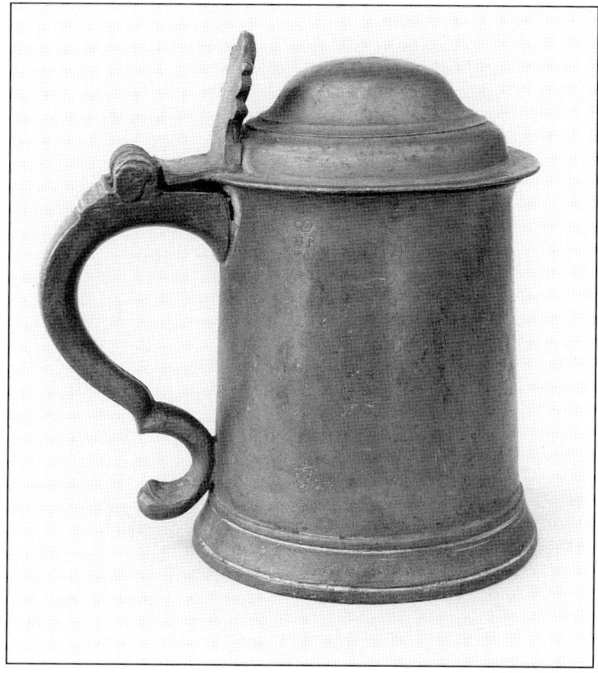

Fig. 269. *Pint tankard. Ingram and Hunt, Bewdley, 1788–1807 (P 2540). H 6", TD 3 3/8". BD 4". Friedens United Church of Christ Church, New Ringgold, Schuylkill County, Pa.*

Ingram and Hunt produced the pint tankard shown in Figure 269. Tankard forms deteriorated at the beginning of the nineteenth century. The heavy, ungraceful handle design lacks the beauty of the handle illustrated in the previous example.

Tankards marked by pewterers from Continental Europe were not found in the survey.

46. Jean Woods, *The Germanic Heritage* (Hagerstown, Md.: Washington County Museum of Fine Arts, 1983), 32.

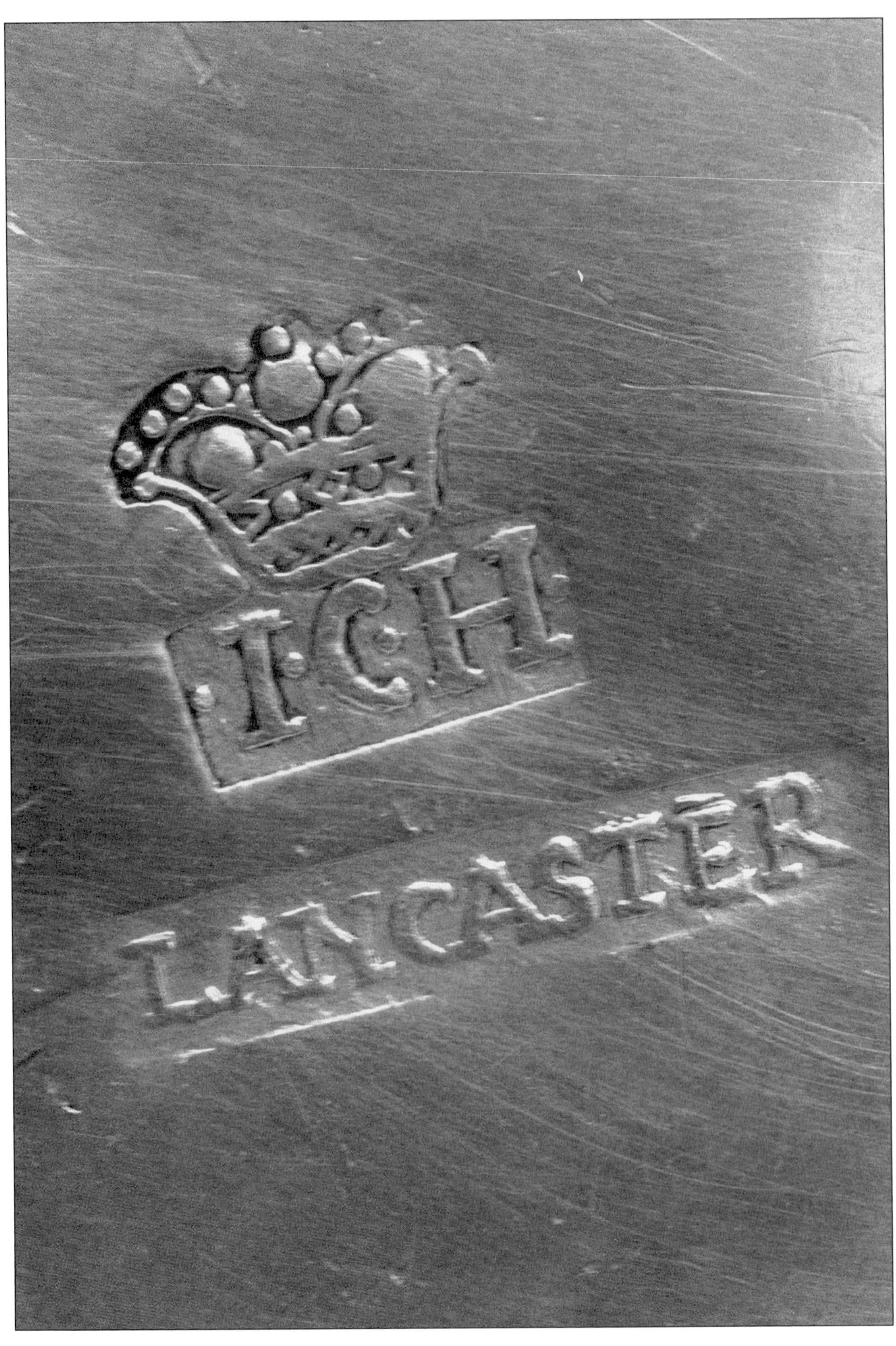

Fig. 270. *Mark of Johann Christoph Heyne on flagon. Brickerville United Lutheran Church, Brickerville, Lancaster County, Pa.*

CHAPTER 6

Pewterers

The intention of this section is to give a brief synopsis of the pewterers whose pieces were found in the survey. Much new information has been learned since the standard reference books (Laughlin's three-volume *Pewter in America* [1940, 1971], Cotterell's *Old Pewter* [1929], and Hintze's seven-volume *Die Deutschen Zinngiesser und ihre Marken* [1921-1931]) were first printed. An attempt was made to update and include the most recent information about makers and their working dates, hence some dates may differ from those in the standard texts. Updates on Townsend and Compton, the Hales, Stynt Duncumb, Bush, Perkins, Samuel Ellis, Ingram and Hart, Henry Joseph, Thomas Byles and others are included and are the result of recent scholarship.

American

Johann Philip Alberti
Alberti took the oath of allegiance in Philadelphia on December 13, 1754, at the age of 32, having recently arrived on the ship *Neptune* from Hamburg. He opened his shop with Christian Horan and after a ten-year partnership worked alone until his death in 1780. His shop inventory, taken September 18, 1780, was appraised by pewterers Christian Horan and Adam Koehler. Forty-six turning tools, two turning wheels, a lot of old iron, a lot of files, a frame of bellows, two vices, 274 pounds of pewter, 31 3/4 pounds of old brass, 149 pounds of lead, two six-plated stoves, several turning blocks, a wheel and grindstone, and 42 3/4 pounds of brass molds are listed in his inventory.[1]

Blakeslee Barnes
Blakeslee Barnes was a tinsmith from Berlin, Connecticut, who employed a pewterer named Nott in Philadelphia from 1812 to 1817. (This was probably William Nott, a pewterer who was working in Wethersfield, Connecticut, about 1810 and may have been hired by Barnes for his Philadelphia shop). Barnes was in Philadelphia during those years, but may have had his employee cast the many plates, dishes, and basins that have survived. Barnes shared an address with pewterer Thomas Danforth III and may have had a partnership or business arrangement with Danforth.[2] Only flatware is known bearing his marks.

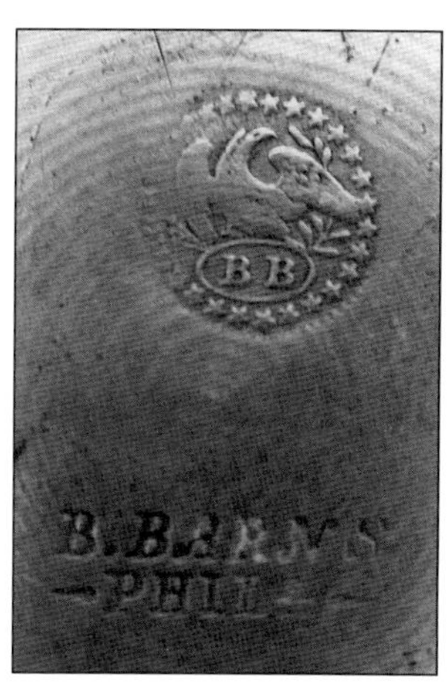

Fig. 271. *Mark of Blakeslee Barnes on plate. St. John's Lutheran Church, Spinnerstown, Bucks County, Pa.*

Stephen Barns
Little is known about Stephen Barns. A Stephen Barns was born February 1777 in Middletown, Connecticut, but his occupation is unknown. He may have served his apprenticeship with Middletown pewterer William Danforth. Flatware marked Stephen Barns is found in the same sizes as those by William Danforth. The style of the Barns mark is of the 1795–1810 period.

1. Philip Alberti's inventory is located in the Manuscript Library of the Winterthur Museum, Winterthur, Del. 56x14.1, Box 11.

2. John Carl Thomas, *Connecticut Pewter and Pewterers,* The Connecticut Historical Society (Hartford: Connecticut Printers, 1976), 85.

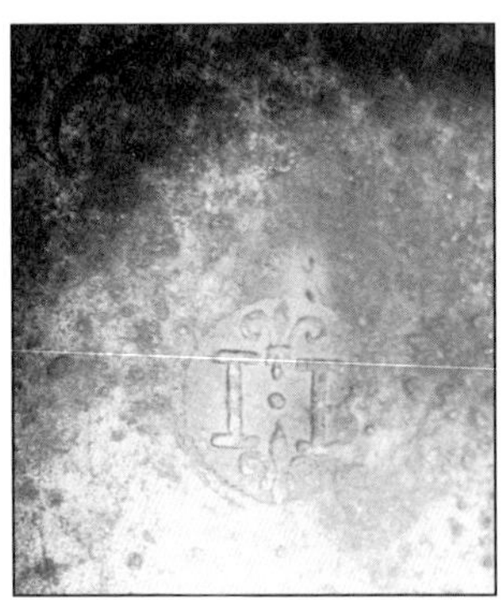

Fig. 272. *Mark of John Bassett on quart tankard. Heidelberg Union Church, Slatington, Lehigh County, Pa.*

Charles E. Barton
Charles E. Barton was a partner in the firm Leonard, Reed, and Barton, which was located in Taunton, Massachusetts. Barton worked for Babbit, Crossman and Company, 1827–1829; Crossman West and Leonard, 1829–1830; Taunton Britannia Manufacturing Company, 1830-1835; Leonard Reed, and Barton, 1835-1840, and its successor firm, Reed and Barton.

Frederick Bassett
Frederick Bassett, youngest son of New York pewterer John Bassett, produced fine quality pewter. He inherited his father's tools at his father's death in 1761. Frederick worked in New York, 1761–1780, and 1785–1799. During the Revolutionary War, he moved to Hartford where he worked from 1780 to 1785.

John Bassett
John Bassett, son of Michael and Elizabeth Bassett, was baptized in 1696. He married Elizabeth Fisher in 1724, and worked in New York City from 1720 to 1761. His oldest and youngest children, Francis and Frederick, carried on the trade.[3] He was a pewterer of the highest order. John Bassett used metal of fine quality. His pewter has substance and readily takes a fine sheen when polished.

Thomas Danforth Boardman and Sherman Boardman
The largest and longest-lived single pewter business in America in the nineteenth century was built by the Boardman brothers.[4] Tremendous quantities of pewter were made and peddled up and down the east coast by this enterprising family. Thomas Danforth Boardman developed a formula that he said would finish up to the sheen of English pewter. He kept the formula a secret for years in order to keep ahead of his competitors.[5]

Thomas Danforth Boardman (1784–1873) was born in Litchfield, Connecticut, the great-grandson of Thomas Danforth I of Norwich, the patriarch of a family of pewterers that spanned five generations and included a total of nineteen pewterers. Thomas apprenticed under his uncles Edward Danforth and Samuel Danforth, and he hired the tools and molds of the former when he began his long and illustrious career on July 21, 1804. His brother Sherman soon joined him and much pewter was made in Hartford marked with the "TD & SB" mark. Sherman and Thomas worked together from about 1808 to 1860. An outlet was opened in New York in 1822 and a younger brother, Timothy, represented the firm. Timothy died two years later. Lucius Hart then managed the firm; he became a partner, and the name of the New York outlet was changed to Boardman & Hart. Pewter may have been manufactured in New York City but more likely was made in Hartford and shipped to the New York branch.

The enterprising Boardman brothers opened a sales outlet in Philadelphia in 1842 under the name Boardman and Hall. Sherman's son Henry S. Boardman and Franklin D. Hall represented the firm. The name was later changed to Hall, Boardman and Company. Hall and Boardman did make the alloy in Philadelphia, as Edwin Freedley commented in his manufacturing treatise of 1856.[6]

Sherman died in March 1861; his brother Thomas operated the factory in Hartford until an illness and his death on September 10, 1873.[7] If one includes Thomas' apprenticeship period, he had been involved with the manufacture of pewter for seventy-six years. He had seen the industry develop from small shops to large manufacturing companies where pewter, now called Britannia, was cast,

3. Ledlie I. Laughlin, *Pewter in America, Its Makers and Their Marks* (Barre, Mass.: Barre Publishers, 1940), 2:5.

4. Thomas, *Connecticut Pewter and Pewterers,* 119.

5. Ibid., 119.

6. Edwin T. Freedley, *Leading Pursuits and Leading Men* (Philadelphia: Edward Young, 1856), 402.

7. Laughlin, *Pewter in America,* 1:129.

spun, stamped and pressed into a multitude of forms unheard of in earlier years.

Over thirty marking dies were used by the Boardmans and most continued to be used for many years. The same marks have been found on early flagons, as well as teapots of late design with copper bottoms.

Parks Boyd

Parks Boyd was born about 1771. He married Sarah Loudon in St. Paul's Episcopal Church in Philadelphia on June 6, 1793. He worked at various locations in that city, including Elfreth's Alley. He died June 6, 1819. Robert Palethorp, Jr., purchased the contents of his shop.

Cornelius Bradford

Cornelius Bradford was born October 18, 1729, in New York City. He served his apprenticeship with his father, William Bradford. In 1752 or 1753 he moved to Philadelphia, having inherited the property of his uncle, Andrew Bradford. He advertised in *The Pennsylvania Journal or Weekly Advertiser*, May 3, 1753:

> Cornelius Bradford, Pewterer in Second Street, Makes and Sells, wholesale and retale, Pewter Dishes, Plates, Tankards, Quart and Pint Muggs, Basons, Porringers, Tea Potts, Cullenders, Spoons, and all other sorts of Pewter. Said Bradford makes WORMS of any Size for Distilling, as also Cranes. Where all Persons may have Pewter mended at a reasonable Price, or old pewter exchanged for new.[8]

Bradford moved back to New York in 1770; he purchased The Merchants' Coffee House and just before the Revolution was a dispatch-bearer between the Committees of Correspondence in New York and Philadelphia and New York and Boston.[9] He is listed in New York's 1786 Directory as a plumber with Malcom McEuen but probably was more active with his Coffee House than as a plumber. He died November 9, 1786, and in his will called himself "Keeper of the Coffee House," suggesting his inactivity as a pewterer. His pewter is generally thought to have been made before the Revolutionary War. Hallmarks with the initials "D S," probably of an as-yet-unidentified pewterer, often accompany Bradford's marks on his flatware. Bradford's working dates were 1752–1753 and 1770–1785, New York, and 1753–1770, Philadelphia.

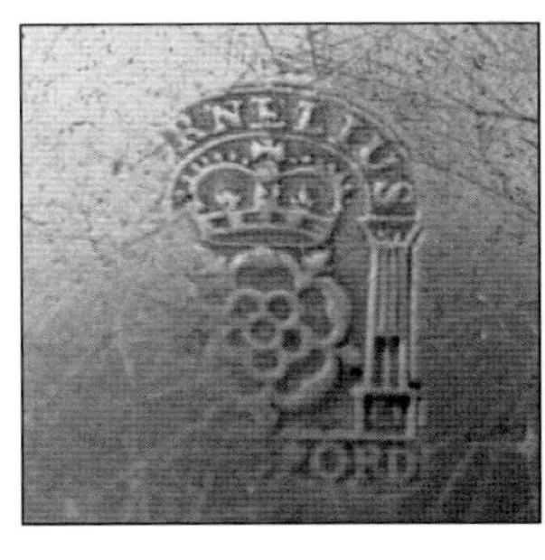

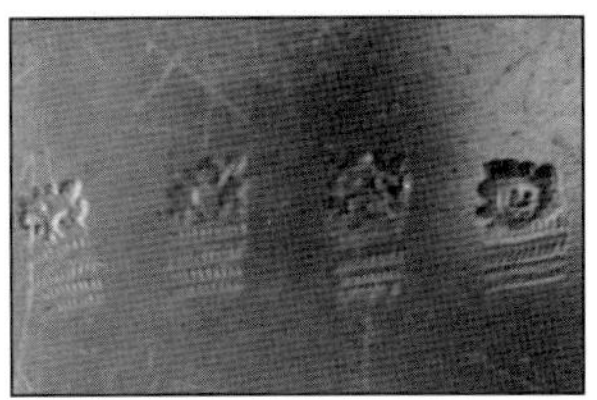

Fig. 273. *Marks of Cornelius Bradford on plate. East Vincent United Church of Christ, Spring City, Chester County, Pa.*

John Andrew Brunstrom

John Andrew Brunstrom was one of the users of the Love mark. A native of Sweden, John Brunstrom married Elizabeth Hasselberg, the daughter of pewterer Abraham Hasselberg.

> On January 16, 1783, in Old Swedes' Church he married Elizabeth, daughter of Abraham Hasselberg, deceased, and stepdaughter of Adam Kehler. Four months later he purchased from Doctor Redman the property in Pewter Platter Alley which Kehler has been occupying. In the deed he was described as a pewterer; also in a deed of 1786 when he bought property on the north side of High Street. The records show that in the same year he was a private in the Philadelphia militia. In the census of 1790 'John Bromstone, Pewterer,' was living in Elfreth's Alley. The city Directory of 1791 shows his residence at the same address, his shop at 133 North Second Street. The yellow fever plague of 1793, which carried off one-tenth of the city's population within a few months, cut short the life of this obscure maker on September 13 of that year. His age at time of death was given as 'about 40.'[10]

Brunstrom took the oath of allegiance on October 10, 1785 and the entry lists

8. *The Pennsylvania Journal or Weekly Advertiser* (Philadelphia), May 3, 1753.

9. Laughlin, *Pewter in America*, 2:10.

10. Laughlin, *Pewter in America*, 2:55, 56.

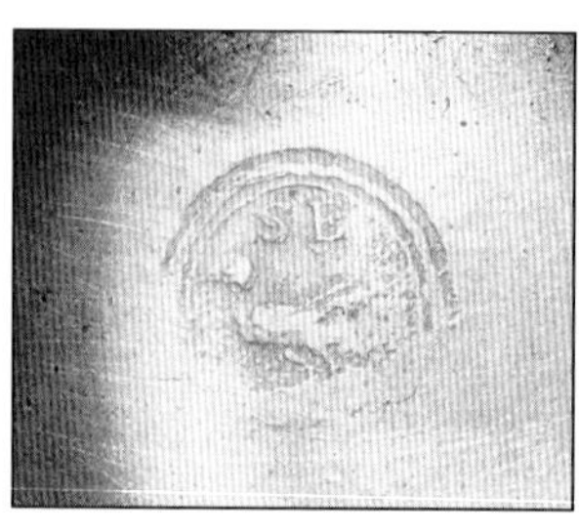

Fig. 274. *Mark of Simon Edgell on pint tankard. Christ Little Tulpehocken United Church of Christ, Bernville, Berks County, Pa.*

"John Brunstrong [*sic*] from Sweden, resident in Philadelphia about four years." He probably learned his trade in Sweden. His father-in-law, pewterer Abraham Hasselberg, died in 1779.

Brunstrom's inventory included large quantities of finished pewter and extensive brass molds and patterns.

A tankard of Swedish design bears the I.Brunstrom mark in addition to the crowned X quality mark commonly found in conjunction with the "Love" mark. The tankard is in the collection of the Winterthur Museum. A quart mug, not in the survey, is similarly marked.

Great quantities of "Love"-marked pewter flatware survive today, seemingly more than Brunstrom could ever have produced in his short ten-year working period. (See Love, page 133).

Thomas Byles

Thomas Byles, son of Josias Byles of Winchester, England, and his wife, Sarah Auber Byles, sailed for Boston in 1693. In his father's will, dated 1704, Thomas is mentioned as being under age, suggesting that he was born between 1683 and 1690.[11] He worked in Newport from 1711 to 1728 and probably later.[12] He purchased property on High (Market) Street in Philadelphia in 1738. Byles advertised in the *Pennsylvania Gazette* of November 26, 1741, "To be SOLD by Thomas Byles, Pewterer, in Market-Street; a good STILL and WORM, containing near 70 gallons, very reasonable."[13] He died in 1770 and his large inventory, presented September 10, 1771, by pewterers Benjamin Harbeson, Jr., and William Will, contained great quantities of finished pewter, pewter molds, and tools.[14] Quart and pint mugs, tankards straight and bellied, chalices, basins and plates are listed. Only one small paten by this maker was found in the survey.

Thomas Danforth III

Thomas Danforth III was born in Middletown, Connecticut, on June 2, 1756. He was the oldest son of pewterer Thomas Danforth II. His grandfather, uncle, cousin, and five brothers were also pewterers. His sister married Oliver Boardman, whose progeny Thomas Danforth Boardman, in partnership with his brother Sherman, enjoyed a large and prosperous pewter business in the nineteenth century. Thomas III apprenticed with his father from 1770 to 1777. He worked in Middletown and moved to the Rocky Hill section of Wethersfield in 1783. He probably shared or owned molds jointly with his brothers. His business relationship with tinsmith Blakeslee Barnes from nearby Berlin may have lured him to Philadelphia, for he opened a shop there in 1806 or 1807 at an address previously used by Barnes.[15] Thomas Danforth III journeyed back and forth between Wethersfield and Philadelphia until about 1812, when he settled in Wethersfield. He died there in January 1840. Based on the number of hollowware and particularly flatware pieces that have survived, Thomas must have enjoyed a large business.

Simon Edgell

Simon Edgell is the earliest Pennsylvania pewterer whose pewter has survived. Edgell was born in England and arrived in Philadelphia in 1713 or earlier. He was admitted a freeman of Philadelphia on May 27, 1717.[16] He purchased property on High (Market) Street in 1718. Edgell was a merchant and sold "Nails, Shot, Window Glass, Looking-Glasses, Irish Linnens, Woollens, and sundry other Merchandize

11. Laughlin, *Pewter in America,* 2:41-42.

12. Joseph O. Reese, "Thomas Byles and the Hell Gate Shipwreck," *Pewter Collectors' Club of America Bulletin,* no. 109 (November 1994): 53.

13. *The Pennsylvania Gazette* (Philadelphia), November 26, 1741.

14. Laughlin, *Pewter in America,* 2:156-158.

15. Thomas, *Connecticut Pewter and Pewterers,* 84.

16. *Minutes of the Common Council of the City of Philadelphia, 1704–1776* (Philadelphia: Crissy and Markley, 1847), 130.

at very reasonable Rates, . . ."[17] He died in 1742. His inventory, taken August 27, 1742, by Evan Morgan and Myles Strickland, included "4 Fine Wrought Plats [*sic*] & 2 Cans for Sacrament Table".[18]

Simon Edgell's pewter is among the earliest and rarest of surviving American pewter.[19] Of the thirteen marked pieces by Edgell, four have had Pennsylvania German church affiliations. Two unmarked but nearly identical pieces of pewter, unquestionably from the same molds used by Edgell, survive in Mennonite and Lutheran churches in southeastern Pennsylvania.

Roswell Gleason

Named after his uncle, Roswell Gleason was born in Putney, Vermont, on April 6, 1799, the eldest son of Reuben Gleason.[20] He worked for a tinsmith in Dorchester, Massachusetts, in 1818. In 1821, he opened his own shop in the same town. His business prospered, for in 1837 he had six employees and at one time had 125 employees.[21] Pewterers who worked for Gleason—and many eventually had their own shops—were George Richardson, Samuel Green, Sr. and Jr., Eli Eldridge, Eli Henry Eldridge, Ephraim Capen, B. F. Knox, and Rufus Dunham.[22] Gleason followed the styles and trends of the time; by the late 1850s, much of his pewter was silver-plated. He died January 27, 1887, a wealthy, prominent and respected citizen.[23]

Ashbil Griswold

Ashbil Griswold worked in Meriden, Connecticut, 1807–1842. He was born in Rocky Hill, Connecticut, April 4, 1784. After serving his apprenticeship with Thomas Danforth III, he established his own shop in Meriden in 1807. Griswold took Ira Couch as a business partner in about 1830 and the business flourished. Finished goods were sold by peddlers who traveled up and down the East Coast. Great quantities of pewter were produced. and except for the Boardmans in Hartford, the firm produced more pewter than any other Connecticut firm.[24] Flatware in large quantities, mugs, beakers, and the entire spectrum of Britannia goods, such as teapots, soap dishes, caster sets, and spittoons, have survived. However, the firm must not have had much contact with the Pennsylvania Germans, for only one plate from this maker was found in the survey. Griswold retired from the business in 1842 and died May 30, 1853.[25]

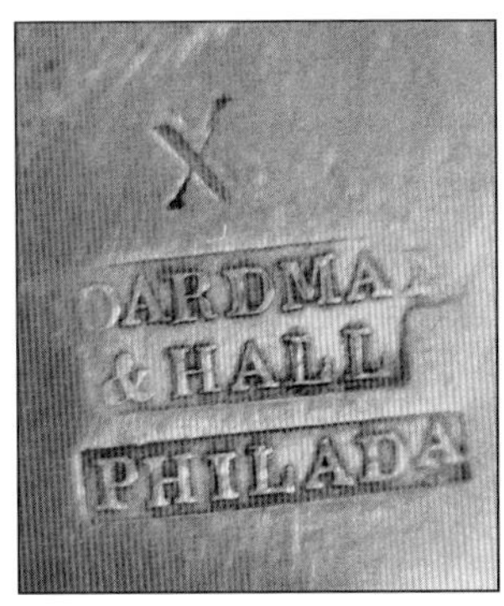

Fig. 275. *Mark of Boardman and Hall on flagon. Christ Lutheran Church, Elizabethtown, Lancaster County, Pa.*

Franklin D. Hall

Hall worked in Hartford, 1840, and Philadelphia, 1842–1857. He was a partner in the Boardman firm. (See Thomas Danforth and Sherman Boardman.)

The Harbesons

Benjamin Harbeson and his sons Benjamin, Jr., Joseph, and Robert, were Philadelphia coppersmiths. In 1793, Benjamin Harbeson, Jr., and his brother Joseph opened a shop of their own.[26] Just which Harbeson made pewter marked "Harbeson Philada" is not known, but it may have been Benjamin Harbeson, Jr., for he and William Will took Thomas Byles' inventory on September 10, 1771.

17. *The Pennsylvania Gazette* (Philadelphia), September 4 to September 11, 1735.

18. Laughlin, *Pewter in America,* 2:154.

19. Donald M. Herr, "A Simon Edgell Beaker," *Pewter Collectors' Club of America Bulletin,* no. 76 (March 1978): 274.

20. Richard L. Bowen, Jr., "Some of Roswell Gleason's Early Workers," *Pewter Collectors' Club of America Bulletin,* no. 83 (September 1981): 157.

21. Laughlin, *Pewter in America,* 2: 102.

22. Bowen, "Some of Roswell Gleason's Early Workers," 148-161.

23. Laughlin, *Pewter in America,* 2: 102.

24. Thomas, *Connecticut Pewter and Pewterers,* 165.

25. Laughlin, *Pewter in America,* 1: 127.

26. Laughlin, *Pewter in America,* 1: 63.

It was the custom that a craftsman's inventory be taken by a member of the same trade. It has been suggested that the pewter was made in the shop of Benjamin, Jr., and Joseph, who worked together from 1793 to 1803.[27] Whatever the case, Harbeson pewter often has a very high lead content, is soft, pits easily, and is frequently of inferior quality. It seems ironic that a finished product of much higher quality could have been obtained by just adding more copper to the mixture.

Lucius D. Hart
Hart managed and became a partner of the Boardman firm's outlet in New York City from 1828 to 1853. The Hartford-based Boardman company changed the name of its New York outlet to Boardman and Hart. (See Thomas Danforth and Sherman Boardman.)

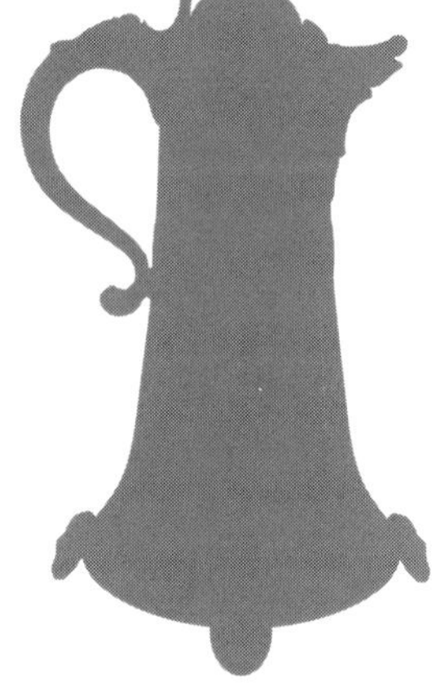

Johann Christoph Heyne
Johann Christoph Heyne was born in Feuntschen, Saxony, on December 3, 1715. It is not known where he served his apprenticeship, but by 1735 he was working as a journeyman pewterer in Stockholm for Maria Sauer, the widow of pewterer Jakob Sauer.[28] He arrived in Philadelphia on June 7, 1742, aboard the ship *Catherine,* as a member of the "First Sea Congregation" of the Moravian Church. He soon left for the Moravian settlement in Bethlehem. In 1746 he married Maria Margaret Schaefer, and they both taught in Moravian schools in Pennsylvania. Heyne traveled to Ireland in 1747 where he helped establish the Moravian church in Ireland. Two years later he returned to Pennsylvania, and in 1752 he and his wife settled in Lancaster.[29] Maria Heyne died in January 1764. Six months later Heyne married Anna Regina Steinmann, a widow, whose son John Frederick Steinman was one of the administrators of Heyne's estate when he died January 11, 1781.

Most of the surviving pewter made by Heyne was for ecclesiastical use. His splendid flagons, with their strongly Germanic elements of cherub's head feet and body combined with a cast hollow English handle, are remarkable examples of cultural assimilation of styles. Heyne made the only known eighteenth-century pewter candlesticks marked by an American maker. Johann Christoph Heyne was a most capable pewterer whose designs differed notably from the English tradition in which the great majority of American pewterers were trained. His ingenuity, versatility, and craftsmanship rank him with the best American pewterers.

William Kirby
William Kirby, son of New York pewterer Peter Kirby, was married to Catherine Roosevelt on February 6, 1760.[30] A merchant, as well as a pewterer, he advertised in *The New York Gazette and The Weekly Mercury,* September 26, 1774, that he had "imported a large and general assortment of London pewter, which he will sell wholesale and retail, on the most reasonable terms . . ." and "He takes old pewter and bees-wax in exchange for new pewter." William continued the pewtering tradition after his father's death in 1788, and sold his property to his son Nicholas Roosevelt Kirby in 1795. Thereafter he is listed as a merchant in city directories, until 1804.

Only one piece of pewter by this rarely represented New York maker was found in the survey. It is a quart tankard with a crenated lip and painted surface,

27. John Barrett Kerfoot, *American Pewter* (New York: Bonanza Books, 1924), 99.

28. Eric de Jonge, "Johann Christoph Heyne, Pewterer, Minister, Teacher," *Winterthur Portfolio 4,* The Henry Francis du Pont Winterthur Museum (Charlottesville: University Press of Virginia, 1968), 169-184. See also Antiques (March 1955), 230-232.

29. In a lecture at the October 25, 1975, meeting of the Pewter Collectors' Club of America at Lancaster, Pa., John J. Snyder, Jr., revealed that Heyne bought property on East King Street from Jacob Fetter on February 29, 1752 (Deed Book D-350, Lancaster County Historical Society). Heyne is not found on the tax list for Lancaster Borough in 1751.

30. Laughlin, *Pewter in America,* 2: 17.

an unusual treatment for domestic pewter and even more rarely a sort found to have been associated with probable ecclesiastical use.

Horatio Leonard
Leonard was a partner in the Massachusetts-based Taunton Britannia Manufacturing Company, 1830–1833, and the majority stockholder of its successor company, Leonard, Reed and Barton, 1835–1840. (See Leonard, Reed and Barton, below.)

Leonard, Reed and Barton
Former employees of the Taunton Britannia Manufacturing Company—Henry G. Reed, spinner; Charles E. Barton, solderer; and Horatio Leonard's son Gustavus—formed a partnership under the name of Leonard, Reed and Barton in 1835. Gustavus Leonard managed the marketing and financial aspects of the business, and Reed and Barton handled production. In 1840, Leonard sold his interest in the company and the name was changed to Reed and Barton. Since 1840, Reed and Barton have continued to the present time to produce Britannia ware.

George Lightner
In the *Baltimore American,* November 21, 1806, George Lightner advertised his "Tin and Pewter Manufactory" on "North Street, Old Town, near the Hay Scales, Baltimore."[31] He died on January 26, 1815, in his sixty-sixth year. Only flatware—plates, dishes and basins—have been found with his marks.

The "Love" (or "Lovebird") Mark
The "Love" or "Lovebird" mark was probably used by a succession of pewterers in southeastern Pennsylvania and likely in the city of Philadelphia. Surviving pieces are similar in form and style to marked pieces by Philadelphia makers. John Andrew Brunstrom was one of the users of this mark. His tankard of Swedish design with raised bands on its body is a form found marked by "Love," Parks Boyd, and later the Palethorps. Both Boyd and the Palethorps very likely used the "Love" mark. Brunstrom's step-father, pewterer Adam Koehler, may have used the "Love" mark, but no pewter signed by Koehler has survived that would definitely link Koehler to that mark. Other pewterers whose names have been suggested as possible users of the "Love" mark are Moravian pewterers Abraham Hasselberg and Johann Christoph Heyne. No pewter with the Hasselberg name has survived. No pewter with Heyne's marks in combination with the "Love" mark has been found. A plate and a dish bear both the "Love" mark and the mark of Philadelphia pewterer Thomas Byles. Footed Queen Anne teapots that are apparently from the same mold have been found with the marks of Cornelius Bradford, Johann Philip Alberti, and "Love," suggesting that Bradford and Alberti had access to the "Love" molds.[32]

In the eighteenth century, it was customary for pewterers to mark their basins on the outside bottom. Basins of nineteenth-century manufacture are usually marked on the inside bottom. Nearly all basins with the "Love" mark are marked on the outside bottom, suggesting that they were produced or marked in the fashion of the earlier century. The fact that the mark was used over a long period of time and well into the nineteenth century is exemplified by the presence of the "Love" crowned X quality mark found on an inverted mold teapot made by Palethorp and Connell in Philadelphia, 1839–1841.[33] In summary, the "Love" mark was probably used by a succession of pewterers in the Philadelphia area beginning in the last half of the

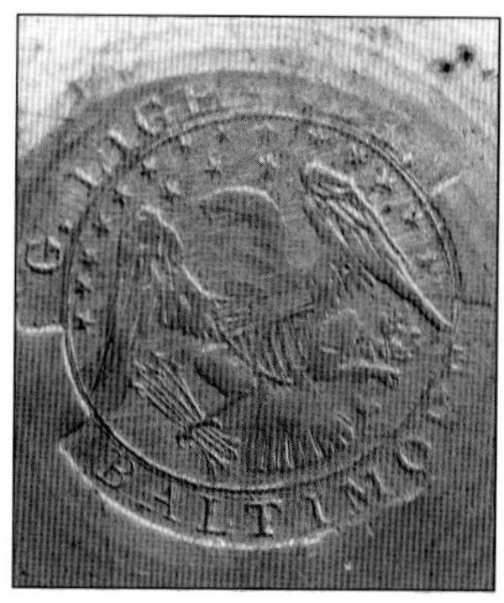

Fig. 276. *Mark of George Lightner on basin. Hummelstown Lutheran Church, Hummelstown, Dauphin County, Pa.*

31. Ibid., 78, 187.

32. Bette A. and Melvyn D. Wolf, "Johann Philip Alberti," *Pewter Collectors' Club of America,* no. 84 (March 1982):177-182.

33. Donald M. Herr, "Palethorp and Connell and the Crowned X," *Pewter Collectors' Club of America Bulletin,* no. 90-91 (September 1986):72.

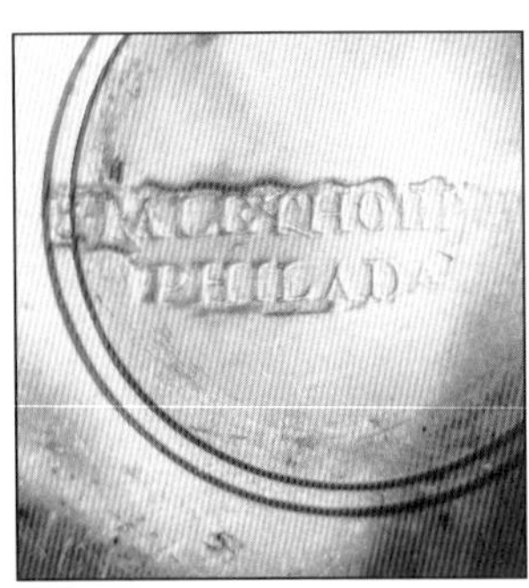

Fig. 277. *Mark of Robert Palethorp on beaker. Blooming Glen Mennonite Church, Blooming Glen, Bucks County, Pa.*

eighteenth century and well into the nineteenth century.

The Palethorps

Robert Palethorp, Jr., was born in 1797, the son of Robert Palethorp, Sr., and Sarah Harrison of Philadelphia. He probably learned the trade from his neighbor, pewterer Parks Boyd. Palethorp opened his shop in 1817, and after Boyd's death in 1819 Palethorp purchased the contents of Boyd's shop. Robert, Jr., took his younger brother John Harrison Palethorp as a partner in 1820. Robert, Jr., died in 1822 at the young age of 25. Robert Palethorp, Sr., then joined his son John Harrison until the elder Palethorp died in 1826. Except for a partnership with Thomas Connell from 1838 to 1841, J. H. Palethorp worked alone until 1845.[34]

D.S.

This as-yet-unidentified pewterer made forms similar to those made in Philadelphia and New York in the second half of the eighteenth century. Smooth rim plates with diameters of $9^{1}/_{4}''$ and marked "D S" appear to have come from the same mold as those marked by Philadelphia makers Simon Edgell, Cornelius Bradford, and Christian and John Hera. Most "D S" plates feature three marks in a triad, positioned in the fashion of the mid-eighteenth century.

A set of four hallmarks, one of which contains the letters "D S" and a quality X mark is found frequently on plates also bearing Cornelius Bradford's marks. The same quality mark has been found in conjunction with the "D S" angel mark found on sugar bowls similar in form to one marked with the "Love" quality mark, suggesting a Philadelphia relationship.[35] Although the "D S" angel mark is Continental in design, the mark is found on straight-sided and tulip-shaped mugs that are typical American and British forms. This suggests that the maker may have had a Continental background but was making forms currently in favor with his American clientele.

Cornelius Bradford, son of New York pewterer William Bradford, worked in New York for two years before moving to Philadelphia in 1753. He worked in Philadelphia until 1780 and then moved back to New York, became involved with running his coffee house and probably produced very little pewter thereafter. It is possible that Bradford acquired the business and tools of an earlier Philadelphia maker whose initials were D.S. It is also possible that he brought molds of a New York pewterer with him to Philadelphia. The New York Bradfords intermarried with women of Dutch lineage. William Bradford, pewterer, married Sytie Sandvoort of New York, and had two sons, Cornelius the pewterer and William. William married Rachel Schuyler, whose brother, Dirck Schuyler, was a merchant who owned property at Maiden Lane and William Street in New York in 1762. It was not unusual for a pewterer to sell goods other than pewter in his shop and to be a merchant. The property adjoining Dirck Schuyler's was owned by a person named King. Recently a pint mug with a high fillet, a design frequently used by New York pewterers, has been found with an unrecorded "R. King" mark, having a handle defect similar to that found on a marked "D S" pint mug. An extensive search of Philadelphia and New York records has not revealed anyone whose occupation is listed as a pewterer having the initials D.S. (See Cornelius Bradford.)

Sheldon and Feltman

Smith Sheldon and J. C. Feltman, Jr., were partners at 35 Dean Street, Albany, N.Y.,

34. A letterhead of Palethorp and Connell dated May 30, 1838 has recently been found that predates the firm one year earlier than is listed in Laughlin's *Pewter in America,* 1:148. Information from Lester P. Breininger, Jr., April 26, 1993. See Lester P. Breininger, Jr., "American Pewter: 1740-1850," *Historical Review of Berks County,* 58, no. 3 (Summer 1993):130, 154.

35. Donald M. Herr, "A Marked Philadelphia Sugar Bowl," *Pewter Collectors' Club of America,* no. 90-91 (September 1986): 5.

from 1847 to 1848. "They made tea-sets, communion flagons, and plates, and other pieces of thin metal and inferior design."[36]

Smith and Feltman
Successors to Sheldon and Feltman, partners George C. Smith and J. C. Feltman, Jr., were Britannia makers at 23 Dean Street, Albany, N.Y., from 1853 to 1856.

John Will
John Will was born in Herborn, Germany, and was baptized there on May 10, 1696. The records of Herborn, which is located about forty miles east of Neuwied on the Rhine, note that John Will married Judith Bomper of Herborn on January 19, 1720. He is recorded as a pewterer and postal officer in Herborn records from 1728 to 1734. After 1734, he is listed as a citizen and pewterer. In 1736, he is listed as a *Kannengiesser* [maker of holloware].[37] About 1736 the Wills moved to Neuwied.[38]

John Will was in New York with his wife and three children in 1750. He was then fifty-six years old. The Reformed Dutch Church records of New York City for February 19, 1750 inform us that:

> on the nineteenth of February, 1750, 'Johannes Will, Junior, van Nieuwied in Hoog Duitschland' joined the church, and that on the twenty-second of September, 1752, 'Johannes Will & Anna Judith Bomper, Egte Lieden met hare 3 kindern, Hendrik Bernhard, Margaretha Elizabeth & Philip Daniel Will van Niewit in Duitsland,' also became members of the congregation.[39]

In 1763, he was a member of a group that separated from the Reformed Dutch Church and established the German Reformed Congregation in New York City.

John Will must have been proud of his country of origin, for he advertised in *The New-York Gazette or Weekly Post-Boy* on February 4, 1760, "This is to give Notice, That John Will, Pewterer, from Germany, living in Smith's Fly, opposite to Mr. Robert Livingston, makes and sells all sorts of Pewter Ware, in the neatest and best Manner."[40]

He last appears in New York records in 1774.

John Will was a pewterer of the highest order. His coffeepot/flagon and oval platter, recorded for the first time in this survey, attest to his awareness of contemporary styles and tastes. His coffeepot is the earliest surviving eighteenth century coffeepot made by an American pewterer and the only existing one known to the author that was made by a New York pewterer. His oval platter, recorded for the first time in this book, probably predates examples known to have been made by both of his sons Henry and William.

John Will was the patriarch of a family of fine pewterers. His sons Henry, Philip, and William carried on the tradition of making pewter of exceptional quality and fine design. Henry worked in New York, 1761–1775, fled to Albany during the Revolution, 1776–1783, and returned to New York and worked there from 1783 to 1793. Philip Will worked in Philadelphia and New York from 1763 to 1787. Only a few plates and a flagon marked by Philip Will have survived. The most innovative Will offspring was William Will of Philadelphia, who worked there from 1764 to 1798.

William Will
William Will, fourth son of pewterer John Will, was born in Neuwied, a city on the Rhine near Koblentz, on January 27, 1742. John Will brought his family to New York in 1752. William learned the

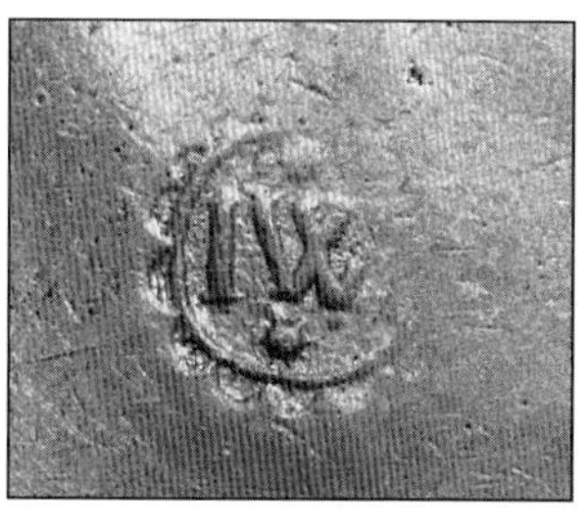

Fig. 278. *Mark of John Will on basin. Zion's (Stone) United Church of Christ, Northampton, Northampton County, Pa.*

36. Laughlin, *Pewter in America.* 2:112.
37. Ibid, 3:102.
38. Ibid, 3:101-102.
39. Ibid, 2:12.
40. *The New York Gazette or The Weekly Post-Boy,* February 4, 1760.

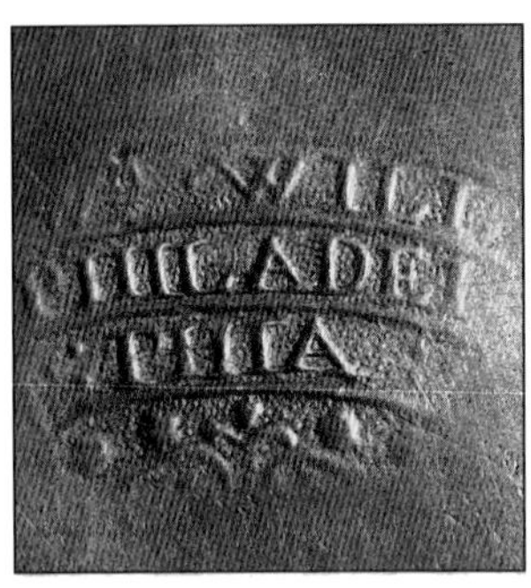

Fig. 279. *Mark of William Will on plate. Zion's (Stone) United Church of Christ, Northampton, Northampton County, Pa.*

trade from his father and brother Henry in New York. He probably moved to Philadelphia with his brother Philip, who advertised himself as a pewterer in the Staatsbote in 1763.[41] William married Barbara Culp the following year in the First (German) Reformed Church of Philadelphia.[42] He apparently prospered, for in the April 28, 1772 issue of the Staatsbote he gave notice that he moved his shop to Second Street "where he practices the pewterer's craft in all its forms."[43]

In addition to being one of the most productive pewterers of colonial America, William Will was a patriot of the first order:

> in 1776 he organized a company of infantry known as 'Captain Will's Company of Associators.' In 1777 he was a Lieutenant-Colonel of the First Battalion, and later of Colonel Jacob's Third Battalion, which he himself afterward commanded, and in 1780 he commanded the Third Regiment of Foot. In 1777 he was appointed with Charles Wilson [*sic*] Peale and four others, 'Commissioner for the Seizure of the Personal Effects of Traitors' for the city of Philadelphia, and in the following year this same committee was put in charge of forfeited estates as well as personal property—the Alien Property Custodians of an earlier day. In the same year the Pennsylvania Council delegated William Will as storekeeper at Lancaster for the Continental Army, and in 1779 'Commissioner for Collecting Salt.' . . . Will found time in 1780 to run for high sheriff of Philadelphia, to which he was duly elected. In 1781 and again in 1782 he was re-elected.[44]
>
> In 1785 the people of Philadelphia elected as councillor their world-citizen, Benjamin Franklin, and at the same election sent as representatives to the General Assembly Robert Morris, 'the financier of the Revolution,' and William Will, the pewterer.[45]

Will traveled in the best of circles. However, he must have fallen on hard times, for in 1789 he declared himself bankrupt and much of his property was sold at sheriff's sales over the next two years.[46] Regardless of his difficulties, Will retained the respect of his community, as noted in his death notice on February 14, 1798.

> On Saturday morning departed this life after a lingering indisposition which he bore with Christian fortitude, Colonel William Will, in the 56th year of his age; a native of the city of Nieuwidt [Neuwied] in Germany; and on Monday his remains were interred in the burial ground of the German reformed congregation attended by the members of the German incorporated society, and a very large number of respectable citizens.[47]

Ledlie I. Laughlin summarized the remarkable qualities of William Will, the man and his pewter.

> William Will is one of the outstanding figures in the history of American pewter. No other has left a more impressive evidence of ability, and few approached the

41. *Staatsbote,* September 19, 1763.

42. Records of the First (German) Reformed Church of Philadelphia, III, 2098, Collections of the Genealogical Society of Pennsylvania, Historical Society of Pennsylvania, Philadelphia.

43. *Staatsbote,* April 28, 1772.

44. Laughlin, *Pewter in America,* 2:52.

45. Ibid., 2:53.

46. Suzanne Hamilton, "William Will, Pewterer: His Life and His Work, 1742-1798." (M.A. diss, University of Delaware, 1967), 21.

47. *Poulson's American Daily Advertiser* (Philadelphia), February 14, 1798.

craftsmanship which his pewter displays. Gifted beyond most of his fellows, he unselfishly subordinated his business to a life of service to his community and demonstrated that he was not only a superior craftsman, but also a splendid soldier, a capable statesman, and an executive of unusual ability.[48]

William Will's pewter is of fine quality and workmanship. He was a highly skilled artisan. His ability to make new designs by using interchangeable parts cast from existing molds was unequaled by any other American pewterer. The body of one of his federal flagon forms was used as the body for his coffeepots. He ingeniously used a measure, pint mug, quart tankard, basin, sugar bowl body, chalice body, and teapot hinge to produce the ambitious flagon forms used in Pennsylvania German churches.

Hiram Yale and Company

Hiram Yale and his brother Charles manufactured pewter in Wallingford, Connecticut, from 1824 to 1835. Hiram, born March 27, 1799, and Charles, born April 20, 1790, were sons of pewter buttonmaker Samuel Yale. The brothers purchased Samuel Danforth's molds. The shop inventory at Hiram's death in 1831 included christening basins, goblets, pitchers, and plates. Charles moved the shop outside of Wallingford to a location later called Yalesville. He died November 2, 1835.

British

Ash and Hutton

Gregory Ash and William Hutton were partners in Bristol, England. William Hutton apprenticed to Edward Gregory and his wife Ann on July 8, 1730. He was free to strike his own mark on October 3, 1739. Gregory Ash, son of Richard Ash, apprenticed to the widow of Edward Gregory on January 7, 1733. He was free to strike his mark on March 24, 1741. Ash and Hutton worked together from 1741 until William Hutton's death in 1768.[49]

William Bancks

The town in which William Bancks worked is unknown. The probable dates of his pewter production are from about 1700 to 1710.[50] The style of his baluster measures is of that period.

William Bartlett

William Bartlett is thought to have worked from about 1740 to 1770. The location of his shop is unknown. He had a London mark, as did many pewterers, whether they worked in London or elsewhere. Bartlett probably did not work in that city, for one of his marks is very explicit: "Wm BARTLETT NOT IN LONDON."[51]

Allen Bright

Allen Bright, son of Henry Bright, worked in Bristol and Colwell, Herefordshire, England. He apprenticed to William Watkins and his wife Mary in Bristol on November 1, 1735. He completed his apprenticeship and was free to strike his own mark November 2, 1742. He died in 1763.[52]

Burford and Green

Thomas Burford and James Green had leave to strike their marks on the London Company touchplate on October 13, 1748. Their business was located in a region of London called The Poultry, and

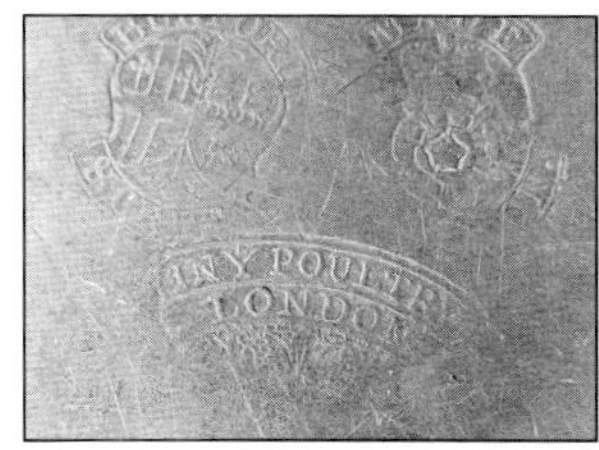

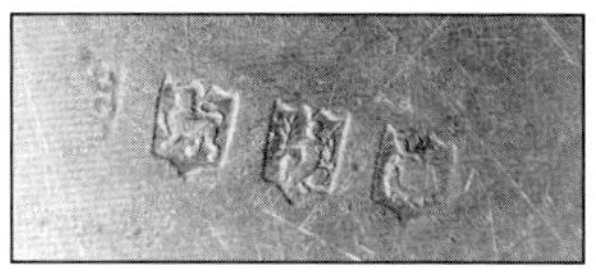

Fig. 280. *Mark of Burford and Green on plate. St. John's Lutheran Church, Palmerton, Carbon County, Pa.*

48. Laughlin, *Pewter in America,* 2:51.

49. Ian D. Robinson, "Antique British Pewter Found Today in New England," *Pewter Collectors' Club of America Bulletin,* no. 89 (September 1984):392.

50. Christopher A. Peel, *More Pewter Marks* (Cringleford, Norwich, England: Peel, 1977):10.

51. Howard H. Cotterell, *Old Pewter: Its Makers and Marks in England, Scotland and Ireland: An Account of the Old Pewterer and His Craft* (London: B. T. Batsford, Ltd., 1929). Reprint, Rutland, Vt. & Tokyo, Japan: Charles E. Tuttle Co., 1963:156.

52. Cotterell, *Old Pewter,* 118.

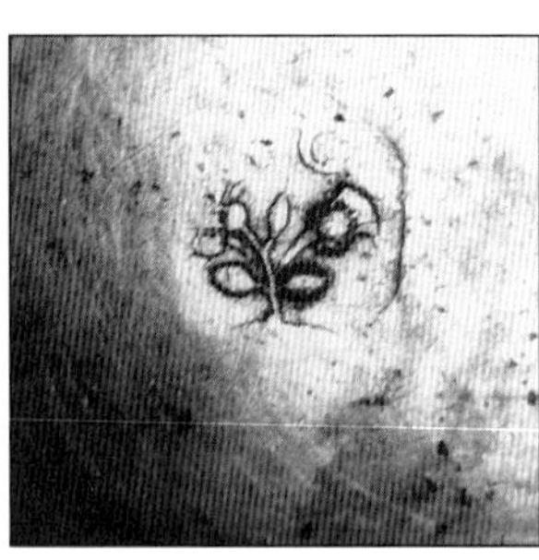

Fig. 281. *Mark of William Charlesley on quart tankard. Hill Lutheran Church, Cleona, Lebanon County, Pa.*

one of their marks denotes their location. The partnership was dissolved in 1780, when James Green retired from the firm.[53]

Burgum and Catcott
Henry Burgum the elder and George Symes Catcott were members of the firm Burgum and Catcott in Bristol and Littledean from 1765 to 1779. Burgum had been apprenticed to Allen Bright, Bristol, and Catcott to Stephen Cox of the same city.

Robert Bush, Sr.
Robert Bush, son of William Bush, was apprenticed to Thomas and Anne Lanyon of Bristol for fifty pounds on June 2, 1748. He completed his apprenticeship and was admitted as a Freeman on June 19, 1755. He advertised in *Felix Farley's Journal* in July and August of 1765 that he sold patent oval pewter dishes invented by Joseph Spackman of London. Bristol directories list the various business associations Robert Bush had with Richard Perkins, Richard Hale, Preston Egar, James Curtis, Robert Bush, Jr., and William Bush.[54] In summary, Robert Bush worked alone, 1755–1771 and 1782–1786. In 1801 the name of the firm was Robert and William Bush, suggesting that Robert, Sr., turned the business over to his sons Robert, Jr., and William.

Robert Bush and Company
Robert Bush and Company is listed in the Bristol directories for the years 1787 to 1795. A notice in the London Gazette of July 30, 1793, for the dissolution of the firm lists partners Preston Edgar and James Curtis. Robert Bush, Sr., continued to use the name Robert Bush & Co., for the firm is listed in Bristol directories until 1795.

Bush, Perkins, and Company
Robert Bush and his apprentice Richard Perkins formed a partnership, marking their pewter with both Bush & Perkins (1771–1773) and Bush, Perkins, and Co. (1774–1781). The Bristol directory for the year 1775 lists Bush, Perkins, and Co., pewterers and coppersmiths, 20 High Street.[55]

John Carr
Little is known about this Bristol pewterer who worked about 1750. He used a "hard metal" touch in addition to his full name touch.

A. Carter
A. Carter was a pewterer who probably worked about 1750 in the West Country, an area west of London that was not under the strict control of pewter guilds, as was often the case in large cities. The Carter plate found in this survey was not hammered. Carter's mark has been found on plates and Guernsey measures found on the Channel Islands suggesting that he, like other mainland pewterers, shipped his ware across the Channel.[56]

William Charlesley
William Charlesley worked in London from 1729 to 1770. He was elected to the Yeomanry of the London Company on June 19, 1729. Charlesley was given leave to strike his mark on the London touchplate on June 15, 1732. He was elected to the office of Upper Warden in the Company in 1764. He died in 1770.[57]

Bourchier and Richard Cleeve
Bourchier Cleeve was elected to the Yeomanry of the London Company on December 16, 1736, and was free to strike his touch on June 22, 1738. Cleeve paid the stipulated fine and was excused

53. Ibid., 171.

54. Richard L. Bowen, Jr. "Bush, Perkins, Edgar, and Curtis: Bristol Pewterers," *Pewter Collectors' Club of America Bulletin,* no. 84 (March 1982):184-186.

55. Ibid, 184.

56. Stanley C. Woolmer and Charles H. Arkwright, *Pewter of the Channel Islands* (Edinburgh: John Bartholomew, 1973), 106.

57. Cotterell, *Old Pewter,* 178.

from serving in the office of Upper Warden in 1757. He lived at Foots-Clay Place, Kent, and was in partnership with Richard Cleeve about 1754.[58]

Thomas Compton
Thomas Compton apprenticed to London pewterer John Townsend in 1763. He married John Townsend's daughter Mary, who was also a pewterer and formed the firm of Townsend & Compton.[59] John Townsend, son of Benjamin Townsend (and not John Townsend, Jr., as previously thought) was likely a member of the firm.[60] They worked from 1785 to 1806. From 1806 to 1810, the firm was called Townsend, Compton & Co. Since no "& Co." marks survive, the Townsend & Compton marks likely continued in use until 1810. The Townsend and Compton firm produced tremendous quantities of pewter and enjoyed their business relationship with fellow Quakers in Philadelphia. (See Townsend and Compton, page 143.)

Thomas and Townsend Compton
Thomas Compton was joined by his second son, Townsend Compton, to form the firm Thomas & Townsend Compton, which was active in London from 1810 to 1815. Thomas died in 1817. Brothers Townsend Compton and Henry Compton and then Henry alone continued the firm until about 1855.[61]

James Dixon and Sons
The James Dixon firm of Sheffield remained under the control of direct descendants of founder James Dixon from 1804 until Milo Dixon's death in 1976.[62]

Born in Sheffield in 1776, James Dixon apprenticed to Samuel Broadhead, Sheffield Plate manufacturer, at the age of fourteen. Seven years later, he finished his apprenticeship. He started his own firm in 1804. After his partnership with Thomas Smith, 1811–1822, was dissolved, his eldest son William Frederick Dixon joined the firm. In 1835 another son, James Willis Dixon, became a partner and the name of the firm became James Dixon & Sons. James Willis Dixon traveled to America and established sales agencies for their wares. James Dixon retired in 1842 and a third son, Henry Isaac Dixon, and son-in-law William Fawcett joined the firm. James Dixon died in 1852.

The firm hired designers to create new patterns and styles to meet the demands of its customers. Electroplated wares were added to their line of goods and nickel silver and Britannia were used as base metals. Eventually highly polished nickel silver was referred to as British Plate.

Chalices in the survey bear marks used by James Dixon & Sons from about 1842 to 1851.

Stynt Duncumb
Stynt Duncumb (often incorrectly called Samuel Duncombe) was the son of Wribbenhall pewterer John Duncumb. He was baptized May 22, 1712, at St. Martin's, Birmingham. He probably began his pewtering career about 1730. His father died in 1745 and in his will bequeathed: "To his son Stent [*sic*] all his household goods, stock in trade and personal effects together with his buildings at Wribbenhall."[63] Wribbenhall is located across the Severn River from Bewdley. Stynt Duncumb died in 1767.

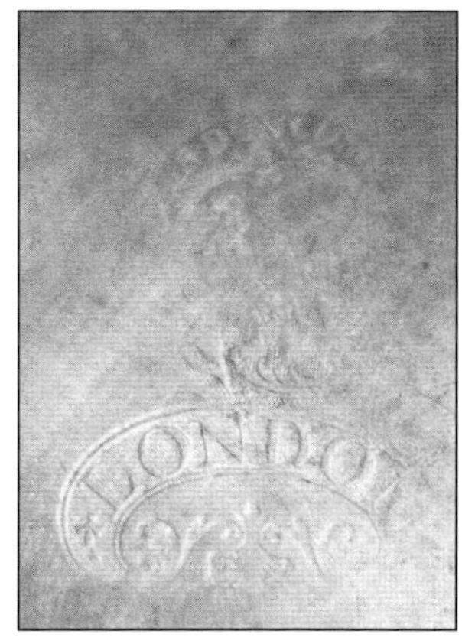

Fig. 282. *Mark of Stynt Duncumb on plate. Christ's Church (Lowhill) United Church of Christ, New Tripoli, Lehigh County, Pa.*

58. Ibid., 182.

59. Richard L. Bowen, Jr., "John Townsend and Associates," *Pewter Collectors' Club of America Bulletin,* no. 104 (June 1992):99. Elsie Englefield, *A Treatise on Pewter* (London, 1933). Elsie's father, William James Englefield, was the last pewterer in a firm that traced its roots back to John Townsend, Sr. (worked 1748–1801) and beyond that to Thomas Scattergood (worked 1703–1724).

60. Ronald F. Homer, "Editor's Note," *Pewter Collectors' Club of America Bulletin,* no. 105 (December 1992):129. From the archives of the Worshipful Company of Pewterers in London.

61. Bowen, "John Townsend and Associates," 100.

62. Jack L. Scott, *Pewter Wares from Sheffield* (Baltimore: Antiquary Press, 1980), 224.

63. Ronald F. Homer and David W. Hall, *Provincial Pewterers: A Study of the Craft in the West Midlands and Wales* (Chichester: Phillimore & Co., 1985), 66.

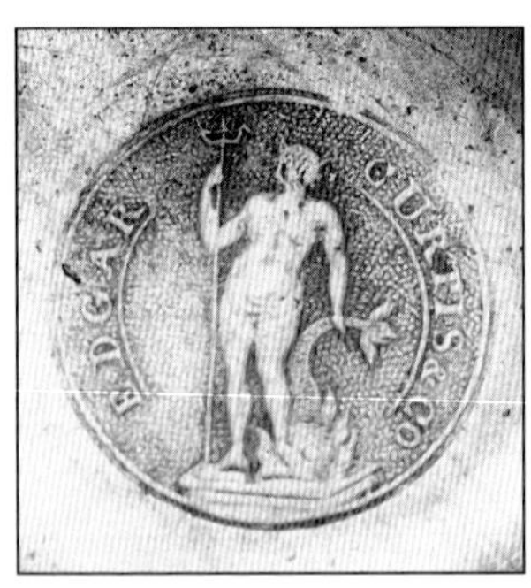

Fig. 283. *Mark of Edgar, Curtis, and company on quart mug. St. Peter's Lutheran Church, Pebersburg, Centre County, Pa.*

William Eddon

William Eddon of London was elected to the Yeomanry and was free to strike his mark on March 20, 1689. He had apprenticed to Peter Duffield, who also incorporated an hourglass in his mark.[64] Eddon was very active in the pewterers' guild and was elected to the office of Renter Warden in 1721 and the office of Upper Warden in 1729. In 1732 and 1737 he was elected to the most important position of the guild, the office of Master. He worked until 1745. William Eddon was a fine pewterer, who made huge three and one-half pint tankards, one of which was found in the survey. This early maker was a prolific exporter to the Colonies.[65]

Edgar, Curtis, and Company

After Robert Bush and Company, the partnership of Robert Bush, Sr., Preston Edgar, and James Curtis, was dissolved in 1793, Edgar and Curtis formed a partnership of their own. Edgar, Curtis, and Company is listed in the Bristol Directories from 1793 to 1809.[66]

Edgar and Son

Preston Edgar left the firm of Edgar, Curtis, and Company and in 1810 formed his own firm Preston Edgar and Son with his son of the same name. The firm is listed as Edgar and Son in the Bristol Directories from 1812 to 1855.[67] They are listed as pewterers, coppersmiths, worm-makers, brass founders, and candlemold makers.

Samuel Ellis

Samuel Ellis had leave to strike his mark on the London touchplate on November 10, 1721. He was elected to the London Company offices of Steward in 1730, Renter Warden in 1737, Upper Warden in 1747, and Master in 1748. He died in 1773. The hallmarks of Samuel Ellis were subsequently used by Thomas Swanson, Fasson and Son, and Fasson and Sons.[68] A plate having hallmarks of Samuel Ellis and Richard King was found in this survey.

Thomas Giffin

Thomas Giffin was elected to the Yeomanry of the London Company on December 13, 1759. He had leave to strike his touch in 1764. On March 10, 1760 he was elected to the Livery. He paid the stipulated fine to be excused from serving in the office of Steward in 1768, and Renter Warden and Upper Warden in 1777. His shop was at 135 Fenchurch Street, ten doors from John Townsend, with whom he was in partnership from 1777 to Townsend's death in 1801. One plate by Thomas Giffin was found in the survey.

Richard Going

This Bristol maker was elected a Freeman on February 7, 1715. In 1734, Going advertised that he lived at the Block Inn on the Quay and had been there for twenty five years. The sale notice of his sizable estate was printed in Felix Farley's Bristol Journal, February 16, 1766.[69]

Hale and Sons

William Hale and his sons Richard and Thomas worked in Bristol from 1778 until about 1822.[70] Thomas Hale had served his apprenticeship under Robert Bush, Sr. William must have left the firm about

64. Stanley Shemmel, "William Eddon, Some Further Information and Comment," *Journal Pewter Society* (Autumn 1979), 13. See also Cotterell, London Touchplate 1, Number 41.

65. Ian Robinson, "William Eddon, Master Pewterer Extraordinary," *Journal Pewter Society* (Autumn 1979), 12.

66. Bowen, "Bush, Perkins, Edgar, and Curtis: Bristol Pewterers," *Pewter Collectors' Club of America Bulletin* no. 84 (March 1982):189.

67. Ibid., 186, 187.

68. Robinson, "Antique British Pewter Found Today in New England," 379.

69. Cotterell, *Old Pewter,* 217.

70. Richard L. Bowen, "The Hales of Bristol, England," *Pewter Collectors' Club of America Bulletin,* no. 84 (March 1982):192. Personal correspondence from Bowen on March, 15 1991, notes that Hale and Sons worked until 1822. This updates the incorrect dates (1852–1870) in Cotterell's Old Pewter, 223.

1782, for the Bristol directory of 1783 lists only Richard and Thomas Hale as coppersmiths, pewterers, and brass founders. The Hales sold their business to Edgar and Son in 1823. A $7\,^{7}/_{8}''$ plate with the enigmatic sheaf-of-wheat mark and the Hale and Sons hallmarks was found in the survey.[71] Recently two other plates have been reported with the same marks[72] The hallmarks are not the same as the Hale and Sons mark that is listed in Cotterell (C 2070).

Robert Iles
Robert Iles had leave to strike his mark on the London touchplate on March 19, 1695. His mark included that year. He was elected to the offices of Yeomanry in the London Company in 1691, Livery in 1713, and Steward in 1717, and paid fines to excuse himself from the offices of Renter Warden in 1728 and Upper Warden in 1735.

Ingram and Hunt
Ingram and Hunt worked in Bewdley from about 1770 to 1803 or 1807.[73] John Ingram, Jr., was born in 1731 and died in 1799. He was the son of John Ingram and his wife Mary Duncumb. He apprenticed to his uncle Stynt Duncumb and later formed a partnership with Charles Hunt. They enjoyed a large trade, for Ingram and Hunt ledgers reveal more than seven hundred customers recorded in about a twenty-year period. They shipped the alloy throughout England and Wales and even to Hamburg, Germany.[74] Based on the frequency of their mark in this country, they also exported a large amount to America.

Samuel Jefferys
Samuel Jefferys was elected to the Yeomanry of the London Company June 13,

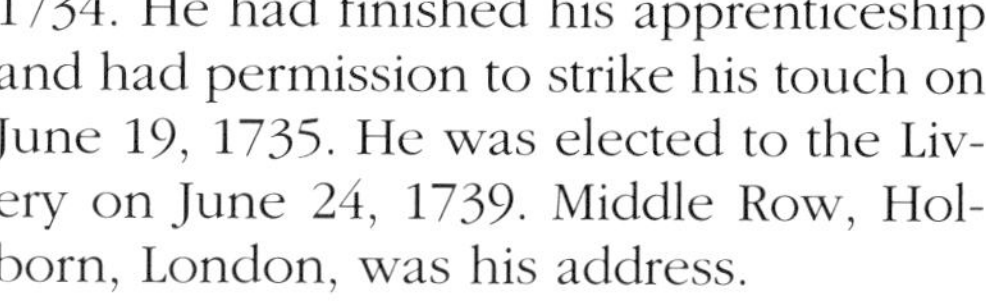

1734. He had finished his apprenticeship and had permission to strike his touch on June 19, 1735. He was elected to the Livery on June 24, 1739. Middle Row, Holborn, London, was his address.

Henry Joseph
Henry Joseph was elected a Yeoman of the London Company on March 24, 1736. He held all the offices of that company including the office of Master in 1771. He worked on New Street, St. Bride's, London. The mark of Francis Piggott has been found with Henry Joseph's on some pieces of pewter, suggesting a business relationship. Henry and Richard Joseph formed their partnership in 1787. Henry Joseph was an able craftsman, and his ecclesiastical wares include handsome spire flagons. Henry Joseph was one of a few British makers who made domestic export wares especially for the American market. His well-designed creamers, not much different from those made by Philadelphia and New York pewterers, have sometimes been erroneously attributed to American makers. Joseph's pewter made for household use includes Queen Anne style teapots, sugar bowls (with and without handles), sauce boats, broth bowls, pepper pots, tankards, and flatware. All of these forms have been found in America but rarely in England, because they were export items made for the American market. Recent scholars have given Henry Joseph his due credit.[75]

Henry and Richard Joseph
Henry and Richard Joseph were partners from 1787 to 1815. Their shop was at 9 New Street, Shoe Lane, London. Richard was elected to all the offices of the London Company, including the office of Master in 1805 and 1806.

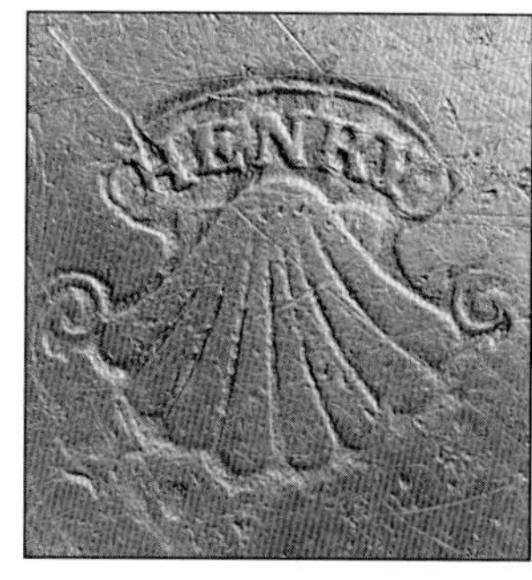

Fig. 284. *Mark of Henry Joseph on basin. Zion's (Stone) United Church of Christ, Northampton, Northampton County, Pa.*

71. In the collection of the Colonial Park United Church of Christ, Harrisburg, Dauphin Co., Pa.

72. Richard L. Bowen, Jr., "The Sheaf of Wheat Mark and the Hales of Bristol," *Pewter Collectors' Club of America Bulletin,* no. 104 (June 1992):102.

73. Robinson, "Antique British Pewter Found Today in New England," 389, 392.

74. Homer and Hall, *Provincial Pewterers,* 68–69.

75. Wayne A. Hilt, "Henry Joseph—Master Pewterer," *Pewter Collectors' Club of America Bulletin,* no. 77 (September 1978):293–300.

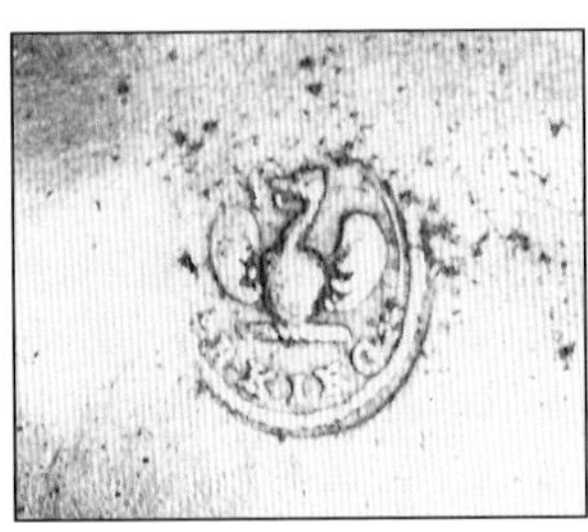

Fig. 285. *Mark of Richard King on three and one-half pint tankard. Muddy Creek Lutheran Church and Peace United Church of Christ, Denver, Lancaster Country, Pa.*

Richard King
Richard King, sometimes called Richard King, Jr., was the son of a pewterer by the same name. In fact, four Richard Kings worked as pewterers in London from the mid-sixteenth century to the end of the eighteenth century. Richard King, Jr., also called Richard King IV, is credited with making the bulk of the surviving pewter with that name. On December 12, 1745, King was granted leave to strike his touch. King was elected to all the offices of the London Company, including Master in 1777. He died in 1798. A variety of both hollow- and flatware by King was found in this study.

John Langford
This early London maker had leave to strike his touch on March 24, 1719. He was elected to the Yeomanry of the London Company in 1719, Livery in 1734, and offices of Steward in 1742, paid the stipulated fine to be excused from serving in the office of Renter Warden in 1746, took the office of Upper Warden in 1755 and Master in 1757. He died in 1757, the same year he was elected to the office of Master. Only one basin by this maker was found in the survey. Another pewterer by the same name worked in London about 1780, but marks ascribed to him were not those found on this basin.

Philip Matthews
Philip Matthews had leave to strike his touch on the London touchplate in 1736. He was elected to the Livery of the London Company on June 23, 1743. He worked until 1755.

Richard Pawson
Richard Pawson was elected to the Yeomanry of the London Company on March 12, 1752. He had leave to strike his mark on March 22, 1753.

Hellier Perchard
Hellier (Hillier, Hellary) Perchard used the year 1709 on one of his marks. It was that year that he was elected to the Yeomanry of the London Company. He was elected to the Livery on June 7, 1714, and the office of Steward in 1728, paid a fine to be excused from serving in the office of Renter Warden in 1728, and was elected to the offices of Upper Warden in 1738 and Master in 1740. Perchard was originally from the Isle of Guernsey but lived and worked in London.[76] Only one piece, a pint mug, was found with his mark in this study.

Francis Piggott
Francis Piggott, elected to the Yeomanry of the London Company on March 24, 1735, had leave to strike his touch on June 22, 1738. He worked until 1773. His mark is sometimes found with those of Henry Joseph, and he probably had a business relationship with Joseph.

Thomas Scattergood
This London pewterer was elected to the Yeomanry of the London Company on December 16, 1736, after having leave to strike his touch on March 24 of the same year. He was elected to the Livery on March 21, 1744, paid the stipulated fine to be excused from the duties of the Steward in 1754, and was elected to the offices of Renter Warden in 1760, Upper Warden in 1773, and Master in the years 1774 and 1775. His trade card gives his location as "at the Blackmoores head near the South Sea House in Bishopsgate street LONDON."[77]

Thomas Swanson
Thomas Swanson was elected to the Yeomanry of the London Company on December 13, 1753 and the Livery on March 15, 1764. He paid the fine to be excused from serving in the office of Steward in 1769 and was elected to the office of Renter Warden in 1777. He died in 1783. He continued the business of Samuel Ellis, and one of his marks reads "Successor to S. Ellis London." He must have been a generous person, for on

76. Woolmer and Arkwright, *Pewter of the Channel Islands,* 125.

77. Cotterell, *Old Pewter,* 74.

June 10, 1783, Swanson gave to the Company Consuls money of which thirty pounds was to be distributed annually among six poor widows of pewterers.[78]

Cornelius Swift
Cornelius Swift was elected to the Yeomanry of the London Company on October 18, 1770. He struck his mark on the London touchplate in 1778. He was elected to the Livery on January 20, 1796. He paid fines to be excused from the duties of the offices of Steward in 1798 and Renter Warden in 1813. He was elected to the office of Master in 1814.

John Townsend
John Townsend was given leave to strike his mark on the London touchplate June 16, 1748, the same day he was elected to the Yeomanry of the London Company. One of his marks bears that year. He was elected to the Livery on January 21, 1754, and to the offices of Steward in 1762, Renter Warden in 1769, Upper Warden in 1782, and Master in 1784. He continued the business started by a Thomas Scattergood in 1703. In 1792 his shop was at 125 Fenchurch Street. Another of his marks bears that location, "Fenchurch Street, London." He died November 25, 1801.

Pewter by John Townsend, his various partnerships and his offspring is found more frequently than that of any other maker in Pennsylvania German churches. The same can be said for pewter in domestic use in southeastern Pennsylvania as well.

John Townsend's name appears in Quaker ministry records as early as 1757. John Townsend and his son-in-law Thomas Compton were active Quakers, having close ties to Friends in Philadelphia. Philadelphia Quakers visited them in London, and John Townsend journeyed to Philadelphia in 1785, traveling from Meeting to Meeting to preach. He ministered to Friends in North Carolina and Virginia. He attended Yearly Meetings in Rhode Island, Nantucket, Halifax, and St. John's, New Brunswick, where he met his brother James in 1786.[79]

John Townsend shipped tremendous quantities of pewter to America. Philadelphia merchant Daniel Wister ordered pewter regularly from his friend John Townsend. The size of his orders is truly staggering. In 1763, Daniel Wister ordered a shipment of 12,916 pieces of pewter—one of three shipments for that year![80]

Townsend and Compton
John Townsend's daughter and son-in-law were also pewterers. John Townsend's daughter, Mary, finished her apprenticeship in 1774 and married pewterer Thomas Compton.[81] The Townsend in the Townsend and Compton firm was very likely John Townsend and after his death in 1801, his daughter Mary Townsend Compton. As the daughter of a liveryman she was automatically a pewterer in her own right and entitled to use her late father's mark.[82] The Townsend and Compton firm produced pewter from 1785 to 1806. The marks used by Townsend and Compton may have been used over a period of twenty five years.[83] The firm, Townsend, Compton & Co., continued until 1810.

The firm continued its profitable relationship with Philadelphia merchants. Large quantities of the finished product must have been exported to this country based on the number of existing pieces marked Townsend and Compton. Pewter

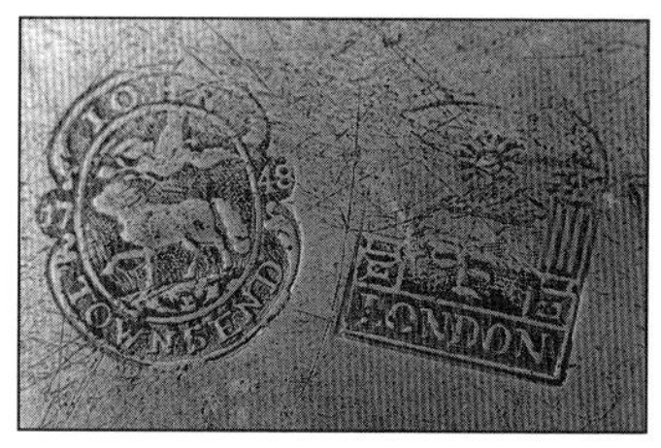

Fig. 286. *Mark of John Townsend on basin. East Vincent United Church of Christ, Spring City, Chester County, Pa.*

78. Ibid., 316.

79. Charles F. Montgomery, "John Townsend, English Quaker with American Connections," *Pewter Collectors' Club of America Bulletin,* no. 51 (December 1964):24–25.

80. Charles F. Montgomery, *A History of American Pewter: A Winterthur Book* (New York: Praeger, 1973), 8.

81. Bowen, "John Townsend and Associates," 99.

82. Homer, "Editor's Note," 129.

83. Bowen, "John Townsend and Associates," 100. From Elsie Englefield, *A Treatise on Pewter* (London, 1933), 21–23.

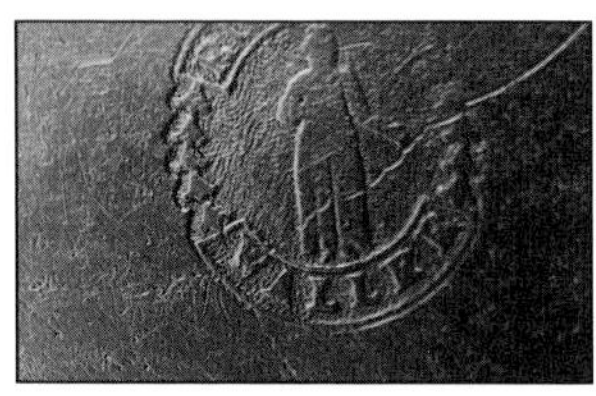

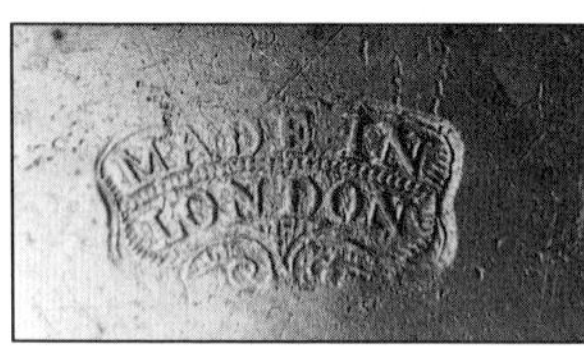

Fig. 287. *Marks of Robert Waller on plate. Paradise-Holzschwamm Union Church, with Lutheran and United Church of Christ congregations, Thomasville, York County, Pa.*

marked Townsend and Compton is found in southeastern Pennsylvania more frequently than any other eighteenth-century maker or firm.

Townsend and Giffin
Another of John Townsend's partnerships was with Thomas Giffin. Townsend and Giffin produced pewter at Fenchurch Street, London, from 1777 to 1801.[84]

Townsend and Reynolds
John Townsend was in partnership with Robert Reynolds in London from 1767 to 1776.[85] They used a lamb-and-dove mark that included the names of both pewterers.

Robert Waller
Robert Waller was elected to the Yeomanry of the London Company on October 21, 1779. He struck his mark on the London touchplates about 1782. He was listed as being in London in 1786.

John Watts
John Watts worked in London from 1725 to 1765. Elected to the Yeomanry of the London Company on October 19, 1725, Watts had leave to strike his touch a few days later on October 29. He was elected to the offices of Livery in 1736, and Steward in 1748, paid a fine to be excused from the office of the Renter Warden in 1750, and was elected Upper Warden in 1758 and Master in 1760. He died in 1765.

John Yates
John Yates, born in 1788, established himself as a spoon and toy maker at 54 Coleskill Street, Birmingham, by 1805. He entered into a partnership with Thomas Birch and Lucas Spooner in 1829 to form the firm of Yates, Birch, and Spooner. His son James joined the firm in 1837. John Yates left pewtering in the 1850s and set up a steel tool manufacturing business.[86]

Richard Yates
Richard Yates was elected to the Yeomanry of the London Company on March 19, 1772. He struck his mark on the London touchplate about 1775. Yates was elected to the Livery on July 4, 1777, and the office of Steward in 1783. His business was at 20 Shoreditch in London from 1792 to 1807.[87]

Continental European

GERMAN

Elias Beyerbach
Elias Beyerbach, from Frankfurt am Main, was a son of Johann Heinrich Beyerbach. He became a master pewterer in 1755 and died in 1783.[88] A flagon of rococo design from his workshop was found in the survey. The flagon, now having a broken stem, was made in the style of contempory silver flagons and has the inclined, sloping body with gadrooning typical of pewter made in the Frankfurt area. The form also was produced in Karlsbad, Bohemia, the western part of Czechoslovakia, now the Czech Republic.

Johann Jacob Bühler
Hintze reported that Johann Jacob Bühler became a master pewterer in 1712 in the city of Heilbronn; however, the mark on a flagon found in the survey clearly included the date 02 for the year 1702. A pewterer frequently included in his mark the year in which he became a Master. This mark with the year designated 1702 reveals that year as the beginning of his pewtering career. This date is substanti-

84. Ian D. Robinson, "Antique British Pewter Found Today in New England," 389. Also see Bowen, "John Townsend and Associates," 100.

85. Bowen, "John Townsend and Associates," 100.

86. Homer and Hall, *Provincial Pewterers,* 90.

87. Cotterell, *Old Pewter,* 343.

88. Information from Karl Schöppl in a letter to the author dated October 19, 1992. From Dietz, *Frankfurter Zinngiesser.*

ated by the complaint of a colleague, Johann Greffe, in 1704 that Bühler traded Frankfurt pewter; a complaint that he repeated in 1718 and 1719.[89] Bühler moved to Karlsruhe in 1733 and continued his profession there.

Johann Michael Dor
Johann Michael Dor was the son of pewterer Veit Conrad Dor of Heilbronn. He was born April 17, 1693, and learned the trade with his father. Johann became a master pewterer in 1725, and married the same year. Dor died August 13, 1756. After his death, Ludwigsburg pewterer Johann Joseph Tambornino, previously from Heilbronn, complained that Dor had kept two pieces of his pewter to be repaired for more than a year.[90]

Johann Dietrich Finck
Johann Dietrich Finck worked in Bamberg, Germany, about 1731.[91] The repoussé gadrooning on the rim and inside bottom of the Finck dish in this survey is frequently found on flatware from southern Germany.

Daniel Heidenreich
Daniel Heidenreich (Heydenreich), from Durlach, was mentioned in local records at his daughter Susanna's birth on April 29, 1705. He probably became a master pewterer the following year.[92] Pewter with the dates 1755 and 1756 have been recorded from his workshop. Both Heidenreich flagons found in the survey are dated 1764. There was, however, probably more than one pewterer with the name Daniel Heidenreich. If the dates are contemporary with the pewter, it is unlikely that one person would have made pewter over a span of fifty-nine years.

Johann Martin Kaller
Born in 1734, Johann Martin Kaller was the third generation of a family of pewterers from Heilbronn. He was the son of Johann Conrad Kaller and the grandson of Johann Martin Kaller of the same name. Johann Martin Kaller had a brother Johann Jacob Christian Kaller and an uncle Johann Jacob Kaller who were pewterers in the same city. Johann Martin Kaller died on January 29, 1784.[93]

Frantz Kurtz
Frantz Kurtz was born in Reutlingen on September 10, 1710, was married on January 20, 1734, and died March 23, 1798. Frantz was the son of Reutlingen pewterer Johannes Kurtz and the grandson of pewterer Michael Kurtz. His brother Urban Kurtz and son Michael Kurtz were also pewterers in Reutlingen.[94]

Heinrich Müller
Heinrich Müller was a pewterer in Rothenburg ob der Tauber, Bavaria. Born in Schneeberg, in the region of Sachsen-Meissen, he was the son of carpenter/cabinetmaker Georg Müller. He married Susanna Margaretha, daughter of pewterer Johann Heinrich Korn in Rothenburg. His mark, dated 1712, suggests that 1712 was the year in which he established his business as a pewterer. He became a citizen of that town on January 16, 1721.[95] He committed adultery in 1726 while

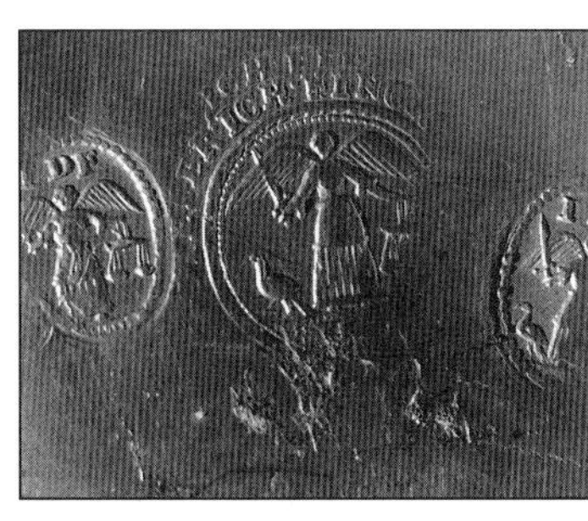

Fig. 288. *Mark of Johann Dietrich Finck on dish. St. Michael's Lutheran Church, Germantown, Philadelphia County, Pa.*

89. Erwin Hintze, *Die Deutschen Zinngiesser und Ihre Marken*. (Osnabruck: Otto Zeller Verlagsbuchhandlung GMBH, 1965). 5:235. Hintze lists the pewterer Bühler but does not illustrate a mark. Karl Schöppl, in a letter dated November 11, 1991, agreed that we now know that Bühler was working ten years earlier than previously recorded.

90. Hintze, *Die Deutschen Zinngiesser und Ihre Marken*. 5:236.

91. Ibid., 5:78.

92. Ibid., 5:139.

93. Ibid., 5:238.

94. Ibid., 5:216–217.

95. Editorial postscript to John J. Evans, Jr., "I.C.H., Lancaster Pewterer," in *American and British Pewter: An Historic Survey*, ed. John Carl Thomas (N.Y.: Universe Books, 1976), 116.

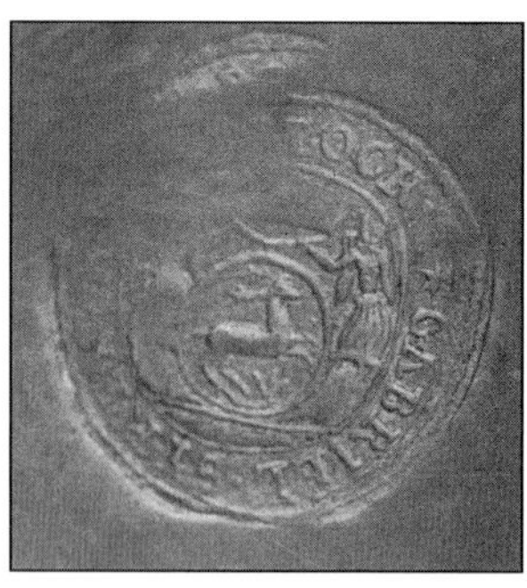

Fig. 289. *Mark of Gabriel Syren on flagon. New Hanover Lutheran Church, Gilbertsville, Montgomery County, Pa.*

drunk and was given "Tower Punishment," a type of jail sentence in a tower not uncommon in eighteenth-century Germany. He lived in the house of his father-in-law Korn and claimed half of the house as dowry. From 1727 to 1744, Korn made a series of attempts to get Müller to buy the house or to move out. Heinrich Müller was buried in Rothenburg on January 22, 1744.[96] The flagon from his workshop in the survey is dated 1733.

Philipp Jacob Schott

Philipp Jacob Schott worked in Frankfurt am Main, Germany, from 1726 to 1765. He is listed as No. 112 in Dietz's Frankfurt Masterlist.[97]

Gabriel Syren

Gabriel Syren went from Karis to Åbo in Finland (at that time Sweden). A document has been located from which it has been ascertained that he was a master pewterer in Frankfurt am Main in 1727.[98] He worked until perhaps 1753, and then his son Johann Valentin Syren became a master in Frankfurt am Main.[99]

NETHERLANDIC

Hendrick Kock

Hendrick Kock was born in 1732 and died in 1787. He worked in Rotterdam.[100] His ENGLES HART TIN mark capitalized on the recognized fine quality of English pewter.

SWISS

Jakob Laufer

Jakob Laufer worked in Zofingen. He was born in 1683, married Susanna Zurlinden in 1721 and died in 1746. A rosette design placed on the inside bottom of a flagon was a method of identification used by pewterers of Switzerland and southern Germany. The five-petaled rosette found in the flagon in this survey is similar to one used by Jakob Laufer.[101] The form of this flagon, or *Stize* as it is called in Switzerland, is similar to marked examples from Luzern and Basel.[102]

---

96. Ludwig Schnurrer, *Das Zinngiesserhandwerk: Rothenburg ob der Tauber* (Rothenburg: Petersche Druckeri, 1981), 96.

97. Letter from Karl Schöppl, December 17, 1991.

98. Information from Karl Schöppl in a letter dated October 20, 1991. From Dietz, *Frankfurter Zinngiesser*.

99. Information from Karl Schöppl, November 11, 1991.

100. B. Dubbe, *Tin en tinnegieters in Nederland* (Lochem: De Tijdstroom, 1978), 370, 373.

101. Hugo Schneider and Paul Kneuss, *Zinn: Die Zinngiesser der Schweiz und ihre Marken* (Olten: Walter-Verlag, 1983), 3:219.

102. Hugo Schneider, *Zinn: Katalog der Sammlung des Schweizerischen Landesmuseums, Zürich* (Olten: Walter-Verlag, 1970), 1:103-104.

APPENDIX 1

Pewter Totals

Churches that have pewter

NUMBER OF PEWTER PIECES BY CHURCH

Lutheran	267	@ 44%
UCC	197	33
Union	84	14
Mennonite	34	6
Ch. of Brethren	14	2
Moravian	6	1
Roman Catholic	4	1
	606 pieces pewter	

Numbers and percentage of churches that have pewter

	# HAVE	# HAVE NOT	% HAVE PEWTER
Lutheran	64	150	30
UCC	54	128	30
Union	13	17	33
Mennonite	24	43	36
Ch. of Brethren	5	18	22
Moravian	4	4	50
Roman Catholic	1	14	7
	165	374	30

Numbers and percentage of congregations that have pewter

	# HAVE	# HAVE NOT	% HAVE PEWTER
Lutheran	77	167	32
UCC	67	145	32
Mennonite	24	43	36
Ch. of Brethren	5	18	22
Moravian	4	4	50
Roman Catholic	1	14	7
	178	391	31

178 of 569 congregations have pewter = 31% have pewter

Pewter: Country of Origin

CHURCH	NUMBER	AM.	AM. OR CONT.	CONT.	ENGLAND	GERMANY	NETH.	OTHER
Luth.	267	136	8	2	104	13	2	2
UCC	197	89	5	2	90	5	2	4
Union	84	46	1	–	32	3	–	2
Mennonite	34	17	–	–	14	1	2	–
Ch. Br.	14	10	–	–	4	–	–	–
Moravian	6	6	–	–	–	–	–	–
Roman Catholic	4	4	–	–	–	–	–	–
	606	307	14	4	244	22	6	8
% of total*	(99.81)	50.57	2.31	.66	40.33	3.63	.99	1.32

* That is at least 50.57% of pewter in the survey is American in origin. Some pewter in the American or Continental category (2.31%) is probably American in origin and would increase the percentage of American pewter one or two points.

40.33% was made in England, 3.63% in Germany, .99% in the Netherlands, .66% on the Continent and 1.32% other or unknown country of origin.

Pewter Forms

Basins	75	(6 footed)
Beakers	24	(1 handled, 1 double hdl.)
Candlesticks	4	
Chalices	112	
Ciboria	2	
Dishes	14	
Plates	207	(3 footed)
Pitchers, ewers	11	(1 covered pitcher)
Flagons	69	(4 two quart, 3 one quart)
Measures	4	(3 quart, 1 pint)
Mugs	24	(6 quart, 17 pint, 1 one-half pint, 16 straight, 8 tulip)
Spoons	7	3 tea, 4 table
Tankards	53	(1 three and one-half pint, 47 quart, 4 pint, 1 one-half pint, 34 straight, 19 tulip)
	606	

In decreasing order, the forms most frequently found are plates (207), chalices (112), basins (75), flagons (69), tankards (53), beakers (24), mugs (24), dishes (14), pitchers, ewers (11), spoons (7), measures (4), candlesticks (4), and ciboria (2).

Number of churches having pewter by State, County.

MARYLAND	
Carroll	2
Frederick	2
Washington	1
PENNSYLVANIA	
Adams	2
Berks	19
Bucks	7
Carbon	1
Centre	2
Chester	2
Cumberland	2
Dauphin	9
Lancaster	29
Lebanon	16
Lehigh	15
Monroe	2
Montgomery	14
Northampton	8
Northumberland	2
Perry	1
Philadelphia	1
Schuylkill	5
Snyder	2
Somerset	1
Washington	1
York	11
	22 of 67 counties in Pennsylvania have pewter

Pewter was found in Pennsylvania churches in the following counties: Lancaster (29), Berks (19), Lebanon (16), Lehigh (15), Montgomery (14), York (11), Dauphin (9), Northampton (8), Bucks (7), Schuylkill (5), Adams (3), Centre (2), Chester (2), Cumberland (2), Monroe (2), Northumberland (2), Snyder (2), Carbon (1), Perry (1), Philadelphia (1), Somerset (1), and Washington (1).

VIRGINIA	
Frederick	3
Rockingham	1
Shenandoah	2
WEST VIRGINIA	
Hampshire	1

APPENDIX 2

List of Churches and Their Pewter

DIMENSIONS	FORM	MAKER	ORIGIN	WORKING	MARK
Carroll County MD					
PIPE CREEK CHURCH OF THE BRETHREN, LINWOOD					
L 7 1/2″	tablespoon	unknown England	England	1750–1800	
L 7 7/8″	tablespoon	unknown England	England	1750–1800	
L 7 3/8″	tablespoon	unmarked probably America	America	1780–1825	
L 5 3/8″	teaspoon	John Yates	England	1805–1852	P 5340A
ST. LUKE'S LUTHERAN CHURCH, NEW WINDSOR					
H 4 3/4″ TD 3 1/4″ BD 3 5/8″	mug	Allen Bright	England	1742–1763	C 574
Frederick County MD					
APPLE'S UNITED CHURCH OF CHRIST, THURMONT					
H 7 1/2″ TD 3 7/8″ BD 3 5/8″	chalice	Hiram Yale and Company	America	1824–1835	L 445
H 7 1/2″ TD 3 7/8″ BD 3 5/8″	chalice	Hiram Yale and Company	America	1824–1835	L 445
H 6 3/8″ TD 3 3/4″ BD 2 7/8″	church cup	att. Boardmans	America	1804–1873	
EVANGELICAL LUTHERAN CHURCH, FREDERICK					
TD 9 1/8″	basin	Townsend and Compton	England	1785–1810	C 4800
GLADE UNITED CHURCH OF CHRIST, WALKERSVILLE					
H 12″ TD 3″ BD 5 5/8″	flagon	unmarked Germany	Germany	1700–1750	

DIMENSIONS	FORM	MAKER	ORIGIN	WORKING	MARK
Washington County MD					
ZION EVANGELICAL & REFORMED UCC, HAGERSTOWN					
TD 8 1/8″	basin	Hale and Sons	England	1778–1822	C 2070
H 1 1/4″ TD 9 1/2″	footed plate	att. William Will	America	1764–1798	
H 7 3/4″ TD 5″ BD 4 1/2″	tankard	Robert Bush and Company	England	1787–1795	C 739
Adams County PA					
BENDER'S LUTHERAN CHURCH, BIGLERVILLE					
TD 9 1/8″	basin	Robert Bush Sr.	England	1755–1801	C 737
EMMANUEL UNITED CHURCH OF CHRIST, ABBOTTSTOWN					
H 8 3/4″ TD 4 1/8″ BD 4 1/2″	chalice	att. Johann Christoph Heyne	America	1752–1781	
FLOHR LUTHERAN CHURCH, MCKNIGHTSTOWN					
H 8″ TD 3 5/8″ BD 4 1/4″	chalice	att. William Will	America	1764–1798	
Berks County PA					
ALLEGHENY UNION LUTHERAN & UCC, ALLEGHENYVILLE					
TD 9″	basin	Bouchier and Richard Cleeve	England	1754	C 963
TD 8″	basin	Philipp Jacob Schott	Germany	1726–1765	
H 7″ TD 3 1/2″ BD 3 5/8″	chalice	att. Boardmans	America	1804–1873	
H 9″ TD 4 1/8″ BD 4 5/8″	chalice	att. Johann Christoph Heyne	America	1752–1781	
H 8 1/4″ TD 3 1/2″ BD 3 1/4″	chalice	unmarked probably Philadelphia	America	1800–1810	
H 11″ TD 4 1/8″ BD 5 7/8″	flagon	Boardman and Hall	America	1804–1873	T 125g
H 9″ TD 3″ BD 5″	flagon	Frantz Kurtz	Germany	1734–1798	H v.6, p.1146
TD 6 3/8″	plate	Johann Christoph Heyne	America	1752–1781	L 532, 533

DIMENSIONS	FORM	MAKER	ORIGIN	WORKING	MARK

Berks County PA

ALLEGHENY UNION LUTHERAN & UCC, ALLEGHENYVILLE

DIMENSIONS	FORM	MAKER	ORIGIN	WORKING	MARK
TD 6″	plate	Love	America	1750–1825	L 868, 869
TD 6 1/8″	plate	Thomas Danforth III	America	1777–1813	L 370
TD 6 1/8″	plate	Thomas Danforth III	America	1777–1813	L 370
TD 6″	plate	Love	America	1750–1825	L 868, 869
TD 6″	plate	Love	America	1750–1825	L 868, 869
H 7″ TD 4 1/4″ BD 5″	tankard	Love	America	1750–1825	L 869

BALLY MENNONITE CHURCH, BALLY

DIMENSIONS	FORM	MAKER	ORIGIN	WORKING	MARK
TD 10 1/4″	basin	Blak(e)slee Barn(e)s	America	1812–1817	L 551
H 5 3/8″ TD 3 3/4″ BD 2 7/8″	beaker	unknown Netherlands	Netherlands	1700–1725	
TD 10 7/8″	dish	Edgar and Son	England	1810–1855	C 1511
H 7 1/4″ TD 4″ BD 4 1/2″	tankard	Love	America	1750–1825	L 869

BERN UNION CHURCH LUTHERAN & UCC, LEESPORT

DIMENSIONS	FORM	MAKER	ORIGIN	WORKING	MARK
H 7 5/8″ TD 4 1/8″ BD 3 7/8″	chalice	unmarked	America or Continental	1750–1800	
TD 10 7/8″	dish	John Townsend	England	1748–1801	C 4795
TD 8 5/8″	plate	Love	America	1750–1825	L 869
TD 8 5/8″	plate	Love	America	1750–1825	L 869
TD 8 5/8″	plate	Love	America	1750–1825	L 869
TD 8 5/8″	plate	Love	America	1750–1825	L 869
TD 8 1/2″	plate	Richard Yates	England	1772–1807	c 5344
H 7″ TD 4 3/8″ BD 5″	tankard	William Eddon	England	1689–1745	C 1503

CHRIST LITTLE TULPEHOCKEN UCC, BERNVILLE

DIMENSIONS	FORM	MAKER	ORIGIN	WORKING	MARK
TD 9 1/8″	basin	att. Love	America	1750–1825	
H 7 5/8″ TD 4 1/8″ BD 4 1/4″	chalice	unmarked	America or Continental	1750–1800	
TD 7 3/4″	plate	John Townsend	England	1748–1801	C 4795
H 5 7/8″ TD 3 3/8″ BD 3 7/8″	tankard	Simon Edgell	America	1713–1742	L 526

DIMENSIONS	FORM	MAKER	ORIGIN	WORKING	MARK
Berks County PA					
CHRIST LUTHERAN CHURCH, SPANGSVILLE					
H 9″ TD 3 7/8″ BD 4 1/4″	chalice	unmarked	America or Continental	1750–1800	
H 7 1/2″ TD 3 3/8″ BD 4 5/8″	flagon	att. Love	America	1750–1825	
TD 7 7/8″	plate	Blak(e)slee Barn(e)s	America	1812–1817	L 556, 553
TD 7 3/4″	plate	Blak(e)slee Barn(e)s	America	1812–1817	L 555, 553
TD 7 3/4″	plate	Blak(e)slee Barn(e)s	America	1812–1817	L 556, 553
EPLER'S UNITED CHURCH OF CHRIST, LEESPORT					
H 5″ TD 7 3/4″ BD 5 1/8″	baptismal basin	att. Boardmans	America	1804–1873	
H 7″ TD 3 5/8″ BD 3 3/4″	chalice	att. Boardmans	America	1804–1873	
H 7″ TD 3 5/8″ BD 3 3/4″	chalice	att. Boardmans	America	1804–1873	
H 11 1/4″ TD 4 1/8″ BD 5 3/4″	flagon	Boardman and Company	America	1825–1827	L 431
H 7 1/2″ TD 4 1/8″ BD 5″	flagon	Boardman and Company	America	1825–1827	L 431
TD 9″	plate	Boardman and Company	America	1825–1827	L 431
TD 8 5/8″	plate	Hale and Sons	England	1778–1822	C 2070
TD 8 5/8″	plate	Hale and Sons	England	1778–1822	C 2070
FRIEDENS LUTHERAN CHURCH, STONY RUN					
TD 8″	basin	Love	America	1750–1825	L 868, 869
H 9 1/8″ TD 4 1/4″ BD 4 1/2″	chalice	Philadelphia	America	1764–1798	
TD 11 7/8″	dish	Townsend and Giffin	England	1777–1801	C 4800, 4801
H 6 3/8″ TD 4 1/8″ BD 4 3/8″	mug	William Will	America	1764–1798	L 535
TD 7 7/8″	plate	Townsend and Giffin	England	1777–1801	C 4800, 4801
JERUSALEM (RED) UNION CHURCH LUTHERAN & UCC, KEMPTON					
H 9″ TD 4″ BD 4 1/2″	chalice	Philadelphia	America	1764–1798	

DIMENSIONS	FORM	MAKER	ORIGIN	WORKING	MARK

Berks County PA

JERUSALEM (RED) UNION CHURCH LUTHERAN & UCC, KEMPTON

DIMENSIONS	FORM	MAKER	ORIGIN	WORKING	MARK
H 1 5/8″ TD 15 1/2″ W 10 1/2″	dish	William Will	America	1764–1798	L 539
H 11 3/4″ TD 3″ BD 5 1/2″	flagon	unmarked Germany	Germany	1700–1750	
H 7″ TD 3 3/8″ BD 4 1/4″	pitcher	att. William Will	America	1764–1798	

MOST BLESSED SACRAMENT CHURCH, BALLY

DIMENSIONS	FORM	MAKER	ORIGIN	WORKING	MARK
H 21 1/4″ BD 8 3/4″	candlestick	Johann Christoph Heyne	America	1752–1781	L 530, 533
H 22 7/8″ BD 8 3/4″	candlestick	Johann Christoph Heyne	America	1752–1781	L 530, 533
H 22″ BD 8 3/4″	candlestick	Johann Christoph Heyne	America	1752–1781	L 530, 533
H 22″ BD 8 3/4″	candlestick	Johann Christoph Heyne	America	1752–1781	L 530, 533

ST. JOHN'S (HAIN'S) UNITED CHURCH OF CHRIST, WERNERSVILLE

DIMENSIONS	FORM	MAKER	ORIGIN	WORKING	MARK
H 8″ TD 4 1/8″ BD 4 1/4″	chalice	att. Johann Christoph Heyne	America	1752–1781	
TD 9 3/8″	plate	Townsend and Compton	England	1785–1810	C 4800
TD 8″	plate	Townsend and Compton	England	1785–1810	C 4800
TD 8″	plate	Townsend and Compton	England	1785–1810	C 4800
TD 8″	plate	Townsend and Compton	England	1785–1810	C 4800
TD 8″	plate	Townsend and Compton	England	1785–1810	C 4800
TD 8″	plate	Townsend and Compton	England	1785–1810	C 4800
H 6 1/2″ TD 4 3/8″ BD 4 3/4″	tankard	Simon Edgell	America	1713–1742	L 526

ST. JOHN'S UNITED CHURCH OF CHRIST, SINKING SPRING

DIMENSIONS	FORM	MAKER	ORIGIN	WORKING	MARK
H 7 7/8″ TD 3 1/2″ BD 4 3/8″	chalice	att. William Will	America	1764–1798	
H 13 3/4″ TD 3 3/8″ BD 4 1/4″	flagon	att. William Will	America	1764–1798	
TD 8 1/4″	plate	John Townsend	England	1748–1801	C 4795
TD 8 1/4″	plate	Townsend and Compton	England	1785–1810	C 4800

DIMENSIONS	FORM	MAKER	ORIGIN	WORKING	MARK
Berks County PA					
ST. MICHAEL'S LUTHERAN CHURCH, HAMBURG					
H 7 5/8″ TD 3 7/8″ BD 4 1/8″	chalice	unmarked	America or Continental	1750–1800	
ST. PAUL'S LUTHERAN CHURCH, HAMBURG					
H 8 1/4″ TD 4″ BD 4 1/2″	chalice	unmarked	America or Continental	1750–1800	
H 7 1/8″ TD 3 1/2″ BD 3 3/4″	chalice	att. Boardmans	America	1804–1873	
H 7 1/8″ TD 3 1/2″ BD 3 3/4″	chalice	att. Boardmans	America	1804–1873	
H 10 3/4″ TD 3 3/4″ BD 5 "	flagon	Boardman and Hart	America	1828–1853	L 437, 438
H 4 3/4″ TD 3 1/2″ BD 3 7/8″	mug	John Townsend	England	1748–1801	C 4795
TD 6 1/8″	plate	Thomas Danforth III	America	1777–1813	L 370
SALEM UNITED CHURCH OF CHRIST, SPANGSVILLE					
H 7 3/8″ TD 4″ BD 3 7/8″	chalice	unmarked	America or Continental	1750–1800	
H 13 1/2″ TD 3 3/8″ BD 4 3/8″	flagon	att. William Will	America	1764–1798	
TD 9″	plate	Townsend and Compton	England	1785–1810	C 4800
TD 9 1/8″	plate	Townsend and Compton	England	1785–1810	C 4800
H 5″ TD 4″ BD 3 7/8″	tankard	John Townsend	England	1748–1801	C 4795
SCHWARZWALD UNITED CHURCH OF CHRIST, READING					
H 12 3/4″ TD 4″ BD 5 3/4″	flagon	Jakob Laufer	Switzerland	1712–1746	S 1603
TRINITY LUTHERAN CHURCH, READING					
TD 11 5/8″	dish	Thomas Danforth III	America	1777–1813	M p. 220
ZION (SPIES) UNITED CHURCH OF CHRIST, READING					
TD 8″	basin	Townsend and Compton	England	1785–1810	C 4800

DIMENSIONS	FORM	MAKER	ORIGIN	WORKING	MARK

Berks County PA

ZION (SPIES) UNITED CHURCH OF CHRIST, READING

DIMENSIONS	FORM	MAKER	ORIGIN	WORKING	MARK
H 7 1/4″ TD 3 7/8″ BD 4 1/8″	chalice	unmarked	America or Continental	1750–1800	

ZION MOSELEM LUTHERAN CHURCH, KUTZTOWN

DIMENSIONS	FORM	MAKER	ORIGIN	WORKING	MARK
H 12 3/4″ TD 4 1/4″ BD 3 7/8″	flagon	William Will	American	1764–1798	L539

ZION ST. JOHN'S (REED'S) LUTHERAN CHURCH, STOUCHSBURG

DIMENSIONS	FORM	MAKER	ORIGIN	WORKING	MARK
TD 8″	basin	Thomas Scattergood	England	1736–1775	C 4139
H 7 5/8″ TD 4″ BD 3 7/8″	chalice	unmarked	America or Continental	1750–1800	
TD 6 3/4″	plate	Thomas Byles	America	1711–1771	L 586
H 6 1/2″ TD 4 1/2″ BD 4 7/8″	tankard	att. Simon Edgell	America	1713–1742	

Bucks County PA

BLOOMING GLEN MENNONITE CHURCH, BLOOMING GLEN

DIMENSIONS	FORM	MAKER	ORIGIN	WORKING	MARK
TD 10 1/4″	basin	John H. and Robert Palethorp	America	1817–1845	L 561
H 4″ TD 3 1/2″ BD 3 1/2″	beaker	Robert Palethorp Jr.	America	1817–1821	L 560

DEEP RUN MENNONITE CHURCH EAST, PERKASIE

DIMENSIONS	FORM	MAKER	ORIGIN	WORKING	MARK
H 4 3/8″ TD 3 5/8″ BD 3 1/4″	beaker	att. Simon Edgell	America	1713–1742	

EAST SWAMP MENNONITE CHURCH, QUAKERTOWN

DIMENSIONS	FORM	MAKER	ORIGIN	WORKING	MARK
TD 10 1/4″	basin	Thomas and Townsend Compton	England	1810–1815	C 1064

LINE LEXINGTON MENNONITE CHURCH, LINE LEXINGTON

DIMENSIONS	FORM	MAKER	ORIGIN	WORKING	MARK
H 5 1/2″ TD 3 5/8″ BD 3 1/4″	beaker	William Will	America	1764–1798	L 539

ST. JOHN'S (SCHUETZ'S) LUTHERAN CHURCH, SPINNERSTOWN

DIMENSIONS	FORM	MAKER	ORIGIN	WORKING	MARK
TD 8″	basin	John Townsend	England	1748–1801	C 4795
TD 8 3/4″	plate	Samuel Ellis	England	1721–1764	C 1547
TD 7 7/8″	plate	Blak(e)slee Barn(e)s	America	1812–1817	L 557, 558

DIMENSIONS	FORM	MAKER	ORIGIN	WORKING	MARK
Bucks County PA					
ST. JOHN'S (SCHUETZ'S) LUTHERAN CHURCH, SPINNERSTOWN					
TD 7 7/8″	plate	Townsend and Compton	England	1785–1810	C 4800
H 6 1/4″ TD 4 1/4″ BD 4 3/4″	tankard	Richard King	England	1745–1798	C 2748, 2749, 2750
SPRINGFIELD MENNONITE CHURCH, PLEASANT VALLEY					
TD 10 7/8″	dish	Townsend and Compton	England	1785–1810	C 4800
H 4 3/4″ TD 3 1/2″ BD 3 3/4″	mug	John Townsend	England	1748–1801	C 4795
SWAMP MENNONITE CHURCH, QUAKERTOWN					
TD 10 3/4″	basin	Townsend and Compton	England	1785–1810	C 4800
H 4 1/4″ TD 3 3/8″ BD 3 1/2″	beaker	Hall, Boardman and Co.	America	1842–1857	M p. 222
Carbon County PA					
ST. JOHN LUTHERAN CHURCH, PALMERTON					
TD 8 1/4″	basin	Townsend and Compton	England	1785–1810	C 4800
H 8 1/4″ TD 3 5/8″ BD 3 1/2″	chalice	unmarked probably Philadelphia	America	1800–1810	
TD 8 1/2″	plate	unmarked probably America	America	1780–1825	
TD 8 1/2″	plate	Burford and Green	England	1748–1780	C 698
TD 8 1/2″	plate	Burford and Green	England	1748–1780	C 698
TD 8 1/2″	plate	Burford and Green	England	1748–1780	C 698
Centre County PA					
ST. PETER'S LUTHERAN CHURCH, REBERSBURG					
H 8 1/2″ TD 3 1/2″ BD 3 1/2″	chalice	unmarked probably Philadelphia	America	1800–1810	
H 6 1/8″ TD 4″ BD 5″	mug	Edgar Curtis and Co.	England	1793–1809	C 1266A, 1508
TD 8 5/8″	plate	Love	America	1750–1825	L 869
TD 8 5/8″	plate	Love	America	1750–1825	L 869
TD 8 5/8″	plate	Love	America	1750–1825	L 869
TD 8 5/8″	plate	Love	America	1750–1825	L 869

DIMENSIONS	FORM	MAKER	ORIGIN	WORKING	MARK

Centre County PA

SALEM LUTHERAN CHURCH, AARONSBURG

DIMENSIONS	FORM	MAKER	ORIGIN	WORKING	MARK
H 1 1/2″ TD 10 5/8″	baptismal basin	William Will	America	1764–1798	L 537, 540
H 7 3/4″ TD 3 1/2″ BD 3 5/8″	chalice	att. William Will	America	1764–1798	
H 13 7/8″ TD 3 3/8″ BD 4 3/8″	flagon	att. William Will	America	1764–1798	
H 10 7/8″ TD 3 3/8″ BD 4 1/4″	pitcher	att. William Will	America	1764–1798	

Chester County PA

EAST VINCENT UNITED CHURCH OF CHRIST, SPRING CITY

DIMENSIONS	FORM	MAKER	ORIGIN	WORKING	MARK
TD 11 1/2″	basin	John Townsend	England	1748–1801	C 4795
H 9 1/8″ TD 3 3/8″ BD 4 1/8″	flagon	Germany, Cologne	Germany	1675–1757	
TD 8″	plate	Cornelius Bradford	America	1753–1785	L 496, 497

PHOENIXVILLE MENNONITE CHURCH, PHOENIXVILLE

DIMENSIONS	FORM	MAKER	ORIGIN	WORKING	MARK
H 5 1/2″ TD 3 5/8″ BD 3 1/8″	beaker	unknown Netherlands	Netherlands	1700–1750	

Cumberland County PA

FRIEDENS PEACE CHURCH, SHIREMANSTOWN

DIMENSIONS	FORM	MAKER	ORIGIN	WORKING	MARK
H 7 3/8″ TD 3 5/8″ BD 4 3/8″	chalice	att. William Will	America	1764–1798	
H 8 1/4″ TD 3 1/8″ BD 4″	chalice	Philadelphia	America	1764–1798	
H 12 1/2″ TD 4 1/8″ BD 6″	flagon	Thomas D and Sherman Boardman	America	1810–1860	L 435
TD 8 5/8″	plate	Townsend and Compton	England	1785–1810	C 4800
TD 8 5/8″	plate	Townsend and Compton	England	1785–1810	C 4800

DIMENSIONS	FORM	MAKER	ORIGIN	WORKING	MARK

Cumberland County PA

SALEM (STONE) UNITED CHURCH OF CHRIST, CARLISLE

DIMENSIONS	FORM	MAKER	ORIGIN	WORKING	MARK
TD 8″	basin	Townsend and Compton	England	1785–1810	C 4800
H 8½″ TD 3⅛″ BD 3½″	chalice	unmarked probably Philadelphia	America	1800–1810	
TD 8⅞″	plate	Love	America	1750–1825	L 868, 869
TD 8⅝″	plate	Love	America	1750–1825	L 868, 869
TD 8⅞″	plate	Love	America	1750–1825	L 868, 869
TD 8⅝″	plate	Love	America	1750–1825	L 868, 869
H 8½″ TD 4″ BD 4⅞″	tankard	Cornelius Swift	England	1770–1814	C 4608

Dauphin County PA

COLONIAL PARK UNITED CHURCH OF CHRIST, HARRISBURG

DIMENSIONS	FORM	MAKER	ORIGIN	WORKING	MARK
TD 8⅛″	basin	Townsend and Compton	England	1785–1810	C 4800
H 8¼″ TD 3¾″ BD 4⅛″	chalice	Philadelphia	America	1764–1798	
H 7⅜″ TD 4⅛″ BD 3⅝″	chalice	att. Palethorps	America	1817–1840	
TD 8¾″	plate	unknown Netherlands	Netherlands	1750–1800	
TD 7⅞″	plate	Hale and Sons	England	1778–1822	C 2070

HANOVERDALE CHURCH OF THE BRETHREN, HUMMELSTOWN

DIMENSIONS	FORM	MAKER	ORIGIN	WORKING	MARK
H 4⅛″ TD 3⅜″ BD 2⅝″	beaker	att. Johann Christoph Heyne	America	1752–1781	
H 4⅛″ TD 3⅜″ BD 2⅝″	beaker	att. Johann Christoph Heyne	America	1752–1781	

HUMMELSTOWN UNITED CHURCH OF CHRIST, HUMMELSTOWN

DIMENSIONS	FORM	MAKER	ORIGIN	WORKING	MARK
H 8¾″ TD 4″ BD 4½″	chalice	att. Johann Christoph Heyne	America	1752–1781	

ST. PAUL'S (SAND HILL) LUTHERAN CHURCH, HERSHEY

DIMENSIONS	FORM	MAKER	ORIGIN	WORKING	MARK
H 8¼″ TD 4⅛″ BD 4½″	chalice	att. Johann Christoph Heyne	America	1752–1781	
TD 6¼″	plate	Johann Christoph Heyne	America	1752–1781	L 530, 432

DIMENSIONS	FORM	MAKER	ORIGIN	WORKING	MARK

Dauphin County PA

ST. THOMAS UNITED CHURCH OF CHRIST, HARRISBURG

DIMENSIONS	FORM	MAKER	ORIGIN	WORKING	MARK
H 7 7/8″ TD 3 1/2″ BD 4 3/8″	chalice	att. William Will	America	1764–1798	
H 6″ TD 4 1/8″ BD 4 7/8″	mug	Edgar Curtis and Co.	England	1793–1809	C 1266A, 1508

SALEM UNITED CHURCH OF CHRIST, HARRISBURG

DIMENSIONS	FORM	MAKER	ORIGIN	WORKING	MARK
H 6 5/8″ TD 3 1/2″ BD 4 1/2″	chalice	att. William Will	America	1764–1798	
H 14″ TD 3 3/8″ BD 4 3/8″	flagon	att. William Will	America	1764–1798	
TD 8 3/4″	plate	Townsend and Compton	England	1785–1810	C 4800
TD 8 3/4″	plate	Townsend and Compton	England	1785–1810	C 4800

STAUFFER MENNONITE CHURCH, HERSHEY

DIMENSIONS	FORM	MAKER	ORIGIN	WORKING	MARK
H 4 1/4″ TD 3 1/2″ BD 4″	mug	John Townsend	England	1748–1801	C 4795

ZION (KLINGERS) LUTHERAN CHURCH, ERDMAN

DIMENSIONS	FORM	MAKER	ORIGIN	WORKING	MARK
TD 8″	basin	Townsend and Compton	England	1785–1810	C 4800
TD 6″	basin	unmarked probably America	America	1780–1825	
TD 6″	basin	unmarked probably America	America	1780–1825	

ZION LUTHERAN CHURCH, HUMMELSTOWN

DIMENSIONS	FORM	MAKER	ORIGIN	WORKING	MARK
TD 7 7/8″	basin	George Lightner	America	1806–1815	L 566
H 8 1/4″ TD 4 1/4″ BD 4 1/2″	chalice	att. Johann Christoph Heyne	America	1752–1781	
H 11 3/8″ TD 3 1/2″ BD 6″	flagon	Johann Christoph Heyne	America	1752–1781	L 530, 532
H 8 1/4″ TD 3 3/4″ BD 4″	measure	unknown England	England	1750–1800	
TD 6 3/8″	plate	Johann Christoph Heyne	America	1752–1781	L 533

DIMENSIONS	FORM	MAKER	ORIGIN	WORKING	MARK
Lancaster County PA					
BERGSTRASSE LUTHERAN CHURCH, EPHRATA					
H 12 1/4″ TD 5 1/4″ BD 4 3/8″	flagon	William Will	America	1764–1798	L 539
BETHANY UNITED CHURCH OF CHRIST, EPHRATA					
TD 9 1/8″	plate	Blak(e)slee Barn(e)s	America	1812–1817	L 551, 553
TD 8 7/8″	plate	William Bartlett	England	c.1740–1770	C 279
TD 8″	plate	Townsend and Compton	England	1785–1810	L 4800
TD 7 7/8″	plate	John Townsend	England	1748–1801	C 4795
BOSSLER'S MENNONITE CHURCH, ELIZABETHTOWN					
H 4 1/2″ TD 3 1/2″ BD 4″	mug	John Townsend	England	1748–1801	C 4975
BOWMANSVILLE MENNONITE CHURCH, BOWMANSVILLE					
H 4 3/8″ TD 3 1/2″ BD 3 1/4″	beaker	Simon Edgell	America	1713–1742	L 526
BRICKERVILLE UNITED LUTHERAN CHURCH, BRICKERVILLE					
TD 7 3/4″	basin	Stephen Barns	America	1795–1810	L 417
H 8 1/8″ TD 3 1/2″ BD 4 1/2″	chalice	att. William Will	America	1764–1798	
H 11 1/2″ TD 3 1/2″ BD 5 3/4″	flagon	Johann Christoph Heyne	America	1752–1781	L 530, 532
H 11 1/2″ TD 3 1/2″ BD 5 3/4″	flagon	Johann Christoph Heyne	America	1752–1781	L 530, 532
TD 7 1/8″	plate	Thomas Giffin	England	1764–1777	C 1861
TD 8 1/2″	plate	John Carr	England	1750	C 813
TD 8″	plate	Townsend and Compton	England	1785–1810	C 4800
TD 8 7/8″	plate	Hellier Perchard	England	1709–1740	C 3611
H 6 3/4″ TD 4″ BD 4 3/4″	tankard	unknown England	England	1750–1800	
CHESTNUT HILL MENNONITE CHURCH, LANDISVILLE					
H 4 5/8″ TD 3 1/4″ BD 4″	mug	William Will	America	1764–1798	L 537

DIMENSIONS	FORM	MAKER	ORIGIN	WORKING	MARK

Lancaster County PA

CHRIST CHURCH UNITED CHURCH OF CHRIST, ELIZABETHTOWN

DIMENSIONS	FORM	MAKER	ORIGIN	WORKING	MARK
TD 9 1/4″	basin	unmarked Germany	Continental	1700–1750	
H 5 1/4″ TD 4 1/8″ BD 2 5/8″	beaker	unmarked Germany	Continental	1700–1750	
H 7″ TD 4 1/4″ BD 3 1/4″	pitcher	att. William Will	America	1764–1798	
TD 9″	plate	unknown England	England	1750–1800	
TD 6 1/4″	plate	Johann Christoph Heyne	America	1752–1781	L 533
H 7 1/4″ TD 4″ BD 4 7/8″	tankard	John Townsend	England	1748–1801	C 4795

CHRIST LUTHERAN CHURCH, ELIZABETHTOWN

DIMENSIONS	FORM	MAKER	ORIGIN	WORKING	MARK
H 7 1/8″ TD 3 1/2″ BD 3 1/4″	chalice	att. Boardmans	America	1804–1873	
H 11 1/4″ TD 4 1/8″ BD 5 7/8″	flagon	Boardman and Hall	America	1804–1873	Lv2p98,T fig125g
H 11″ TD 4″ BD 5 7/8″	flagon	Boardman and Hall	America	1804–1873	Lv2p98,T fig123g
H 4 3/4″ TD 3 1/2″ BD 3 3/4″	mug	Burford and Green	England	1748–1780	C 698
TD 6 1/2″	plate	Boardman and Hall	America	1804–1873	Lv2p98,T fig125g
TD 8 1/8″	plate	Townsend and Compton	England	1785–1810	C 4800
TD 8 1/8″	plate	Townsend and Compton	England	1785–1810	C 4800
TD 6 1/2″	plate	Johann Christoph Heyne	America	1752–1781	L 533

EAST PETERSBURG MENNONITE CHURCH, EAST PETERSBURG

DIMENSIONS	FORM	MAKER	ORIGIN	WORKING	MARK
H 3 1/4″ TD 2 3/4″ BD 3″	mug	Boardman and Hart	America	1828–1853	L 437, 438

EPHRATA CLOISTER, GERMAN SEVENTH DAY BAPTISTS,EPHRATA

DIMENSIONS	FORM	MAKER	ORIGIN	WORKING	MARK
TD 13 1/8″	dish	Townsend and Compton	England	1785–1810	C 4800
H 7 3/4″ TD 3 3/4″ BD 4 5/8″	tankard	William Will	America	1764–1798	L 541

DIMENSIONS	FORM	MAKER	ORIGIN	WORKING	MARK

Lancaster County PA

GOOD MENNONITE CHURCH, BAINBRIDGE

DIMENSIONS	FORM	MAKER	ORIGIN	WORKING	MARK
H 4″ TD 3 1/4″ BD 3 7/8″	mug	D S	America	1750–1790	L 888

HOLY TRINITY LUTHERAN CHURCH, LANCASTER

DIMENSIONS	FORM	MAKER	ORIGIN	WORKING	MARK
TD 6″	basin	Blak(e)slee Barn(e)s	America	1812–1817	L 557
H 4 3/8″ TD 3 3/8″ BD 2 7/8″	beaker	unknown England	England	1750–1800	
H 12 1/2″ TD 3 1/2″ BD 6 1/2″	flagon	Heinrich Muller	Germany	1712–1744	H v.6, 1199
H 12 1/2″ TD 3 1/2″ BD 6 1/2″	flagon	Johann Christoph Heyne	America	1752–1781	L 530 ,531,532
H 12 1/2″ TD 3 1/2″ BD 6 1/2″	flagon	Johann Christoph Heyne	America	1752–1781	L 530, 531,532
H 13 1/2″ TD 3 3/8″ BD 4 3/8″	flagon	att. William Will	America	1764–1798	

JERUSALEM UNITED CHURCH OF CHRIST, MANHEIM

DIMENSIONS	FORM	MAKER	ORIGIN	WORKING	MARK
TD 8″	basin	Frederick Bassett	America	1761–1799	L 468
H 10 7/8″ TD 4″ BD 4 1/2″	chalice	att. Johann Christoph Heyne	America	1752–1781	
H 8 3/4″ TD 4″ BD 4 1/2″	chalice	att. Johann Christoph Heyne	American	1752–1781	
H 12 1/8″ TD 3″ BD 5 1/4″	flagon	unmarked Germany	Germany	1700–1750	
H 11 1/2″ TD 3 1/2″ BD 6″	flagon	Johann Christoph Heyne	America	1752–1781	L 530, 532
TD 8 1/2″	plate	John Townsend	England	1748–1801	C 4795
TD 8 1/8″	plate	Townsend and Compton	England	1785–1810	C 4800
H 7 1/4″ TD 4 1/4″ BD 5″	tankard	Philip Matthew(s)	England	1736–1755	C 3135

LANDSIVILLE MENNONITE CHURCH, LANDISVILLE

DIMENSIONS	FORM	MAKER	ORIGIN	WORKING	MARK
H 4 1/4″ TD 3 1/8″ BD 3 3/4″	mug	att. Palethorps	America	1817–1840	

DIMENSIONS	FORM	MAKER	ORIGIN	WORKING	MARK

Lancaster County PA

LITITZ MORAVIAN CHURCH, LITITZ

DIMENSIONS	FORM	MAKER	ORIGIN	WORKING	MARK
H 11 1/8″ TD 4 3/8″ BD 4 1/2″	chalice	att. Johann Christoph Heyne	America	1752–1781	

MAYTOWN UNITED CHURCH OF CHRIST, MAYTOWN

DIMENSIONS	FORM	MAKER	ORIGIN	WORKING	MARK
H 11 1/2″ TD 3 1/2″ BD 6″	flagon	Johann Christoph Heyne	America	1752–1781	L 530, 532

MELLINGER MENNONITE CHURCH, LANCASTER

DIMENSIONS	FORM	MAKER	ORIGIN	WORKING	MARK
H 4 3/4″ TD 3 1/2″ BD 4 3/8″	mug	Richard Pawson	England	1753	C 3562

MUDDY CREEK LUTHERAN & PEACE UCC, DENVER

DIMENSIONS	FORM	MAKER	ORIGIN	WORKING	MARK
TD 10 7/8″	basin	Townsend and Compton	England	1785–1810	C 4800
H 11 3/4″ TD 4 1/8″ BD 4 1/2″	chalice	Johann Christoph Heyne	America	1752–1781	L 533
H 8 3/8″ TD 4 1/8″ BD 4 12″	chalice	att. Johann Christoph Heyne	America	1752–1781	
TD 9 1/4″	plate	Richard King	England	1745–1798	C 2750
TD 9 1/4″	plate	Thomas Danforth III	America	1777–1813	T fig. 58,59
TD 9 1/4″	plate	Thomas Danforth III	America	1777–1813	T fig. 58,59
H 7 7/8″ TD 4 5/8″ BD 5 5/8″	tankard	Richard King	England	1745–1798	C 2750

NEW DANVILLE MENNONITE CHURCH, NEW DANVILLE

DIMENSIONS	FORM	MAKER	ORIGIN	WORKING	MARK
H 5 3/8″ TD 3 1/4″ BD 3 1/8″	beaker	Robert Iles	England	1695–1735	C 2522

RISSER'S MENNONITE CHURCH, MT. JOY

DIMENSIONS	FORM	MAKER	ORIGIN	WORKING	MARK
H 4 1/2″ TD 3 5/8″ BD 3 3/4″	mug	Philip Matthew(s)	England	1736–1755	C 3135

ST. JOHN'S LUTHERAN CHURCH, MAYTOWN

DIMENSIONS	FORM	MAKER	ORIGIN	WORKING	MARK
TD 9 3/8″	basin	Burgum and Catcott	England	1765–1779	C 709
H 8 3/4″ TD 4 1/8″ BD 4 1/2″	chalice	att. Johann Christoph Heyne	America	1752–1781	
H 7 1/8″ TD 4 1/8″ BD 4 1/4″	tankard	John Townsend	England	1748–1801	C 4795

DIMENSIONS	FORM	MAKER	ORIGIN	WORKING	MARK
Lancaster County PA					
ST. MICHAEL'S LUTHERAN CHURCH, STRASBURG					
TD 8″	basin	Townsend and Compton	England	1785–1810	C 4800
H 8″ TD 3 1/2″ BD 4 1/4″	chalice	att. William Will	America	1764–1798	
H 7 1/8″ TD 4 1/4″ BD 4 1/8″	ciborium	att. William Will	America	1764–1798	
H 13 5/8″ TD 3 3/8″ BD 4 1/4″	flagon	att. William Will	America	1764–1798	
H 10 3/4″ TD 3 3/8″ BD 4 1/4″	pitcher	att. William Will	America	1764–1798	
TD 6 3/8″	plate	Johann Christoph Heyne	America	1752–1781	L 532, 533
ST. STEPHEN'S UNITED CHURCH OF CHRIST, NEW HOLLAND					
H 8 1/2″ TD 4 1/8″ BD 4 1/2″	chalice	att. Johann Christoph Heyne	America	1752–1781	
SALEM (HELLER'S) UNITED CHURCH OF CHRIST, LEOLA					
H 3 1/8″ TD 2 3/4″ BD 2 1/8″	beaker	unmarked probably America	America	1780–1825	
H 10 1/4″ TD 5 7/8″ BD 5 1/2″	pitcher	Boardman	America	1804–1873	L 435
SWAMP UNITED CHURCH OF CHRIST, REINHOLDS					
TD 10 1/4″	basin	John Townsend	England	1748–1801	C 4795
H 7 3/8″ TD 4 3/8″ BD 4 1/2″	chalice	unmarked England or Continenta	England or	1750–1775	
TD 8 5/8″	plate	Love	America	1750–1825	L 868, 869
TD 8 5/8″	plate	Love	America	1750–1825	L 868, 869
TD 8 5/8″	plate	Love	America	1750–1825	L 868, 869
H 7 1/2″ TD 4 1/8″ BD 4 1/4″	tankard	Ash and Hutton	England	1741–1768	
TRINITY LUTHERAN CHURCH, NEW HOLLAND					
TD 10 1/4″	basin	Townsend and Compton	England	1785–1810	C 4800
H 7 7/8″ TD 3 1/8″ BD 4 1/8″	chalice	unmarked	unknown	1750–1790	

DIMENSIONS	FORM	MAKER	ORIGIN	WORKING	MARK

Lancaster County PA

TRINITY LUTHERAN CHURCH, NEW HOLLAND

DIMENSIONS	FORM	MAKER	ORIGIN	WORKING	MARK
H 11 3/4″ TD 3 1/4″ BD 5 3/8″	flagon	unmarked Germany	Germany	1700–1750	
H 11 3/4″ TD 3 1/4″ BD 5 5/8″	flagon	unmarked Germany	Germany	1700–1750	
TD 6 3/8″	plate	Johann Christoph Heyne	America	1752–1781	L 533
TD 8 1/2″	plate	Simon Edgell	America	1713–1742	L 526
TD 8″	plate	Townsend and Compton	England	1785–1810	C 4800
H 7 1/4″ TD 4 3/8″ BD 5″	tankard	William Eddon	England	1689–1745	C 1503

ZION LUTHERAN CHURCH, MANHEIM

DIMENSIONS	FORM	MAKER	ORIGIN	WORKING	MARK
H 10 1/4″ TD 4″ BD 4 1/2″	chalice	att. Johann Christoph Heyne	America	1752–1781	
H 11 3/8″ TD 3 1/2″ BD 6″	flagon	Johann Christoph Heyne	America	1752–1781	L 530, 532

Lebanon County PA

BINDNAGLE LUTHERAN CHURCH, PALMYRA

DIMENSIONS	FORM	MAKER	ORIGIN	WORKING	MARK
TD 11 3/4″	basin	John Langford	England	1719–1757	C 2823
H 8 7/8″ TD 4 1/8″ TD 4 1/2″	chalice	att. Johann Christoph Heyne	America	1752–1781	
H 11 3/4″ TD 3 1/2″ BD 5 7/8″	flagon	Johann Christoph Heyne	America	1752–1781	L 530, 532
H 11 3/4″ TD 3 1/2″ BD 5 7/8″	flagon	Johann Christoph Heyne	America	1752–1781	L 530, 532
H 8 7/8″ TD 3 1/4″ BD 4 5/8″	flagon	Johann Michael Dor	Germany	1725–1756	H v.5 1186
TD 7 7/8″	plate	Blak(e)slee Barn(e)s	America	1812–1817	L 551, 553
TD 7 7/8″	plate	Blak(e)slee Barn(e)s	America	1812–1817	L 551, 553
TD 7 7/8″	plate	Francis Piggott	England	1738–1773	C 3682

DIMENSIONS	FORM	MAKER	ORIGIN	WORKING	MARK

Lebanon County PA

GINGRICH'S MENNONITE CHURCH, LEBANON

DIMENSIONS	FORM	MAKER	ORIGIN	WORKING	MARK
H 4 1/4″ TD 3 1/2″ BD 4″	mug	Townsend and Compton	England	1785–1810	C 4800

GRUBBEN UNION CHURCH LUTHERAN & UCC, LEBANON

DIMENSIONS	FORM	MAKER	ORIGIN	WORKING	MARK
TD 14 7/8″	dish	Townsend and Compton	England	1785–1810	C 4800
H 6 1/4″ TD 3 1/4″ BD 3″	measure	unknown England	England	1750–1800	

HILL LUTHERAN CHURCH, CLEONA

DIMENSIONS	FORM	MAKER	ORIGIN	WORKING	MARK
TD 12″	basin	Samuel Ellis	England	1721–1764	C 1547
H 11 3/4″ TD 4 3/4″ BD 3 7/8″	chalice	unmarked England or Scotland	Scotland or	1750–1800	
H 8 1/8″ TD 3″ BD 4 1/4″	chalice	att. William Will	America	1764–1798	
H 7 1/4″ TD 3 1/2″ BD 4 5/8″	chalice	unmarked	Continental	1744	
H 11″ TD 4 1/8″ BD 4 1/2″	chalice	Johann Christoph Heyne	America	1752–1781	L 523
H 5 1/2″ TD 4 1/4″ BD 3 1/4″	ciborium	Johann Christoph Heyne	America	1752–1781	L 533
H 13 3/4″ TD 3 3/8″ BD 4 3/8″	flagon	att. William Will	America	1764–1798	
H 11 1/4″ TD 3 1/2″ BD 5 7/8″	flagon	Johann Christoph Heyne	America	1752–1781	L 530, 532
H 11 1/4″ TD 3 1/2″ BD 5 7/8″	flagon	Johann Christoph Heyne	America	1752–1781	L 530, 532
TD 8 1/2″	plate	A. Carter	England	1750	C 825
TD 8″	plate	Townsend and Compton	England	1785–1810	C 4800
TD 7 5/8″	plate	Townsend and Compton	England	1785–1810	C 4800
TD 7 3/4″	plate	Love	America	1750–1825	L 868, 869
TD 6 1/2″	plate	Johann Christoph Heyne	America	1752–1781	L 533
H 7 1/4″ TD 4 3/8″ BD 5″	tankard	William Eddon	England	1689–1745	C 1503

DIMENSIONS	FORM	MAKER	ORIGIN	WORKING	MARK

Lebanon County PA

HILL LUTHERAN CHURCH, CLEONA

DIMENSIONS	FORM	MAKER	ORIGIN	WORKING	MARK
H 7 1/8″ TD 4 1/8″ BD 5″	tankard	William Charesley	England	1729–1770	C 888

MILLCREEK LUTHERAN CHURCH, NEWMANSTOWN

DIMENSIONS	FORM	MAKER	ORIGIN	WORKING	MARK
TD 6″	plate	Love	America	1750–1825	L 868, 869
TD 7 5/8″	plate	Thomas, Townsend & Henry Compton	England	1810–1855	C 1063
H 7 1/2″ TD 4″ BD 4 1/4″	tankard	Ash and Hutton	England	1741–1768	C 118

ST. JACOB'S (KIMMERLING'S) UNITED CHURCH OF CHRIST, LEBANON

DIMENSIONS	FORM	MAKER	ORIGIN	WORKING	MARK
H 8 3/8″ TD 4 1/8″ BD 4 1/2″	chalice	att. Johann Christoph Heyne	America	1752–1781	
TD 8 3/8″	plate	Love	America	1750–1825	L 868, 869
TD 8 7/8″	plate	Love	America	1750–1825	L 868, 869
TD 8 5/8″	plate	Love	America	1750–1825	L 868, 869
TD 8 5/8″	plate	Love	America	1750–1825	L 868, 869

ST. LUKE'S LUTHERAN CHURCH, SCHAEFFERSTOWN

DIMENSIONS	FORM	MAKER	ORIGIN	WORKING	MARK
H 9″ TD 4″ BD 4 1/2″	chalice	Johann Christoph Heyne	America	1752–1781	L 533, 532
H 14 1/2″ TD 4″ BD 5 1/2″	flagon	Daniel Heidenreich	Germany	1764	H v.5 No 709
H 14 1/2″ TD 4″ BD 5 1/2″	flagon	Daniel Heidenreich	Germany	1764	H v.5 No.709
H 7 1/2″ TD 4 1/8″ BD 4 7/8″	tankard	John Townsend	England	1748–1801	C 4795

ST. PAUL'S UNITED CHURCH OF CHRIST, SCHAEFFERSTOWN

DIMENSIONS	FORM	MAKER	ORIGIN	WORKING	MARK
H 8 3/4″ TD 4″ BD 4 1/2″	chalice	Johann Christoph Heyne	America	1752–1781	L 533

ST. PAUL'S UNITED CHURCH OF CHRIST, NEWMANSTOWN

DIMENSIONS	FORM	MAKER	ORIGIN	WORKING	MARK
TD 7 5/8″	plate	Townsend and Compton	England	1785–1810	C 4800
TD 7 5/8″	plate	Townsend and Compton	England	1785–1810	C 4800
TD 7 5/8″	plate	Townsend and Compton	England	1785–1810	C 4800

DIMENSIONS	FORM	MAKER	ORIGIN	WORKING	MARK

Lebanon County PA

SALEM (WALMER'S) UNION CHURCH LUTHERAN & UCC, ANNVILLE

DIMENSIONS	FORM	MAKER	ORIGIN	WORKING	MARK
TD 10 3/8″	basin	Robert Waller	England	1782–1786	C 4934
TD 5 3/4″	basin	unmarked probably America	America	1780–1825	
TD 5 3/4″	basin	unmarked probably America	America	1780–1825	
TD 5 3/4″	basin	unmarked probably America	America	1780–1825	
H 8″ TD 3 1/8″ BD 3 3/4″	chalice	att. William Will	America	1764–1798	
TD 7 7/8″	plate	Ashbil Griswold	America	1807–1830's	L 418
H 7 1/4″ TD 4 1/4″ BD 4 3/4″	tankard	unknown England	England	1750–1800	P 5836b

SALEM LUTHERAN CHURCH, LEBANON

DIMENSIONS	FORM	MAKER	ORIGIN	WORKING	MARK
TD 8″	basin	Thomas Danforth III	America	1777–1813	L 373
H 3 5/8″ TD 3″ BD 2 1/8″	beaker	att. Boardmans	America	1804–1873	
H 3 5/8″ TD 3″ BD 2 1/8″	beaker	att. Boardmans	America	1804–1873	
H 8 7/8″ TD 4″ BD 4 5/8″	chalice	att. Johann Christoph Heyne	America	1752–1781	
H 13 3/4″ TD 3″ BD 5 1/2″	flagon	Hendrick Kock	Netherlands	1752–1787	D 519
H 13 1/2″ TD 3″ BD 5 1/2″	flagon	Hendrick Kock	Netherlands	1752–1787	D 519
H 11″ TD 3 3/4″ BD 5″	flagon	att. Boardmans	America	1804–1873	
H 11″ TD 3 3/4″ BD 5″	flagon	att. Boardmans	America	1804–1873	
TD 6 3/8″	plate	Johann Christoph Heyne	America	1752–1781	L 532, 533
H 7 3/8″ TD 4 1/8″ BD 4 5/8″	tankard	John Townsend	England	1748–1801	L 4795

SALEM UNITED CHURCH OF CHRIST, CAMPBELLTOWN

DIMENSIONS	FORM	MAKER	ORIGIN	WORKING	MARK
TD 9 1/8″	basin	Townsend and Compton	England	1785–1810	C 4800
H 8″ TD 3 1/2″ BD 4 1/4″	chalice	att. William Will	America	1764–1798	

DIMENSIONS	FORM	MAKER	ORIGIN	WORKING	MARK

Lebanon County PA

SALEM UNITED CHURCH OF CHRIST, CAMPBELLTOWN

DIMENSIONS	FORM	MAKER	ORIGIN	WORKING	MARK
H 8 1/8″ TD 3 3/8″ BD 3 1/4″	chalice	unmarked probably Philadelphia	America	1800–1810	
H 6″ TD 4 1/8″ BD 4 7/8″	mug	Thomas and Townsend Compton	England	1810–1815	C 1064
H 6 3/8″ TD 4 1/8″ BD 4 1/2″	mug	John Townsend	England	1748–1801	C 4795

TABOR UNITED CHURCH OF CHRIST, LEBANON

DIMENSIONS	FORM	MAKER	ORIGIN	WORKING	MARK
H 8 1/2″ TD 4 1/8″ BD 4 1/2″	chalice	att. Johann Christoph Heyne	America	1752–1781	
H 6 3/4″ TD 4″ BD 4 7/8″	tankard	unknown England	England	1750–1800	C 5952

TRINITY LUTHERAN CHURCH, COLEBROOK

DIMENSIONS	FORM	MAKER	ORIGIN	WORKING	MARK
TD 7 7/8″	basin	Burford and Green	England	1748–1780	C 698
H 8 7/8″ TD 4 1/8″ BD 4 1/2″	chalice	att. Johann Christoph Heyne	America	1752–1781	
H 11 1/4″ TD 3 1/2″ BD 5 7/8″	flagon	Johann Christoph Heyne	America	1752–1781	L 530, 532
H 7 1/2″ TD 3 3/4″ BD 4 3/4″	tankard	William Will	America	1764–1798	L 539

ZION LUTHERAN CHURCH, JONESTOWN

DIMENSIONS	FORM	MAKER	ORIGIN	WORKING	MARK
TD 9 1/4″	basin	Townsend and Reynolds	England	1767–1776	C 4797
TD 5 3/4″	basin	unmarked probably America	America	1780–1825	
H 7″ TD 3 1/2″ BD 4 3/4″	chalice	unmarked	Germany	1744	
H 12 3/4″ TD 3 1/2″ BD 5 1/2″	flagon	Johann Martin Kaller	Germany	1752–1784	H v.5 No. 1194
H 10 1/4″ TD 3 1/8″ BD 4 3/8″	flagon	Johann Martin Kaller	Germany	1752–1784	H v.5 No. 1194
TD 8″	plate	Townsend and Compton	England	1785–1810	C 4800
H 7 3/8″ TD 4″ BD 5″	tankard	unknown England	England	1750–1800	

DIMENSIONS	FORM	MAKER	ORIGIN	WORKING	MARK

Lebanon County PA

A LUTHERAN CHURCH

DIMENSIONS	FORM	MAKER	ORIGIN	WORKING	MARK
H 7″ TD 3 1/2″ BD 3 3/8″	chalice	att. Palethorps	America	1817–1840	
TD 6 3/8″	plate	Johann Christoph Heyne	America	1752–1781	L 533
TD 8 5/8″	plate	Love	America	1750–1825	L 868, 869
TD 8″	plate	Townsend and Compton	England	1785–1810	C 4800
TD 8″	plate	Townsend and Compton	England	1785–1810	C 4800
TD 8″	plate	Townsend and Compton	England	1785–1810	C 4800
TD 8″	plate	Townsend and Compton	England	1785–1810	C 4800
H 7 1/4″ TD 4″ BD 4 7/8″	tankard	Townsend and Compton	England	1785–1810	C 4800

Lehigh County PA

BEN SALEM UNITED CHURCH OF CHRIST, ANDREAS

DIMENSIONS	FORM	MAKER	ORIGIN	WORKING	MARK
TD 8 1/2″	plate	Townsend and Compton	England	1785–1810	C 4800
TD 8 1/2″	plate	Townsend and Compton	England	1785–1810	C 4800
TD 8 1/2″	plate	Townsend and Compton	England	1785–1810	C 4800

CHRIST'S CHURCH (LOWHILL) UNITED CHURCH OF CHRIST, NEW TRIPOLI

DIMENSIONS	FORM	MAKER	ORIGIN	WORKING	MARK
H 7 1/2″ TD 4″ BD 4″	chalice	unmarked	Pa. or Continental	1750–1800	
H 12 3/4″ TD 4 3/8″ BD 4 5/8″	flagon	att. William Will	America	1764–1798	
H 1 1/8″ TD 9 3/4″	footed plate	att. William Will	America	1764–1798	
H 4 5/8″ TD 3 1/2″ BD 3 5/8″	mug	Johann Philip Alberti	America	1754–1780	
TD 8 1/2″	plate	Stynt Duncumb	England	1730–1767	C 1466
TD 7 5/8″	plate	Townsend and Compton	England	1785–1810	C 4800
TD 8″	plate	Townsend and Compton	England	1785–1810	C 4800

EGYPT UNITED CHURCH OF CHRIST, WHITEHALL

DIMENSIONS	FORM	MAKER	ORIGIN	WORKING	MARK
TD 10 1/2″	basin	Thomas Swanson	England	1753–1783	C 4801
H 8 1/8″ TD 3 1/4″ BD 4 1/4″	chalice	att. William Will	America	1764–1798	

DIMENSIONS	FORM	MAKER	ORIGIN	WORKING	MARK

Lehigh County PA

EGYPT UNITED CHURCH OF CHRIST, WHITEHALL

DIMENSIONS	FORM	MAKER	ORIGIN	WORKING	MARK
H 10 3/4″ TD 3 1/4″ BD 4 1/4″	pitcher	att. William Will	America	1764–1798	
TD 12 1/8″	plate	Townsend and Compton	England	1785–1810	C 4800
TD 7 5/8″	plate	Townsend and Compton	England	1785–1810	C 4800
TD 8″	plate	Townsend and Compton	England	1785–1810	C 4800
TD 8″	plate	Townsend and Compton	England	1785–1810	c 4800
H 7 1/4″ TD 4 3/8″ BD 5″	tankard	unknown England	England	1750–1800	
H 8″ TD 4 1/4″ BD 4 3/4″	tankard	Richard King	England	1745–1798	C 2750

EMMAUS MORAVIAN CHURCH, EMMAUS

DIMENSIONS	FORM	MAKER	ORIGIN	WORKING	MARK
H 7″ TD 4 3/8″ BD 5″	tankard	William Kirby	America	1760–1793	L 499

FRIEDENS LUTHERAN CHURCH, CENTER VALLEY

DIMENSIONS	FORM	MAKER	ORIGIN	WORKING	MARK
H 8 3/4″ TD 3 3/8″ BD 3 1/4″	chalice	unmarked probably Philadelphia	America	1800–1810	
TD 8 1/4″	plate	Townsend and Compton	England	1785–1810	C 4800
H 7 3/4″ TD 4″ BD 4 1/2″	tankard	Philadelphia	America	1764–1798	

HEIDELBERG UNION LUTHERAN & UCC, SLATINGTON

DIMENSIONS	FORM	MAKER	ORIGIN	WORKING	MARK
TD 10 3/4″	basin	Samuel Jefferys	England	1734–1739	C 2607
H 7 5/8″ TD 4″ BD 3 7/8″	chalice	unmarked	Pa. or Continental	1750–1800	
H 7 3/8″ TD 3 1/4″ BD 4 1/2″	chalice	att. William Will	America	1764–1798	
H 12 7/8″ TD 4 1/2″ BD 4 5/8″	flagon	att. William Will	America	1764–1798	
H 12″ TD 3 3/8″ BD 4″	flagon	William Will	America	1764–1798	L 538, 541
H 5/8″ TD 9″	footed plate	att. William Will	America	1764–1798	

DIMENSIONS	FORM	MAKER	ORIGIN	WORKING	MARK

Lehigh County PA

HEIDELBERG UNION LUTHERAN & UCC, SLATINGTON

DIMENSIONS	FORM	MAKER	ORIGIN	WORKING	MARK
TD 6¼″	plate	Philadelphia	America	1764–1798	
TD 8⅜″	plate	Townsend and Compton	England	1785–1810	C 4800
TD 8⅛″	plate	Townsend and Compton	England	1785–1810	C 4800
H 6¾″ TD 4″ BD 4⅞″	tankard	John Bassett	America	1720–1761	L 458

JACOB'S UNITED CHURCH OF CHRIST, JACKSONVILLE

DIMENSIONS	FORM	MAKER	ORIGIN	WORKING	MARK
TD 9¼″	basin	John Townsend	England	1748–1801	C 4795
H 7″ TD 4″ BD 3⅞″	chalice	unmarked	Pa. or Continental	1750–1800	
H 8½″ TD 3⅝″ BD 3½″	chalice	unmarked probably Philadelphia	America	1800–1810	
TD 8¾″	plate	John Carr	England	1750	C 813
TD 7⅝″	plate	Townsend and Compton	England	1785–1810	C 4800
TD 8⅜″	plate	William Bartlett	England	c.1740–1770	C 279
H 6⅜″ TD 3½″ BD 3⅝″	tankard	John Townsend	England	1748–1801	C 4795

JORDAN LUTHERAN CHURCH, OREFIELD

DIMENSIONS	FORM	MAKER	ORIGIN	WORKING	MARK
H 7⅛″ TD 3⅝″ BD 3¾″	chalice	att. Boardmans	America	1804–1873	
TD 9¾″	plate	Francis Piggott	England	1738–1773	C 3682

NEFFS UNION CHURCH LUTHERAN & UCC, NEFFS

DIMENSIONS	FORM	MAKER	ORIGIN	WORKING	MARK
TD 10⅜″	basin	Thomas Scattergood	England	1736–1775	C 4139
H 7⅝″ TD 4″ BD 4¼″	chalice	unmarked	Pa. or Continental	1750–1800	
H 4⅝″ TD 3⅓″ BD 4″	mug	John Will	America	1752–1774	L 481
TD 8″	plate	Townsend and Compton	England	1785–1810	C 4800
TD 8″	plate	Townsend and Compton	England	1785–1810	C 4800
TD 8″	plate	Townsend and Compton	England	1785–1810	C 4800
TD 8″	plate	Townsend and Compton	England	1785–1810	C 4800
TD 8″	plate	Townsend and Compton	England	1785–1810	C 4800

Lehigh County PA

A UNION CHURCH

DIMENSIONS	FORM	MAKER	ORIGIN	WORKING	MARK
TD 11 3/4″	basin	unmarked probably America	America	1780–1825	
H 7 5/8″ TD 3 1/4″	chalice	att. Love	America	1750–1825	
H 12 3/4″ TD 3 7/8″ BD 4 1/2″	flagon	William Will	America	1764–1798	L 539
T 4 1/8″	plate	unmarked probably America	America	1780–1825	
TD 4 1/8″	plate	unmarked probably America	America	1780–1825	
TD 6″	plate	unmarked probably America	America	1780–1825	
TD 7 5/8″	plate	Thomas, Townsend & Henry Compton	England	1810–1855	C 1063
TD 8 3/8″	plate	Townsend and Compton	England	1785–1810	C 4800
TD 8 7/8″	plate	Richard King	England	1745–1798	C 2750, 1547
TD 8 3/8″	plate	Townsend and Compton	England	1785–1810	C 4800
TD 8 3/8″	plate	Thomas and Townsend Compton	England	1810–1815	C 1064
H 7 7/8″ TD 4″ BD 4 3/8″	tankard	Cornelius Bradford	America	1753–1785	L 496

ST. PAUL'S LUTHERAN CHURCH, ALLENTOWN

DIMENSIONS	FORM	MAKER	ORIGIN	WORKING	MARK
H 14″ TD 3 3/8″ BD 4 1/4″	flagon	att. William Will	America	1764–1798	
TD 8 5/8″	plate	Townsend and Compton	England	1785–1810	C 4800
TD 8 5/8″	plate	Townsend and Compton	England	1785–1810	C 4800
TD 8 5/8″	plate	Townsend and Compton	England	1785–1810	C 4800
TD 8 5/8″	plate	Townsend and Compton	England	1785–1810	C 4800

ST. PAUL'S UNITED CHURCH OF CHRIST, TREXLERTOWN

DIMENSIONS	FORM	MAKER	ORIGIN	WORKING	MARK
H 9 1/2″ TD 3 7/8″ BD 4 1/4″	chalice	unmarked	Pa. or Continental	1750–1800	

WEISENBERG LUTHERAN CHURCH, NEW TRIPOLI

DIMENSIONS	FORM	MAKER	ORIGIN	WORKING	MARK
TD 9 1/8″	plate	John Townsend	England	1748–1801	C 4795
H 5 6/8″ TD 3 1/8″ BD 4 1/8″	tankard	Philip Matthew(s)	England	1736–1755	C 3135

ZION LUTHERAN CHURCH, OLD ZIONSVILLE

DIMENSIONS	FORM	MAKER	ORIGIN	WORKING	MARK
TD 9 1/8″	basin	John Watts	England	1725–1765	C 4991

DIMENSIONS	FORM	MAKER	ORIGIN	WORKING	MARK

Lehigh County PA

ZIONS UNITED CHURCH OF CHRIST, ALLENTOWN

DIMENSIONS	FORM	MAKER	ORIGIN	WORKING	MARK
H 7¾″ TD 3¾″ BD 4¼″	chalice	att. John Will	America	1752–1774	
TD 7⅝″	plate	Townsend and Compton	England	1785–1810	C 4800
TD 7⅝″	plate	Townsend and Compton	England	1785–1810	C 4800

Monroe County PA

CHRIST UNITED LUTHERAN CHURCH, STROUDSBURG

DIMENSIONS	FORM	MAKER	ORIGIN	WORKING	MARK
H 9⅞″ TD 4⅜″ BD 5⅞″	flagon	Roswell Gleason	America	1821–1871	L. v.II, p.102
TD 8″	plate	Townsend and Compton	England	1785–1810	C 4800
TD 9⅛″	plate	Roswell Gleason	America	1821–1871	L v.II, p. 102
TD 9¼″	plate	Roswell Gleason	America	1821–1871	L. v.II, p.102

ZION LUTHERAN CHURCH, MID. SMITHFIELD

DIMENSIONS	FORM	MAKER	ORIGIN	WORKING	MARK
TD 10¼″	basin	Bush and Perkins	England	1771–1773	C 740
H 8″ TD 4″ BD 4⅛″	chalice	att. William Will	America	1764–1798	
TD 8″	plate	Blak(e)slee Barn(e)s	America	1812–1817	L 551
H 7½″ TD 4″ BD 4¾″	tankard	Love	America	1750–1825	L 869

Montgomery County PA

BOEHMS REFORMED UNITED CHURCH OF CHRIST, BLUE BELL

DIMENSIONS	FORM	MAKER	ORIGIN	WORKING	MARK
H 6½″ TD 3½″ BD 5″	pitcher	att. Johann Philip Alberti	America	1754–1780	
H 9″ TD 4⅝″ BD 4½″	pitcher covered	att. Boardmans	America	1804–1873	
TD 8″	plate	Richard King	England	1745–1798	C 2570

EMMANUEL LUTHERAN CHURCH, POTTSTOWN

DIMENSIONS	FORM	MAKER	ORIGIN	WORKING	MARK
TD 11¾″	basin	Thomas Swanson	England	1753–1783	C 4801
H 9″ TD 4⅛″ BD 4½″	chalice	Philadelphia	America	1764–1798	

DIMENSIONS	FORM	MAKER	ORIGIN	WORKING	MARK

Montgomery County PA

EMMANUEL LUTHERAN CHURCH, POTTSTOWN

DIMENSIONS	FORM	MAKER	ORIGIN	WORKING	MARK
H 9 1/8″ TD 3 7/8″ BD 4 1/4″	chalice	unmarked	America or Continental	1750–1800	
H 13″ TD 3 3/4″ BD 5″	flagon	Johann Philip Alberti	America	1754–1780	
H 6 1/8″ TD 4″ BD 4 7/8″	mug	Townsend and Compton	England	1785–1810	C 4800
TD 9 1/8″	plate	Townsend and Compton	England	1785–1810	C 4800
TD 9 1/8″	plate	Townsend and Compton	England	1785–1810	C 4800
TD 9 1/8″	plate	Townsend and Compton	England	1785–1810	C 4800
TD 7 7/8″	plate	Blak(e)slee Barn(e)s	America	1812–1817	L 556
TD 7 7/8″	plate	Blak(e)slee Barn(e)s	America	1812–1817	L 556

LOWER SKIPPACK MENNONITE CHURCH, SKIPPACK

DIMENSIONS	FORM	MAKER	ORIGIN	WORKING	MARK
TD 11 3/4″	basin	Thomas Swanson	England	1753–1783	C 4593
H 5 1/4″ TD 3 3/8″ BD 3 1/8″	beaker	Robert Iles	England	1695–1735	C 2522

NEW GOSHENHOPPEN REFORMED UCC, EAST GREENVILLE

DIMENSIONS	FORM	MAKER	ORIGIN	WORKING	MARK
TD 10 1/2″	basin	Samuel Ellis	England	1721–1764	C 1547
H 10 1/2″ TD 3 5/8″ BD 5 1/8″	flagon	Johann Jacob Buhler	Germany	1702–1733	
TD 8 5/8″	plate	Townsend and Compton	England	1785–1810	C 4800
TD 8 5/8″	plate	Townsend and Compton	England	1785–1810	C 4800
TD 8 5/8″	plate	Townsend and Compton	England	1785–1810	C 4800
TD 8 5/8″	plate	Townsend and Compton	England	1785–1810	c 4800
H 7 1/4″ TD 4 1/4″ BD 5″	tankard	unknown England	England	1750–1800	

NEW HANOVER LUTHERAN CHURCH, GILBERTSVILLE

DIMENSIONS	FORM	MAKER	ORIGIN	WORKING	MARK
H 7 1/2″ TD 4 1/8″ BD 4 1/4″	chalice	unmarked	Continental	1744	
TD 14 5/8″	dish	Thomas Scattergood	England	1736–1775	C 4139
H 15″ TD 4 5/8″ BD 5 3/4″	flagon	Gabriel Syren	Germany	1727–1753	
H 7 1/4″ TD 4 1/4″ BD 4 7/8″	tankard	unknown England	England	1750–1800	

DIMENSIONS	FORM	MAKER	ORIGIN	WORKING	MARK
Montgomery County PA					
PLAINS MENNONITE CHURCH, HATFIELD					
H 4″ TD 3 3/8″ BD 2 7/8″	beaker	Robert Palethorp Jr.	America	1817–1821	M p.225
ST. LUKE'S UNITED CHURCH OF CHRIST, TRAPPE					
H 6 1/8″ TD 4 1/8″ BD 3″	chalice	att. Roswell Gleason	America	1821–1871	
TD 8 3/8″	plate	Townsend and Compton	England	1785–1810	C 4800
ST. PAUL'S LUTHERAN CHURCH, ARDMORE					
H 5 1/8″ TD 8 3/8″ BD 5 1/8″	baptismal basin	att. Leonard, Reed and Barton	America	1835–1840	
H 7 1/2″ TD 3 3/4″ BD 3 3/4″	chalice	James Dixon and Sons	England	1842–1851	ST p.224
H 11 1/2″ TD 2 7/8″ BD 5″	flagon	unmarked Germany	Germany	1700–1750	
H 6 5/8″ TD 4 3/4″ BD 4 3/8″	pitcher	John H. Palethorp	America	1820–1845	L.v.II p.108
ST. PAUL'S LUTHERAN CHURCH, RED HILL					
H 2 1/4″ TD 6 1/4″ BD 4 1/2″	baptismal basin	att. Hiram Yale and Company	America	1824–1835	
TD 11 1/8″	dish	Hiram Yale and Company	America	1824–1835	L 445
H 14 1/4″ TD 5 1/2″ BD 5″	flagon	Hiram Yale and Company	America	1824–1835	L 445
TD 7 7/8″	plate	John Townsend	England	1748–1801	C 4795
ST. PETER'S LUTHERAN CHURCH, NORTH WALES					
H 7 3/4″ TD 3 5/8″ BD 4 1/8″	chalice	att. William Will	America	1764–1798	
H 12 3/4″ TD 3 7/8″ BD 4 3/4″	flagon	William Will	America	1764–1798	L 541
TD 8″	plate	Townsend and Compton	England	1785–1810	C 4800
H 8″ TD 4 1/4″ BD 4 1/2″	tankard	John Townsend	England	1748–1801	C 4795

DIMENSIONS	FORM	MAKER	ORIGIN	WORKING	MARK

Montgomery County PA

SALFORD MENNONITE CHURCH, HARLEYSVILLE

DIMENSIONS	FORM	MAKER	ORIGIN	WORKING	MARK
H 4″ TD 3 1/2″ BD 2 7/8″	beaker	John H. and Robert Palethorp	America	1817–1845	L v.2, p.108

TOWAMENCIN MENNONITE CHURCH, KULPSVILLE

DIMENSIONS	FORM	MAKER	ORIGIN	WORKING	MARK
H 6 1/8″ TD 3 1/2″ BD 2 7/8″	beaker	City mark of Horb A. Neckar	Germany	1730–1760	H 1270, 1271

UPPER SKIPPACK MENNONITE CHURCH, SKIPPACK

DIMENSIONS	FORM	MAKER	ORIGIN	WORKING	MARK
TD 11 3/4″	basin	John Townsend	England	1748–1801	C 4795
H 6 3/4″ TD 3 5/8″ BD 3 5/8″	chalice	Leonard, Reed and Barton	America	1835–1840	L.v.II p. 106

WENTZ'S UNITED CHURCH OF CHRIST, WORCESTER

DIMENSIONS	FORM	MAKER	ORIGIN	WORKING	MARK
H 8″ TD 4″ BD 4 3/8″	chalice	att. John Will	America	1752–1774	
H 1 3/8″ TD 14 1/4″ W 10 1/4″	dish	John Will	America	1752–1774	L 481, 482
H 13 3/8″ TD 4 1/8″ BD 5″	flagon	John Will	America	1752–1774	L 479
H 9 1/8″ TD 3 3/8″ BD 3 3/8″	pitcher	att. John Will	America	1752–1774	
TD 8 3/8″	plate	John Townsend	England	1748–1801	C 4795
TD 8 7/8″	plate	John Townsend	England	1748–1801	C 4795

Northampton County PA

CENTRAL MORAVIAN CHURCH, BETHLEHEM

DIMENSIONS	FORM	MAKER	ORIGIN	WORKING	MARK
H 4 1/2″ TD 8″ BD 5 1/8″	baptismal basin	Boardman and Company	America	1825–1827	L 433
H 8 1/8″ TD 4 1/8″ BD 4 3/8″	chalice	att. Johann Christoph Heyne	America	1752–1781	
H 8 1/4″ TD 4 1/8″ BD 5″	flagon	Boardman and Company	America	1825–1827	L 431

DIMENSIONS	FORM	MAKER	ORIGIN	WORKING	MARK

Northampton County PA

EMANUEL LUTHERAN CHURCH, BATH

DIMENSIONS	FORM	MAKER	ORIGIN	WORKING	MARK
H 8″ TD 4 1/8″ BD 4 1/8″	chalice	att. Smith and Feltman	America	1849–1852	
H 8″ TD 4 1/4″ BD 4 1/8″	chalice	att. Smith and Feltman	America	1849–1852	
TD 10 1/4″	dish	Sheldon and Feltman	America	1847–1848	L. v.2, p. 112
TD 10 1/4″	dish	Sheldon and Feltman	America	1847–1848	L. v.2, p. 112
H 12″ TD 4 3/4″ BD 7″	flagon	Smith and Feltman	America	1849–1852	L v.2. p.113
TD 7 7/8″	plate	Richard Yates	England	1772–1807	C 5344
TD 7 7/8″	plate	Ashbil Griswold	America	1807–1842	L 418

FIRST UNITED CHURCH OF CHRIST, EASTON

DIMENSIONS	FORM	MAKER	ORIGIN	WORKING	MARK
H 9 1/8″ TD 4″ BD 4 1/4″	chalice	unmarked	America or Continental	1750–1800	
H 11″ TD 3 1/8″ BD 4 7/8″	flagon	unmarked Germany	Germany	1700–1750	
H 7 1/2″ TD 4″ BD 4 5/8″	tankard	Ash and Hutton	England	1741–1768	C 118

HOPE LUTHERAN CHURCH, CHERRYVILLE

DIMENSIONS	FORM	MAKER	ORIGIN	WORKING	MARK
H 8″ TD 4″ BD 4 1/4″	chalice	att. John Will	America	1752–1774	
H 4 3/4″ TD 3 1/2″	mug	John Townsend	England	1748–1801	C 4795
TD 7 3/4″	plate	Robert Bush and Company	England	1787–1795	C 739
TD 7 3/4″	plate	Robert Bush and Company	England	1787–1795	C 739

NAZARETH MORAVIAN CHURCH, NAZARETH

DIMENSIONS	FORM	MAKER	ORIGIN	WORKING	MARK
TD 8 7/8″	plate	Love	America	1750–1825	L 868, 869

TRINITY LUTHERAN CHURCH, BETHLEHEM

DIMENSIONS	FORM	MAKER	ORIGIN	WORKING	MARK
H 7 5/8″ TD 4″ BD 4 1/8″	chalice	att. John Will	America	1752–1774	
H 8 3/4″ TD 3 3/4″ BD 3 1/4″	chalice	att. John Will	America	1752–1774	

DIMENSIONS	FORM	MAKER	ORIGIN	WORKING	MARK

Northampton County PA

TRINITY LUTHERAN CHURCH, BETHLEHEM

DIMENSIONS	FORM	MAKER	ORIGIN	WORKING	MARK
H 12″ TD 4″ BD 5″	flagon	Germany, Cologne	Germany	1675–1757	
TD 8 3/8″	plate	Love	America	1750–1825	L 868, 869
TD 8 3/8″	plate	Love	America	1750–1825	L 868, 869
H 7 1/4″ TD 4 1/4″ BD 5″	tankard	William Eddon	England	1689–1745	C 1503

A UNITED CHURCH OF CHRIST

DIMENSIONS	FORM	MAKER	ORIGIN	WORKING	MARK
TD 8″	plate	Benjamin and Joseph Harbeson	America	1793–1807	L 549
TD 8 1/4″	plate	Townsend and Compton	England	1785–1810	C 4800
TD 7 3/4″	plate	Townsend and Compton	England	1785–1810	C 4800
H 6 3/4″ TD 4 1/8″ BD 4 3/4″	tankard	Burgum and Catcott	England	1765–1779	C 708
TD 8″	basin	Burgum and Catcott	England	1765–1779	C 708
H 8 7/8″ TD 3 7/8″ BD 4 1/4″	chalice	unmarked	America or Continental	1750–1800	
H 8 1/8″ TD 3 7/8″ BD 4 1/8″	chalice	Philadelphia	America	1764–1798	

ZION'S (STONE) UNITED CHURCH OF CHRIST, NORTHAMPTON

DIMENSIONS	FORM	MAKER	ORIGIN	WORKING	MARK
TD 7 7/8″	basin	John Will	America	1752–1774	L 481
TD 9″	basin	Henry Joseph	England	1736–1785	C 2686
H 8 1/2″ TD 3 7/8″ BD 4 3/8″	chalice	att. William Will	America	1764–1798	
H 8″ TD 4″	chalice	att. John Will	America	1752–1774	
TD 6 1/4″	plate	William Will	America	1764–1798	L 534
TD 8 5/8″	plate	Love	America	1750–1825	L 868, 869
TD 8 5/8″	plate	Love	America	1750–1825	L 868, 869
TD 8 5/8″	plate	Love	America	1750–1825	L 868, 869
H 8 1/8″ TD 4 1/8″ BD 4 3/8″	tankard	William Will	America	1764–1798	L 535
H 8 1/8″ TD 4 1/8″ BD 4 3/8″	tankard	att. William Will	America	1764–1798	

DIMENSIONS	FORM	MAKER	ORIGIN	WORKING	MARK
Northumberland County PA					
FIRST UNITED CHURCH OF CHRIST, SUNBURY					
H 8 7/8″ TD 4 1/8″ BD 4 1/2″	chalice	att. Johann Christoph Heyne	America	1752–1781	
HIMMEL'S UNION CHURCH LUTHERAN & UCC, REBUCK					
TD 8″	basin	Townsend and Compton	England	1785–1810	C 4800
H 8 7/8″ TD 4 1/8″ BD 4 1/4″	chalice	att. Johann Christoph Heyne	America	1752–1781	
TD 6 3/8″	plate	Johann Christoph Heyne	America	1752–1781	L 533
H 7 1/8″ TD 4 1/8″ BD 4 1/4″	tankard	John Townsend	England	1748–1801	C 4795
Perry County PA					
TRINITY UNITED CHURCH OF CHRIST, NEW BLOOMFIELD					
H 7 3/4″ TD 3 7/8″ BD 4 3/8″	chalice	att. William Will	America	1764–1798	
Philadelphia County PA					
ST. MICHAEL'S LUTHERAN CHURCH, GERMANTOWN					
TD 12 5/8″	dish	Johann Dietrich Finck	Germany	1731	H v.5, p.78
H 13″ TD 3 7/8″ BD 4 3/8″	flagon	att. Love	America	1750–1825	
TD 9 1/8'	plate	John Townsend	England	1748–1801	C 1795
TD 4 3/8″	plate	unmarked	America, England, or Continental	1750–1850	
Schuylkill County PA					
CHRIST UNITED CHURCH OF CHRIST, NEW RINGGOLD					
H 4 7/8″ TD 7 5/8″ BD 5 1/4″	baptismal basin	att. Parks Boyd	America	1795–1819	
TD 8 7/8″	plate	Love	America	1750–1825	L 868, 869
TD 8 7/8″	plate	Love	America	1750–1825	L 868, 869
TD 8 7/8″	plate	Love	America	1750–1825	L 868, 869

DIMENSIONS	FORM	MAKER	ORIGIN	WORKING	MARK

Schuylkill County PA

FRIEDENS LUTHERAN CHURCH, NEW RINGGOLD

DIMENSIONS	FORM	MAKER	ORIGIN	WORKING	MARK
TD 10 1/8″	basin	Bouchier and Richard Cleeve	England	1754	C 962
H 7 1/2″ TD 4″ BD 4 1/8″	chalice	unmarked	America or Continental	1750–1800	
TD 9 1/4″	plate	unknown England	England	1750–1800	

FRIEDENS UNITED CHURCH OF CHRIST, NEW RINGOLD

DIMENSIONS	FORM	MAKER	ORIGIN	WORKING	MARK
TD 8″	basin	unknown England	England	1750–1800	
H 12″ TD 3 1/2″ BD 4 3/4″	flagon	Elias Beyerbach	Germany	1755–1783	
TD 8 3/8″	plate	William Will	America	1764–1798	L 537, 540
H 6″ TD 3 3/8″ BD 4″	tankard	Ingram and Hunt	England	1788–1807	P 2540A

ST. JOHN'S LUTHERAN CHURCH, FRIEDENSBURG

DIMENSIONS	FORM	MAKER	ORIGIN	WORKING	MARK
H 7 3/4″ TD 3 1/2″ BD 3 1/2″	chalice	att. William Will	America	1764–1798	
H 10 3/4″ TD 3 1/4″ BD 4 1/4″	pitcher	att. William Will	America	1764–1798	
TD 8″	plate	Townsend and Compton	England	1785–1810	C 4800

ZION (RED) UNION CHURCH LUTHERAN & UCC, ORWIGSBURG

DIMENSIONS	FORM	MAKER	ORIGIN	WORKING	MARK
H 7 1/8″ TD 4 1/8″ BD 4 3/8″	tankard	Townsend and Compton	England	1785–1810	C 4800

Snyder County PA

CROSS ROADS MENNONITE CHURCH, RICHFIELD

DIMENSIONS	FORM	MAKER	ORIGIN	WORKING	MARK
H 3 3/4″ TD 3″ BD 2 1/8″	beaker	unmarked	America	1780–1825	

ST PETER'S LUTHERAN CHURCH, FREEBURG

DIMENSIONS	FORM	MAKER	ORIGIN	WORKING	MARK
TD 8 1/4″	basin	unknown England	England	1750–1800	
H 7 7/8″ TD 3 1/2″	chalice	att. William Will	America	1764–1798	
H 10 1/2″ TD 4 1/4″ BD 4 3/8″	chalice	att. Johann Christoph Heyne	America	1752–1781	

DIMENSIONS	FORM	MAKER	ORIGIN	WORKING	MARK

Snyder County PA

ST PETER'S LUTHERAN CHURCH, FREEBURG

DIMENSIONS	FORM	MAKER	ORIGIN	WORKING	MARK
H 13 3/4″ TD 3 1/4″ BD 4 1/4″	flagon	att. William Will	America	1764–1798	
TD 8 3/4″	plate	unknown England	England	1750–1800	C 6039

Somerset County PA

HOLY TRINITY LUTHERAN CHURCH, BERLIN

DIMENSIONS	FORM	MAKER	ORIGIN	WORKING	MARK
TD 7 3/4″	plate	Townsend and Compton	England	1785–1810	C 4800
H 7 3/4″ TD 4 1/4″ BD 4 7/8″	tankard	Townsend and Compton	England	1785–1810	C 4800

TRINITY UNITED CHURCH OF CHRIST, BERLIN

DIMENSIONS	FORM	MAKER	ORIGIN	WORKING	MARK
TD 8″	basin	Stynt Duncumb	England	1730–1767	C 1466

Washington County PA

BETHLEHEM LUTHERAN CHURCH, SCENERY HILL

DIMENSIONS	FORM	MAKER	ORIGIN	WORKING	MARK
TD 8″	basin	Henry and Richard Joseph	England	1787–1815	C 2687
H 4 5/8″ TD 3 3/8″ BD 3 7/8″	mug	Edgar Curtis and Co.	England	1793–1809	C 1266A
TD 8 1/2″	plate	Townsend and Compton	England	1785–1810	C 4800

York County PA

BLACK ROCK CHURCH OF THE BRETHREN, BRODBECKS

DIMENSIONS	FORM	MAKER	ORIGIN	WORKING	MARK
H 5 1/8″ TD 3 1/2″ BD 2 7/8″	beaker	att. Boardmans	America	1804–1873	
H 5 1/8″ TD 3 1/2″ BD 3″	beaker	att. Boardmans	America	1804–1873	
L 7 3/4″	tablespoon	Thomas D and Sherman Boardman	America	1810–1860	
L 5 3/8″	teaspoon	John Yates	England	1805–1852	P 5340A
L 5 1/4″	teaspoon	Thomas D and Sherman Boardman	America	1810–1860	

DIMENSIONS	FORM	MAKER	ORIGIN	WORKING	MARK

York County PA

CANADOCHLY LUTHERAN CHURCH, DELROY

DIMENSIONS	FORM	MAKER	ORIGIN	WORKING	MARK
TD 10 7/8″	basin	Richard Going	England	1715–1766	C 1909
H 10″ TD 4 1/8″ BD 4 1/4″	chalice	att. Johann Christoph Heyne	America	1752–1781	
H 11 1/4″ TD 3 1/2″ BD 5 7/8″	flagon	Johann Christoph Heyne	America	1752–1781	L 530, 531, 532
TD 8 3/8″	plate	Richard King	England	1745–1798	C 2750
TD 6″	plate	Johann Christoph Heyne	America	1752–1781	L 533
H 7 1/4″ TD 4 1/4″ BD 5″	tankard	William Eddon	England	1689–1745	C 1503

CHRIST LUTHERAN CHURCH, YORK

DIMENSIONS	FORM	MAKER	ORIGIN	WORKING	MARK
TD 9 1/8″	plate	James Dixon and Sons	England	1842–1851	ST 154

CODORUS CHURCH OF THE BRETHREN, LOGANVILLE

DIMENSIONS	FORM	MAKER	ORIGIN	WORKING	MARK
H 4 1/8″ TD 3 3/8″ BD 2 5/8″	beaker	Johann Christoph Heyne	America	1752–1781	L 530
H 4 1/8″ TD 3 3/8″ BD 2 5/8″	beaker	Johann Christoph Heyne	America	1752–1781	L 530

EMMANUEL UNITED CHURCH OF CHRIST, FREYSVILLE

DIMENSIONS	FORM	MAKER	ORIGIN	WORKING	MARK
TD 10″	basin	Burgum and Catcott	England	1765–1779	C 708
H 7 3/8″ TD 4 1/8″ BD 3 3/8″	chalice	John H. and Robert Palethorp	America	1817–1845	L v.2, p.108
TD 8 1/8″	plate	Townsend and Giffin	England	1777–1801	C 4801
H 6 3/4″ TD 4 1/8″ BD 4 7/8″	tankard	unknown England	England	1750–1800	

FRIEDENSAAL LUTHERAN CHURCH, SEVEN VALLEYS

DIMENSIONS	FORM	MAKER	ORIGIN	WORKING	MARK
H 7 7/8″ TD 4″ BD 4 3/8″	tankard	Philadelphia	America	1764–1798	

PARADISE-HOLTZSCHWAMM UNION LUTHERAN & UCC, THOMASVILLE

DIMENSIONS	FORM	MAKER	ORIGIN	WORKING	MARK
TD 11 1/2″	basin	Samuel Ellis	England	1721–1764	C 1547
TD 7 7/8″	plate	Robert Waller	England	1782–1786	C 4934
TD 7 7/8″	plate	Robert Waller	England	1782–1786	C 4934

DIMENSIONS	FORM	MAKER	ORIGIN	WORKING	MARK

York County PA

PARADISE-HOLTZSCHWAMM UNION LUTHERAN & UCC, THOMASVILLE

DIMENSIONS	FORM	MAKER	ORIGIN	WORKING	MARK
H 8″ TD 4″ BD 4 3/4″	tankard	Philadelphia	America	1764–1798	

ST. PAUL'S (WOLF'S) UNITED CHURCH OF CHRIST, YORK

DIMENSIONS	FORM	MAKER	ORIGIN	WORKING	MARK
TD 9 1/4″	basin	John Townsend	England	1748–1801	C 4795
H 7 5/8″ TD 4″ BD 4 1/4″	chalice	unmarked	America or Continental	1750–1800	
H 8″ TD 3 7/8″ BD 4″	measure	unknown England	England	1750–1800	
TD 9 1/8″	plate	Richard Yates	England	1772–1807	C 5344
TD 7 5/8″	plate	Richard Yates	England	1772–1807	C 5344
TD 7 5/8″	plate	Townsend and Compton	England	1785–1810	C 4800

ST. PAUL'S (ZEIGLER'S) LUTHERAN CHURCH, SEVEN VALLEYS

DIMENSIONS	FORM	MAKER	ORIGIN	WORKING	MARK
TD 8 1/2″	plate	Townsend and Giffin	England	1777–1801	C 4801

ST. PETER'S (LISCHEY'S) UNITED CHURCH OF, SPRING GROVE

DIMENSIONS	FORM	MAKER	ORIGIN	WORKING	MARK
H 8 7/8″ TD 4 1/8″ BD 4 5/8″	chalice	Johann Christoph Heyne	America	1752–1781	L 533
H 7 1/4″ TD 4 1/4″ BD 5 1/8″	tankard	Robert Bush Sr.	England	1755–1801	C 737

TRINITY (ROTH'S) UNITED CHURCH OF CHRIST, SPRING GROVE

DIMENSIONS	FORM	MAKER	ORIGIN	WORKING	MARK
H 8 1/4″ TD 3 7/8″ BD 4 1/8″	measure	W. Bancks	England	1700–1710	C 240

Frederick County VA

CENTENARY UNITED CHURCH OF CHRIST, WINCHESTER

DIMENSIONS	FORM	MAKER	ORIGIN	WORKING	MARK
H 10 3/4″ TD 4 1/8″ BD 4 1/2″	chalice	att. Johann Christoph Heyne	America	1752–1781	
TD 10″	dish	Leonard, Reed and Barton	America	1835–1840	L v2, p.106
H 10 1/8″ TD 4″ BD 5 1/4″	flagon	att. Leonard, Reed and Barton	America	1835–1840	

DIMENSIONS	FORM	MAKER	ORIGIN	WORKING	MARK
York County PA					
TRINITY LUTHERAN CHURCH, STEPHENS CITY					
H 8 3/8″ TD 3 1/2″ BD 3 3/4″	chalice	James Dixon and Sons	England	1842–1851	S p.225
H 8 3/8″ TD 3 1/2″ BD 3 3/4″	chalice	James Dixon and Sons	England	1842–1851	S p.225
TD 9 1/8″	plate	James Dixon and Sons	England	1842–1851	S p.225
Rockingham County VA					
RADER'S LUTHERAN CHURCH, TIMBERVILLE					
TD 11 3/4″	basin	Love	America	1750–1825	L 868, 869
Shenandoah County VA					
ST. PAUL'S UNITED CHURCH OF CHRIST, WOODSTOCK					
H 7 1/2″ TD 3 5/8″ BD 4 1/2″	chalice	att. William Will	America	1764–1798	
ZION LUTHERAN CHURCH, EDINBURG					
H 4 5/8″ TD 3 1/2″ BD 3 3/4″	mug	Richard Yates	England	1772–1807	C 5344
Hampshire County WV					
HEBRON LUTHERAN CHURCH, WARDENSVILLE					
TD 9 1/4″	basin	Townsend and Compton	England	1785–1810	C 4800

APPENDIX 3

Eighteenth Century Churches That No Longer Have Pewter

The churches listed here were founded in the eighteenth century but currently do not own pewter made in that century, as reported by the pastor, church historian, church secretary, or as determined by an on-site visit by the author. Included are churches that have a history of being in existence in the eighteenth century. Churches with unsubstantiated claims of being founded in the eighteenth century were not included in the survey.

Reasons for the absence of pewter vessels include the use of other materials, such as ceramics, glass, wood, tin, and silver. Ceramic pitchers were frequently used by Mennonite congregations. The Amish groups used only ceramic cups and pitchers. Glass decanters were favored by the Church of the Brethren and glass chalices were occasionally used by the Moravians. The German Seventh Day Baptists probably used wood. Tin cups and pouring vessels were frequently found in Mennonite and Brethren Churches. Eighteenth-century silver was noted in only one Lutheran and one Reformed church. The Pennsylvania Germans clearly preferred pewter for their communion and baptismal vessels, perhaps because of its durability, availability, and affordability.

On more than one occasion it was reported that the pewter pieces were in the hands of various parishioners for safekeeping. Unfortunately, in some cases they became separated from the church forever. Congregations frequently merged, sometimes with other denominations, and with the merger went the pewter. When Union church agreements dissolved, the denomination that remained in the old building frequently retained the old pewter. A few congregations reported the loss of their pewter to fire, the Civil War, and occasionally theft. On several occasions, it was given to the minister upon his retirement. The old pewter was frequently replaced by a new set as styles changed. Many churches listed below do own pewter (frequently silver-plated and not within the time period of this project) that was made in the late nineteenth century.

Maryland

BALTIMORE COUNTY

First and St. Stephen's United Church of Christ, Baltimore; St. Paul's Lutheran Church, Upperco; Zion Lutheran Church, Baltimore.

CARROLL COUNTY

Benjamin's (Kreider's) United Church of Christ, Westminster; Emmanuel Lutheran Church, Tyrone; Emmanuel United-Church of Christ, Westminster; Grace United Church of Christ, Taneytown; Immanuel Lutheran Church, Manchester; St. Benjamin's Lutheran Church, Westminster; St. Mary's Lutheran Church, Westminster; St. Mary's United Church of Christ, Westminster; Trinity Lutheran Church, Taneytown; Trinity United Church of Christ, Manchester.

FREDERICK COUNTY
Christ United Church of Christ, Middletown; Church of the Incarnation United Church of Christ, Emmitsburg; Elias Lutheran Church, Emmitsburg; Evangelical United Church of Christ, Frederick; Grace Lutheran Church, Keymar; Grace Moravian Church, Thurmont; Pleasant View Church of the Brethren, Burkittsville; St. John's Lutheran Church, Creagerstown; St. John's Lutheran Church, Thurmont; Zion Lutheran Church, Middletown.

WASHINGTON COUNTY
Beaver Creek Church of the Brethren, Hagerstown; Christ United Church of Christ, Sharpsburg; Holy Trinity Lutheran Church, Sharpsburg; Miller Mennonite Church, Leitersburg; St. John's Lutheran Church, Hagerstown; St. Paul's Lutheran Church, Clear Spring; St. Paul's Lutheran Church, Funkstown; St. Paul's United Church of Christ, Clear Spring; Salem United Church of Christ, Maugansville; Trinity Lutheran Church, Boonsboro; Trinity United Church of Christ, Boonsboro; Zion Lutheran Church, Williamsport.

New Jersey

HUNTERDON COUNTY
Zion Lutheran Church, Oldwick.

MORRIS COUNTY
Zion Lutheran Church, Long Valley.

WARREN COUNTY
St. James' Lutheran Church, Phillipsburg.

Pennsylvania

ADAMS COUNTY
Bair's (Hostetter's) Mennonite Church, Hanover; Basilica of the Sacred Heart of Jesus Catholic Church, Hanover; Bermudian Church of the Brethren, East Berlin; Christ United Church of Christ, Littlestown; Lower Bermudian Lutheran Church, York Springs; Mount Olivet United Church of Christ, York Springs; Mummasburg Mennonite Church, Gettysburg; St. John's Lutheran Church, Abbottstown; St. John's Lutheran Church, Littlestown; Trinity Lutheran Church, Arendtsville; Trinity United Church of Christ, Biglerville; Trinity United Church of Christ, Gettysburg; Upper Bermudian Lutheran Church, Gardners; Zion United Church of Christ, Arendtsville.

ALLEGHENY COUNTY
Smithfield United Church of Christ, Pittsburgh.

ARMSTRONG COUNTY
Christ Lutheran Church, Kittanning.

BEDFORD COUNTY
Friends Cove United Church of Christ, Bedford; Messiah Lutheran Church, Bedford; New Enterprise Church of the Brethren, New Enterprise; St. John's United Church of Christ, Bedford; Trinity Lutheran Church, Bedford.

BERKS COUNTY
Alsace Lutheran Church, Reading; Altalaha Lutheran Church, Rehrersburg; Boyertown Mennonite Church, Boyertown; Christ Little Tulpehocken Lutheran Church, Bernville; Christ Lutheran Church, Fleetwood; Christ Lutheran Church, Womelsdorf; Christ United Church of Christ, Bowers; First United Church of Christ, Hamburg; First United Church of Christ, Reading; Friedens Lutheran Church, Bernville; Grace (Alsace) United Church of Christ, Reading; Huff's United Church of Christ, Alburtis; Little Swatara Church of the Brethren, Bethel; Longswamp United Church of Christ, Mertztown; Mt. Zion Lutheran Church, Krumsville; New Bethel Lutheran Church, Kempton; New Bethel United Church of Christ, Kempton; New Jerusalem Zion United Church of Christ, Krumsville; Roberson Lutheran Church, Plowville; St. Daniel's Lutheran Church, Robesonia; St. John's Lutheran Church, Birdsboro; St. John's Lutheran Church, Hamburg; St. John's Lutheran Church, Kutztown; St. John's Lutheran Church, Shoemakersville; St. John's United Church of Christ, Birdsboro; St. John's United Church of Christ, Kutztown;

St. John's (Gernant's) United Church of Christ, Leesport; St. John's (Host) United Church of Christ, Bernville; St. Joseph's Lutheran Church, Boyertown; St. Joseph's (Hill's) United Church of Christ, Boyertown; St. Michael's United Church of Christ, Hamburg; St. Paul's Lutheran Church, Douglassville; St. Paul's United Church of Christ, Athol; St. Peter Catholic Church, Reading; St. Peter's United Church of Christ, Fleetwood; Schwarzwald Lutheran Church, Jacksonwald; Zion Lutheran Church, Shoemakersville; Zion Lutheran Church, Womelsdorf; Zion (Blue Mountain) United Church of Christ, Strausstown; Zion (Spies) Lutheran Church, Reading; Zion United Church of Christ, Hamburg; Zion United Church of Christ, Womelsdorf.

BLAIR COUNTY
Clover Creek Church of the Brethren, Martinsburg; Martinsburg Mennonite Church, Martinsburg; Zion Lutheran Church, Williamsburg.

BUCKS COUNTY
Christ Lutheran Church, Pipersville; Christ Lutheran Church, Trumbauersville; Christ United Church of Christ, Trumbauersville; Doylestown Mennonite, Doylestown; Durham Lutheran Church, Durham; Peace (Tohicken) Lutheran Church, Hagersville; Ridge Valley United Church of Christ, Sellersville; Rockhill Mennonite Church, Telford; St. John the Baptist Catholic Church, Revere; St. John's Lutheran Church, Sellersville; St. Luke's Lutheran Church, Ferndale; St. Luke's United Church of Christ, Ferndale; St. Luke's United Church of Christ, Ottsville; St. Matthew's Lutheran Church, Perkasie; St. Peter's United Church of Christ, Perkasie; Tinicum United Church of Christ, Pipersville; Trinity Lutheran Church, Pleasant Valley; Trinity United Church of Christ, Pleasant Valley.

CAMBRIA COUNTY
First Congregational United Church of Christ, Ebensburg; St. Michael's Catholic Church, Loretto.

CARBON COUNTY
Zion's (Snyder's) United Church of Christ, Lehighton.

CENTRE COUNTY
Emmanuel Lutheran Church, Spring Mills; Emmanuel United Church of Christ, Spring Mills; Holy Cross Lutheran Church, Spring Mills; St. John Lutheran Church, Spring Mills; St. Luke Lutheran Church, Centre Hall; St. Peter's United Church of Christ, Aaronsburg.

CHESTER COUNTY
Brownback's United Church of Christ, Spring City; St. Agnes Catholic Church, West Chester; St. Peter's Lutheran Church, Chester Springs; Vincent Mennonite Church, Spring City; Zion Lutheran Church, Spring City.

CUMBERLAND COUNTY
First Lutheran Church, Carlisle; First United Church of Christ, Carlisle; Diller Mennonite Church, Newville; Grace United Church of Christ, Shippensburg; Memorial Lutheran Church, Shippensburg; Mt. Zion Lutheran Church, Boiling Springs; St. Patrick's Catholic Church, Carlisle; St. Peter Lutheran Church, Newville; St. Stephen's Lutheran Church, New Kingston; Trindle Springs Lutheran Church, Mechanicsburg; Zion Lutheran Church, Newville.

DAUPHIN COUNTY
Big Swatara Church of the Brethren, Hershey; Christ Lutheran Church, Linglestown; David's United Church of Christ, now nondenominational, Millersburg; St. John's Lutheran Church, Berrysburg; St. Mark's Lutheran Church, Harrisburg; St. Peter's Lutheran Church, Halifax; St. Peter's Lutheran Church, Middletown; St. Peter's (Hoffman's) United Church of Christ, Lykens; Salem Lutheran Church, Millersburg; The Valleys United Church of Christ, Halifax; Zion Lutheran Church, Harrisburg.

DELAWARE COUNTY
St. Thomas the Apostle Catholic Church, Chester Heights.

FAYETTE COUNTY
Jacob's Lutheran Church, Masontown.

FRANKLIN COUNTY
Antietam (Price's) Church of the Brethren, Waynesboro; Chambersburg Mennonite Church, Chambersburg; Corpus Christi Catholic Church, Chambersburg; Evangelical Lutheran Church, Greencastle; First Lutheran Church, Chambersburg; Grace United Church of Christ, Greencastle; Salem Lutheran Church, Pleasant Hall; Salem United Church of Christ, Waynesboro; Solomon's Lutheran Church, Chambersburg; Solomon's United Church of Christ, Chambersburg; Trinity United Church of Christ, Mercersburg; Zion United Church of Christ, Chambersburg.

GREENE COUNTY
St. Ann Catholic Church, Waynesburg.

HUNTINGTON COUNTY
Christ Reformed United Church of Christ, Alexandria.

JUNIATA COUNTY
Bunkertown Church of the Brethren, Bunkertown; Free Spring Church of the Brethren, Mifflintown.

LANCASTER COUNTY
Assumption of the Blessed Mary Catholic Church, Lancaster; Byerland Mennonite Church, Willow Street; Conestoga Church of the Brethren, Leola; Erb Mennonite Church, Manheim; Erisman Mennonite Church, Mount Joy; Gehmans Mennonite Church, Reinholds; Groffdale Mennonite Church, New Holland; Habecker Mennonite Church, Lancaster; Hammer Creek Mennonite Church, Lititz; Hernley Mennonite Church, Manheim; Hershey Mennonite Church, Lancaster; Hess Mennonite Church, Lititz; Indiantown Mennonite Church, Ephrata; Lancaster Moravian Church, Lancaster; Lichty Mennonite Church, East Earl; Masonville Mennonite Church, Washington Boro; Metzler Mennonite Church, Ephrata; Millersville Mennonite Church, Millersville; Mount Joy Mennonite Church, Mount Joy; New Providence Mennonite Church, New Providence; Paradise Mennonite Church, Paradise; River Corner Mennonite Church, Quarryville; Rohrerstown Mennonite Church, Rohrerstown; St. Paul's Lutheran Church, Penryn; St. Paul's United Church of Christ, Manheim; St. Peter's Catholic Church, Elizabethtown; Strasburg Mennonite Church, Strasburg; Stumptown Mennonite Church, Leola; Swamp Lutheran Church, Reinholds; United Church of Christ Church at Conestoga; Weaverland Mennonite Church, East Earl; White Oak Church of the Brethren, Penryn; Willow Street Mennonite Church, Willow Street; Zion United Church of Christ, New Providence.

LEBANON COUNTY
Hill United Church of Christ, Cleona; Kralls Mennonite Church, Myerstown; St. John Lutheran Church, Fredericksburg; St. John's United Church of Christ, Fredericksburg; St. John's United Church of Christ, Jonestown; St. Paul's United Church of Christ of Hamlin, Fredericksburg; Tulpehocken Trinity United Church of Christ, Richland.

LEHIGH COUNTY
Chestnut Hill United Church of Christ, Coopersburg; Christ Church (Schoenersville) United Church of Christ, Allentown; Christ Lutheran Church, Allentown; Ebenezer Lutheran Church, New Tripoli; Ebenezer United Church of Christ, New Tripoli; Faith United Church of Christ, Center Valley; Jerusalem Lutheran Church, Allentown; Jerusalem United Church of Christ of Eastern Salisbury, Allentown; Jordan United Church of Christ, Allentown; Lower Saucon United Church of Christ, Hellertown; Old Zionsville United Church of Christ, Old Zionsville; St. Paul's (Blue) Lutheran Church, Coopersburg; St. Peter's United Church of Christ, Macungie; Saucon Mennonite Church, Coopersburg; Shepherd of the Hills Lutheran Church, Whitehall; Trinity or Great Swamp United Church of Christ, Spinnerstown; Upper

Milford Mennonite Church, Zionsville; Ziegel United Church of Christ, Breinigsville; Ziegel's Lutheran Church, Fogelsville, Ziegel's United Church of Christ, Fogelsville; Zion Lehigh Lutheran Church, Alburtis.

LUZERNE COUNTY
St. John's Lutheran Church, St. Johns; St. John's United Church of Christ, St. Johns.

MIFFLIN COUNTY
St. John's Lutheran Church, Lewistown.

MONROE COUNTY
St. Matthew's United Church of Christ, Kunkletown.

MONTGOMERY COUNTY
Augustus Lutheran Church, Trappe; Christ United Church of Christ, Telford; Coventry Church of the Brethren, Pottstown; Falkner Swamp United Church of Christ, Gilbertsville; Franconia Mennonite Church, Souderton; Indian Creek Church of the Brethren, Harleysville; Little Zion Lutheran Church, Telford; Methacton Mennonite Church, Norristown; Old Goshenhoppen Lutheran Church, Woxall; Old Goshenhoppen United Church of Christ, Woxall; Providence Mennonite Church, Collegeville; St. Luke's United Church of Christ, North Wales; St. Paul's United Church of Christ of Whitemarsh, Ft. Washington; Schwenkfelder United Church of Christ, Palm; Trinity United Church of Christ, Pottstown; Upper Dublin Lutheran Church, Ambler; Zions United Church of Christ, Pottstown.

NORTHAMPTON COUNTY
Christ Lutheran Church, Mount Bethel; Dryland United Church of Christ, Nazareth; Good Shepherd Lutheran Church, Northampton; Holy Cross Lutheran Church, Nazareth; Hope United Church of Christ, Wind Gap; Lower Saucon United Church of Christ, Hellertown; St. John's Lutheran Church, Easton; St. Luke's Lutheran Church, Hellertown; St. Paul's of Indianland United Church of Christ, Cherryville; Schoeneck Moravian Church, Nazareth; Trinity United Church of Christ, Mt. Bethel.

NORTHUMBERLAND COUNTY
Follmer Lutheran Church, Potts Grove; St. James Lutheran Church, Pitman; St. Peter's Lutheran Church, Red Cross; Trinity Lutheran Church, Milton; Zion Lutheran Church, Hickory Corners; Zion Lutheran Church, Sunbury; Zion United Church of Christ, Hickory Corners.

PERRY COUNTY
Christ United Church of Christ, Duncannon; Good Shepherd Lutheran Church, Liverpool; Lebanon United Church of Christ, Loysville; Messiah Lutheran Church, Elliottsburg; Tressler Memorial Lutheran Church, Loysville; Zion United Church of Christ, Blain.

PHILADELPHIA COUNTY
Germantown Church of the Brethren, Germantown; Germantown Mennonite Church, Germantown; Holy Trinity German Catholic Church, Philadelphia; Immanuel Lutheran Church, Philadelphia; Old First Reformed United Church of Christ, Philadelphia; Old St. Mary's Catholic Church, Philadelphia.

SCHUYLKILL COUNTY
Jacob's Lutheran Church, Pine Grove; St. John United Church of Christ, Friedensburg; St. Johns United Church of Christ, Palmerton; St. Paul's Lutheran Church, Auburn; St. Paul's (Summer Hill) United Church of Christ, Auburn; St. Peter's United Church of Christ, Pine Grove; Salem (Hetzel's) Lutheran Church, Pine Grove; Salem (Hetzel's) United Church of Christ, Pine Grove; Zion Lutheran Church, Snyders.

SNYDER COUNTY
Botschaft Lutheran Church, Mt. Pleasant Mills; Christ (White) Lutheran Church, Middleburg; First United Church of Christ, Middleburg; St. John's Lutheran Church, McClure; St. Paul's United Church of

Christ, Selinsgrove; St. Peter Lutheran Church, Kreamer; Salem Lutheran Church, Kreamer; Zion Lutheran Church, Kratzerville; Zion United Church of Christ, Kratzerville.

SOMERSET COUNTY
Brothers Valley Church of the Brethren, Berlin; Friedens Lutheran Church, Friedens; Messiah Lutheran Church, New Centerville; St. John's Lutheran Church, Salisbury; St. John's United Church of Christ, Salisbury; St. Luke's Lutheran Church, Rockwood; St. Michael's Lutheran Church, Berlin; St. Paul's United Church of Christ, Somerset; St. Paul's United Church of Christ, Stoystown; Samuel's Lutheran Church, Rockwood.

UNION COUNTY
Dreisbach's United Church of Christ, New Berlin; Emmanuel United Church of Christ, New Berlin; Faith Lutheran Church, Lewisburg; First Lutheran Church, Mifflinburg; Messiah Lutheran Church, New Berlin; St. John's United Church of Christ, Mifflinburg.

WASHINGTON COUNTY
Ten Mile Church of the Brethren, Marianna.

WESTMORELAND COUNTY
Brush Creek Lutheran Church, Irwin; Brush Creek, Salem United Church of Christ, Irwin; First Lutheran Church, Greensburg; First United Church of Christ, Greensburg; Harrold Zion Lutheran Church, Greensburg; Mt. Zion Lutheran Church, Donegal; St. John's Lutheran Church, Mt. Pleasant; St. John's United Church of Christ, Mt. Pleasant; St. John's (Harrold's) United Church of Christ, Greensburg; St. Paul's Lutheran Church, Latrobe; St. Paul's United Church of Christ, Latrobe.

YORK COUNTY
Bethlehem United Church of Christ, Glen Rock; Canadochly United Church of Christ, Hellam; Emanuel Lutheran Church, Freysville; Emmanuel United Church of Christ, Hanover; First Moravian Church, York; Jerusalem Lutheran Church, Glen Rock; Jerusalem United Church of Christ, Glen Rock; North Hartman Street Mennonite Church, Spring Grove; Quickel Lutheran Church, Zion View; St. David's (Sherman's) Lutheran Church, Hanover; St. David's (Sherman's) United Church of Christ, Hanover; St. Jacob's (Stone) Lutheran Church, Brodbecks; St. Jacob's (Stone) United Church of Christ, Brodbecks; St. James Lutheran Church, Hellam; St. John's Lutheran Church, Stewartstown; St. John's (Franklin) Lutheran Church, Dillsburg; St. Johns United Church of Christ, Dallastown; St. Luke's Lutheran Church, Red Lion; St. Matthew's Lutheran Church, Hanover; St. Patrick's Catholic Church, York; St. Paul's Lutheran Church, York; St. Paul's United Church of Christ, Shrewsbury; St. Peter's United Church of Christ, Seven Valleys; Salem Lutheran Church, Dover; Salem United Church of Christ, Dover; Stony Brook Mennonite Church, York; Trinity United Church of Christ, Hellam; Trinity United Church of Christ, York; Zion United Church of Christ, York.

Virginia

AUGUSTA COUNTY
Christ Lutheran Church, Staunton; Mt. Tabor Lutheran Church, Staunton; St. John's United Church of Christ, Middlebrook; St. Peter's Lutheran Church, Churchville.

FREDERICK COUNTY
Grace Lutheran Church, Winchester; St. John's Lutheran Church, Winchester.

LOUDOUN COUNTY
St. James United Church of Christ, Lovettsville.

PAGE COUNTY
St. Peter's Lutheran, Shenandoah.

ROCKINGHAM COUNTY
Brown Memorial United Church of Christ, McGaheysville; Friedens United Church

of Christ, Mt. Crawford; Trinity Lutheran Church, Harrisonburg; Trinity Lutheran Church, Timberville.

SHENANDOAH COUNTY
Emanuel Lutheran Church, Woodstock; Flat Rock Church of the Brethren, Quicksburg; Grace United Church of Christ, Mt. Jackson; Reformation Lutheran Church, New Market; St. Mary's Lutheran Church, Mt. Jackson; St. Paul's Lutheran Church, Strasburg.

West Virginia

BERKELEY COUNTY
Christ United Church of Christ, Martinsburg; St. John's Lutheran Church, Martinsburg.

JEFFERSON COUNTY
Christ United Church of Christ, Shepherdstown; St. Peter's Lutheran Church, Shepherdstown.

Glossary

Alloy. A substance formed of two or more metals usually fused together when molten.

Baluster. A vaselike or turned outline.

Beading. A type of decoration that gave the appearance of beads. The decoration was frequently made with a knurling tool that incised small lines into the metal. The design was sometimes present in the molds used to make the finished product.

Beaker. A flared cylindrical drinking vessel having a body that tapers out toward the top, so that its top diameter is larger than its base diameter. Some beakers have handles.

Booge. The curved part of a plate, dish, or basin between the rim and the bottom or base.

Britannia metal. An alloy that is hard and thin and can be made into sheets for mass production.

Ciborium. A vessel used to contain the eucharistic wafers. Also known as a pyx or host box.

Ewer. A vessel having a handle and a lip or spout with a wide mouth used for holding liquid. A pitcher often had a narrow spout. The terms ewer and pitcher are frequently interchanged.

Flecheltechnik. Wrigglework.

Fillet. A raised band of metal on the body of a mug or tankard.

Finial. The uppermost ornament on a vessel.

Flagon. A tall receptacle having a lid, from which wine or other liquid is poured into smaller vessels for convenient drinking.

Flatware. A name given to pewter plates and dishes that are flat, as opposed to hollow-ware. Also known as "sad-ware."

Gadrooning. Ornamental notching in a rounded molding. A type of decoration based on curves.

Hollowware. Pewter vessels that are made in multiple molds such as flagons, tankards, mugs, chalices and beakers.

Mark. The design struck on a piece of pewter by its maker to identify his ware. Also called hallmark, maker's mark, touch, and touchmark.

Mug. A flared cylindrical drinking vessel that has a base larger than its top.

Knop. An enlargement found on the stem of a chalice.

Paten. A small plate used to hold bread or wafers for communion.

Pyx. Ciborium.

Sadware. Another term for flatware.

Strike. To apply a mark.

Stitze, Stize. A flagon in the German pewter vocabulary.

Tankard. A one-handled drinking vessel with a lid.

Thumbpiece. A lever found on the lid of a flagon, tankard, or measure used as an aid to raise the lid.

Touchmark. Mark.

Vessel. A hollow receptacle or container for liquids such as communion wine.

Wrigglework. Engraving in which the engraving instrument is moved back and forth in a rocking motion, producing a zig-zag line. *Flechеltechnik* in the German pewter vocabulary.

Bibliography

Barkin, Kenneth. *European Pewter in Everyday Life (1600–1900).* Riverside, Calif.: University of California, 1988.

Barquist, David L. *American and English Pewter at the Yale University Art Gallery: A Supplementary Checklist.* New Haven, Conn.: Yale University Art Gallery, 1985.

Bauer, Dirk. *Kirchliches Zinngerät aus dem Kreise Marburg.* Marburg: Marburger Universitätsmuseum für Kunst und Kulturgeschichte, 1970.

———. *Kirchliches Zinngerät: Katalog zur Ausstellung kirchliches und bürgerliches Zinngerät im Altkreis Wolfhagen.* Wolfhagen: Schneidmüller, 1982.

Benes, Peter, and Philip D. Zimmerman. *New England Meeting House and Church: 1630–1850.* A Loan Exhibition held at the Currier Gallery of Art, Manchester, N.H. *The Dublin Seminar for New England Folklife.* Boston: Boston University and The Currier Gallery of Art, 1979.

Beyer, Paul. *Das Erzgebirge.* Leipzig: F. A. Brockhaus, 1973.

Boehm, John Philip. *Life and Letters of the Rev. John Philip Boehm: Founder of the Reformed Church in Pennsylvania 1683–1749.* edited by William J. Hinke. Philadelphia: Reformed Church in the United States, 1916.

Boucaud, Philippe, and Claude Frégnac. *Les Étains: Des origines au début du XIX siècle.* Fribourg: Office du Livre, 1978.

Bowen, Richard L., Jr. "Bush, Perkins, Edgar, and Curtis: Bristol Pewterers." *Pewter Collectors' Club of America Bulletin,* no. 84 (March 1982).

———. "John Townsend and Associates." *Pewter Collectors' Club of America Bulletin,* no. 104 (June 1992).

———. "John Townsend and Associates: A Rejoinder." *Pewter Collectors' Club of America Bulletin,* no. 105 (December 1992).

———. "Some of Roswell Gleason's Early Workers." *Pewter Collectors' Club of America Bulletin,* no. 83 (March 1978).

———. "The Hales of Bristol, England." *Pewter Collectors' Club of America Bulletin,* no. 84 (March 1982).

———. "The Sheaf of Wheat Mark and the Hales of Bristol." *Pewter Collectors' Club of America Bulletin,* no. 104 (June 1992).

Brendle, A. S. *A Brief History of Schaefferstown.* Schaefferstown, Pa.: Historic Schaefferstown, Inc., 1979. First edition published by Hiram Young, York, Pa., 1901.

Brener, David. *The Jews of Lancaster, Pennsylvania: A story with two beginnings.* Lancaster, Pa.: Congregation Shaarai Shomayim, Lancaster, Pa. in association with The Lancaster County Historical Society, 1979. First edition published in 1976.

The Brethren Encyclopedia. 3 vols. Philadelphia and Oak Brook, Ill.: The Brethren Press, 1983–1984.

Brett, Vanessa. *Phaidon Guide to Pewter.* Englewood Cliffs, N.J.: Prentice–Hall, 1983. Originally pub. by Phaidon Press Ltd., Littlegate House, St. Ebbe's Street, Oxford, 1982.

Bruzelli, Birger. *Länsing För Tennvänner.* Stockholm: Askild & Karenkull, 1978.

———. *Tenngjutare I Sverige: Verksamhet Föremal Stämplar.* Stockholm: Alb. Bonniers boktryckeri, 1967.

Carlson, Janice H. "Analysis of British and American Pewter by X-Ray Fluorescence Spectroscopy." *Winterthur Portfolio 12.* The Henry Francis du Pont Winterthur Museum, Charlottesville: University Press of Virginia, 1977, 65–85.

Cassell, C. W., W. J. Finck, and Elon O. Henkel, eds. *History of The Lutheran Church in Virginia and East Tennessee.* Strasburg, Va.: Shenandoah Publishing House, Inc., 1930.

Cole, Milton H. *History of Zion (Stone) Church near Kreidersville, Pa. In Commemoration of The One Hundreth Anniversary of the Building of the Present Church Edifice, 1836–1936.* Allentown, Pa.: Schlechters, 1936.

Cortelyou, Roland G., Jr. "The Pewterer's Oval Machine." *Pewterer Collectors' Club of America Bulletin,* no. 103 (December 1991).

Cotterell, Howard H., Adolphe Riff, and Robert M. Vetter. *National Types of Old Pewter: A revised and expanded edition.* Princeton, N.J.: The Pyne Press, 1972.

Cotterell, Howard H. *Old Pewter: Its Makers and Marks in England, Scotland and Ireland: An Account of the Old Pewterer and His Craft.* London: B. T. Batsford, Ltd, 1929. Rutland, Vt., and Tokyo, Japan: Charles E. Tuttle Co., 1963.

Croll, P. C. *Annals of the Oley Valley in Berks County, Pa.* Reading, Pa.: Reading Eagle Press, 1926.

Currier Gallery of Art. *British Pewter: 1600–1850.* Manchester, N.H.: The Currier Gallery of Art, 1974.

de Jonge, Eric. "Johann Christoph Heyne: Pewterer, Minister, Teacher." *Winterthur Portfolio 4,* The Henry Francis du Pont Winterthur Museum, Charlottesville: University Press of Virginia, 1968, 169–184.

Dolz, Renate. *Zinn.* Antiquitäten series, no. 8. München: Wilhelm Heyne Verlag, 1983.

Dubbe, B. *Tin en tinnegieters in Nederland.* Zeist, 1965. Lochem BV: De Tijdstroom 1978.

Ebert, Katherine. *Collecting American Pewter.* New York: Charles Scribner's Sons, 1973.

Esner, Bernard. "The Cause of a Skipped Heartbeat (Almost)!" *Pewter Collectors' Club of America Bulletin,* no. 9 (March 1979).

Evans, John J. Jr. "I.C.H., Lancaster Pewterer." *The Magazine Antiques,* September 1931.

Fennimore, Donald L. "A Marbleized Pewter Tankard." *Pewter Collectors' Club of America* Bulletin, no. 88 (March 1984).

Fennimore, Donald L. "Religion in America: Metal Objects in Service of the Ritual." *American Art Journal* 10 (November 1978), 20–43.

Freedley, Edwin T. *Leading Pursuits and Leading Men.* Philadelphia: Edward Young, 1856.

Friesen, Steve. *A Modest Mennonite Home.* Intercourse, Pa.: Good Books, 1990.

Garvan, Beatrice B., and Charles F. Hummel. *The Pennsylvania Germans: A Celebration of Their Arts 1683–1850.* An Exhibition organized by The Philadelphia Museum of Art and The Henry Francis du Pont Winterthur Museum. Philadelphia: Philadelphia Museum of Art, 1982.

Glatfelter, Charles H. *Pastors and People: German Lutheran and Reformed Churches in the Pennsylvania Field, 1717–1793,* vol. 1 of *Pastors and Congregations.* Breinigsville, Pa.: Pennsylvania German Society, 1980.

———. *Pastors and People: German Lutheran and Reformed Churches in the Pennsylvania Field, 1717–1793,* vol. 2 of *The History.* Breinigsville, Pa.: Pennsylvania German Society, 1981.

Goll, George Philip. *The History of the St. John Evangelical Lutheran Church, Maytown, Lancaster Co., Pa. 1765–1904.* Lancaster, Pa.: Wickersham Printing Co., 1904.

Goyne, Nancy A. "Britannia in America: The Introduction of a New Alloy and a New Industry." *Winterthur Portfolio 2.* Winterthur, Del.: The Henry Francis du Pont Winterthur Museum, 1965.

Gudehus, Jonas Heinrich. "Journey To America," translated by Larry M. Neff. *Ebbes fer Alle-Ebber Ebbes fer Dich: Something for Everyone—Something for You.* Breinigsville, Pa.: Pennsylvania German Society, 1980.

Haedeke, Hanns-Ulrich. *Altes Zinn.* 42 Bildtafeln. Leipzig: Insel, 1969.

———. *Zinn.* Braunschweig: Klinkhardt and Bierman, 1963. Reprint, München: Klinkhardt and Biermann, 1983.

———. *Zinn: Kataloge des Kunstgewerbemuseums Köln,* vol. 3. Köln: J. P. Bachem, 1976.

Haedeke, Hanns-Ulrich, and Walter Danz. *Sächsisches Zinn.* Leipzig: Prisma, 1975.

Haller, Mabel. *"Early Moravian Education in Pennsylvania"* n. D. diss. University of Pennsylvania. Nazareth, Pa.: Moravian Historical Society, 1953.

Hamilton, Suzanne. "The Pewter of William Will: A Checklist." *Winterthur Portfolio 7,* The Henry Francis du Pont Winterthur Museum. Charlottesville, Va.: University Press of Virginia, 1972.

———. *William Will, Pewterer: His Life and His Work, 1742–1798.* Master's diss., University of Delaware, 1967.

Harbaugh, H[enry]. *The Life of Rev. Michael Schlatter with a full account of his travels and labors among the Germans in Pennsylvania, New Jersey, Maryland and Virginia including his services as chaplain in the French and Indian War, and in the War of the Revolution. 1716–1790.* Philadelphia: Lindsay and Blakiston, 1857.

Herman, Theodore F., and John S. Stahr, eds. *The Reformed Church Review.* Philadelphia: The Reformed Church Publication Board, 1914.

Herr, Donald M. "A Marked Philadelphia Sugar Bowl." *Pewter Collectors' Club of America Bulletin,* no. 90–91 (March–September 1985).

———. "A Simon Edgell Beaker." *Pewter Collectors' Club of America Bulletin,* no. 76 (March 1978).

———. "Another Flagon Form by William Will." *Pewter Collectors' Club of America Bulletin,* no. 97 (December 1988).

———. "Johann Christoph Heyne, Lancaster, Pennsylvania, pewterer." *The Magazine Antiques* (January 1980).

———. "Marked American Beakers." *Pewter Collectors' Club of America Bulletin,* no. 84 (March 1982).

———. "Palethorp and Connell and the Crowned X." *Pewter Collectors' Club of America Bulletin,* no. 90–91 (September 1986).

———. "Pewter Services on View at Lancaster." *Pewter Collectors' Club of America Bulletin,* no. 72 (February 1976).

———. "Two More Forms by William Will." *Pewter Collectors' Club of America Bulletin,* no. 67 (December 1972).

Hilt, Wayne A. "Henry Joseph—Master Pewterer." *Pewter Collectors' Club of America Bulletin,* no. 77 (September 1978).

Hintze, Erwin. *Die Deutschen Zinngiesser Und Ihre Marken.* 1921–1931. Reprint, 7 vols. Aalen: Otto Zeller Verlagsbuchhandlung, 1964.

Homer, Ronald F. "Editor's Note." *Pewter Collectors' Club of America Bulletin,* no. 105 (December 1992).

Homer, Ronald F. *The Stanley E. Thomas Collection of Pewter in the Museum of North Devon, Barnstaple, with an Account of the Pewterers of Barnstaple.* N.P.: The Pewter Society, 1993.

Homer, Ronald F., and David W. Hall. *Provincial Pewterers: A Study of the Craft in the West Midlands and Wales.* London and Chichester: Phillimore & Co. Ltd., 1985.

Hornsby, Peter R. G. *Pewter of the Western World (1600–1850).* Exton, Pa.: Schiffer Publishing, Ltd., 1983.

Hornsby, Peter R. G., Rosemary Weinstein, and Ronald F. Homer. *Pewter: A Celebration of the Craft 1200–1700.* London: The Museum of London, 1989.

Hostetler, John A. *Amish Roots: A Treasury of History, Wisdom, and Lore.* Baltimore and London: The Johns Hopkins University Press, 1989.

———. *Amish Society.* 4th ed. Baltimore: The Johns Hopkins University Press, 1993.

Jacobs, Carl. *Guide to American Pewter.* New York: The McBride Company, 1957.

Jacobs, Celia. *The Pocket Book of American Pewter: The Makers and the Marks.* Rev. 2nd ed. Boston: Cahners, 1970.

Kauffman, Henry J. *The America Pewterer: His Techniques and His Products.* Camden, N. J.: Thomas Nelson, Inc., 1970.

Kerfoot, John Barrett. *American Pewter.* New York: Bonanza Books, 1924.

Kidd, H. S. *Lutherans in Berks County: Two Centuries of Continuous Organized Church Life 1723–1923.* Kutztown and Reading, Pa.: William S. Rhode Pub. Co., 1923.

Kohlmann, Theodore. *Zinngiesserhandwerk und Zinngerät in Oldenburg, Ostfriesland und Osnabrück (1600–1900).* Göttingen: Otto Schwartz & Co., 1972.

Laughlin, Ledlie I. *Pewter in America: Its Makers and Their Marks.* Vols. 1 and 2, Boston, Mass.: The Houghton Mifflin Co., 1940. Reprint, Barre, Mass.: Barre Publishers, 1969. Vol. 3, Barre, Mass.: Barre Publishing Co., Inc., 1971.

Lipman, Jean, and Alice Winchester. *The Flowering of American Folk Art 1776–1876.* New York: Viking Press, 1974.

Masse, H. J. L. J. *Chats on Old Pewter.* 3rd ed. New York: Dover Publications, Inc., 1971.

Mead, Frank S. *Handbook of Denominations in the United States.* 7th ed. Nashville: Abingdon, 1980.

The Mennonite Encyclopedia: A Comprehensive Reference Work on the Anabaptist–Mennonite Movement. 4 vols. Scottdale, Pa.: Mennonite Publishing House, 1955–1959.

Michaelis, Ronald F. *British Pewter.* London: Cox and Wymann, Ltd., 1969.

[Lewis Miller] *Lewis Miller: Sketches and Chronicles: The Reflections of a Nineteenth Century Pennsylvania German Folk Artist.* York, Pa.: Historical Society of York County, 1966.

Minutes of the Common Council of the City of Philadelphia: 1704–1776. Philadelphia: Crissy and Markley, 1847.

Montgomery, Charles F. *A History of American Pewter: A Winterthur Book.* New York: Praeger, 1973.

———. "John Townsend, English Quaker with American Connections." *Pewter Collectors' Club of America Bulletin,* no. 51 (December 1964).

Montgomery, Morton L. *History of Berks County in Pennsylvania.* Philadelphia: Everts, Peck & Richards, 1886.

Mory, Ludwig. *Schönes Zinn: Geschichte Formen und Probleme.* München: Bruckmann, 1972.

Muhlenberg, Henry Melchior. *The Journals of Henry Melchior Muhlenberg.* Translated by Theodore G. Tappert and John W. Doberstein. 3 vols. Philadelphia: Muhlenberg Press, 1942–1958.

Peal, Christopher A. *Addenda to More Pewter Marks.* Cringleford, Norwich, England: Peal, 1977.

———. *British Pewter and Britannia Metal: for Pleasure and Investment.* New York and London: Pebbles Press, 1973.

———. *More Pewter Marks.* Cringleford, Norwich, England: Peal, 1976.

Pewter Collectors' Club of America, Inc. *Pewter in American Life.* Providence, R.I.: Mowbray Co., 1984.

The Pewter Society. *Exhibition of British Pewterware Through the Ages: From Romano–British Times to the Present Day.* Reading Museum and Art Gallery Catalogue. Reading: The Pewter Society, 1969.

Quarles, Garland R. *The Churches of Winchester, Virginia: A Brief History of Those Established Prior to 1825.* Winchester, Virginia: The Farmers and Merchants National Bank, 1960.

Rader, Gladys C., and Lorraine J. Weida, comps. *History of Jerusalem Lutheran Church of Western Salisbury and Jerusalem Western Salisbury United Church of Christ, Allentown, Pennsylvania 245th Anniversary 1741–1986.* Allentown, Pa.: Western Salisbury Union Church, 1987.

Rasmussen, Holger. *Gammelt Dansk Tin: Kandestoberne og deres arbejder.* Kobenhavn (Copenhagen): Arnold Busck, 1987.

Reese, Joseph O. "Thomas Byles and the Hell Gate Shipwreck." *Pewter Collectors' Club of America Bulletin,* No. 109 (November 1994).

Robinson, Ian D. "Antique British Pewter Found Today in New England." *Pewter Collectors' Club of America Bulletin,* no. 89 (September 1984).

———. "William Eddon, Master Pewterer Extraordinary." *Journal Pewter Society,* Autumn 1979.

Schneider, Hugo. *Zinn: Katalog der Sammlung des Schweizerischen Landesmuseums, Zürich.* Vol. 1. Olten: Walter–Verlag AG., 1970.

Schneider, Hugo and Paul Kneuss. *Zinn: Die Zinngiesser der Schweiz und ihre Marken.* Vol. 3. Olten: Walter–Verlag AG., 1983.

Schumacher, Daniel. *Daniel Schumacher's Baptismal Register.* Translated by Frederick S. Weiser. Allentown, Pa.: Pennsylvania German Society, 1968.

Schnurrer, Ludwig. *Das Zinngiesserhandwerk: Rothenburg ob der Tauber.* Rothenburg, Germany: Petersche Druckeri, 1981.

Scott, Jack L. *Pewter Wares from Sheffield.* Baltimore: Antiquary Press, 1980.

Shelley, Donald A. *The Fraktur–Writings or Illuminated Manuscripts of the Pennsylvania Germans.* Allentown, Pa.: Pennsylvania German Folklore Society, 1961.

Shemmel, Stanley. "William Eddon: Some Further Information and Comment." *Journal Pewter Society,* Autumn 1979.

Smucker, David J. Rempel, introduction and transcription, and Noah G. Good, translation. "Church Practices of Lancaster Mennonites: Writings by Christian Nissley (1777–1831)." *Pennsylvania Mennonite Heritage.* Vol. 13, no.3 (July 1990).

Stara, D. *Pewter Marks of the World.* London: Hamlyn, 1978.

Stocker, Henry Emilius. *Moravian Customs and Other Matters of Interest.* Bethlehem, Pa.: Times Publishing Co., 1918.

Strassburger, Ralph Beaver, and William J. Hinke. *Pennsylvania German Pioneers,* edited by William J. Hinke. 3 vols. Norristown, Pa.: Pennsylvania German Society, 1934.

Stravinskas, Peter M. J., ed. *Our Sunday Visitor's Catholic Encyclopedia.* Huntington, Ind.: Our Sunday Visitor, Inc., 1991.

Swain, Charles V. "Interchangeable Parts in Early American Pewter." *The Magazine Antiques* (February 1963).

———. "Three Flagons Attributed to John Will." *The Magazine Antiques* (May 1972).

———. "Varying Forms from One Mold." *Pewter Collectors' Club of America Bulletin,* no. 48 (March 1963).

Swank, Scott T. *Arts of the Pennsylvania Germans.* A Winterthur Book, New York: W. W. Norton & Co., 1983.

Tappert, Theodore G., and John W. Doberstein, trans. *The Journals of Henry Melchior Muhlenberg.* Philadelphia: Muhlenberg Press, 1942–1958.

Tardy. *Les Étains Francais.* Paris: Tardy, 1959.

Thomas, John C. "A Marked Boardman Chalice." *Pewter Collectors' Club of America Bulletin,* no. 49 (September 1963).

———. *Connecticut Pewter and Pewterers.* Hartford: The Connecticut Historical Society, 1976.

———, ed. *American and British Pewter: An Historical Survey.* New York: Universe Books, 1976.

Thormann, Dagmar. *Silber und Zinn aus Windsheim.* Bad Windsheim, Germany: Delp, 1991.

Tischer, Friedrich. *Böhmisches Zinn und seine Marken.* Leipzig: Karl W. Hiersemann, 1928.

Twelve Views of Churches, Schools and Other Buildings Erected by the United Brethren in America; with Brief Descriptions Annexed. New York: Lithography of Endicott, 1836.

Upton, Dell. *Holy Things and Profane: Anglican Parish Churches in Colonial Virginia.* The Architectural History Foundation. Cambridge, Mass.: MIT Press, 1986.

Verster, A. J. G. *Das Buch vom Zinn.* Hannover: Fackelträger-Verlag Schmidt-Küster GmbH, and Amsterdam: J.H. de Bussy, 1963.

Vetter, Robert M., and Georg Wacha. *Linzer Zinngiesser: Herausgegeben vom Stadtmuseum Linz.* Wien und München: Anton Schroll & Co., 1967.

Wagner, Margarete. *Nürnberger Handwerker: Bilder und Aufzeichnungen aus den Zwölfbrüderhäusern 1388–1807.* Wiesbaden: Guido Pressler, 1977.

Ward, Barbara M. "In a Feasting Posture: Communion Vessels and Community Values in Seventeenth- and Eighteenth-Century New England," *Winterthur Portfolio 23.* Winterthur Museum, Chicago: The University of Chicago Press, 1988.

Weeks, Eve B., and Mary B. Warren. *Materials Towards a History of the Baptists by Morgan Edwards.* Vol. 1. Danielsville, Ga.: Heritage Papers, 1984. Reprint of 1857 edition.

Weigelt, Horst. "The Emigration of the Schwenkfelders from Silesia to America." *Schwenkfelders in America: Papers Presented at the Colloqium on Schwenkfeld and the Schwenkfelders, Pennsburg, Pa. September 17–22, 1984,* Edited by Peter C. Erb. Pennsburg, Pa.: Schwenkfelder Library, 1987.

Weiser, Frederick S. *A Congregation Named Saint John's: Two Hundred Years of Parish Life in Saint John's Evangelical Lutheran Church, Maytown, Pennsylvania, 1767–1967.* Maytown: Church Council, 1967.

Weiser, Frederick S. "The Use of Pewter Sacramental Vessels in American Lutheranism in the Eighteenth Century." *Pewter Collectors' Club of America Bulletin,* no. 67 (December 1972).

Wenger, John C. *History of the Mennonites of the Franconia Conference.* Telford, Pa.: Franconia Mennonite Historical Society, 1937.

Wilsdorf, H., W. Quellmalz, and G. Schlegel. *Das erzgebirgische Zinn in Natur, Geschichte und Technik.* Altenberg, Germany: Altenberg Museum, 1983.

Wiswe, Mechthild. *Historische Zinngiesserei im sudöstlichen Niedersachsen.* Braunschweig: Braunschweigisches Landesmuseum, 1981.

Wolf, Bette A., and Melvyn D. "Johann Philip Alberti." Pewter Collectors' Club of America Bulletin, no. 84 (March 1982).

Wolf, Melvyn, and Bette A. "Nineteenth Century American Chalices." *Pewter Collectors' Club of America Bulletin,* no. 79 (September 1979).

Woods, Jean. *The Germanic Heritage.* Hagerstown: Washington County Museum of Fine Arts, 1983.

Woolmer, Stanley C., and Charles H. Arkwright. *Pewter of the Channel Islands.* Edinburgh: John Bartholomew and Son, Ltd., 1973.

Worshipful Company of Pewterers of London. *A Short History of The Worshipful Company of Pewterers of London and a Catalogue of Pewterware in Its Possession.* London: Percy Lund, Humphries & Co., Ltd., 1968.

Worshipful Company of Pewterers of London. *Supplementary Catalogue of Pewterware, 1979.* London and Bradford: Lund Humphries, 1978.

Yates, W. Ross, ed. *Bethlehem of Pennsylvania: The First One Hundred Years.* Bethlehem, Pa.: Bethlehem Book Committee, Chamber of Commerce, Bethlehem, Pa., 1968.

Yoder, Don. "Sects and Religious Movements of German Origin." In *Encyclopedia of the American Religious Experience,* New York: Charles Scribner's Sons, 1988. edited by Charles H. Lippy and Peter W. Williams, 2:615–633.

Zimmerman, Philip D. "The Lord's Supper in Early New England: The Setting and the Service." In *New England Meeting House and Church: 1630–1850. The Dublin Seminar for New England Folklife Proceedings 1979,* edited by Peter Benes. Boston: Boston University, 1979.

Index

N

O

P

R